Twentieth Century Etiquette

and Deportment

Or the Lady and Gentleman at Home and Abroad; Containing Rules of Etiquette for All Occasions, Including Calls; Invitations; Parties; Weddings; Receptions; Dinners and Teas; Etiquette of the Street; Public Places, Etc., Etc. Forming a Complete Guide to Self-Culture; the Art of Dressing Well; Conversation; Courtship; Etiquette for Children; Letter-Writing; Artistic Home and Interior Decorations, Etc.

Maud C. Cooke

Alpha Editions

This edition published in 2024

ISBN : 9789362516800

Design and Setting By
Alpha Editions
www.alphaedis.com
Email - info@alphaedis.com

As per information held with us this book is in Public Domain. This book is a reproduction of an important historical work. Alpha Editions uses the best technology to reproduce historical work in the same manner it was first published to preserve its original nature. Any marks or number seen are left intentionally to preserve its true form.

PREFACE.

THERE is much truth and force in the old saying that "Manners make the man." All persons should know how to appear to the best advantage in polite society. This very attractive volume furnishes rules of etiquette for all occasions, and is a complete guide for daily use in all matters pertaining to social intercourse.

The first department treats of Introductions and Salutations. The rules given under this head are those constantly observed in the best society. The same is equally true of all the instructions throughout the book, which is the most complete work on this subject ever issued.

The next department treats of the very important Art of Conversation. It has been said, with truth, that "a good talker is always a social success." The reader is here taught how to converse agreeably and with ease. To be a bright, witty, interesting talker, is a most charming accomplishment. This volume is a help in this respect, the value of which cannot be overestimated.

Visiting Cards and Customs are next treated, and all the perplexing questions which they occasion are fully answered. With this very comprehensive volume at hand, no person will be guilty of blunders and humiliating mistakes.

Invitations, Formal and Informal, Acceptances and Regrets, form another topic. The work furnishes full information and is authority upon all matters of social etiquette.

All young persons, and some older ones, are deeply interested in the Etiquette of Courtship and Marriage, Weddings and Wedding Anniversaries. These subjects are treated in a manner at once practical and instructive.

The usages of the best society in giving Parties, Dinners, Teas, Receptions, Breakfasts, Luncheons, etc., are minutely described. Also, Home Etiquette and Etiquette for Children. With this volume in the home, parents can easily teach the young polite and winning manners.

Miscellaneous Entertainments form a department that is bright and sparkling. The dark side of life is not overlooked, Etiquette of Funerals forming a separate topic. How the young lady should "come out" is stated in full, with invaluable instructions to her parents and herself.

Then we come to Etiquette of Public Places, followed by that of Walking, Riding, Boating, Driving, etc. Etiquette for Bicycle Riders receives full attention. Here are Hints for Travelers, for Hostess and Guest, General Etiquette and Delsarte Discipline, Musicales, Soirées, Lawn Parties, etc.

Washington Etiquette is described and all the proper titles for professional and public men are given.

The Art of Dress receives exhaustive treatment, and the rules to be observed by those who would dress tastefully are very complete. They who are well dressed have already made a favorable impression upon others. Suggestions and rules upon this subject are important to all who would shine in social life.

Letter-Writing makes constant demands upon nearly all persons, yet its difficulties are perplexing. Here are plain directions upon this subject, which should be studied and followed by all who would succeed in the great art of elegant correspondence. It is essential often to have the best Forms for Letters, happily expressed, choice in the use of words and easy and correct in grammatical construction.

Artistic Home Decorations are fully treated, showing how to have a pretty, tasteful and inviting home at least expense. This subject is receiving great attention everywhere, and this delightful volume should be in every household in the land, as it furnishes just the information needed. Fireplaces and Windows, Stairways, Woodwork, Doors, Lighting, Decorating, Furniture and Paintings, are among the topics treated in this part of the volume.

In short, this work is a treasury of rules and information on every subject of Social Etiquette, Self-Culture and Home Life.

An entirely new and very important feature is the beautiful Phototype Engravings in rich colors. The publishers consider themselves fortunate in being able to present these new and admirable embellishments, which have been pronounced gems of art.

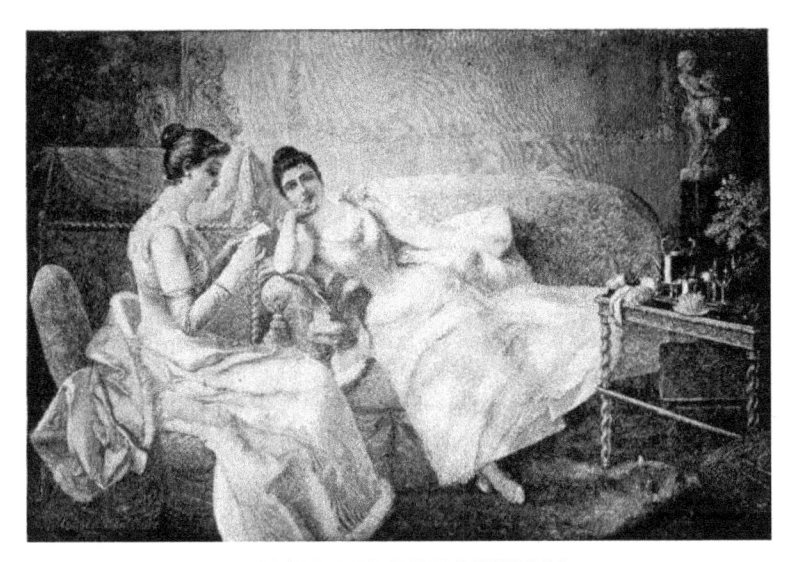

VOTARIES OF FASHION

THE AFTERNOON MUSICAL CONCERT

THE ESSENCE OF ETIQUETTE.

THE old chronicler says, "Manners maketh man." "Manners are not the character, but they are the dress of character," adds a modern writer. Manners are not the pure gold of the mind, but they set the mint stamp upon the crude ore and fit it for circulation, and few there be who may dare to set aside their valuation. To genius only is this privilege granted, and genius is exceeding rare.

It should be remembered that more people can give the list of Dr. Samuel Johnson's sins against good manners than can quote from his "Rasselas" and "Rambler," while there will always be more who can descant upon the selfish, tyrannical ill-breeding of Thomas Carlyle than can estimate the value and immensity of his literary labors.

The essence of all etiquette will be found in that Golden Rule from Holy Writ that enjoins upon us to "do unto others as we would that they should do unto us," and whereon Lord Chesterfield based his maxim for the cultivation of manners:

"Observe carefully what pleases or displeases you in others, and be persuaded that, in general, the same things will please or displease them in you."

The social code, even in its smallest particulars, is the outgrowth of a kindly regard for the feelings of others, even in the little things of life, and a kindly sympathy for all that interests your companions.

"Be hospitable toward the ideas of others," says Dr. George Ripley, "Some people," he asserts, "only half listen to you, because they are considering, even while you speak, with what wealth of wit they will reply." Such people may be brilliant, but they can never be agreeable. You feel that they are impatient to have their own turn come, and have none of the gentle receptiveness so pleasing to our own ego that rebels against their egotism.

It is the kind and sympathetic soul that wins friends, and

"He who has a thousand friends

Has not a friend to spare,

But he who has an enemy

Will find him everywhere."

Our first impressions of a man are impressions of his manners. We designate him from the first glimpse of his face, first sound of his voice, as an affable, agreeable and sincere individual; or as crabbed, cross-grained and suspicious in his temperament, and are attracted by, or repelled from him, according to the characteristics with which his manners have clothed him.

The Influence of Good Manners.

So potent is this power exercised over the world by the gentle sway of manners that their possession is worthy the cultivation and care we put forth for the attainment of all gracious, pleasant things, and to their possessor is given the key to which all doors open.

Emerson was one of the most acute observers of manners that culture has ever produced, and he wrote: "The longer I live the more I am impressed with the importance of manners. When we reflect upon their persuasive and cheering force, how they recommend, prepare and draw people together; when we think what keys they are, and to what secrets; what high and inspiring character they convey, and what divination is required of us for the reading of this fine telegraphy, we see what range the subject has."

Manners, with some, are the gracious legacy of inheritance, education and environment; with others they are the growth of the careful cultivation of years, and carry with them the calm self-poise of the man who has conquered circumstances and established his own position. In such as these there inheres a certain power that impresses itself upon all who come in contact with its influence.

The self-possession and certainty stamped upon the face of a man who inherited, or won for himself, the sure and perfect armor of good-breeding, is but the outer stamp of the man himself.

Manners are profitable as well as pleasant. They carry with them a measureless weight of influence. A gentleman once brought into his library a costly subscription book. "My dear," said his wife, "you already had a copy of that work." "I knew I did," he replied, "but the manners of the lad who sold it were so elegant that it was a pleasure to purchase it."

The charm of good manners is not a qualification belonging to any particular station in life, for, to the poor and unlettered oftimes may be traced deeds and actions that mark them as nature's noblemen. Education, wealth and social station do not always confer them, but the outer grace may be acquired by all.

In this way it has come to be known that a refinement of laws in any country indicates that a gradual refinement of manners has led up towards, and finally crystallized into a refinement of the hearts and the laws of the people.

The Marks of True Politeness.

True politeness is always known by its lack of assumption. President Tyler, in advising his daughter-in-law previous to her taking her position as lady of the White House, used these noteworthy words: "It is, I trust, scarcely necessary to say that, as upon you will devolve the duty of presiding at the White House, you should be equal and untiring in your affabilities to all. You should remember that nothing shows a little soul so much as the exhibition of airs or assumptions under any circumstances."

The minor observances have much to do with the polishing and perfecting of the manners of men. These little things that mark one as being "to the manor born" are not the growth of moments but the slow accretions of years; neither can their use be dropped in the privacy of home to be assumed at pleasure for the outside world to admire, else they will fit but illy, as borrowed plumes are wont to do.

The best-intentioned and best-hearted people that the world has ever known are too often careless in the slight observances that mean so much to the cultivated. Thoreau says, "I could better eat with one who did not respect the truth or the laws than with a sloven and unpresentable person. Moral qualities rule the world, but at short range the senses are despotic."

"The code of society is just a little stronger with some individuals than the code of Sinai, and many a man who would not scruple to put his fingers in your pocket, would forego peas rather than use his knife as a shovel."

The Great Value of Courtesy.

"Be courteous," is an apostolic command that too many earthly followers of the Twelve would do well to consider. They are just, they are truthful, sometimes aggressively so; they are conscientious, they weary not in well-doing, but—they are not courteous. They are not good mannered, and by so much as they sin in this regard do they lose their power to win.

"Good manners," says one, "are more serviceable than a passport, than a bank account, than a lineage. They make friends for us; they are more potent than eloquence or genius without them." They add to beauty, they detract from personal ugliness, they cast a glamour over defects, in short, they work the miracle of mind over matter exemplified in the case of the extremely plain Madame de Staël, who was reputed to "talk herself beautiful in five minutes."

They teach us the beauty of self-sacrifice, they constrain us to listen, with an appearance of interest to a twice-told tale, they teach the wife to smile over the somewhat worn jest of the husband, as she smiled in like fashion in the days of auld lang syne, or, harder still, they enjoin upon us to follow the Duc de Morny's definition of a polite man, as "one who listens with interest to things he knows all about, when they are told by a person who knows nothing about them."

They impress upon us to guard the feelings of others, they warn us to avoid the familiarity that breeds contempt, and, above all, they are contagious!

There is much to be said as to the true definition of those beautiful but abused terms, lady and gentleman, each with its strong, sweet meaning.

"A lady is one who, to inbred modesty and refinement, adds a scrupulous attention to the rights and feelings of others, and applies the Golden Rule of doing as she would be done by, to all who are connected with her, both at home and in society."

While a gentleman has been described as: "Whoever is true, loyal and candid; whoever possesses a pleasing, affable, demeanor; whoever is honorable in himself and in his judgment of others and requires no law but his word to make him fulfil all engagements."

Such men and such women are "ladies" and "gentlemen" whether they are found in the peasant's hut or the prince's palace.

Rules of Etiquette.

The following rules, published some time ago as a receipt for that beauty of expression so much more lasting and attractive than mere beauty of feature, were written originally for the guidance of woman, but they are equally applicable to the needs of man.

"1. Learn to govern yourself and to be gentle and patient.

"2. Guard your temper, especially in seasons of ill-health, irritation, and trouble, and soften it by a sense of your own shortcomings and errors.

"3. Never speak or act in anger.

"4. Remember that, valuable as is the gift of speech, silence is often more valuable.

"5. Do not expect too much from others, but forbear and forgive, as you desire forbearance and forgiveness yourself.

"6. Never retort a sharp or angry word. It is the second word that makes the quarrel.

"7. Beware of the first disagreement.

"8. Learn to speak in a gentle tone of voice.

"9. Learn to say kind and pleasant things when opportunity offers.

"10. Study the characters of those with whom you come in contact, and sympathize with them in all their troubles, however small.

"11. Do not neglect little things if they can affect the comfort of others in the smallest degree.

"12. Avoid moods, and pets, and fits of sulkiness.

"13. Learn to deny yourself and prefer others.

"14. Beware of meddlers and tale-bearers.

"15. Never charge a bad motive, if a good one is conceivable."

Courtesy, charity and love are one, and, when all good deeds are done the warning comes: "If ye have not charity" all is naught. Therefore:

"A sweet, attractive kind of grace,

A full assurance given by looks,

Continual comfort in a face,

The lineaments of gospel-books."

Do ye all things courteously, founding precept and practice upon that old rule, the Golden Rule, which is the Alpha and the Omega of all good manners and the very Essence of all Etiquette.

INTRODUCTIONS AND SALUTATIONS

INDISCRIMINATE introductions are always in bad taste, yet, since the sweetest of our friendships are wont to reach us through the medium of a formal presentation, it is well that we understand how, when and where these introductions should properly take place.

As a rule, introductions, to be agreeable, should be desired before being given; and since we are, or should be, in a measure, the endorsers of those whom we present to our friends, a due degree of care should be exercised in so doing, lest inadvertently we force upon another what may prove an undesirable acquaintance.

Introductions are given in cases of necessity, such as business transactions, or emergencies that may arise in traveling, as when we wish to consign some friend to the care of another. They are given at balls, that partners may be found for all the dancers. Here, however, care must be taken beforehand to ascertain if the parties will dance, for such is the selfishness and, shall it be said, ill-breeding of our society young men that not unfrequently they will walk away without even offering the lady the courtesy of the next dance. In this way her hostess unwittingly exposes her to a marked slight, since the ballroom introduction is supposed to mean an intention on the part of the gentleman to show some attention to the lady, with whom he should either dance, promenade, or talk through one set.

Neither are young ladies quite guiltless in this respect, since it often happens that they refuse partners from simple caprice, and no gentleman likes to be refused, even for a quadrille. It may be added that these introductions necessitate no after acknowledgments on either side unless mutually agreeable.

Introductions are given at card parties when necessary to fill out tables for a game, and they occur also where one person especially wishes another to become acquainted with a friend.

An English Custom.

Strangers are always introduced to visitors, and at dinners, if previously unacquainted, the gentleman is introduced, a few minutes beforehand, to the lady he is to take out to the table. In England, however, where they exercise great care in giving introductions, even this formality is not always complied with. Richard Grant White speaks of being informed at the last moment, in some house whose owner boasted many titles, that he was to take down "the lady in pink over there in the bay window," to whom, therefore, he duly went, and, bending an inviting elbow, said in his most persuasive tones: "May I have the pleasure?" The proffered honor was accepted, and he and the lady, each equally ignorant as to the other's identity, went out to spend a long two hours in entertaining one another.

The one redeeming feature of this English custom is that everyone, at private entertainments, talks to everyone else without an introduction, considering that the fact of their being guests under the same roof is a species of endorsement for all, and, better still, this sociability carries with it no after obligations, because, since they are not introduced, they are not acquainted. In this country, owing probably to the unfortunate frequency of introductions among us, a certain chill pervades the atmosphere when a portion of the guests are unacquainted with one another, for, as a rule, no one here attempts to converse without having been properly presented.

In metropolitan circles, however, this is not so much the case, and as our country grows older it is to be hoped that "a change will come o'er the spirit of our dream" in this respect, thus lessening the present responsibility of our hostesses, who, torn between two opposing factions, feel that "If I introduce Mrs. So-and-so to Mrs. Blank she will never forgive me, and if I do not introduce Mrs. Blank to Mrs. So-and-so I shall have made a mortal enemy."

At a party given in behalf of a *débutante* she is to be introduced to every lady present, and every gentleman is to be presented to her. In case there should be a distinguished guest present at any entertainment, all other guests must be made acquainted with the favored one.

You May Introduce Yourself.

There are also times when it is eminently proper to introduce one's self, such as when you find upon entering a drawing room that the hostess has forgotten your name; or if it should have been wrongly announced; or if you are an entire stranger to the hostess, it is not only proper, but imperative, to introduce yourself at once. Then, too, it occasionally happens that a gentleman, wishing to render some assistance to a lady who is traveling alone, prefers to introduce himself beforehand. This, of course, leaves the lady perfectly free to recognize him or not at any future time. Occasions such as these are constantly arising, and tact and judgment must be used to decide the question for one's self.

Watering-place introductions are frequently given for the convenience and pleasure of the time being. They are usually made by the eldest lady of either party and further recognition in the future is optional.

Do not introduce people in public places. Do not, even if a friend should overtake you and walk by your side for some distance, or should meet and talk with you, introduce him to another friend with whom you are also walking. You may do it, however, in exceptional cases. Do not, as a rule, introduce two people who are inhabitants of the same town; it is to be supposed that they could have known one another had they cared so to do. Still, it is well to exercise judgment in this one particular, since what could be done unquestioned in a city parlor cannot always be accomplished without exciting comment and ill-feeling in a country town.

Do not introduce gentlemen to ladies without first being sure that the acquaintance will be agreeable to the lady, since it is much more difficult for a lady to shake off an undesirable acquaintance than it is for a gentleman. In the case of foreigners it is always well to be careful before introducing them to young ladies at their own request, since it often happens that foreign titles, found upon this side of the water, are extremely dubious. Hence one is clearly justified in referring them to her parents or guardians for the required favor.

A Custom Out of Date.

Introductions at evening parties are, fortunately, very much out of date, except it is for partners in dancing, or unless there should be so many strangers present as to threaten overwhelming the entire party in speechless gloom. Occasionally in the country some old-fashioned hosts persist in handing each newcomer around the room like refreshments for an introduction to each one present. This custom puts the later arrivals in the position, as some one says, "of making a semi-circular bow like a concert singer before an audience," and this, to non-professionals, is not a little embarrassing.

Timid people, and people unaccustomed to the rules of social etiquette, always feel a certain dread in going through the slight formality of an introduction. Nothing, however, if one remembers a few timely hints, can be simpler than this little ceremony so necessary for each of us to perform many times in our intercourse with others. Recollect always to introduce the gentleman to the lady, never the lady to the gentleman, except in the case of very exalted rank, extreme age or the possession of great eminence in intellectual or artistic life; otherwise, the rule is inflexible save in introducing a youthful "rosebud" formally to an elderly gentleman, in which case you would present her to him. The chivalry of etiquette assumes that a man is always honored by presentation to a lady.

In introducing ladies, present the younger to the elder, unless in case of some marked exception such as those given above.

The simplest form in presenting one person to another is always the best. A wife presents her husband as "Mr. North," "Colonel North," or "Doctor North," always giving him his rightful titles. The wife of the President should introduce him as "The President," while we should address him as "Mr. President."

In introducing a gentleman to a lady one should say, "Mrs. A. allow (or permit) me to introduce (or present) Mr. B.; Mr. B., Mrs. A.," being sure that the names are distinctly pronounced. If this should not be the case, let the parties themselves ask it at once, a simple "I beg pardon, I did not understand the name," saving much future annoyance.

Forms of Introduction.

In introducing two ladies the same formula may be used, as: "Mrs. Y. allow me to introduce Mrs. Z.; Mrs. Z., Mrs. Y." Or one may say: "Mrs. Y., this is my friend Mrs. Z.; Mrs. Z., Mrs. Y." A still further variation is to say: "Mrs. Y., I believe you have never met Mrs. Z.; Mrs. Z., Mrs. Y." In introducing two gentlemen any of the above forms may be used. If the introduction is given simply for business purposes it should be short and concise, as: Mr. A., Mr. B.; Mr. B., Mr. A.

In introducing a stranger it will always be well to make some little explanatory remark that may be used as a stepping-stone toward beginning a conversation, thus: "Miss S., allow me to present Mr. T., who is just back from Africa," or, "Miss E., this is my friend Mr. F., the composer of that little song you sang just now." Any remark like this always serves to make the opening of the conversation easier.

An introduction received, or solicited, simply for your own convenience, as a business recommendation, or otherwise, entitles you to no after benefits, or social recognition.

Where there are several waiting for an introduction to the same individual, name the latter first, then in succession name the others, bowing slightly, as each name is pronounced, in the direction of the one named. Thus: "Colonel Parker, allow me to present to you Mrs. Roe, Miss Doe, and Doctor Brown," being sure always to give every one their full honorary title in making the introduction.

In introducing relatives be very sure to give their full name. A sister, for instance, should be introduced as, "My sister, Miss Roe;" or, "Miss Mary Roe," or, "My sister, Mrs. Doe," as the case may be, making sure always never to say "My sister Mary," or, "My brother Joe," thereby leaving the stranger ignorant as to name or estate.

A mother is always at liberty to introduce her son or daughter; a husband is supposed always to introduce his wife, and a wife her husband.

What Should Follow the Introduction.

Nowadays, the usual recognition of an introduction is by a formal bow. Handshaking rarely occurs and a gentleman introduced to a lady never offers his hand unless she should first extend her own. The inclination on the part of the lady is slight, that of the gentleman deeper. The custom of a courtesy by the lady has scarcely taken root in this country.

A hostess receiving in her own parlors is at liberty, if she should wish, to extend her hand to all comers.

A gentleman upon being introduced to a lady usually suggests that he is "Happy to make her acquaintance," or, "Delighted to make the acquaintance of Miss B———," though, if he choose, he may simply bow, repeating her name. A lady, upon introduction to a gentleman, simply bows, possibly repeating his name, but never is "happy" or "delighted" to make his acquaintance. The pleasure is supposed to be upon his part, the condescension upon her side. She should, however, upon his expression of pleasure, bow, with a slight smile, or a murmured "Thank you," in return, though, a married lady, especially if she be a little the elder, may cordially say she is "glad to meet him."

It is the place of a gentleman, after an introduction to a lady, to make some remark calculated to set the conversational ball rolling, and she should endeavor to supplement his efforts sufficiently to keep up the conversation. If, however, the gentleman be younger than the lady and somewhat embarrassed, she should show sufficient tact to open the conversation herself. If the introduction is between two ladies, the one who is introduced should make the first remark.

Letters of Introduction are fully commented upon and explained in this volume in the Department on Correspondence, where the proper forms for such letters are given.

All introductions, however annoying, should be received pleasantly and acknowledged fully while under the roof where they are given, though, an hour after, the two might pass one another in speechless silence. This is for the hostess' sake, and so great is this solicitude on the part of the well-bred that mortal enemies have met and smiled across the mahogany of a mutual friend, thus preventing the utter chagrin of a hostess who discovers, by frowning faces and averted gaze, that her carefully arranged dinner is a partial failure.

A Lady's Wishes Should be Respected.

Gentlemen rarely ask for introductions to one another, but, should a lady, for any cause, express a desire to present two men of her acquaintance to one another, they must, even if not anxious for the honor, acquiesce instantly in her request.

An introduction given between two visitors calling at the same house need not carry with it any weight unless both parties so desire. At the time, a bow is the most that is demanded; afterward, it is the individual having the most social prestige, or, if there is no difference in standing, the one having most confidence, to whom this privilege is given of acknowledging or ignoring the introduction. A bowing acquaintance with a person thus introduced cannot in the least injure the social position of an individual.

An introduction given on the street needs no after recognition. At the time, a gentleman simply lifts his hat, a lady bows, and that is all.

After any introduction (except the one just mentioned) never give the cut direct save for very good cause. It is too often an uncalled-for insult.

SALUTATIONS.

The style of salutation differs among nations, but there have been none yet discovered so low in the social scale as to be entirely destitute of some sign for expressions of respect or fear between man and man. Fear is, perhaps, the origin of respect, for every form of salutation among us to-day may be traced back to a source that plainly affirms it to be the survival of some attitude of deference from the conquered to the conqueror, or some habit of adoration of an unseen Power.

In our own customs of salutation we bare the head in token of respect, never thinking that in the olden time it was an act of adoration practiced before gods and rulers. Our formal bow is simply the modification of a servile prostration, and the graceful bow of a lady of society is but the last remaining trace of a genuflection. When we rise and stand as our friends enter, or leave, our reception-room, it is an act of respect, it was once an act of homage. The throwing of a kiss is an imitation of an act of worship that devout Romans practiced before their gods, and the wave of the hand to a friend across the street is a modification of the same custom.

The removal of a gentleman's glove in shaking hands with a lady is the relic of a habit based on necessity, and dating back to a day when the knight of old removed his iron gauntlet, lest he crush the maiden's hand within its grasp. The removal of the glove was practiced between men also at a later date, when, too often, beneath the heavily embroidered gauntlet, lurked the assassin's dagger, so that to unglove before a hand-clasp grew to be considered an act of good faith.

The bow, the hand-clasp, and the kiss are the principal methods of salutation employed by the most highly civilized nations of this era of the world.

The bow is the most proper salutation among friends and acquaintances meeting in public. It is also frequently resorted to on private occasions.

The bow should never degenerate into a nod; this is both ungracious and ungentlemanly. The hat should be lifted sufficiently to clear the head, and the bow, in the reception-room, should slightly incline the body also. Ladies should incline their heads gracefully and smile upon their friends pleasantly, but not broadly.

Removing the Hat.

A gentleman should remove his hat from his head with the hand farthest from the person saluted. This turns the hat from instead of towards them. If you see that the person saluted is going to stop to shake hands, use the left in order to leave the right free.

A gentleman, in giving assistance to a lady in any difficulty (which should be offered immediately), should do so courteously, lifting his hat and requesting the pleasure of assisting her. This rule, unfortunately, is much more frequently observed on the Continent of Europe than in England or America.

Gentlemen meeting and passing ladies on hotel stairs, or in the corridors, should lift their hats, whether acquainted or not. The same courtesy should be observed on entering an elevator where there are one or more ladies, or in opening a door for a lady and giving her precedence in entering.

All these observances, slight as they are, mark the thorough gentleman who respects all women, whether or not there has been a formal presentation between them.

In giving up a seat to a lady in a street car, or a crowded room, a gentleman will do so with a slight bow. Such a kindness should always be acknowledged by the lady with a bow and a polite "Thank you." American women are too prone to take this altogether optional courtesy on the part of men as a matter of course, deserving no thanks at their hands, or to look upon its omission as an infringement of their rights. No true lady will ever fail to acknowledge such courtesies. Any aid given, or information furnished, should also call forth her thanks.

A gentleman walking with a lady will salute with a bow any person they may meet to whom she extends the same courtesy, even should the party be quite unknown to him.

Where two gentlemen are walking together and they chance to meet a lady with whom one is acquainted and the other not, both should bow, the one because of his acquaintance and the other out of respect.

The Privilege of Recognition.

A gentleman should usually wait for a lady to recognize him first on the street. This privilege of recognition is her prerogative. Especially is this the case if he is simply the acquaintance of a single evening's entertainment. Acquaintances of long standing, however, do not wait for such formalities, usually speaking at about the same moment.

When a gentleman and lady are walking together and another gentleman, also a friend of the lady, should meet or overtake the couple, a bow and smile and a word of greeting are all that can be permitted the newcomer, when he should at once pass on. By doing otherwise he affronts the lady's escort, and should she, by word or look, endeavor to retain him at her side, she also sins against that conventional code which argues that by her own consent she has granted her company, for the time being, to her first escort.

As before said, introductions are not to be given in public places, but should it happen that a lady walking with a gentleman meet another lady, and either pause for a few words, or else walk on beside her for a few steps, the gentleman, at her departure, should lift his hat politely in farewell.

If a gentleman should stop a lady on the street for conversation, and she should be desirous of discontinuing it, she should bow slightly, whereupon the gentleman must instantly take his leave. If she should walk on without breaking up the conversation, he is bound to accompany her.

Absolute good form, however, demands that a gentleman, wishing to converse with a lady on the street, should, instead of stopping her, turn and walk with her for a short distance in the direction in which she may be going. When the conversation is finished, he should lift his hat, bow, wish her "Good morning" or "Good afternoon," as the case may be, and retrace his footsteps in the direction in which he was previously going.

Young ladies show the same deference in awaiting a bow from a woman much their senior that a gentleman does towards a lady.

A gentleman, in bowing to a lady, if he should be smoking, removes his cigar from his lips; and if, alas! his hand or hands should be in his pockets, withdraws them immediately.

Returning Salutations.

A lady's bow should always be returned by a gentleman; if he should be determined not to recognize her he should take the pains of crossing the street or in some other manner avoiding the meeting. Bows from persons not recognized at the moment should be returned, as it may be some one, not recalled at the moment, yet who has a claim upon your politeness.

If the same friend is met several times in the course of a walk or drive, the first bow is all that is required, a smile, or a glance answering all purposes of recognition at after meetings.

A gentleman lifts his hat on passing a funeral procession or a group of mourners; he removes it entirely on entering a church, and he should remove it on entering a private office; he should remain uncovered while talking to a lady at a door, unless, after the kindly custom of French ladies, she should request him to replace his hat, on account of wind or weather; in short, he should be with uncovered head much more than American men are apt to be.

Gentlemen, who are acquainted, should lift their hats slightly upon meeting one another, but should never fail to do so should either one be walking with a lady. Under such circumstances a simple nod would be a slight towards her.

A recognition, by bow or smile, is not required from opposite sides of the street, or across hotel dining rooms. Gentlemen riding or driving, and having both hands occupied, are not compelled to lift the hat on bowing.

If saluted by an inferior, do not fail to return the courtesy in kind, remembering Henry Clay, who, when asked why he lifted his hat to an old colored man who had paid him the same deference, replied, "I never allow a negro to outdo me in politeness, sir."

Shaking Hands.

Gentlemen, as a rule, shake hands upon being introduced to one another. The lady of a house usually shakes hands with all guests whom she receives in her house for the first time. Gentlemen do not, however, offer to shake hands with the hostess, leaving it to her to put the stamp of cordiality upon the ceremony of introduction, or to simply pass it with courtesy.

If a lady extends her hand to a gentleman, he does not, as of old, remove his glove, nor does he make use of the out-of-date formula, "Excuse my glove." At his departure the lady bows her adieu, but does not again extend her hand.

The hand-clasp is a cordial expression of good will, but there are degrees of cordiality to be observed in the performance of this ceremony. Every one knows, and shudders at, the woman who gives two, or at most, three fingers of a cold and lifeless hand for a moment into your keeping, and every one recognizes and fears the man who swallows up and crushes the entire hand within his powerful grasp. Each extreme is to be avoided.

A lady should give her whole hand, not her fingers; a gentleman should receive it cordially, holding it neither too tightly nor too loosely, shaking it very slightly and not presuming to retain it. Should a gentleman sin against any of these particulars, a lady is justified in refusing to offer her hand next time.

A young lady simply gives her hand to a gentleman, neither pressing nor shaking his, unless it be in the case of especial friends. Two ladies shake hands quietly. Both ladies and gentlemen always rise to shake hands. Elderly people, or invalids, are permitted to excuse themselves and keep their seats.

Ball-room introductions for dancing do not necessitate hand-shaking, a bow being all that is required. A very particular introduction, wherever given, such as one prefaced by some remark like, "I want you to know my friend So-and-So," merits a hand-shake on your part, together with some cordial remark.

Inferiors in social position should always wait until their superiors offer the hand, never taking the initiative in this respect. This precaution will sometimes save them the pain of a marked slight.

Words of Salutation.

Verbal greetings ought always to be quiet and respectful; they should never be shouted across streets, nor called when the parties are at any distance from each other. Nicknames should not be used publicly and promiscuously, in short, all possible respect should be paid to the feelings of other persons on public occasions.

The phrases, "Good morning," "Good evening," "Good afternoon," "How do you do?" "How are you?" are the usual forms employed. Sometimes the name of the person addressed is added, thus: "Good morning, Mrs. Smith."

Replies to these salutations are sometimes simply a bow from a lady to a gentleman, or perhaps a bow and a repetition of his greeting, as: "Good morning, Mr. Jones." "How do you do," should be replied to by the same phrase, never, as is often the case with the novice in social arts, by: "I am very well, thank you." A special inquiry after one's health, however, as: "How do you do, Mrs. Jones?" followed, after her acknowledgment, by: "How are you?" or, "How is your health?" should receive the response, "I am very well, thank you." After an acquaintance has been ill, the first inquiry by a friend should be one concerning health. This is a rule that should never be neglected: to do so would be an oversight.

Kissing is a custom which the code of English and American etiquette relegates as much as possible to the privacy of home. A kiss, the outward expression of our closest affection and our warmest love, should never be made a public show whereat the outside world may smile. Hence, the effusive kissing between girls and women at their meeting and their parting, is to be regretted as a specimen, to say the least, of very bad taste on their part. Indiscriminate kissing of children and infants is also objectionable on the score of health. Happily, kisses and embraces among men are never seen in this country, though, in some parts of Europe they are constantly to be observed, both in public and private.

**CHICAGO'S WELCOME TO PRESIDENT MCKINLEY—
ETIQUETTE OF THE BANQUETING ROOM**

AN AFTERNOON TEA

ART OF CONVERSATION

"TALK often," says Lord Chesterfield, "but never long; in that case if you do not please, at least you are sure not to tire your hearers. Pay your own reckoning, but do not treat the entire company: this being one of the very few cases in which people do not care to be treated, every one being fully convinced that he has the wherewithal to pay."

All other arts pale before the art of conversation as a source of popularity, and no other accomplishment tends so much toward social success. The contact of many minds is a constant stimulus to mental activity and its outward expression in animated conversation. It lends new power to brilliancy of talent, and quickens, to a certain extent, even then the lowest and dullest of intellects.

Everyone has been surprised and delighted at times by some unexpectedly brilliant remark that has flashed from his lips during the course of some animated exchange of badinage and repartee, and there is no one but realizes how the mind acquires breadth and the opinions grow tolerant as one converses with persons of intelligence and culture.

Since, however, according to Cicero, "Silence is one of the greatest arts of conversation," there may be added, with equal wisdom, to the above counsel, "Listen often and well." Be not an impatient listener, nor yet an impassive one, but pay the compliment of attention and interest to the subject in hand, and your company will be sought as an acquisition.

Any lady, by profound attention to, and a pleased interest in the subject under consideration, may promote the conversation most skillfully and delightfully. Knowledge of the subject is not always necessary. An English savant, deeply interested in Egyptology, once escorted a young lady out to dinner. His conversation, as a matter of course, turned entirely upon excavations, hieroglyphics, and kindred topics. Upon all these the young lady was profoundly ignorant, but, if unversed in Egyptian lore, she was most thoroughly versed in conversational arts, and, by her speaking glances of intelligence and her pleased smile, so fascinated the man of science that he enthusiastically declared afterward that "Miss L—— was one of the best conversationalists and the most intelligent young lady he had ever met, and that her knowledge of Egyptology was something wonderful." This, to one who had sat opposite them at table, and could have vouched that the lady in question had not spoken a single word through the entire dinner, was slightly amusing. So strong, however, was the impression left upon the mind of the savant by her interested attention, that it would have been difficult to convince him of the fact.

The Good Listener.

This, even if an exception, shows what attentive listening may accomplish toward social success. Let it be mentioned here, however, that no one individual should be so carried away by a pet hobby as to force conversation into a monologue. A very well-bred man, no matter how great his interest in or eloquence upon any topic may be, always catches at the slightest hint to close the conversation.

A man will always bear in mind that the greatest compliment he can pay a woman is a respectful, deferential attention to her words. There are men whose very manner of listening conveys, in itself, the most delicate flattery.

A woman, in her turn, should always remember that, however interesting her conversation may be, there is always danger that a man may possibly weary of its protracted continuance, and so she should forebear leaving him no loophole for escape. Louise Chandler Moulton enjoins one thing on women which they would do well to recollect, and that is, "if they want a man to stay with them to make it evidently and entirely easy for him to get away. There is something lawless and rebellious in even the best of men; they hate doing things because they are obliged."

Suitable Topics.

To render conversation agreeable, suitable topics for the company present, if possible, must be chosen. Neither soar above the level of their conversation, nor sink so far beneath it, as to lead them to infer that you possess a very slight opinion of their merits.

In conversing, too many educated men fall into the error of talking commonplaces to all women alike, as if "small talk," to the exclusion of all weightier matters, were the only species of conversation suited to a woman's ear. On the contrary, she is more often either hurt or angered at your evident condescension, or, on the other hand, she credits you with just the amount of knowledge that you have evinced in your conversation with her.

In the search after suitable topics it is well to remember that all are pleased by a display of interest in their especial affairs. Thus, by leading the artist to talk of his pictures, the lady amateur of her music, the *prima donna* of her successes, the mother of her children, the author of his book, you may rest assured that they will always speak of you as a person of great discrimination and a very interesting conversationalist. They in their turn, unless extremely devoid of tact and eminently selfish, will display sufficient regard for your feelings to give an opportunity for waxing eloquent on your part over your own pet topics. Be very careful then not to fall into that besetting fault of good talkers, a monologue, which is fatal to all conversation.

Richard Steele gave a most desirable maxim for conversation when he said: "I would establish one great rule in conversation, which is this, that men should not talk to please themselves, but those that hear them—adapting their words to the place where, the time when, and the person to whom they are spoken."

Misuse of Quotations.

Do not use classical quotations before a woman unless you know that, by virtue of a classical education on her own part, she is capable of appreciating the point. Remember, too, that there are a great many men who, not having enjoyed your educational advantages, are annoyed, rather than edified by your display of learning.

Do not make a point of exhibiting your learning aggressively anywhere. "Classical quotation is the literary man's parole the world over," says Dr. Samuel Johnson, but he savored somewhat of the pedant, and his imitators, by too frequent an indulgence in this habit, may run the risk of aping his pedantry without possessing his genius. Neither is it well to interlard conversation with too frequent quotations from English authors, no matter how well they may fit the occasion. This is a habit that easily becomes tiresome.

"Small Talk."

The current change of society is the light coin of "small talk" that breaks with chink and shimmer the heavy bills of large denomination, that else would overwhelm social conversation with their size.

Wiseacres may meet and learnedly discourse on all manner of sage subjects, but that is discussion, debate, argument, what you will, not conversation. Conversation is light, brilliant, and tossed back and forth from one to another with the grace and ease of the feathered shuttlecock.

A lady of high literary attainments was seen in a gay gathering sitting quietly by herself in a corner, and, being questioned by a friend as to her silence, replied, half bitterly, "I have no 'small change,' and my bank bills are all of too large denomination for the occasion." This is a difficulty that one should strive to overcome, for, after all, it is small change, rather than bank bills, that society in general requires.

Given the foundation of even a moderate education, the aspirant for social success will gain more ideas from modern fiction than from any other source whatever. No historian presents the social manners and customs of his time with half the accuracy displayed by our best fiction writers. A well-known society woman, familiar with its usages both at home and abroad, declares that "a course of Anthony Trollope is as good as a London season," and we all know that Howells and James and other authors of that ilk have lifted the *portières* of our own drawing rooms and shown us what is transpiring therein. Gail Hamilton says that to be "well-smattered" is next best to being deeply learned, and nowhere can a smattering of almost everything be better gained than from the modern works of fiction.

A Valuable Source of Knowledge.

A friend of the writer, a talented elocutionist, and socially brilliant, once said with reference to her quiet country home and her sudden emergence therefrom to mingle in Washington society, that she found herself perfectly at ease in those circles so widely different from her previous experience of life, and that "she attributed it wholly to her knowledge of social customs and the social atmosphere, as gained from the best society stories." It was in this manner that she served her social novitiate and the result bore testimony to its efficacy.

Where one is not quite sure of rising to the occasion it is well to be provided, before attending a social gathering, with several topics that will be suitable to bring forward in conversation. Many are in the habit of doing this constantly. Some new book, one that created a little sensation, some course of lectures, some late theatrical or operatic entertainment, anything, in short, that is generally popular. Be careful, however, in broaching such subjects not to egotistically give your own opinion at the outset by saying decidedly, "I think that book is a perfect failure, quite absurd in fact. What is your opinion?" This course of action, if your companion is younger or more timid than yourself, will probably reduce him to the point of having no opinion whatever, or at least to being afraid to express it, and the conversation, as such, will fail completely. Whereas, if you had quietly asked him if he had read the book, how he enjoyed it, etc., you would have gradually entered upon a conversation wherein you would have drawn out his ideas and at the same time have been enabled to display your own.

Cultivate Your Mind.

One of the first requisites of social success is a cultivated mind. You cannot hope to hold your own in society without at least a general knowledge of the events of the last few years in historical, scientific, artistic and social fields. Such knowledge is easily gained by a little study and a great deal of observation, the pains taken being more than recompensed by the ease and assurance with which one enters society.

If a musician or an artist, you should be sure to know something of your chosen art aside from the mere technicalities. Be well versed in the various schools of painting, the varied merits of the musical masters of the past and present. Be filled with the spirit as well as the technique of your profession and you cannot fail to converse pleasantly upon these subjects. Always remember, however, not to advance your opinions to the utter exclusion of every one else, or your companionship will become tiresome to the best of listeners.

"Drawing Out Others."

The very essence of the art of conversation is to draw others out and cause them to shine; to be more anxious, apparently, to discover other people's opinions than to advance your own.

Who does not remember gratefully and admiringly the sympathetic people who seem to draw out the very best there is in us—in whose company we appear almost brilliant, and actually surprise ourselves by the fluency and point of our remarks? Such people are a boon to society. No one sits dull and silent in their presence, or says unpleasant, sarcastic things before them, and, while never seeming to advance any views of their own, and certainly never forcing them upon our attention, we involuntarily learn of them and love them, scarcely knowing why.

Malebranche showed his knowledge of human nature when he wrote: "He who has imparted to others his knowledge without any one perceiving it and without drawing from it any advantage, necessarily gains all hearts by his virtuous liberality. Those who would be loved, and who have much wit, should thus impart it to others."

The Passion for Argument.

Never permit yourself to be drawn into an argument in general society. Nothing can be more provocative of anger on one side or another, or more destructive to conversation, than a lengthy and, too often, bitter argument. Good breeding would suggest that the subject be changed at once before the controversy becomes heated. Especially should any debate upon politics or religion be avoided as subjects upon which two seldom agree, but which are so close to the hearts of the majority as to cause serious annoyance if their pet beliefs are touched upon or questioned. Be careful, also, not to take the opposite side of *every* question that is brought up in conversation.

Wit and Humor.

Sidney Smith once said: "Man could direct his ways by plain reason and support his life on tasteless food; but God has given us wit and flavor, and laughter and perfumes, to enliven the days of man's pilgrimage, and to charm his pained footsteps over the burning marl." And Sidney Smith was so much the life and soul of every social gathering that, while the English language is spoken, his witty remarks will be quoted with delight.

Wit, however, is too often but another name for sarcasm and ridicule, that, like a barbed arrow, rankles long in the soul of its victim. True humor, it should be remembered, is neither scathing nor insolent; it is simply that bright repartee that someone aptly calls the "spice of conversation." Hence it would be well to smother the temptation to be witty at the expense of another, and crush back the brilliant but cutting retort meant only to wound, not to amuse.

Evil Speaking.

Beware of evil speaking. In the eyes of all right-minded persons much that you have said recoils upon your own head, for no one has quite the same opinion of an individual after having listened to a series of scandalous stories from his lips. Hence, for your own sake, as well as for that of others, eschew the vice of evil speaking as a very pestilence.

Let young ladies have a care how they speak lightly or contemptuously of one another at any time, but more especially when conversing with men. Nothing, as a rule, is more prejudicial to a woman, in the estimation of a man, than this all-too-prevalent habit. No matter what the faults of your sister-woman may be, condone them gently, or, if this be impossible, let a silence that is golden fall about the subject.

Unhesitatingly acknowledge a woman's beauty or talent, and, instead of detracting from your own merits, it will enhance them in the eyes of all. A young man was once heard by the writer counselling his sister from the depths of his own experience as a social favorite. "Never," said he, "say one word against a girl to any young man. It only puts you down in their estimation. Say something pretty and complimentary about them if you can; if not, keep still." And his advice was words fitly spoken, that are, indeed, "like apples of gold in pictures of silver."

"Telling Stories."

Stories should never be introduced into general conversation unless they meet several requirements. In the first place, they should be short and well told. Secondly, they should be new to the company where they are told. Nothing is more tiresome than listening to a twice-told tale, though the height of good breeding is to smile over its tediousness.

One way to avoid inflicting this martyrdom is to ask beforehand if any one present has heard such and such a story. Then, in the third place, it must be straight to the point, and directly called for as an illustration of the case in hand.

A PROMENADE AT THE OPERA

CONSULTING HER PROGRAMME

Do not tell more than two or three stories or anecdotes in the same evening. Never be guilty of relating in company a narrative that is in the least questionable in its import. This is utterly inexcusable, and, to so sin, is to render one's self unfit for social companionship. Avoid repetition. If some portion of an anecdote has met with applause, do not repeat it. Its unexpectedness was its only charm.

Absent-Mindedness.

This is a sin against good manners which cannot be too greatly condemned, being, as it is, in some measure an insult to the company in which you find yourself. No one cares to be of so little importance as to find the person addressed totally oblivious of his presence or remarks, and no one can blame him if, as Chesterfield suggests, "finding you absent in mind, you should speedily find them absent in body."

Profuse Compliments.

To be endurable, compliments should be made use of in a very cautious and artful manner. If permitted to degenerate into gross flattery they are far from complimentary to the understanding of the individual addressed. The day, happily, is long since past when conversation between men and women was confined to unmixed flattery on the one side and blushing acceptance on the other. That "the best flattery is that which comes at second hand," no one can deny, yet, judicious praise is not only acceptable but useful many times in giving the needed incentive, without which the flagging footsteps might have faltered on their way.

Contradictions and Interjections.

Never be guilty of abrupt contradictions. If you differ decidedly from some given opinion, soften the expression of your difference by such modifications as, "I hardly think so," or, "My idea is rather different," or, "I beg to differ." This is much more polite and less likely to arouse antagonistic feelings.

In conversation never allow yourself to fall into the habit of using constantly such phrases as "You don't say!" "Do tell!" "Did you ever?" "Is that so?" and many others that will come to mind as you recall your own faults in this respect, and the faults of your friends. An equal avoidance should be cultivated of such interjections as "Say," "Well," etc., with which we often begin our sentences. These habits are all to be condemned and should be corrected as speedily as possible.

Voice and Manner.

Let your voice be low and pleasantly modulated and your enunciation clear, distinct and musical. All these things are marks of good breeding, and, if not yours by birthright, may be acquired by patience and perseverance. Avoid high tones and nasal tones. Do not talk rapidly, or in a hesitating, stumbling fashion. A partial course in elocution and voice training will work wonders in this direction, and any one determined to succeed will never regret the time or money so spent.

Cultivate also, if shy and timid by nature, self esteem sufficient to imagine that you are quite the equal of those with whom you are about to meet. This resolution will enable you to say what you wish without fear of mistake, and without showing too much respect of persons. The above-mentioned elocutionary lessons will also be an aid toward acquiring self-possession.

Repose of manner should be assiduously cultivated. Do not fidget or loll about in your chair, or twist your fingers constantly, or play with something while you talk, or restlessly beat a tattoo with fingers or feet. All such faults render your companionship a burden to those about you.

Indulge in no facial contortions, as they rapidly become habits difficult to break and usually leave their traces on the face in lines impossible to efface. Lifting the eyebrows, rolling the eyes, opening them very widely, twisting the mouth and opening it so as to show the tongue in talking, are all disagreeable habits, that, once acquired, can only be broken by ceaseless vigilance. Practice talking without moving the facial muscles but slightly. Do this before your mirror daily, if necessary, and before the same faithful mentor learn to open the eyes less widely, parting the lids only just so far as to show the colored iris without a glimpse of the white portion, or cornea, of the eye above or below it. The time thus spent will result in a change most gratifying to yourself and friends.

Conversational Sins.

Never interrupt a person who is talking. Never take the words out of anyone's mouth and finish the sentence for them. To do this is ill-bred and does not bespeak your superior discernment, but your ignorance of polite society.

Puns, unless exceptionally witty, are to be carefully avoided. Young ladies, especially, should beware of establishing any reputation for punning. At all events, puns should never be far-fetched.

Do not whisper in company; nothing can be more vulgar. Neither should two in a gathering converse together in a foreign language, not understood by the others present, or talk blindly in a manner unintelligible only to themselves. Should, however, a distinguished foreigner to whom the language is almost unknown be among the guests, it is a mark of courtesy for as many as possible to converse in his native tongue.

Do not immediately break off the conversation upon persons entering the room. It is too apt to leave the impression upon their minds that the discourse was of them. In carrying on a conversation after newcomers enter the room, briefly recapitulate what has gone before, that the thread of the story may be complete for them. Look at those with whom you are talking, but never stare.

Profanity is the last and most inexcusable sin committed against good manners and propriety. The man who will deliberately use profane language in the drawing-room, or before women and children, or aged men, should be considered without the pale of good society.

Language coarse in its tendency is open to the same criticism, and remarks and stories that carry a double meaning cannot be too severely condemned. If it is at any time possible for a woman to receive such a story in its innocent sense, let her do it, showing by some remark the light in which it is taken; otherwise, she should be apparently blind and ignorant as to its meaning.

Avoid affectations. In conversation make use of long words as little as possible, and wherever a short and easily understood one is suitable to express your meaning, choose it in preference to one of polysyllabic proportions.

Use of the Lips and Facial Expressions.

Do not cover the lips with the hand, or a fan, while speaking. To do so shows nervousness and a lack of social training. Besides this, much of the expression of the face lies in the mouth. This is shown by all actors, readers and public speakers, who, as a rule, appear before their audiences with closely-shaven faces, that no portion of the varying changes of the lips may be lost.

Never, if you are a man, speak lightly of women. Nothing so surely lowers your own standard in the eyes of all sensible people. Never hurt the feelings of others. Never allude publicly to times when you have known them in less affluent circumstances than the present.

Be very careful to guard against over much laughing. Nothing gives a sillier appearance than spasms of laughter upon the slightest provocation. It soon grows into a very disagreeable habit. Smile frequently, if need be, but be moderate in laughter. A very little reasoning will serve to do this; and the reflection that few grown people laugh well will aid still farther in curbing the propensity.

Let your greeting of acquaintances be free from boisterousness and familiarity. Do not bring your hand down heavily upon their shoulder, nor emphasize your sentences with pushes and punches of an active elbow, nor fling your arms about their necks or shoulders. To some fastidious persons these boorish acts are a positive insult. An affectation of boisterous familiarity more often betrays a feeling of social inferiority than absolute shyness or timidity does.

Never permit yourself to correct other people in matter or manner, unless it should be absolutely necessary to protect some one else. Under all ordinary circumstances do not betray a confidential communication made you by a friend. Set the seal of the confessional upon it. If it should be sorrowful in its nature, do not mention it even to the friend who has confided it to your keeping unless he or she should first refer to it. It may have been confessed in a moment of confidence and regretted almost as soon as spoken, hence, do not revive the memory yourself.

Control Your Temper.

Keep your temper under all circumstance while in company. Even if some remark has been made with plain intent to injure your feelings, an absolute ignoring of the intended sting will prevent others, and, most of all, the guilty party, from perceiving the depth of the wound. A true gentleman, or lady, is never quick to take offense.

Never ask impertinent or personal questions, unless these latter are called for by the nature of the conversation. Be careful not to give advice unless it is sought, and remember then that it is a commodity of which a very little goes a long way.

And last, but not least, utterly eschew all slang. There are some young ladies who apparently think that a little slang, to spice their remarks, is piquant and saucy, but, in the majority of cases they so soon overstep the mark and fall into the deplorable habit of constantly and copiously interlarding their speech with all manner of slang phrases, that one is forced to advocate total abstinence as the only safeguard.

The too common habit of exaggeration, on the part of so many schoolgirls and young ladies is also to be deplored, a quiet unobtrusiveness of speech always marking the true lady.

Do not, in speaking, too frequently mention your hearer by name. To do so implies either great familiarity on your part, or social inferiority on theirs. In this latter case it savors strongly of patronage.

In speaking to people always give them their proper titles, as: "Colonel," "Doctor Jones," "Professor Gray." Never make a practice of saying: "That is so, Colonel," but, "That is so, Colonel Sharp."

In mentioning a married daughter, unless to a very intimate friend, give her married title, as: "Mrs. Miller," or, "My daughter, Mrs. Miller." In speaking of unmarried daughters, or of sons (unless to servants), give them their

Christian name, as Hattie or George, or else mention them, and this is better before strangers, as: "My daughter," or, "My son."

Misuse of Initials.

Never address persons by their initials, as: "Mrs. W.," "Miss C.," "Mr. D.;" give them instead their full name. Neither should you call young ladies, "Miss Mollie," or "Miss Jennie;" "Miss Smith," or, "Miss Brown," being in much better taste. Their Christian names should only be used to distinguish them from other sisters. Never address people by their Christian names unless very familiarly acquainted. This practice savors of ill-breeding and is often very annoying to the person so addressed.

In speaking of persons who are absent, mention them by their last name, as: "Mrs. Roe," "Mr. Doe," unless the intimacy is very great; even then care should be taken not to use their Christian names too freely among persons to whom they may be strangers.

A wife in speaking of her husband should rather say "Mr. Smith," than "My husband;" but, above all, let her refrain from referring to her liege lord as "he," as if the whole wide world possessed no other mortal to whom that pronoun was applicable. Husbands should follow the same rules in referring to their wives.

Be careful not to interlard conversation with "sir," or "ma'am." In Europe these terms are relegated to the use of the lower classes.

VISITING CARDS.

CARDS are the sign manual of society. Their use and development belongs only to a high order of civilization. They accompany us, as one writer has justly remarked, all the way from the cradle to the grave. They begin with engraved announcements of the birth of a child, then cards for its christening, and, later on, dainty little cards of invitation for children's parties, until, in due time, the girl crosses that line

"Where the brook and river meet

Womanhood and childhood sweet,"

sets up a card of her own, and blossoms forth into a young lady.

They announce the gaieties, the pleasures, the anniversaries of life: they inquire for us during our illness and sorrow, they return thanks for our gifts and attentions, and, finally, they commemorate to our friends the last, sad earthly scene and ring the curtain down.

The stress laid by society upon the correct usage of these magic bits of pasteboard will not seem unnecessary when it is remembered that the visiting card, socially defined, means, and is frequently made to take the place of, one's self. It will be seen, therefore, that one of the first requisites for social success is to understand the language, so to speak, of the visiting card. With this end in view the following suggestions on the subject have been carefully arranged with due regard to brevity, accuracy and ease of reference.

Style of the Card.

The card should be perfectly plain, fine in texture, thin, white, unglazed and engraved in simple script without flourishes. Gilt edges, rounded or clipped corners, tinted surfaces or any oddity of lettering, such as German or Old English text, are to be avoided. A photograph or any ornamentation whatever upon a card savors of ill-breeding or rusticity. Have the script engraved always, never printed. The engraved autograph is no longer considered in good taste, neither are written cards as elegant as those that are engraved.

Size of the Card.

The regulation size, both in this country and England, for a lady's visiting card is three and one-half inches in length and two and one-half inches in width. This oblong form is most generally used, but there is an almost square shape, two and a half inches by three, also in favor, and especially used by unmarried ladies where the shortness of their name would be too much emphasized in the longer card. For instance: "Miss Ray" would be quite justified in choosing the square style, while "Miss Ethelinda Crane" or "Mrs.

Algernon Spenser" would find the length of their names displayed to better advantage on the oblong card.

A NAVAL BALL ON SHIPBOARD

AN ABSORBING STORY.

Cards for gentlemen are much smaller than those for ladies. This holds good in both England and America, where the required size is three inches one way by one inch and a half the other.

William L. Smith

The largest card in use is the one sometimes adopted by the newly-married and engraved with their joint names. Thus:

MR. AND MRS. GRANT TROWBRIDGE

may make use of a card four inches long by three and one-half in width, but a lady and her daughter, where their names appear together, should use the first-mentioned oblong size for ladies.

Engraving the Name.

Married ladies make a point of using their husband's name or initials upon their cards instead of their own, as:

Mrs. George B. Cleveland,

Or:

Mrs. G. B. Cleveland,

Instead of:

Mrs. Grace E. Cleveland.

It occasionally, however, happens that some lady, unwilling to so lose the identity of her own name, prefers this latter form. Or, if her family name be an old and honored one, she frequently retains it, thus:

Mrs. Grace Ethridge Cleveland.

But, though the married woman make use of her husband's name, she has no claim to his titles; so that while others may address her as "Mrs. Judge So and So," "Mrs. Dr. So and So," she must carefully avoid all such display. Let her be comforted, however, as her just pride in her husband's honors is easily gratified, since she is expected, on all formal occasions, to leave one of his cards, wherein his titles are set forth, with her own.

Occasionally a lady contents herself with having engraved upon her cards a simple:

Mrs. Courthope.

This, however, is unwise unless the name is a very uncommon one, and even then, should there be more than one branch of the family in the vicinity, the wife of the oldest member of the family only would have a right to make use of it.

Newly married couples frequently send out for their first cards the largest size mentioned engraved thus:

Mr. and Mrs. Holman B. Hunt.

Occasionally they preserve this custom throughout the entire first season. But this is all; from thenceforth husband and wife have their own separate cards. They may, however, be used at times throughout the married life to convey messages of sympathy, congratulation, or to accompany gifts.

Widows have always hesitated about exchanging the beloved and accustomed name upon their cards for their own signature. This, however, in many cases, is a necessity, especially where there is a son bearing the father's name. This is sometimes thought to be avoided by the use of the distinctive "Senior" or "Junior," a custom obviously wrong, since after the death of Francis Brown, Senior, Francis Brown, Junior, becomes at once Francis Brown, and his wife, Mrs. Francis Brown. Hence, while we have no such convenient title as

"Dowager," the widowed Mrs. Francis Brown will be obliged to drop her husband's name in favor of her son's wife and thenceforth appear before the world as Mrs. Mary E. Brown. Where there are no children, or immediate relatives, change of title on the part of the widow is a mere matter of sentiment.

The black border upon a widow's cards should never be over a quarter of an inch in depth: more than this savors of ostentation rather than affliction.

Young ladies, especially if it is their first season in society, will find it the best form to have their names engraved upon the visiting card of their mother. Thus, if it is the eldest daughter:

Mrs. Wilfrid Ferguson.
Miss Ferguson.

If a younger daughter:

Mrs. Wilfrid Furguson.
Miss Ethel Furguson.

And if it should chance that two daughters "come out" in consecutive seasons both of their names are frequently engraved upon their mother's card, thus:

Mrs. Wilfrid Furguson.
Miss Furguson.
Miss Ethel Furguson.

Though it often happens that, for convenience sake, by the time the second rosebud is "out," the first has established a cardcase of her own. Yet as neither custom nor etiquette sanctions young girls in having cards of their own, a mother often continues to have the name of her young daughters engraved upon her own card.

Young ladies should always prefix "Miss" to their names, as:

Miss Alice Creighton Wright,

there being a certain forwardness about announcing one's self as:

Alice Creighton Wright.

Especially is this so among strangers, the prefix "Miss" carrying with it a certain quiet reserve and dignity.

The eldest daughter of a family announces herself upon her cards as "Miss Wright," unless there are several of the same name in town, while the others are respectively "Miss Alice Creighton Wright" and "Miss Ethel May Wright." Occasionally a card is used for sisters engraved as follows:

MISSES WRIGHT.

All pet names are to be avoided upon visiting cards and "Nettie Cranston" very properly becomes "Miss Annette Cranston" upon her cards.

Neither are initials good form for young ladies, though after an unmarried lady has reached a certain, or rather an "uncertain," age, she may, if she choose, be permitted to place upon her visiting cards:

MISS A. C. WRIGHT.

If the young lady be motherless she often has her name engraved beneath that of her father, using not the smaller card of a gentleman but the first given oblong card for ladies. In England unmarried ladies, unless they have reached a very "uncertain" age indeed, follow the above fashion, and quite young ladies leave their chaperon's card as well. This fashion is often followed here, and when so done signifies that they will be inseparable for the season.

Address on Cards.

There is much question as to whether the address should be engraved on a lady's card, some very exclusive circles prohibiting it entirely on a young lady's card and questioning its use for a married lady, suggesting that in case a young lady desires to give her address to any particular individual it may be easily pencilled on one of her cards for the occasion, and that married ladies have the privilege of leaving one of their husband's, with engraved address, in connection with their own. This custom, while it may seem an over-nicety to those outside the great centers of metropolitan life, will be appreciated by all those to whom the "ins and outs" of city life are familiar. It should be said that while engraving the address is still a mooted question, except for young ladies, each individual is at liberty to use her own judgment on the question.

Cards for Gentlemen.

The size and style of a gentleman's card has been already given, but a few words as to name and titles will be necessary here. Custom, with reference to the cards that a man must carry, is considerably less arbitrary than towards women in the same respect. He may use his initials or his full name, as it pleases him. He may inscribe himself "Mr. John Smith," or simply "John Smith," and be quite correct in so doing, though just now there is a little inclination in favor of the more formal "Mr." an English custom we do well in copying.

Military, not militia, naval and judicial titles, may always be used. Physicians and clergymen have the same privilege; honorary titles, however, should be avoided.

A private gentleman would have his card as: MR. HOWARD MASON, 24 Union Square. If he were a club man, the club name, providing it were a very fashionable one, would take the place of the address, as: MR. HOWARD MASON, Union League Club. For a military card: CAPTAIN ARTHUR COLEMAN, U. S. A. For a naval card: ADMIRAL PORTER, U. S. N. A medical man might use the following: GEORGE H. HARRISON, M.D.

Some eminent men go to extreme simplicity, as, for instance, "Mr. Webster" being all that graced the cards of that celebrity.

It is hardly necessary to say that a business card should never be used as a visiting card. A gentleman carries his cards either in his pocket or in a small leather case sold for that purpose.

Cards for Receptions.

Cards used for receptions, lawn-tennis parties, afternoon teas, etc., in place of more formal invitations, have been fully described under "Invitations." One example will suffice here: MRS. LAWRENCE BARRETT, July 1st, at 4. P. M. The object of the entertainment being written in the corner of the engraved card.

Cards for receptions are a necessary convenience in this era of lengthy visiting lists. Without them there would be no possibility of leisure or of seeing one's friends at their own homes. The following is an example: MRS. EMMONS B. CHURCHILL, Thursdays. Or: Thursdays, Three o'clock to five, may be substituted; the latter form, however, usually meaning that a simple afternoon tea will be served on the day mentioned.

A young lady never sends out a reception card in her own name alone, but her name is engraved upon her mother's card or that of her chaperon, thus: MRS. HAROLD GRAY; MISS GRAY, Wednesdays, Four o'clock to seven. Or, in case of a chaperone: MRS. GEORGE M. JANSEN; MISS ALICE LEVICTOIRE, Wednesdays, Three o'clock to five.

Foreign Phrases.

There are a certain number of French phrases that custom has declared shall take the place of that "pure English undefiled" whereof Spenser wrote. In a few cases these chance to be shorter, more euphonious, and more directly to the point than the corresponding English phrase. For instance, the word "chaperon," so important in its signification at the present, has no adequate

English translation. Below is given an alphabetical list of those phrases in most frequent use, together with the abbreviations that ofttimes serve in place of the full phrase:

FRENCH PHRASES.	ABBREVIATIONS.	TRANSLATIONS.
Bal masque		A masquerade ball.
Chaperon		An older woman attending a girl in society.
Costume de rigueur		Costume to be full dress.
Debut		First appearance.
Debutante		A young girl making her first social appearance.
En ville	E. V.	In town or city.
Fete Champetre		A rural or outdoor entertainment.
Matinee		A morning or daylight entertainment.
Matinee musicale		A daylight musical entertainment.
Musicale		Musical entertainment.
Pour dire adieu	P. D. A.	To say farewell.
Pour prendre conge	P. P. C.	To take leave.
Protege		One under protection.
Repondez s'il vous plait	R. S. V. P.	Reply if you please.
Soirée		An evening party.
Soirée dansante		A dancing party.
Soirée musicale		A musical entertainment.

The term *en ville*, when used in the place of "city," in addressing a note that is to pass through the postman's hands, is a needless and annoying affectation, since it is hardly to be expected that a knowledge of the French language forms one of the qualifications for a letter-carrier's position, and if delay ensues in delivery, the writer, not the carrier, is to blame.

P. P. C. Cards.

In the event of leaving town for a long absence, P. P. C. cards are frequently sent out. This is especially convenient where the length of one's visiting list renders the personal making of farewell calls an impossibility. The cards are sent out upon the eve of departure, and all persons receiving them are expected, upon the arrival of the absentee, to return the courtesy by cards (which may also be sent by mail) and by invitations. The ordinary engraved visiting card is used, and the initials P. P. C. (an abbreviation of the French phrase "to take leave") are written in capitals in the lower left hand corner of the card. P. D. A. (to say farewell) is occasionally used, but is not in general favor. If the address should happen to be engraved in the lower left hand corner, P. P. C. may be written in the lower right hand corner, either way being permissible at any time. The large card inscribed jointly with the name of husband and wife is frequently used in this connection. P. P. C. cards are especially appropriate where there are no calls due. If possible, unpaid personal calls should be answered in person on the eve of departure.

Turning Down the Corners.

This custom is almost out of date, and in consequence of the various interpretations liable to be given to the act, its disuse is a satisfaction to all parties concerned. To briefly explain the custom, a card turned down at the corner, or across one end, signifies that the call was made in person, and is sometimes very convenient when one wishes it distinctly understood that the card was brought in person, not sent; while one folded through the center denotes that the call includes all members of the family. A man should not turn down the corners of his cards.

Minor interpretations, such as which end or which corner is to be turned down on different occasions, even the surviving adherents of the custom do not pretend to agree upon.

How to Leave Cards.

In leaving cards follow the fashion of those who have paid you the same courtesy. If a call has been made upon you, return it by a call, as to return a personal visit by the sending of a bit of pasteboard would partake of the nature of a slight. If cards only have been sent you by a servant, return cards in the same manner by messenger or servant; if they were sent by mail, return by mail. If the cards of any of the gentlemen of a house are left, always leave the cards of any gentleman of your family in return.

Of course first calls should be made and returned in person, the card-leaving formalities coming later on. This rule is departed from only by a few ladies whom age, health, social or literary duties will excuse from making personal calls. These frequently permit themselves to send out cards in place of a first call, either accompanying them with, or immediately following them by an invitation to some entertainment. This attention should receive the same notice as a first call; cards should be sent in return, together with an answer to the invitation, if it is of a nature to require it, and a personal call must be made thereafter, unless it was simply an afternoon tea, and an invitation sent in return speedily as possible.

A SOCIAL CHAT.

A LEISURE HOUR IN THE PARK.

A lady leaves a card for a lady only, a gentleman leaves cards for the host and hostess of a house. Some authorities assert that a man making the first call of ceremony should, in addition to the first-mentioned cards, if none of the family are at home, leave another folded down through the center for the other members of the family. The folding, however, is questionable taste and the requisite number of cards would be better left in their original state. Cards should be left for the daughters of a house; if there are sons, a lady may leave one of her husband's for them also.

Number of Cards to be Left.

After this first visit of ceremony it is only necessary to leave one card at any following call throughout the season. As a rule in country towns but one card is left at any call, unless it is at the first calls of a bride, when, if her husband's name is not engraved upon her card, she leaves one of his with her own.

A gentleman and lady calling together and finding the mistress of the house, only, at home, would leave but one card, that of the gentleman for the master of the house. Finding no one at home, they would leave three cards, one of hers and two of his. A lady calling under the same circumstances would leave one of her own cards and two of her husband's.

When one lady calls upon another, if the hostess be at home she does not send in her card (unless she is an entire stranger), nor does etiquette strictly enjoin her to leave it in the hall, unless it is upon her hostess' reception day, when, on account of the large number of visitors, it would be difficult to remember all. It then becomes a very desirable custom for a lady to leave a card, together with two of her husband's. Also when the servant is somewhat dull of comprehension as to the name it will be well to send in a card to prevent mistakes. On reception days in very fashionable houses it is the custom to announce the guests by name as they enter the room, so that cards need not be sent in.

Never hand your own card to your hostess. If it be necessary, introduce yourself verbally, doing so quickly and clearly, and being sure to mention yourself, if a young lady, as "Miss."

Busy, elderly, and even young men are very prone to leaving their cards in the hands of mother, sister, wife, or any other lady of the house for distribution, though after an elaborate entertainment it is much more indicative of good breeding that a young man should pay his respects in person to his hostess.

Calls upon Young Ladies.

Young men in this country leave cards for the young ladies of a house, but they should always leave one at the same time for her mother or chaperon. In Europe they are never permitted to leave a card for a young lady at all. They call upon the mother or chaperon, and while they may offer to send for the young lady, she is never asked after.

If a gentleman, in calling where there are several young ladies, especially wishes to see one of the number, he may ask for her, but, before the call is over, should say he would be pleased to see the other ladies; more especially is there no excuse for ignoring the existence of the mother or chaperon of the young girl.

If a gentleman knows the ladies of the house well, it is not necessary for him to send in a card if they are at home, unless it be the first call of the season, when it is well to leave one in the hall. In a household consisting of two or more ladies not closely related a card should be left for each one.

When ladies are visiting in a house where the caller, whether man or woman, is unacquainted, he or she always leaves a card for the lady of the house and requests to see her: a request which she may not grant, but one which it would be a marked slight to omit.

In leaving a card for a friend visiting at a private house, never write her name upon it; depend upon the servant, or whoever opens the door, to remember for whom it is intended. This is only permissible when your friend is at a hotel. In doing this write the name above yours.

When a newly-married man sends cards immediately after his marriage to his bachelor friends it may be expected that he wishes to retain them as such in his new life. Upon the reception of these cards they are expected to call upon the bride at once.

How to Send Cards.

Cards sent by messenger are enclosed in a single unsealed envelope; sent by mail this envelope is enclosed within another and larger one which is sealed. Cards handed in at the door are received by the servant on a salver to prevent being soiled by handling.

When to Leave Cards.

First Calls of the season necessitate the leaving of cards. Let them be left quietly in the hall. This custom assists the lady of the house in revising her visiting list.

Letters of Introduction necessitate that those who have received courtesies in response to such, should, upon their departure, send P. P. C. cards to those that have thus remembered them.

A Change of Residence renders it desirable to send cards by mail to one's friends with the new address engraved thereon. However, should there be unpaid calls, the cards to these should be left in person.

The Return from an Absence, including any length of time, should be announced by sending out cards having the address and reception day engraved upon them. Where P. P. C. cards have been issued previous to departure these should always follow the return.

Preceding a Debut. Previous to the date decided upon for the presentation of a *débutante* to the social world, the young girl's mother calls upon those of her friends whom she desires to be present upon the occasion and leaves them her own and her husband's cards, and, if she have grown sons, their cards also.

Reception Invitations to a full dress reception are preceded by a call by card upon all the acquaintances to whom the hostess may be indebted.

After Cards is the name applied to those that are sent to friends after a marriage and are engraved thus:

MR. AND MRS. CHARLES E. SMITH.

Later on, however, when the bride returns visits, she usually leaves her own card with her married name engraved upon it, thus:

at the same time leaving her husband's separate card with her own.

Before Marriage, the bride expectant in paying her farewell calls, leaves her own separate card, together with that of her mother or chaperon, with all acquaintances she may wish to retain in her new life.

Entertainments and Calls.

After Entertainments, a card, in large cities, is sufficient, unless it be after a dinner or a wedding reception, when a personal call is made. If the wedding invitations have been to the church only, not including the gathering at the house, some most exclusive people send cards to the bride's parents, afterwards inviting the young people to their entertainments. But a dinner absolutely requires a personal call.

Even gentlemen, usually so remiss in such matters, are rather expected to leave a card in person after a dinner. Any invitation, however, coming from a new acquaintance, necessitates a personal call, unless the intercourse is not to be kept up. In towns and smaller cities, a personal call is made after entertainments of any size.

After a Tea a visit is paid and thus the visiting etiquette for a year is established. Before the season is over, however, the lady, if she expects to retain her position in society for the next season, must give a tea, or a series of teas, inviting all who have similarly honored her. This must be done before the season closes. Where the tea is not attended, cards should be sent to the house the same day.

Special Receptions, such as those dress affairs given once or twice in a season, require a personal card.

General Receptions, or "at homes," given in a series, the dates of which are all mentioned on one card, need neither cards nor calls in return. Your presence there is a call in itself. A card may be left in the hall upon the day of reception to assist the memory of the hostess.

Other Hints.

Ladies in a strange city, staying either with friends or at a hotel, are privileged to send cards, giving their address, to any acquaintances, either lady or gentleman, from whom they may wish to receive a call. If desirable, they may send a note in preference, giving date or hour when they will be at home.

Special Pursuits. Ladies having special pursuits, literary, or professional, often permit this fact to cover remission in social demands, in fact do not "visit" at all.

For a Son, upon his introduction to society here in America, there is very little display made. His *entrée* is usually very gradual, but if he has been closely kept at school his freedom from this is often announced by his mother leaving his card with her own when she makes her visits at the beginning of the season. This is taken as a suggestion that, in future, his name is to be included among the invited members of the family.

Cards for an unmarried gentleman should never be left by a lady, except in the case of his having given an entertainment at which ladies were present. In this case the lady of the house should drive to his door with her own cards and those of her family. Names of the young ladies should be engraved for the occasion upon the card of their mother or chaperon. The cards should be sent in by a servant. If a call is made upon a lady's regular reception day, it is rude to leave a card only, without entering and inquiring for the hostess. The time spent inside the house may be very brief, but even a few moments will satisfy the demands of etiquette, which without these would be rudely violated.

Cards may be made to accomplish so much of the multifarious duties of society that one can scarcely imagine the social world revolving safely upon its axis without their intervention. Far be it from any to look upon the custom as a hollow mockery, for, without the system of formal visiting, or calling, society as it now stands could not exist. Such, too, are the complexities of modern existence that life would be all too short for the fulfillment of its demands were it not for these useful bits of pasteboard that do so much of our work by proxy and dispose of our undesirable acquaintances so speedily by the simple cessation, on our part, of leaving cards at their door.

Various Cards.

Among the cards as yet not referred to in this department may be mentioned the following:

Cards of Congratulation, such as those sent the parents of a newly-betrothed couple upon the announcement of the betrothal; those sent the happy parents of a lately arrived son or daughter, etc. Cards of this description should be left in person, though it is not expected that you should enter and make a formal visit. The leaving in person, however, is a compliment.

Cards of Betrothal are distributed by the parents of the newly-engaged pair, leaving their cards with their own on all friends of the family. Individuals receiving these cards should call as soon as possible.

Cards of Courtesy are sent on many occasions. For instance, to a house where the children or youth of their family have been invited without including the elders. This is done in acknowledgment of the courtesy extended to their children. Again, a gift however simple, even flowers, should always be accompanied by a card of courtesy. The simple visiting card is usually sufficient, though a "Merry Christmas," "Happy New Year," or "Many happy returns of the day," may be penciled beneath the name. If there are many words to be written, however, a little note of courtesy is far better. (See Notes.) The recipient of the gift should answer by a note of thanks, never by a card simply. Cards should also accompany, or be attached to, flowers sent to a funeral, that the family may know friends remembered them in their sorrow.

Cards of Inquiry are frequently sent, or better still, left in person, at the homes of friends prostrated by severe illness, or by recent bereavement. These usually have the words, "To inquire," or "With kind inquiries," pencilled above the name. These are many times a source of relief during the weary days of convalescence, or the heavy hours of seclusion after affliction, when the voices of friends would be too hard to bear, but the thought of their loving remembrance yields a healing balm. In cases of bereavement the cards should be sent about one week after the sad occasion that called them forth.

Acknowledgment of Inquiry Cards.

Cards of Thanks are usually sent out in reply to these cards of inquiry, since the answering in any other fashion would prove too great a task. The regular visiting card may be used in this case, pencilling the words "With thanks for kind inquiries," or, "With thanks for the kind inquiries of Mrs. ——," beneath the engraved name; or cards especially engraved for the occasion may be substituted, thus: "Mrs. —— presents her sincerest thanks for recent kind inquiries." These may be sent by mail, but really should be carried by special messenger. Enclose in two envelopes. There is another method of acknowledging attentions during a period of bereavement, viz., the notice in the daily papers. This, however, does not usually meet with favor in large cities, but the example set by Mr. and Mrs. Secretary Blaine upon the death of their son, is, from its heartfelt pathos, worthy of imitation. The card appeared in all the Washington papers as follows:

> "The sympathy of friends has been so generously extended to Mr. and Mrs. Blaine in the great grief which has befallen their household that they are unable to make personal response to each. They beg, therefore, that this public

recognition be accepted as the grateful acknowledgment of a kindness that has been most helpful through the days of an irreparable loss."

Birth cards are frequently sent to all friends, at home and abroad, as soon as the child is named. One very pretty style now in mind reads as follows: ETHEL MAY TOUCEY, Half-past twelve o'clock, January 12, 1895. This was enclosed in two small envelopes and sent by mail. These are more especially useful for sending to friends at a distance.

Christening and Funeral Cards are considered in their respective departments. Families in deep mourning are not expected to send out return cards under the first year. Some prefer, however, to send cards of thanks very soon to those who have inquired, leaving ordinary visiting cards unanswered the usual length of time.

VISITING CUSTOMS

THE customs of society in regard to visiting or "calling," and the rules that govern these customs, are well worthy of our attention and care, since they in a great measure underlie and uphold the structure of our social life. No one, therefore, need consider these details trivial or of little account, since, according to Lord Chesterfield, "Great talents are above the appreciation of the generality of the world, but all people are judges of civility, grace of manner, and an agreeable address, because they feel the good effects of them as making society easy and pleasing."

Length of Visits.

Ceremonious visits should always be short, fifteen to twenty minutes being the outside limit, and a shorter time often sufficing. Even should the conversation become very animated, do not prolong your stay beyond this period. It is far better that your friends should regret your withdrawal than long for your absence. A lull in the conversation, a rising from her seat, or some pretext on the part of the hostess, or the arrival of a guest, all give an opportunity for leave-taking which should be made use of at once.

The Art of Leaving.

Cultivate the art of leaving; nothing will contribute more to your social success. It is said of so brilliant a woman as Madame de Staël that she failed lamentably in this particular, and, on the occasion of her visit to Weimar, made with the avowed intention of intellectually captivating the literary lions of the age, Goëthe and Schiller, she made one fatal mistake, she stayed too long! Goëthe wrote to Schiller: "Madame de Staël is a bright, entertaining person, but she ought to know when it is time to go!" It is also evident from her own statement that she did not know *how* to go. She lingered after she had started, and if this were an unpardonable sin on the part of so marvelous a woman, it is surely a capital crime on the part of ordinary mortals.

The art of leaving is more thoroughly understood by men than by women. The necessities of business life teach the value of time, and the press and hurry of city circles teach them the art of leaving quickly, so that a social call on the part of a business man is a model of good manners. When he has "had his say" and politely listened to yours, he takes his hat, says "good day," and is gone from your presence without giving opportunity for those tedious commonplaces of mutual invitations and promises to come again which seem a social formula with so many women.

When Ready to Leave, Go at Once.

Never say, "I must go," but, when you have finished your visit and rise to depart, go! Never permit yourself to be drawn into touching upon any subject at this critical moment that will necessitate lengthy discourse for yourself and hostess, or force upon you the awkward alternative of reseating yourself to finish the conversation. There is always a certain awkwardness in thus repeating the ceremony of leave-taking which may be avoided by a quick and graceful departure that leaves both host and guest with feelings of the utmost amiability toward one another.

On the other side it is necessary that the host and hostess supplement this laudable endeavor on the part of their guests in order that the departure may be gracefully accomplished. Never detain the visitor, who is attempting to leave, by protests, by inquiries, or by the introduction of new subjects. One writer very pertinently says: "The art of leaving on the part of the guest needs to be supplemented by the art of letting go on the part of the host."

First Calls.

There is, possibly, more difference of opinion on the subject of *who* shall make the first visit or call and *when* it shall be made, than almost any other point of etiquette. At the same time more importance is attached to it than to almost any other social question, and it touches more uniformly every phase of city or country life than any other canon of courtesy.

Neither neighborliness, nor good-Samaritan feeling, can exist without the civility of a call, and, when there is too great a hesitancy on the part of a resident to call upon the newcomer, one is reminded either of the priest or the Levite as they "passed by upon the other side," or is forced to recall the parvenue's dread of losing a footing in social circles.

Common sense and kindliness of heart are always to be relied upon in matters of this nature, and the initiative may safely be taken by those who have social position, age, or length of residence on their side. Of course in large cities the immense demands of social life give a certain immunity from anything like promiscuous calling to those whose circle of acquaintance has already grown beyond the limits of their time. In towns and villages, however, no such immunity exists, and a call may be easily made, or a card left, while, on the other hand, should the new acquaintance prove "pushing," or in any way obnoxious, one simply ceases to leave one's cards and the evil is done away with.

Many elderly ladies, and others whose time is very much occupied by social or other duties, excuse themselves from calling customs. Under such circumstances, they frequently send their cards, accompanied by an invitation, to newcomers younger in years, thus entirely omitting the personal visit. Such invitations, whether accepted or not, should be honored in the same manner as if preceded by a call.

If two people meet pleasantly at a friend's house and wish to continue the acquaintance so begun, let them not hesitate, should none of the before-mentioned distinctions exist, as to which should make the first visit. Still, it is ofttimes wise not to call too hastily upon the newcomer, especially in cities, where it is well first to be properly introduced, and further still to have some assurance that your acquaintance is desired by them as well. As before stated, priority of residence, age, or pre-eminence in social position, should properly be upon the side of the one making the first advances. If none of these exist, let the braver of the two break the social ice.

The etiquette of summer resorts demands that the owners of cottages call first upon renters, and afterward that both unite in calling upon later comers and arrivals at hotels or boarding houses. Of course, such intercourse is simply for the pleasure of the time being, and carries with it no responsibility of recognition in the future, unless such recognition should be satisfactory to both parties. It would be well for the "summer girl" and the "summer young man" to remember this canon whereby "society" guards the doors of its exclusiveness, enjoy the "good that the gods give" and expect no more.

Substitute for First Call.

In continental countries, and in cosmopolitan Washington, newcomers make the first advances themselves, leaving cards with those whom they wish to number among their acquaintances. Every one returns these cards, and invitations flow in upon the aspirant for social honors. This custom, unfortunately, does not hold good anywhere else in this country, though a polite expedient is sometimes adopted by persons entering upon life in a new city. This consists in the newcomer sending out her cards for several reception days in a month. These may be accompanied, or not, by the card of some friend well known in social circles, if such she have, to serve as voucher. If not, she relies upon her own merits and sends out her cards unaccompanied. According to the varied authorities recommending this course of action, those rudely ignoring this suggestion are few in number, and the lady is permitted at once to feel that she has commenced her social career.

Morning and Evening Visits.

Any visit made between the hours of twelve and six is to be looked upon as a morning visit, though there is a little difference in various cities with regard to the exact time. Where one expects to touch upon reception hours, from three to five is usually a safe limit. In country towns or the small cities, from two to five are the usual hours for paying visits. Evening visits should be made between the hours of eight and nine, and ordinarily should never extend in length beyond the hour of ten.

Sunday Visits.

Gentlemen are permitted to call upon lady friends, Sundays after church and Sunday evenings, business cares being their excuse for not availing themselves of the other days of the week. Of course, if there exists any known objection in the family to Sunday visiting all their friends are bound to respect it.

Reception Days.

If a lady have a known reception day, callers are bound, in common politeness, to make their visits, as far as possible, upon that day. If this is not done, either a card only should be left, or, if a personal visit is intended, particular instructions should be given to the servant to the effect that if "Mrs. Brown is otherwise engaged she is not to trouble herself to come down." For which thoughtfulness, "Mrs. Brown," if she be a busy woman, and troubled with many social cares, will cordially thank you.

Unfortunately, it often happens that many of our friends have the same reception day, and one's own "day" may conflict with that of one's nearest friend, so that, where the circle of acquaintance is large, much good nature, a few apologies and a great many cards are needed to safely balance the social accounts.

It is considered a rudeness to simply leave a card, when one happens to arrive upon a lady's reception day, without entering the room for a few moments' visit.

"Not at Home," "Engaged."

The simple and necessary formulæ of, "Not at home," or "Engaged," are more frequently questioned than any other social custom. Nevertheless their use is often a necessity, while, on the contrary, their abuse is to be regretted. No suspicion of an untruth need apply to either, for the phrase, "Not at home," is used with the accepted signification of, "Not at home, for the time being, to any visitors." If, however, conscience rebels against this so transparent fraud, there is always the alternative of "Engaged," which carries not the least suspicion of deception with it, but is somewhat less gracious to the ear.

Indeed, were it not for these safeguards, the woman of society must bid goodby to all opportunities for solitude, self-improvement, or the fulfillment of her own social duties.

The servant should be very carefully instructed each morning as to the formulæ to be employed through the day, or such portion of the day as the lady of the house shall require to herself. No lady, after a servant has informed her that the mistress of the house is "not at home," will question as to her whereabouts, or the probable length of her absence. If she should so far forget her dignity, the well-trained servant will answer all inquiries with a respectful, "I do not know, Madame," adding, if such be the case, "Mrs. Brown receives on Thursdays."

Should a servant show evident hesitation upon receiving your card, and say, "I will see if Mrs. Brown is in," enter the parlor, at the same time saying, "If Mrs. Brown is otherwise engaged, or going out, beg her not to trouble herself."

Never, except upon urgent necessity, insist upon pencilling a word or two upon a visiting card and sending it up, where a lady is "engaged," as a demand upon her attention. If a servant has said the lady is "not at home," she has a perfect right to refuse the message.

In suburban towns and small cities, where reception days are not common, the lady of the house must be very careful how and when she denies herself to visitors. Indeed, in all cases much discrimination must be shown in this respect, as great inconvenience may result, and some injustice be done, by an indiscriminate denial. But, as before said, in towns, it is better, if possible, to receive guests. Even if no servant is kept, the mistress can usually, by the exercise of a little care, keep herself neat and presentable. If at any time some slight alterations are necessary to the toilet, let the interval thus employed be very short.

Some one has said that it would be well for a lady having a reception day to devote a part of the morning of the same day to business calls, and to instruct her servants to inform all comers of this custom.

Visiting List.

It is well for all ladies having a large list of acquaintances to keep a carefully revised visiting list to assist their memories as to addresses, names of persons to invite, reception days of acquaintances, and, if possible, a list of their own ceremonious visits for the season, noting those that have been returned. The time thus expended is amply repaid by the convenience of reference and the avoidance of the possibility of making a second visit when the first is unreturned. Also this list serves as a basis for the visiting list of the next season; those having failed to return calls or cards being dropped from the new list.

Visits Between Ladies and Gentlemen.

A gentleman, as a rule, should not ask a lady for permission to call upon her. It is very easy for her, if she desires his company, to say: "I receive Thursdays," or, "I shall be at home Monday." It is a great discourtesy for a gentleman not to call at the time mentioned, or in a very few days, after being thus invited by a lady. Some gentlemen, if simply asked to "call sometime," will ask, "when may I have the pleasure of seeing you?" To this question a definite answer should be returned, if possible. Very young ladies do not thus invite gentlemen; the invitation coming from either father, mother, or chaperon.

A gentleman does not call upon a lady without some intimation of her wishes in the matter, unless he is the bearer of a letter of introduction, or is taken to her home by some friend sufficiently well acquainted to warrant the liberty. He may, however, seek an introduction through some mutual acquaintance.

Ladies may express regret at being out when a gentleman called; he also should regret the absence. If it should happen that a gentleman should call several times in succession and be so unfortunate as to miss the lady each time, it would be quite proper for her to write him a note, regretting her absence and appointing an evening when she would be at home for his next call. This would remove any feeling of annoyance on his part that perhaps her absence had been premeditated.

Gentlemen frequently call upon their married lady friends, doing so without the slightest appearance of secrecy and with full knowledge of all parties concerned. Indeed, the right of entrance to some of these pleasant home parlors is a great boon to the unmarried men of our cities. Ladies do not call upon gentlemen except professionally or officially, or, it may be, in some cases of protracted invalidism.

"Out of Society."

It sometimes happens that a newly-married lady, or a newcomer in some city, through severe illness, a season of mourning, or devotion to home duties, finds herself, in a year or so, completely "out" of a society with which she had scarcely become acquainted. If she be timid and non-assertive, she will sink back dismayed at the prospect, but if energetic and aspiring, she will at once win her way back by giving a series of receptions, either formal or informal, to all her old-time friends; or, by entering into charities, or joining literary or musical clubs, she will quickly reinstate herself in the memory of society.

Conduct of the Hostess.

A hostess does not necessarily advance to receive her guests, simply rising and moving forward a step in order to shake hands (if she should so wish), remaining standing till they are seated, and, if possible, keeping the latest comer near her side. Gentlemen should always permit the lady to make the first advance in the matter of hand-shaking. It is her prerogative.

As the guests depart, the hostess does not accompany each one to the door, but rising, remains standing until the guests have quite left the room, when it is to be supposed they will be met by a servant. In country towns the hostess usually accompanies the guest to the door, if there are others present, excusing herself to them and remaining out of the room but a moment.

Entertaining Callers.

Where there are several guests in the room at once the hostess should try to make the conversation general and pay equal attention to all, save that for a few moments, the latest arrival engages her more intimately, or some guest of great intellectual or artistic genius may be honored among the rest, as a lion of the hour.

If you should chance to find, at once, in your reception room, two friends with whom you are upon equal terms of intimacy, treat them with the most absolute impartiality, being demonstrative toward neither, for there is too much truth in the saying that "there is always a feeling of jealousy on the part of each, that another should share your thoughts and feelings to the same extent as themselves." There are other occasions where the same care against wounding their feelings should be observed.

If there should be any preference with regard to seats, one suggestion is that a lady should be seated on a couch or sofa, unless advanced in years, when she should be asked to accept an easy chair; an elderly gentleman should be treated in the same manner. If a young lady should be occupying a particularly comfortable seat, she must at once arise and offer it to an older lady entering the room.

Should the hostess, upon the arrival of occasional visitors, be engaged upon work requiring any attention, she must at once relinquish it; but should it be light, ornamental, and not at all confining, she may continue it, if so requested. It would be well, however, to drop it at intervals, lest it appear as if there were more interest in the work than the visitor.

Refreshments are not offered to visitors unless it is a regular reception day with afternoon tea.

Conduct of the Guests.

If a visitor on entering the room finds that name or face has not been remembered by the hostess, let the difficulty be rectified by the guest pronouncing the name instantly and distinctly, the hostess, on her part, to remember names and faces. A bad memory is inconsistent with good manners. In very fashionable houses a servant announces the name of each guest as they enter, thus saving any confusion.

Should you find yourself ushered into a room where there are several inmates, all strangers, ask for the individual you wish to see and introduce yourself distinctly.

If your friend is at a hotel, wait in the parlor until the servant who carries up your card has returned to tell you whether you can be admitted. Never follow him as he goes to make the announcement. A little formality is the best preservative of friendship.

If, while you are paying a visit, other guests arrive, you should, providing your stay has been sufficiently long, arise so soon as they are quietly seated, make your adieus to your hostess, bow politely to the other inmates of the room and take your departure. If you should be calling upon a lady and meet a lady visitor in her drawing room, you should rise when that lady takes her leave.

The style of conversation should always be in keeping with the circumstances under which the visit is made. Common sense alone should teach us that where a short morning call is in question, light, witty and quickly-changed subjects only should be entered upon, the nature of the case plainly prohibiting discussions on many topics.

Gentlemen are expected not to use classical quotations before ladies without a slight apology and a translation, unless they are aware that the lady's educational training has made it possible for her to appreciate them. It would be well if they would use the same courtesy toward other men not gifted like themselves. For a general maxim, it may be here recommended not to air one's classical learning unnecessarily, lest it savor of pedantry.

Guests should greet their hostess cordially, but a bow is usually sufficient to include the others present.

Young ladies visiting a strange city should not receive calls from a gentleman without requesting the privilege from their hostess, and hostess and daughters should be introduced to him. Always avoid the slightest appearance of seeming to use your friend's house for a rendezvous.

Deference to Ladies.

A gentleman rises when ladies leave the room. Ladies bow if it is a gentleman, rising if it is a lady acquaintance, or a lady much older than themselves. A gentleman rises when ladies enter a room, but never offers them his chair unless there should be no other in the room.

A gentleman carries his hat and cane into the drawing room with him in making a visit. His hostess should no more offer to relieve him of them that she would take fan and handkerchief from the hands of her lady guests. If he wears an outer coat he leaves that in the hall; if there should be no hall the hostess may ask him to put it on a chair or in another room. His hat and cane he either holds if he chooses, or places beside him on the floor, never on a chair or other article of furniture. If he intends spending the evening, he can, if he choose, leave hat and cane in the hall. Gentlemen should never bring friends with them to call upon ladies unless they have first received permission from them so to do.

After escorting a lady on the previous evening the gentleman should make a call upon her the following day, if possible. Gentlemen should not consult their watches during a ceremonious visit. If some pressing engagement should render this necessary, they should offer both an apology and an explanation.

A gentleman, unless invited, should never seat himself beside his hostess, but should take the chair pointed out to him.

Gentlemen, in receiving other gentlemen, go to the door to meet them and furnish them with seats.

The man of the house should escort ladies to their carriage, should they call while he is at home. If it be raining or otherwise disagreeable, and they have their own coachman, they should, however, beg him not to trouble himself.

Gentlemen should decline an invitation to spend the evening when making a first visit; indeed, such an invitation should never be given.

A man is usually asked to repeat his visit by the mistress of the house, not by the daughters, or else it is given by their chaperon.

What Not to Do.

Do not, according to the author of "Don't," be in haste to seat yourself; one appears fully as well and talks better, standing for a few moments. A man should always remain standing as long as there are any women standing in the room. A man should never take any article from a woman's hands—book, cup, flower, etc.—and remain seated, she standing. This rule is an imperative one; he must always rise to receive it.

Do not take young children when making formal calls; the hostess will be in terror as to the fate of her bric-a-brac, and the mother in dread as to what her young hopefuls may say or do.

Do not take pet dogs with you into the drawing room. Their feet may be dusty, they may be boisterous in expressing their feelings, and besides, some people have a perfect aversion to dogs, so that your visit, thus accompanied, is likely to be far from pleasant.

Do not meddle with, nor stare at the articles in the room. Do not toss over the cards in the card receiver, if there be one, and, while your name is being announced, do not wander impatiently around the room handling everything within reach.

Do not loll about in your chair, if a gentleman (a lady scarcely needs this caution), keep your feet squarely in front of you, not crossing them; ladies would do well to heed this also. Do not torment pet dogs or cats, or tease the children. Do not call the length of the room if you wish to address any one, but cross the room and speak to him quietly. Neither should you whisper to some one of the company, twist or curl your thumbs or hands, or play with the tassels on the furniture or window curtains, or commit any of the thousand and one blunders that mark the underbred and nervous visitor and render his presence an unwelcome trial.

There are a few other rules that would seem unnecessary to mention here were it not that they are so constantly sinned against. Among others it may be suggested not to do anything disagreeable in company. Do not scratch the head or use a toothpick, earspoon or comb; these are for the privacy of your own apartment. Use a handkerchief whenever necessary, but without glancing at it afterwards, and be quiet and unobtrusive in the action as possible. Do not slam the door, do not tilt your chair back to the loosening of its joints, do not lean your head against the wall, as it will soil the papering; in short, do unto others as you would be done by.

Do not tell long stories, more especially if they are about yourself; do not argue; do not talk scandal, and be sure not to attack the religious beliefs of any one present. Do study the chapter on the "Art of Conversation," and cultivate, as much as possible, that self-repose of manner that is, above all things, a sign of the lady or gentleman.

The Reception-Room.

The arrangement of the reception-room itself has much to do with the pleasure of the visitor. Who does not remember those delightful parlors where the guests dropped into pleasant conversational groups as by magic, and contrast them mentally with those other chilly apartments where a sort of mental frost seems to settle over one's faculties and incapacitate them for use. Much of this may be avoided by a judicious arrangement of chairs and couches, just where people drop naturally into easy groups, or, for the time being, surround their hostess.

Propinquity is a great incentive to pleasant conversation, for there are few people that can talk the pretty nothings and sparkling witticisms, whereof parlor conversation properly consists, across space to people stranded against the opposite wall. Therefore let the hostess, who would have her symposiums remembered with delight, see to it that she has an abundance of chairs, both easy and light, easy ones for the refreshment of the weary in body and light ones that may be quickly moved when the spirit moves toward some other group.

A clever woman, to whom all social arts were long-solved problems, once said that she always observed how the chairs were left in a drawing room where several people had been sitting and put them in the same position next time. A group near the door where the casual caller will naturally drop into one and the hostess into another without the least effort, will be placed in the best possible position for a little chat. Fulfill these conditions and your drawing room will be often filled and the fame of it will go abroad.

Formal calls, as a rule, are at best but a duty performed that brings a satisfaction in itself, but it sometimes happens that, as a reward for our well-doing, some word may be said, some friend may be met by a happy chance that is like a gleam of sunshine on a cloudy day.

INVITATIONS FORMAL AND INFORMAL

THERE are certain rules to be observed in the writing of invitations that cannot be transgressed without incurring a just suspicion as to the degree of one's acquaintance with the laws and canons that govern our best society. For instance, Mrs. John Doe issues invitations for a ball or evening party; these, if issued in her own name or in the name of herself and daughter, or lady friend, would, very properly, find them "at home" on a certain evening. Should, however, the invitations be sent out in the name of herself and husband, then it is that "Mr. and Mrs. John Doe request the pleasure of Mr. and Mrs. Richard Roe's company" at a certain date. We will also find that Mr. Dick Roe is never "at home," but "requests the pleasure of your company."

To widely depart from any of these received canons of etiquette is to commit a decided solecism and to discover an utter unfitness for the desired social rank. Fortunately, there is no need, even for those not to the manor born, of displaying any ignorance in this matter when the simple consultation of a standard work on social etiquette will give the needed information and save the credit of the individual.

At first sight, it would seem a very easy thing to invite a friend to come to you at a given day and hour, and to accept or decline said invitation would appear a matter scarcely worth considering. This rash conclusion, however, disappears from view when it is recollected that the proper phrasing, the suitable signature, and the appropriate paper, are all matters of the nicest choice, and indicate with the most unerring accuracy the good or ill breeding of the parties interested.

From two to three persons only are invited from one family to the same entertainment, and, in the event of a small dinner party, two would be the limit. The invitations would be addressed, not to Mr. Coates and family, but one to "Mr. and Mrs. Coates," another to "The Misses Coates," or to "Miss Coates." If there are brothers, and they are to be invited, a separate invitation is required for each one of them; a single one addressed to the "Messrs. Coates" being considered in bad taste. To one son and one daughter a joint invitation may be extended in the name of "Miss Coates and Brother." On rather informal occasions where the family, and perhaps their guests also, are desired to be present, the invitation may be sent in the name of "Mr. and Mrs. James B. Coates and Party."

Note Paper for Invitations.

Note paper for invitations should be plain, unruled, heavy in texture, creamy-white in tint, and of a size to fold once to fit the large, square envelope of the same size and tint. Monogram, if used, or crests, if they may be rightfully claimed, should be stamped or embossed in white directly in the center of the upper portion of the sheet and on the upper flap of the inner envelope only. This envelope should bear the name simply of the invited guest, and is to be enclosed in a perfectly plain, somewhat larger envelope, which bears the entire address and protects the enclosure from the soil of frequent handling by postman or messenger.

Invitation Cards.

Invitation cards, if they are used, should be heavy, creamy-white, and of a size to fit the large, square envelope. Such a card is sufficiently large to contain any ordinary invitation, and should be enclosed, as above, in two envelopes.

Writing the invitation should receive the greatest care, especial attention being given to securing each phrase a line to itself. For instance, the names of host and hostess should never be separated, but given an entire line, the same rule applying to the names of the invited guests.

COOLING DRAUGHT AFTER A TEN MILE RUN

THE COTILLION

Invitations written in the third person should always be replied to in the third person, care being taken to permit no change of person from beginning to end of the note. This rule holds good in whatever person the invitation may have been written; regrets or acceptances must be sent in the same manner.

No one, nowadays, "presents his (or her) compliments" in giving or accepting an invitation; neither is "your polite invitation" any longer the best form. "Your kind," or "your very kind invitation," being the most graceful manner of acknowledging the courtesy extended.

Written Regrets.

Always, if possible, accept a first invitation if the new acquaintance is to be kept up. In case inexorable circumstances prevent this acceptance, the regret sent should explain these circumstances fully and be very cordially written; while the earliest opportunity must be taken of extending some courtesy in return.

Even should you not desire the acquaintance, your regrets should be courteous and cards should be left at the house in response to their civility. It is then at your own option whether or not to acknowledge the acquaintance farther.

Invitations can be written or engraved on the large cards, or small sheets of note paper, that are used for this purpose, though, on all formal occasions, engraved forms in clear, fine script are preferable, and for weddings absolutely necessary. If written, black ink should be invariably used.

A young lady never sends out invitations in her own name; instead, "Mrs. and Miss Hoyt" are "at home," or the name of the young lady's chaperon appears with her own, as: "Mrs. Haviland and Miss Hoyt, at home, etc."

Uninvited Guests.

Should it so happen that an uninvited guest finds, accidentally, his way into the festivities, let the strictest politeness mark his reception, neither word nor glance betraying the slightest surprise at the unexpected arrival.

Inviting Married People.

A married man should never be invited to an entertainment without his wife, nor a married woman without including her husband also in the invitation. An invitation erring in this particular should be looked upon as an insult, and should never be honored by an acceptance. This category, however, does not include gatherings, such as ladies' luncheons or gentlemen's game suppers, that are wholly confined to the members of one sex.

Dinners.

Ladies who give many dinner parties usually keep on hand the engraved invitation cards, with blanks left for the insertion of name and date. The invitation for a dinner party is always sent out in the name of both host and hostess, and the usual form is as follows:

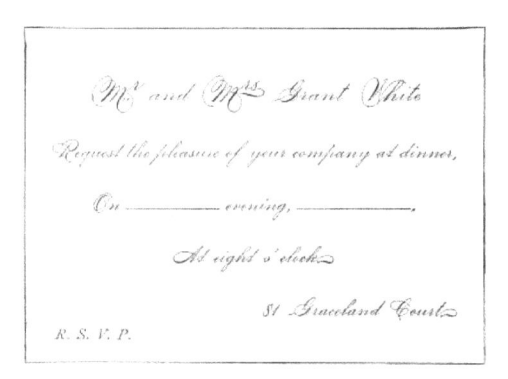

> Mr. and Mrs. Grant White
> Request the pleasure of your company at dinner,
> On ———— evening, ————.
> At eight o'clock
> 81 Graceland Court
> R. S. V. P.

The letters R. S. V. P. are simply the initials of the French words, *Repondez s'il vous plait*, meaning, "Reply, if you please."

Some very stylish people now use, in place of these letters, the English phrase: "The favor of answer is requested."

Written invitations, or those engraved for a single occasion, would read as follows:

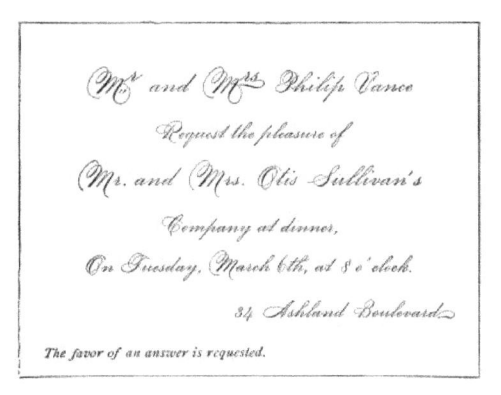

> Mr. and Mrs. Philip Vance
> Request the pleasure of
> Mr. and Mrs. Otis Sullivan's
> Company at dinner,
> On Tuesday, March 6th, at 8 o'clock.
> 34 Ashland Boulevard
>
> *The favor of an answer is requested.*

R. S. V. P. can be substituted for the last phrase, if desired. If the host be a widower with a young lady daughter, the invitation can be issued in the name of father and daughter, as: "Mr. and Miss Van Vleit, etc.," or, a lady and her daughter, under similar circumstances, would issue invitations in the name of "Mrs. Holt and Miss Holt."

Persons who make a point of strictly observing the usages of polite society are extremely careful, having received any invitation, to take immediate notice of it, according to proper form. This is only a courtesy due to the one who has sent the invitation, which should be accepted or declined promptly, in order that the hostess may know what to depend upon.

If the dinner party is given to introduce either a friend or some person of distinction, an extra card, inscribed as follows, is enclosed in the same envelope: To meet MR.———. Another form would be:

> Mr. and Mrs. Jackson
> Request the pleasure of
> Mr. and Mrs. Brown's
> Company at dinner,
> To meet Robert Browning,
> Thursday, October 8th, at seven o'clock
> 642 Arch Street
>   R. S. V. P.

It is well, if the party is given in honor of some celebrated person, to give them the choice of several dates before issuing the general invitation, thus assuring yourself that no conflicting engagement will rob the entertainment of its bright, particular star. An invitation to a dinner is the highest social compliment that can be offered. It should be sent out about ten days in advance, and requires an immediate and positive answer, for it is to be supposed that the hostess wishes to make up her table at once. Both invitation and answer should be sent by messenger; all other invitations, and replies to the same, may be sent by mail. In London, however, where distances are so great, all invitations, without exception, are sent by post.

In case of an informal dinner, a verbal invitation is sometimes sent, one or two days beforehand, by a servant, and a verbal answer is given at the time. The principal objection against this method is that the date, having no written reminder, may be confounded with some other engagement. Where the affair is not too stately, an informal invitation, written in the first person, may be pleasantly exchanged between friend and friend. For instance:

> MY DEAR MRS. ROE:
>
> My aunt, Mrs. LeFevre, of New York City, is here with me for a short stay, and Mr. Doe and I hope that you and Mr. Roe can give us the pleasure of your company at dinner, on Tuesday, October ninth, at seven o'clock, when, with a few other friends, we hope to pass a pleasant hour in your society.Cordially yours,
>
> MARIAN DOE.

Mrs. Marian Doe, St. Caroline's Court.

Asking for Invitations.

Asking for invitations for one's visiting friends, while permissible on some occasions, such as requesting the favor of bringing a gentleman to a ball where dancing men are always at a premium, or an unexpected guest of your family to a reception or evening party, should never be resorted to when a dinner party is in question, for, to gratify the request would, in all probability, throw the whole of a carefully arranged table into disorder. This rule is only to be broken when the guest to be included is some really celebrated character whose addition to the company would compensate for the extra covers to be laid and the re-arrangements to be made before the unexpected guest can be accommodated. No one, however, should feel offense when a request of this nature is refused. The hostess, in all probability, had good and sufficient reasons for her course of action. Invitations for a married couple should never be requested.

Evening Parties, Balls and "At Homes."

Invitations to these entertainments are issued in the name of the hostess only, and are sent out from ten days to two weeks in advance. Informal occasions, however, give very short notice, and it is well to use the word "informal" in the invitation, that guests may not put themselves to inconvenience as regards dress. It must be remembered that this term is too often misleading in its nature, and many a sensitive guest has been seriously annoyed by finding herself, after a too literal interpretation of the "informal" character of the entertainment, in a crowd of gay butterflies, a misuse of the word that should be seriously protested against.

Invitations to evening parties and private balls are less elaborate than formerly; the word "party" or "ball" is never used unless on the occasion of some public affair, such as a charity ball, but any especial feature of the evening may be mentioned in the invitation.

To an evening party where dancing may, or may not, be a feature of the entertainment, the following, either engraved or written on a small sheet of note paper, is a very good form:

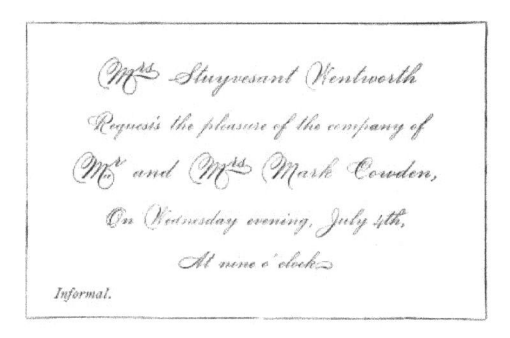

> *Mrs. Stuyvesant Wentworth*
> *Requests the pleasure of the company of*
> *Mr. and Mrs. Mark Cowden,*
> *On Wednesday evening, July 4th,*
> *At nine o'clock*
>
> Informal.

All invitations are to be considered as "formal" unless the word "informal" appears on the card. If the card states that the entertainment is to be "informal," the invited guest is fully justified in considering it so, and dressing accordingly. Neither host, hostess, nor other guests can take any exception if the invitation is treated just as it reads.

If dancing is the feature of the evening, the same form may be used with the word "Dancing" added in the lower left hand corner. Or:

> Mrs. John Burrows,
> At Home,
> Thursday evening, October first,
> At nine o'clock.
> 1080 LaFrance Avenue
> Quadrilles at ten.

If the ball is at a public place, as at Delmonico's, in New York, the following form is appropriate, always making use, in case of so public an entertainment, of the host's name in connection with that of the hostess:

> Mr. and Mrs. George Douglas
> Request the pleasure of your company,
> Thursday evening, December twelfth,
> At nine o'clock
> Delmonico's.

Another form that would be equally appropriate is as follows:

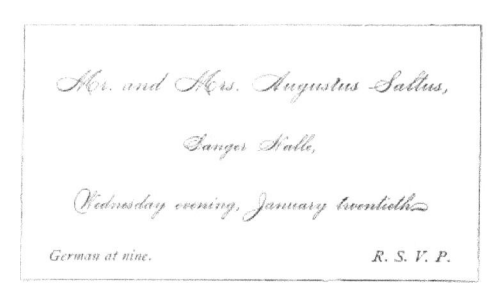

> Mr. and Mrs. Augustus Saltus,
> Sanger Halle,
> Wednesday evening, January twentieth
> German at nine.   R. S. V. P.

If any of these occasions are intended to introduce a *débutante*, her card may be enclosed. If they are given in honor of a friend, or some celebrated individual, the following form is appropriate:

Mrs. Henry Alexander
Requests the favor of your company on
Tuesday evening, October tenth,
From eight to eleven o'clock,
To meet the
Rev. Prof. Dr. Kemp,
Of the Princeton Theological Seminary

684 West 49th Street.   R. S. V. P.

FREE FROM THE RESTRAINTS OF SOCIETY.

OUT FOR HEALTHFUL EXERCISE

Or, if very formal, the name of the guest may be given first, as: To meet the CHIEF JUSTICE OF THE UNITED STATES and MRS. FULLER. MRS. HAROLD COURTRIGHT, At Home, from eight to eleven o'clock, Thursday, February seventh. R. S. V. P.

This same precedence may be given to the name of an honored guest in a dinner or other invitation. Still another form is where the name of the guest is written on a separate card, thus: To meet MRS. SUMMERVILLE. Enclose this in the same envelope.

For a club party the following may be used: THE LA SALLE CLUB requests the pleasure of your attendance Wednesday evening, June eight, at nine o'clock. 555 West 51st Street. R. S. V. P.

A still more simple form for a party invitation is an "At Home" card filled out thus: MRS. DON CARLOS PORTER, At Home, Tuesday evening, March fourth. 1021 Broadway. Cotillion at ten. R. S. V. P.

Masquerades.

The entire invitation for a masquerade may be engraved, or it may be written, with the exception of the word "Masquerade," which should be engraved on the card. For example:

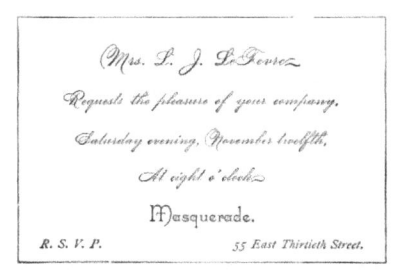

Musicales, Soirées and Matinées.

Invitations to a Musicale are simply written on "At Home" cards, thus:

Or: MRS. P. V. VANVECHTON, At Home, Tuesday afternoon, April second, from half-past three to five o'clock. *Matinee Musicale.*

If the Musicale is to be an evening affair, and dancing is to follow the music, the following form of invitation may be used: MRS. HERBERT HUGHES, At Home, Friday evening, January tenth, at eight o'clock. 200 Winchester Avenue. Music. Dancing at ten.

Precisely the same form is to be used in giving out invitations for a *soirée*, save that the word "*soirée*" is substituted for that of "*Musicale*" or "*matinée musicale.*" It may be farther added that the term "*matinée*" applies exclusively to entertainments given in the morning, or at any time before dinner, a distinction to which our custom of late dinners gives a wide latitude, so that any entertainment up to eight o'clock in the evening may receive the name of *matinée*, notwithstanding the fact that drawn curtains and gas-lighted rooms may give all the semblance of night-time. "*Soiree*," however, is used only where an evening party of a semi-informal character is denoted.

Garden Parties.

Precisely the same form of "At Home" cards can be used for these entertainments, substituting the words "Garden Party" in the left hand corner and sending them out some two or three days in advance. Or, if a more formal affair is intended, use the following: MRS. WAITE TALCOTT requests the pleasure of the company of MR. and MRS. JOHN CLAY, on Monday, August fifth, at four o'clock. Garden Party. "The Oaks."

If it should be desirable to include the entire family in the invitation, the wording would be as follows:

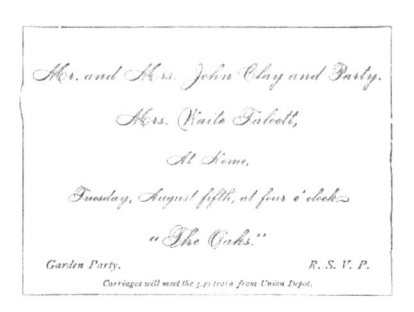

> Mr. and Mrs. John Clay and Party.
> Mrs. Waite Talcott,
> At Home,
> Tuesday, August fifth, at four o'clock
> "The Oaks."
> Garden Party.   R. S. V. P.
> *Carriages will meet the 3.45 train from Union Depot.*

This clause to be added only when the party is to be given at some distance from the station. If preferred, these directions may be written on a separate small card and enclosed in the same envelope.

In this country we are not so accustomed to giving garden parties as people are in England, but a garden party may easily be made one of the most inviting and enjoyable of any.

Breakfasts, Luncheons and Suppers.

Breakfast invitations may be engraved or written upon a lady's visiting card, thus:

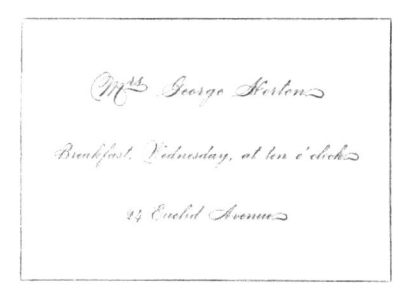

> Mrs. George Kirlen
> Breakfast, Wednesday, at ten o'clock
> 24 Euclid Avenue

A written invitation is usually in the first person, and should read somewhat as follow:

> DEAR MRS. GRACIE:

I should be pleased to have the company of you and your husband at breakfast with us, Wednesday morning at ten o'clock.

Cordially yours,
Mrs. George Horton. Gertrude Horton.

The invitations should be sent out a week or five days in advance, and should be answered at once.

Luncheons, in this country, are very apt to possess much of the formality of a dinner, and are written or engraved, according to the degree of stateliness that is to mark the occasion. Very formal invitations are sent out ten days or two weeks in advance, and are couched in precisely the same terms as a dinner invitation, save that the word "Luncheon" is substituted for "Dinner." Written invitations, also, follow the same plan as those written for dinners, and are not usually issued more than a week or five days in advance. Some ladies use their visiting card, thus: Mrs. Frank E. Wentworth. Luncheon, Wednesday, at one o'clock.

A later hour, say two o'clock, is usually adopted for a more formal affair. Replies should be sent at once that the hostess may be enabled to make up her table.

Teas and "Kettledrums."

Teas and "Kettledrums," High Tea and Afternoon Receptions, have come to bear a strong resemblance one to another, in fact to infringe so much upon the same territory that it is very difficult at times to distinguish between them sufficiently to apply the appropriate name. A simple affair is announced thus by those ladies who have a regular reception day: Mrs. John St. John. Thursdays. Tea at five o'clock. 40 West 49th Street.

Or: Mrs. John St. John. Five o'clock tea. Thursday, February fifth. 40 West 49th Street.

The words "kettledrum" or "afternoon tea" are not to be used, and these cards may be sent by mail, enclosed in a single envelope. They require no answer. Where the lady has not a regular reception day and wishes to give an afternoon tea, an engraved card, like the following, is usually sent out: Mrs. Arthur Merrill. Miss Merrill. Monday, February third, from four to seven o'clock. 274 Chestnut Street.

In case of the hostess having no one to receive with her, her name would appear alone upon the card. The name of any friend may take the place of a daughter's. Such an entertainment partakes more of the nature of an afternoon reception, or high tea. It may be adapted also to other occasions, such as the introduction to one's friends of a guest who is to make a prolonged stay, as for instance: MRS. ARTHUR MERRILL, At Home, Monday, December seventh, from one until seven o'clock. To meet MRS. FRANCES ELMER. 55 Vine Street.

Invitations like this and the one just above are to be enclosed in two envelopes, same as for dinners and sent out ten days or two weeks in advance.

Kaffee Klatsch.

This furnishes very much the same class of entertainment that is to be found at an afternoon tea, save that coffee is the predominating beverage. The invitation is precisely the same as for teas, simply substituting the words "Kaffee Klatsch."

Suppers.

For the evening supper, invitations are issued in some one of the forms presented for dinner parties, substituting the word "Supper." Answers should be returned at once.

Coming-out Parties.

These special festivities may take almost any form, so that the presentation of the blushing *débutante* may be at a dinner, ball, reception, evening party or afternoon tea; which latter custom has become very frequent of late. So much is this the case that it is somewhat to be reprehended as rendering afternoon teas too ceremonious in character. There is this in its favor, however; it relieves young girls from the strain incident upon a large party or ball. In some cases, the invitations preserve their usual form (whatever that may be) and the card of the *débutante* is enclosed in the same envelope. Even this distinction is sometimes wanting. Again, in the case of "At Homes" and "Teas," the name of the young lady is engraved beneath that of her mother; if it is the eldest daughter, the form would be: MRS. ARTHUR HOLT. MISS HOLT.

A younger daughter, under the same circumstances, would pose as: MISS EDITH MAY HOLT.

Such cards do not need a reply, but the guest will remember to leave cards in the hall for the *débutante* as well as her mother or *chaperon*. It may be said here that, should it for any reason occur that the young lady is "brought out" under the wing of some friend instead of under her mother's care, the relative position their names will occupy on the cards is precisely the same, as: MRS. D. G. HAVILAND. MISS HOLT.

A more formal presentation would be in the style of an engraved note sheet:

> Mrs. Arthur Nolt
> Requests the pleasure of introducing her daughter,
> Edith May,
> To
> Mr. and Mrs. Ross Clark,
> On Thursday evening, December fifth.
> At nine o'clock
>
> 28 St. Caroline's Court.   R. S. V. P.

This invitation, of course, implies a large evening party, reception or ball, and should be sent out ten days or two weeks in advance of the event.

Receptions.

Informal receptions and full-dress occasions of the same kind are announced somewhat differently. In the first case the affair partakes so closely of the nature of an afternoon tea that the same form of invitation is used: MRS. HOWARD POST, At Home, Tuesday, October second, from four to seven.

If a series of receptions are planned the form would be: MRS. HOWARD POST, At Home, Tuesdays in November, from four to six o'clock.

Full-dress receptions are frequently given both afternoon and evening, sometimes in the evening only. Invitations to these should be engraved on square cards or note sheets, and sent out two weeks previous to the reception day. A very good form is:

> Mrs. Jerome Hastings
> Requests the pleasure of your company,
> On Thursday, November twelfth,
> From five until ten o'clock
>
> 711 DuPage Street.   R. S. V. P.

If a daughter or a friend is to assist in receiving, the invitation should include her name also: MRS. JEROME HASTINGS, MISS HASTINGS, At Home, Thursday, November twelfth, from five until ten o'clock. 711 DuPage Street.

When the reception is given by a gentleman, and its object is to enable his friends to meet some distinguished guest, the following form is used: MR. HOWARD POST requests the pleasure of the company of MR. ALONZO METCALF to meet GENERAL E. L. BATES. Union League Club. 100 Cedar Street. R. S. V. P.

Though some prefer placing the name of the honored guest first, according to the form given under dinner invitations. The answer should be:

> Mr. Alonzo Metcalf accepts with pleasure Mr. Howard Post's kind invitation to meet General E. L. Bates.

Weddings.

Wedding invitations are issued two weeks in advance, sometimes earlier to friends at a distance, in order that they may lay their plans accordingly. They are engraved in fine script on small sheets of cream note, and the form most used for church weddings is as follows:

> Mr. and Mrs. Richard Earle
> Request the pleasure of your company
> At the marriage of their daughter,
> Guendolen,
> To
> Mr. Egbert Ray Cranston
> On Tuesday, June Eighteenth, 1895,
> At half-past twelve o'clock,
> Christ Church,
> Binghamton

Still another form would give the daughter's name as "Miss Guendolen Earle."

There may or may not be a monogram on the sheet of paper, but, if used there, one to correspond must be placed on the inner envelope also. The envelope, however, may be stamped with a monogram and the paper left plain, this latter style being much in favor. Where the wedding is in church, it is usually followed by an after-reception, cards for which are engraved in some similar form to the following: Reception from one until three o'clock, 107 Washington Street. Or: At Home after the ceremony. 107 Washington Street.

A still more ceremonious invitation to the reception may be issued in the parents' name, and in the usual form of similar invitations, as: MR. and MRS. RICHARD EARLE request the pleasure of your company at the wedding reception of their daughter, GUENDOLEN, and MR. EGBERT RAY CRANSTON, Tuesday evening, June eighteenth, 1895, from nine to eleven o'clock. 107 Washington Street.

If there is reason to believe that the church will be crowded with uninvited guests, admission cards are engraved as follows: Christ Church. Please present this card to the usher. Tuesday, June eighteenth.

How Invitations are Sent.

Several of these cards are usually enclosed for distribution to friends of the invited and for the use of servants that have accompanied guests to the church. This custom is hardly necessary in country towns. All of the cards and the invitation are enclosed in one envelope superscribed with the name only of the person invited, and re-inclosed in another envelope bearing the full address. All formal invitations are to be enclosed in the two envelopes as above; less stately affairs requiring but one envelope; send by mail.

In England, wedding invitations are issued in the name of the mother of the bride only; here custom sanctions the use of the father's name as well. If the invitation is issued in the name of some other relative, then the word "granddaughter," "niece," etc., should be substituted for that of "daughter." If the future home of the young couple is decided upon, "At Home" cards also should be enclosed for all the invited guests that the bride desires to retain upon her visiting list. The following form is appropriate: MR. and MRS. EGBERT RAY CRANSTON, At Home, Thursdays in September, from four until six o'clock. 48 Washington Street.

Or, in place of designating especial days, it may read: MR. and MRS. EGBERT RAY CRANSTON, At Home, after September first. 48 Washington Street.

Where the list of acquaintances is very large it sometimes happens that a portion of the guests are invited to the church only. When this is the case the reception card is omitted from the envelope; but if a visiting acquaintance is to be maintained, "At Home" cards must be enclosed.

Wedding Invitations.

The home wedding is, perhaps, less stately in appearance, but, involving as it does, less care on the part of friends and less nervous strain on that of the bride, is frequently adopted. The invitations are precisely the same as for a church wedding, merely inserting street and number in place of designating the church, omitting, of course, the card of admittance and that for reception. The "At Home" card of the newly-married couple should always be enclosed lest doubt as to their new address prove perplexing to their friends.

Sometimes, where life is to be commenced in their own home, the wedded pair, soon after their establishment therein, send out "At Home" cards for a few evenings after this style: MR. and MRS. EGBERT RAY CRANSTON, At

Home, Tuesday evenings in September, from eight to eleven o'clock. 48 Washington Street.

Gatherings such as these partake of the nature of semi-formal receptions and present a delightful opportunity for welcoming friends to the new home, and at the same time arranging a visiting list for the season, no one receiving a card to these entertainments that is not to be honored with a place thereon. These invitations are to be sent out after the return from the bridal tour, and, when thus used, the first-given "At Home" card is omitted in sending out the wedding invitation.

If the wedding is to be a morning affair from the church, followed by a breakfast, the first given invitation is issued and the following engraved card enclosed in the same envelope: MR. and MRS. RICHARD EARLE request the pleasure of your company at breakfast, Tuesday, June twentieth, at half past twelve o'clock. 107 Washington Street.

"At Home" cards and cards to the church should be enclosed as before. The time should be carefully arranged so that not more than half an hour is allowed to elapse between the ceremony at the church and the reception or breakfast at the house.

A home wedding with a breakfast simply sends out the ordinary wedding invitation, indicating the hour and giving the street and number.

Sometimes, at a home wedding, it is desired that no one but relatives or very particular friends should be present at the ceremony. Under these circumstances the usual invitations are issued. Then, for the favored few, ceremony cards are enclosed, on which the words are engraved: Ceremony at half past eight.

"At Home" cards may be enclosed as before.

Where the wedding has been entirely private, the mother, or some other relative of the bride, frequently gives a reception upon the return home of the young couple, invitations to which are issued as follows: MRS. RICHARD EARLE, MRS. EGBERT RAY CRANSTON. At Home, Wednesday, September first, from four to ten o'clock. 107 Washington Street.

For an evening reception the form is a little different: MR. and MRS. RICHARD EARLE request the pleasure of your company, Thursday, September second, from nine to eleven o'clock. 107 Washington Street. Enclosing the card of Mr. and Mrs. Egbert Ray Cranston.

Announcement Cards.

Announcement cards, where the wedding has been strictly private, are sent out after the following style: MR. and MRS. RICHARD EARLE announce the marriage of their daughter, GUENDOLEN, to MR. EGBERT RAY CRANSTON, Tuesday, November nineteenth, 1895. 107 Washington Street.

The before-given "At Home" cards maybe enclosed, or the necessary information conveyed by having engraved in the lower left hand corner of the sheet of note paper: At Home, after December first, at 48 Washington Street.

Another form of announcement is also used: EGBERT RAY CRANSTON. GUENDOLEN EARLE. Married, Tuesday, November nineteenth, 1895. Binghamton. With this form use "At Home" cards, or engrave the street and number in the lower left hand corner of the announcement card. This form is permissible in any case, but is more frequently employed where there are neither parents nor relatives to send out the announcement.

If the wedding should have taken place during a season of family mourning or misfortune, the bridegroom himself issues the following announcement: MR. and MRS. EGBERT RAY CRANSTON, 48 Washington Street.

These cards are large and square, and in the same envelope with them is enclosed a smaller card engraved with the maiden name of the bride: MISS GUENDOLEN EARLE.

Wedding Anniversaries.

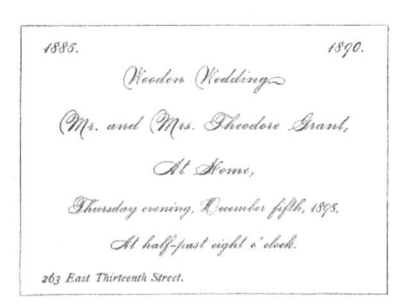

```
1885.                                    1890.
            Wooden Wedding
       Mr. and Mrs. Theodore Grant,
               At Home,
     Thursday evening, December fifth, 1895.
            At half-past eight o'clock.
263 East Thirteenth Street.
```

In sending out invitations for the various anniversaries that pleasantly diversify the years of a long wedded life, the simplest form will always be found in the best taste. There are varied devices for rendering these invitations striking in effect, such as silvered and gilded cards for silver and golden weddings, thin wooden cards for the wooden wedding, etc., but good taste would indicate that none of these, not even gold and silver lettering (though this last is least objectionable of all), should be used. The large engraved "At Home" card, or the small sheet of heavy note paper, also engraved, are the most elegant.

"No Presents Received."

The words, "No presents received," are sometimes engraved in the lower left hand corner of the note sheet, or card. A much-to-be-admired custom, since the multiplicity of invitations requiring gifts, is, in more cases than one, burdensome to the recipient.

Revise the Visiting List.

Now, that it has become the custom to engage the services of an amanuensis to direct the invitations for a crush affair by the hundred, it would be well for every hostess to frequently revise her visiting list, in order that the relatives of lately deceased friends may not be pained by seeing the dear lost name included among the invitations of the family; also, this care is necessary to remove the names of those who have recently departed from the city, and those whose acquaintance is no longer desired.

ACCEPTANCES AND REGRETS

THE essence of all etiquette is to be found in the observance of the spirit of the Golden Rule. Perhaps in no one point is the "do unto others as ye would that they should do unto you," more applicable than in the prompt acknowledgment of either a formal or a friendly invitation. This acknowledgment may be either denial or assent, but whatever the form, it is requisite that the proffered courtesy should be answered by a prompt and decisive acceptance or refusal. This is a duty owed by an invited guest to his prospective host or hostess and one that should never be neglected.

Answering an Invitation.

In accepting or declining an invitation close attention should be paid to the form in which it is written and the same style followed in the answer. For instance: should the invitation be formal, the answer should preserve the same degree of formality; while a friendly invitation in note form should meet with an acceptance or regret couched in the same terms. Another rule to be rigidly observed is, that the acceptance or refusal must be written in the same person that characterized the invitation. For instance: if "Mr. and Mrs. Algernon Smith request the pleasure of the company of Mr. and Mrs. Joseph Bronson at dinner, etc.," with equal stateliness "Mr. and Mrs. Joseph Bronson accept with pleasure the kind invitation of Mr. and Mrs. Algernon Smith." To do otherwise would imply ignorance of the very rudiments of social or grammatical rules.

A friendly note of invitation, beginning somewhat after this fashion: "Mr. Smith and I would be pleased to have you and Mr. Brown, etc.," would be accepted or declined in the same fashion and person, as: "Mr. Brown and I accept with pleasure your kind invitation, etc." To answer such an invitation with a formal acceptance, or regret, written in the third person, as given above, would display profound ignorance of social customs.

An acceptance or regret, written in the first person, receives the signature of the writer, but one written in the third person remains unsigned. To sign it would produce a confusion of persons and be ungrammatical to the last degree. Another error to be avoided is that of beginning in this fashion: "I accept with pleasure the kind invitation of Mr. and Mrs. John Jones," this also producing a change of person altogether inadmissible. Neither must one be betrayed into the mistake of using the words, "will accept," thus throwing the acceptance into the future tense, when, in reality, you *do* accept, in the present tense, at the moment of writing.

Accepting a Dinner Invitation.

Incumbent upon us as it is to answer the majority of our invitations in either the affirmative or negative, there are degrees of necessity even here, for, sin as we may in all other particulars, there is an unwritten code like unto the laws of the Medes and Persians which declareth that the invitations to a dinner are not to be lightly set aside. First, an invitation to a dinner is the highest social compliment that a host and hostess can pay to those invited, and, second, the guests are limited in number and painstakingly arranged in congenial couples by the careful hostess. Judge, then, of her disappointment, when, at the last moment, some delinquent sends in a hasty regret leaving little or no time to fill that terror of all dinner-givers, that skeleton at the feast, an empty chair. One such failure is sufficient to ruin the most carefully-arranged table and is an injury to host and hostess that only the occurrence of some unforeseen calamity can justify.

ANSWERING AN INVITATION.

In answering an invitation it is well to repeat the date, as: "Your kind invitation for Tuesday, May fifth." This will give an opportunity, if any mistakes have been made in dates, to rectify them at once. This caution it would be well to observe in answering any invitation.

Answer decisively as well as promptly. Do not, if there is a doubt as to your being able to attend, selfishly keep the lists open in your favor by suggesting that "You hope to have the pleasure," etc., or, if married, that "one of us will come." This is an injustice to those inviting you, who, to make a success of their entertainment, must know at once the number to be depended upon.

Say "yes" or "no" promptly and abide by your decision. To do this will, in case of refusal, give time to fill your place at table.

Accepting a Dinner Invitation.

In accepting a dinner invitation the following form is very suitable. This, of course, pre-supposes that the invitation has also been written in the third person. (See Invitations.)

> Mr. and Mrs. Harvey Pratt accept with pleasure the kind invitation of Mr. and Mrs. Paul Potter for dinner on Tuesday, December fifteenth, at eight o'clock. 24 Abercrombie Street. Wednesday.

A gentleman might respond thus:

> Mr. Fremont Miller has much pleasure in accepting the very kind invitation of Mr. and Mrs. Paul Potter for dinner on Tuesday, December fifteenth, at eight o'clock. Union League Club. Wednesday.

To answer a formal invitation carelessly and familiarly is to show a degree of disrespect to the sender, but, if the invitation be in note form, first person, answer in same fashion, it being usually safe to follow the style of invitation in either accepting or refusing the proffered pleasure.

Never "present one's compliments" in response to an invitation. It is entirely out of date; neither should one say "the *polite* invitation of Mr. John Jones." All invitations are presupposed to be "polite." "Your kind" or "very kind invitation" is a gracefully-turned and amply sufficient phrase for all occasions.

Declining a Dinner Invitation.

An unexplained regret is often (as before mentioned) wounding to the feelings of a sensitive person, leaving at times the impression that one did not care to come. This can always be avoided by particularizing the cause of refusal. A plea of expected absence, a previous engagement to dine elsewhere, a recent bereavement, or sudden illness in the family, are each of them good and sufficient reasons for non-acceptance and should always be mentioned. Thus, in reply to a formal dinner invitation, a "regret" might be sent in the following terms:

> Mr. and Mrs. Harvey Patten sincerely regret that, owing to the sudden illness of their daughter Eleanor they will be deprived of the pleasure of accepting the very kind invitation of Mr. and Mrs. Paul Potter for dinner on Tuesday, December fifteenth. 24 Abercrombie street. Wednesday.

This form of refusal will be found suitable for all formal occasions, varying the name of the entertainment and the cause for non-acceptance to suit the circumstances.

Persons in Mourning.

Invitations to those in mourning should be sent as a matter of course, except during the first few weeks of deep bereavement, when their sorrows are not to be intruded upon by the gayeties of the outer world. After this first season of sorrow, invitations, which neither custom nor their own feelings permit them to accept, should be sent, that they may know that they are not forgotten in their solitude.

To these there is always given the privilege of declining all invitations without any specified cause therefor, their black-bordered stationery showing all too plainly the sad reason that prompted their refusal. They should then send their cards (black-bordered) by mail enclosed in two envelopes. These will take the place of a personal call and should be the same in number. It may be mentioned here that while people in deep mourning are not usually invited to dinners or luncheons, it is customary for them to receive invitations to all weddings and other social gatherings, and though they may not accept, still it is gratifying for them to know that they are remembered in their seclusion.

"WILL YOU ENTERTAIN THE COMPANY?"

Addressing the Answer.

The answer to an invitation should always be addressed to the person in whose name it is sent. If "Mr. and Mrs. Richard Roe request the pleasure," etc., address the answer to "Mr. and Mrs. Richard Roe." If "Mrs. Richard Roe is At Home" on a certain date, address the reply to her alone. In case of wedding invitations, address all answers to the parents of the bride, in whose name they are sent out, never to the bride, although she may be your only personal acquaintance in the family, the civility being due to the issuers of the invitation. This is customary in the case of all invitations.

Wedding Invitations.

Wedding invitations are usually thought to require no answer unless it be to a sit-down wedding breakfast. In this case the same exactness in reply and the same form is demanded as for a dinner invitation. If the invitation is extended to friends at a distance and pre-supposes an intention to entertain the recipients for any length of time, the obligation for speedy reply is equally necessary.

If the invitation is given by an informal note, as is the case with some very quiet weddings, an answer must always be returned and in the same note form. This attention is demanded by courtesy.

To a large crush wedding a regret, accompanied or not by a gift, may be sent if desired; an acceptance is not necessary. Where the invitations are to the church only, they are amply answered by sending or leaving cards at the house. To receive a card stating that the wedded pair will be "At Home" on certain dates, means that they desire to continue their acquaintance with the parties thus invited, who should either call in person or send cards promptly.

Wedding Anniversaries.

Anniversary invitations require an answer, thus giving a very pleasant opportunity for congratulating the happy couple. The following forms are suitable:

> Mr. and Mrs. Arthur Cummings accept with pleasure the kind invitation of Mr. and Mrs. Kennet Wade for Thursday evening, October tenth, and present their warmest congratulations on their Silver Wedding Anniversary. 45 Church Street. Thursday.

For a refusal:

> Mr. and Mrs. Arthur Cummings sincerely regret that, owing to an unexpected absence from town, they are unable to

accept the very kind invitation of Mr. and Mrs. Kennet Wade for Thursday evening, October tenth, but beg to present to them their warmest congratulations on this occasion of their Silver Wedding Anniversary. 24 Church Street. Wednesday.

The same formulæ in answering will apply to any of the anniversary festivities.

Theater and Opera Parties.

These parties are frequently made up on rather short notice and the invitations are then sent to the house by special messenger who awaits the reply, which must be written at once, that the lady or gentleman giving the entertainment may be sure of a certain number to fill the box or stalls, engaged for the evening. Occasionally, when the party is given by a gentleman, he takes a carriage and gives out the invitations in person when a verbal answer is returned.

Luncheons and Suppers.

Invitations for these are written in the same form as for a dinner, merely substituting the word "luncheon" or "supper" for "dinner," and should be accepted or refused in precisely the same style. Answers also should be sent with the same promptness that the hostess may be certain of arranging her table satisfactorily.

Other Invitations.

Other invitations, aside from those already specified in this department, scarcely demand an answer, except they bear the words: "The favor of an answer is requested," or the initials, "R. S. V. P." Simple "at home" affairs never need an answer, though cards must always be sent, or left in person, immediately afterward. Garden parties, where they are held at any distance from the city and carriages are to be sent to convey the guests thither, always require an answer; this, however, is usually indicated upon the card.

Refusing After Acceptance.

Should it unfortunately occur, after accepting an invitation, that, by one of the sorrowful happenings so often marring our best laid plans, we are prevented from fulfilling our promise, let the regret sent be prompt, that your hostess, especially if the entertainment be a dinner or luncheon, may possibly, even at the eleventh hour, be able to supply the vacancy. Make it explanatory as well, that she may feel positive that no mere whim has caused the disarrangement of her plans.

What Not to Do.

Never write the word "accepts," "regrets" or "declines" upon your visiting card and send in lieu of a written note. To do so is not only an insult to your hostess but a mark as well of your own ill-breeding. An invitation, which is always an honor and implies the best that your host is able to offer, should always receive the courtesy of a civil reply.

ETIQUETTE OF COURTSHIP AND MARRIAGE

"COURTSHIP," according to Sterne, "consists in a number of quiet attentions, not so pointed as to alarm, nor so vague as not to be understood."

In this little quotation lies the spirit and the letter of all etiquette regarding courtship. The passion of love generally appearing to everyone save the man who feels it, so entirely disproportionate to the value of the object, so impossible to be entered into by any outside individual, that any strong expressions of it appear ridiculous to a third person. For this reason it is that all extravagance of feeling should be carefully repressed as an offense against good breeding.

Man was made for woman, and woman equally for man. How shall they treat each other? How shall they come to understand their mutual relations and duties? It is lofty work to write upon this subject what ought to be written. Mistakes, fatal blunders, hearts and lives wrecked, homes turned into bear-gardens, tears, miseries, blasted hopes, awful tragedies—can you name the one most prolific cause of all these?

If our young people were taught what they ought to know—if it were told them from infancy up—if it were drilled into them and they were made to understand what now is all a mystery to them—a dark, vague, unriddled mystery—hearts would be happier, homes would be brighter, lives would be worth living and the world would be better.

"Good Night! Good Night! Parting is such sweet sorrow, That I shall say good night till it be morrow."

A POLITE ESCORT.

This is now the matter—matter grave and serious enough—which we have in hand. There are gems of wisdom founded on health, morality, happiness, which should be put within reach of every household in our whole broad land. It is a most important, yet neglected subject. People are squeamish, cursed with mock modesty, ashamed to speak with their lips what their Creator spoke through their own minds and bodies when he formed them. It is time such nonsense—nonsense shall we say?—rather say it is time such fatal folly were withered and cursed by the sober common sense and moral duty of universal society.

Courtship! Its theme, how delightful! Its memories and associations, how charming! Its luxuries the most luxurious proffered to mortals! Its results how far reaching, and momentous! No mere lover's fleeting bauble, but life's very greatest work! None are equally portentous, for good and evil.

Errors of Love-Making.

God's provisions for man's happiness are boundless and endless. How great are the pleasures of sight, motion, breathing! How much greater those of mind! Yet a right love surpasses them all; and can render us all happier than our utmost imaginations can depict; and a wrong more miserable.

Right love-making is more important than right selection; because it affects conjugal life for the most. Men and women need knowledge concerning it more than touching anything else. Their fatal errors show their almost universal ignorance concerning it. That most married discords originate in wrong love-making instead of selection, is proved by love usually declining; while adaptation remains the same.

Right courtship will harmonize natural discordants, much more concordants, still more those already in love; which only some serious causes can rupture. The whole power of this love element is enlisted in its perpetuity, as are all the self-interests of both. As nature's health provisions are so perfect that only its great and long-continued outrage can break it; so her conjugal are so numerous and perfect that but for outrageous violation of her love laws all who once begin can and will grow more and more affectionate and happy every day.

Any man who can begin to elicit any woman's love, can perfectly infatuate her more and more, solely by courting her right; and all women who once start a man's love—no very difficult achievement—can get out of him, and do with him, anything possible she pleases. The charming and fascinating power of serpents over birds is as nothing compared with that a woman can wield over a man, and he over her. Ladies, recall your love hey-day. You had your lover perfectly spell-bound. He literally knew not what he did or would do. With what alacrity he sprang to indulge your every wish, at whatever cost, and do exactly as you desired! If you had only courted him just right, he would have continued to grow still more so till now. This is equally true of a man's power over every woman who once begins to love him. What would you give to again wield that same bewitching wand?

How to Carry on Courtship.

Intuition, our own selfhood, is nature's highest teacher, and infallible; and tells all, by her "still, small voice within," whether and just wherein they are making love right or wrong. Every false step forewarns all against itself; and great is their fall who stumble. Courtship has its own inherent consciousness, which must be kept inviolate.

Then throw yourself, O courting youth, upon your own interior sense of propriety and right, as to both the beginning and conducting of courtship, after learning all you can from these pages, and have no fears as to results, but quietly bide them, in the most perfect assurance of their happy eventuality!

"What can I do or omit to advance my suit? prevent dismissal? make my very best impression? guarantee acceptance? touch my idol's heart? court just right?" This is what all true courters say.

Cultivate and manifest whatever qualities you would awaken. You inspire in the one you court the precise feeling and traits you yourself experience. This law effects this result. Every faculty in either awakens itself in the other. This is just as sure as gravity itself. Hence your success must come from *within*, depends upon yourself, not the one courted.

Study the specialties, likes and dislikes in particular, of the one courted, and humor and adapt yourself to them.

Be extra careful not to prejudice him or her against you by awakening any faculty in reverse. Thus whatever rouses the other's resistance against you, antagonizes all the other faculties, and proportionally turns love for you into hatred. Whatever wounds ambition reverses all the other feelings, to your injury; what delights it, turns them in your favor. All the faculties create, and their action constitutes human nature; which lovers will do right well to study. To give an illustration:

A Case to the Point.

An elderly man with points in his favor, having selected a woman eighteen years younger, but most intelligent and feminine, had two young rivals, each having more points in their favor, and came to his final test. She thought much of having plenty of money. They saw they could "cut him out" by showing her that he was poor; she till then thinking his means ample. All four met around her table, and proved his poverty. His rivals retired, sure that they had made *"his* cake dough," leaving him with her. It was his turning-point. He addressed himself right to her *affections*, saying little about money matters, but protesting an amount of devotion for her to which she knew they were strangers; and left his suit right on this one point; adding:

"You know I can make money; know how intensely I esteem, admire, idolize, and love you. Will not my admitted greater affection, with my earnings, do more for you than they with more money, but less love?"

Her clear head saw the point. Her heart melted into his. She said "yes." He triumphed by this affectional spirit alone over their much greater availability.

Manifesting the domestic affections and virtues, a warm, gushing friendly nature, fondness for children and home, inspires a man's love most of all, while evincing talents by a man peculiarly enamors woman.

Relations, you shall not interfere, where even parents may not. Make your own matches, and let others make theirs; especially if you have bungled your own. One *such* bungle is one too many.

The parties are betrothed. Their marriage is "fore-ordained" by themselves, its only rightful umpires, which all right-minded outsiders will try to promote, not prevent. How despicable to separate husbands and wives! Yet is not parting those married by a love-*spirit*, equally so? Its mere legal form can but increase its validity, not create it. Marriage is a divine institution, and consists in their own personal betrothal. Hence breaking up a true love-union before its legal consummation, is just as bad as parting loving husband and wife; which is monstrous. All lovers who allow it are its wicked partakers.

Choice of Associates.

The first point to be considered on this subject is a careful choice of associates, which will often, in the end, save future unhappiness and discomfort, since, as Goldsmith so truthfully puts it, "Love is often an involuntary passion placed upon our companions without our consent, and frequently conferred without even our previous esteem."

This last most unhappy state of affairs may, to a great extent, be avoided by this careful choosing of companions. Especially is this true on the part of the lady, since, from the nature and constitution of society, an unsuitable acquaintance, friendship, or alliance, is more embarrassing and more painful for the woman than the man. As in single life an undesirable acquaintance is more derogatory to a woman than to a man, so in married life, the woman it is who ventures most, "for," as Jeremy Taylor writes, "she hath no sanctuary in which to retire from an evil husband; she may complain to God as do the subjects of tyrants and princes, but otherwise she hath no appeal in the causes of unkindness."

First Steps.

To a man who has become fascinated with some womanly ideal, we would say, if the acquaintanceship be very recent, and he, as yet, a stranger to her relatives, that he should first consider in detail his position and prospects in life, and judge whether or not they are such as would justify him in striving to win the lady's affections, and later on her hand in marriage. Assured upon this point, and let no young man think that a fortune is necessary for the wooing of any woman worth the winning, let him then gain the needful introductions through some mutual friend to her parents or guardians.

If, on the other hand, it is a long acquaintance that has ripened into admiration, this latter formality will be unnecessary.

As to the lady, her position is negative to a great extent. Yet it is to be presumed that her preferences, though unexpressed, are decided, and, if the attentions of a gentleman are agreeable, her manners will be apt to indicate, in some degree, the state of her mind.

Prudence, however, does, or should, warn her not to accept too marked attentions from a man of whose past life she knows nothing, and of whose present circumstances she is equally ignorant.

Character.

There is one paramount consideration too often overlooked and too late bewailed in many a ruined home, and that is the character of the man who seeks to win a woman's hand. Parents and guardians cannot be too careful in this regard, and young women themselves should, by refusing such associates, avoid all danger of contracting such ties. Wealth, nor family rank, nor genius, availeth aught if the character of the man be flawed.

Let parents teach their daughters and let girls understand for themselves that happiness, or peace, in married life is impossible where a man is, in any wise, dissipated, or liable to be overcome by any of the fashionable vices of the day. Better go down to your grave a "forlorn spinster" than marry such a man.

Disposition.

As to temper or disposition, the man or woman can easily gain some insight into the respective peculiarities of another's temperament by a little quiet observation. If the gentleman be courteous and careful in his attentions to his mother and sisters, and behave with ease and consideration toward all women, irrespective of age, rank, or present condition, she may feel that her first estimate was a correct one. On the other hand, should he show disrespect toward women as a class, sneer at sacred things, evince an inclination for expensive pleasures in advance of his means, or for low amusements or companionship; be cruel to the horse he drives, or display an absence of all energy in his business pursuits, then is it time to gently, but firmly, repel all nearer advances on his part.

As to the gentleman, it will be well for him also to watch carefully as to the disposition of the lady and her conduct in her own family. If she be attentive and respectful to her parents, kind and affectionate toward her brothers and sisters, not easily ruffled in temper and with inclination to enjoy the pleasures of home; cheerful, hopeful and charitable in disposition, then may he feel, indeed, that he has a prize before him well worth the winning.

If, however, she should display a strong inclination towards affectation and flirtation; be extremely showy or else careless in her attire, frivolous in her tastes and eager for admiration, he may rightly conclude that very little home happiness is to be expected from her companionship.

Trifling.

A true gentleman will never confine his attentions exclusively to one lady unless he has an intention of marriage. To do so exposes her to all manner of conjecture, lays an embargo on the formation of other acquaintances, may very seriously compromise her happiness, and by after withdrawal frequently causes her the severest mortification. Hence a gentleman with no thought of marriage is in honor bound to make his attentions to ladies as general as possible.

Still more reprehensible is the conduct of the man who insinuates himself into the affections of a young girl by every protestation and avowal possible, save that which would be binding upon himself, and then withdraws his attentions with the boastful consciousness that he has not committed himself.

Again, the young lady who willfully, knowingly, deliberately, draws on a man to place hand and heart at her disposal simply for the pleasure of refusing him and thus adding one more name to her list of rejected proposals, is utterly unworthy the name of woman.

Etiquette of Making and Receiving Gifts.

On the question of gifts there is a point of etiquette to be observed. Gentlemen, as a rule, do not offer ladies presents, save of fruits, flowers, or confections; which gifts, notwithstanding that a small fortune may be lavished upon their purchase, are supposed, in all probability from their perishable character, to leave no obligation resting upon the lady.

Should the conversation, however, turn upon some new book or musical composition, which the lady has not seen, the gentleman may, with perfect propriety, say, "I wish that you could see such or such a work and, if you will permit, I should be pleased to send you a copy." It is then optional with the lady to accept or refuse.

Should a gentleman persist in offering other gifts there must be no secrecy about it. She should take early opportunity of saying, in the presence of her father and mother, "I am very much obliged to you for that ring, pin (or other gift) which you were so kind as to offer me the other day, and I shall be happy to accept it if Papa or Mamma does not object." If the lady is positive in her objections to receiving gifts, it is easy to say, "I thank you for the kindness but I never take expensive presents;" or, "Mamma never permits me to accept expensive presents." These refusals are always to be taken by the gentleman in good part. Where a present has been unadvisedly accepted, it is perfectly proper for the mother to return it with thanks, saying, "I think my daughter rather young to accept such expensive gifts."

After an engagement is formally made the etiquette of gifts is somewhat altered, though even then expensive presents, unless it be the engagement ring, are not in the best taste. These should be reserved for the marriage gifts.

Proposals of Marriage.

The proposal itself is a subject so closely personal in its nature that each man must be a law unto himself in the matter, and time and opportunity will be his only guides to success, unless, mayhap, his lady-love be the braver of the two and help him gently over the hardest part, for there be men and men; some who brook not "no" for an answer, and some that a moment's hesitation on the part of the one sought would seal their lips forever.

A woman must always remember that a proposal of marriage is the highest honor that a man can pay her, and, if she must refuse it, to do so in such fashion as to spare his feelings as much as possible. If she be a true and well-bred woman, both proposal and refusal will be kept a profound secret from every one save her parents. It is the least balm she can offer to the wounded pride of the man who has chosen her from out all women to bear his name and to reign in his home. A wise woman can almost always prevent matters from coming to the point of a declaration, and, by her actions and her prompt acceptance of the attentions of others, should strive to show the true state of her feelings.

A gentleman should usually take "no" for an answer unless he be of so persevering a disposition as to be determined to take the fort by siege; or unless the "no" was so undecided in its tone as to give some hope of finding true the poet's words:

"He gave them but one tongue to say us, 'Nay,'

And two fond eyes to grant."

On the gentleman's part, a decided refusal should be received as calmly as possible, and his resolve should be in no way to annoy the cause of all his pain. If mere indifference be or seem to be the origin of the refusal, he may, after a suitable length of time, press his suit once more; but if an avowed or evident preference for another be the reason, it becomes imperative that he should at once withdraw from the field. Any reason that the lady may, in her compassion, see fit to give him as cause for her refusal, should ever remain his inviolable secret.

SOCIAL PASTIME ON RETURN VOYAGE

DECLINED WITH REGRETS.

As whatever grows has its natural period for maturing, so has love. At engagement you have merely selected, so that your familiarity should be only intellectual, not affectional. You are yet more acquaintances than companions. As sun changes from midnight darkness into noonday brilliancy, and heats, lights up, and warms *gradually*, and as summer "lingers in the lap of spring;" so marriage should dally in the lap of courtship. Nature's adolescence of love should never be crowded into a premature marriage. The more personal, the more impatient it is; yet to establish its Platonic aspect takes more time than is usually given it; so that undue haste puts it upon the carnal plane, which soon cloys, then disgusts.

Unbecoming Haste.

Coyness and modesty always accompany female love, which involuntarily shrink from close masculine contact until its mental phase is sufficiently developed to overrule the antagonistic intimacies of marriage.

Besides, why curtail the luxuries of courtship? Should haste to enjoy the lusciousness of summer engulf the delights of spring? The pleasures of courtship are unsurpassed throughout life, and quite too great to be curtailed by hurrying marriage. And enhancing or diminishing them redoubles or curtails those of marriage a hundredfold more. A happy courtship promotes conjugal felicity more than anything else whatever. A lady, asked why she didn't marry, since she had so many making love to her, replied: "Because being courted is too great a luxury to be spoilt by marrying."

No man should wait to make his pile. Two must *acquire* a competence conjointly, in order fully to really *enjoy* it together. This alone can give full zest to whatever pleasures it produces.

A formal proffer of marriage naturally follows a man's selection and decision as to whom he will marry. Consent to canvass their mutual adaptations implies consent to marry, if all is found satisfactory; yet a final test and consummation now become necessary, both to bring this whole matter to a focus, and allow both to state, and obviate or waive, those objections which must needs exist on both sides; including any improvements possible in either.

How to Deal with Objections.

The best time to state and waive or remove all objections, seeming and real, not already adjusted, is at his proposal, and her acceptance. A verbal will do, but a written is much better, by facilitating future reference. A long future awaits their marriage; hence committing this its initial point to writing, so that both can look back to it, is most desirable. And he can propose, and she accept, much better when alone, and they have all their faculties under full control, than verbally, perhaps, when excited. Those same primal reasons for reducing all other contracts to writing obtain doubly in reference to marriage.

You who fear awkwardness on paper, remember that true human nature always appears well, even when poorly dressed. A diamond is no less brilliant because set in clay. Mode is nothing, reality everything. All needed to appear well is to *feel* right, and express naturally what is felt. Saying plainly what you have to say, is all required.

The acceptance or rejection should also be unequivocal, or any contingencies stated, and waived if minor, but if they can neither be obviated nor compromised, should terminate their relations, that both may look elsewhere. If any bones of contention exist, now is the time to inter them finally, and to take the initiatory steps for perfecting both in each other's eyes. Bear in mind that as yet your relations are still those of business merely, because neither has acquired or conceded any right to love or be loved. Without pretending to give model letters of proposal, acceptance, or rejection, because varying circumstances will vary each *ad infinitum*, the following may serve as samples from which to work:

> "MUCH ESTEEMED FRIEND: As we have agreed to canvass our mutual adaptations for marriage, and my own mind is fully made up, a final decision now becomes necessary.
>
> "What I have learned of and from you confirms that high opinion of you which prompted my selection of you, and inspires a desire to consummate it. Your pleasing manner and mode of saying and doing things; your intelligence, taste, prudence, kindness, and many other excellencies, inspire my highest admiration.
>
> "Will you let me love what I so much admire?
>
> "But my affections are sacred. I can bestow them only on one who *reciprocates* them; will bestow them upon you, if you will bestow yours on me; not otherwise; for only *mutual* love can render either happy. I can and will love you alone, with all my heart, provided you can and will love only me, with all of yours. Do you accord me this privilege, on this condition, for life, forever? I crave to make you my wife; to live with and for you, and proffer you my whole being, with honest, assiduous toil, fidelity to business, what talents I possess, and all I can do to contribute to your creature

comforts. Do you accord me this privilege, on this condition? May I enshrine you as queen of my life?

"Say wherein you find me faulty, or capable of improvement in your eyes, and I will do my utmost, consistently with my conscience, to render myself worthy and acceptable to you.

"I wish some things were different in you—that you had better health, arose earlier, were less impulsive, knew more about keeping house, etc.; yet these minor matters sink into insignificance in comparison with your many excellences, and especially that whole-souled affection obviously inherent in you.

"Deliberate fully, for this is a life affair, and if, in order to decide judiciously, you require to know more of me, ask me, or —— and ——. Please reply as soon as you can well decide.

"Decline unless you accept cordially, and can love me truly and wholly; but if you can and will reciprocate my proffered affection, say yes, and indicate your own time and mode of our marriage. Meanwhile, with the highest regards, I am, and hope ever to remain, Yours truly,

A. B."

A true woman could give a better answer than the following, which does not claim to be a model. It is hardly time yet for a gushing love-letter, or we would not profane this sacred subject by making the attempt; yet should like to receive one in spirit somewhat as follows:

"DEAR SIR: Your proffer of your hand and heart in marriage has been duly received, and its important contents fully considered.

"I accept your offer: and on its only condition, that I *reciprocate your love*, which I do completely; and hereby both offer my own hand and heart in return, and consecrate my entire being, soul and body, all I am and can become, to you alone; both according you the 'privilege' you crave of loving me, and 'craving' a like one in return.

"Thank Heaven that this matter is settled; that you are in very deed mine, while I am yours, to love and be loved by, live and be lived with and for; and that my gushing affections have a final resting-place on one every way so worthy of the fullest reciprocal sympathy and trust.

"The preliminaries of our marriage we will arrange whenever we meet, which I hope may be soon. But whether sooner or later, or you are present or absent, I now consider myself as wholly yours, and you all mine; and both give and take the fullest privilege of cherishing and expressing for you that whole-souled love I find even now gushing up and calling for expression. Fondly hoping to hear from and see you soon and often, I remain wholly yours forever,

C. D."

Sealing the Vow.

The vow and its tangible witnesses come next. All agreements require to be attested; and this as much more than others as it is the most obligatory. Both need its unequivocal and mutual mementos, to be cherished for all time to come as its perpetual witnesses. This vow of each to the other can neither be made too strong, nor held too sacred. If calling God to witness will strengthen your mutual adjuration, swear by Him and His throne, or by whatever else will render it inviolable, and commit it to writing, each transcribing a copy for the other as your most sacred relics, to be enshrined in your "holy of holies."

Two witnesses are required, one for each. A ring for her and locket for him, containing the likeness of both, as always showing how they now look, or any keepsake both may select, more or less valuable, to be handed down to their posterity, will answer.

Your mode of conducting your future affairs should now be arranged. Though implied in selection, yet it must be specified in detail. Both should arrange your marriage relations; say what each desires to do, and have done; and draw out a definite outline plan of the various positions you desire to maintain towards each other. Your future home must be discussed: whether you will board, or live in your own house, rented, or owned, or built, and after what pattern; or with either or which of your parents. And it is vastly important that wives determine most as to their domiciles; their internal arrangements, rooms, furniture, management; respecting which they are consulted quite too little, yet cannot well be too much.

Family rules, as well as national, state, corporate, financial, must be established. They are most needed, yet least practiced in marriage. Without them, all must be chaotic. Ignoring them is a great but common marital error. The Friends wisely make family method cardinal.

A Full Understanding.

Your general treatment of each other now especially requires to be mutually agreed upon. Each should say, "I should like to treat and be treated by you thus, but not so; and let you do this but not that;" and both mutually agree on a thousand like minor points, better definitely arranged at first than left for future contention; each making requisitions, conceding privileges, and stipulating for any fancies, idols, or "reserved rights."

Differences must needs arise, which cannot be adjusted too soon. Those constitutionally inherent in each should be adjusted in love's *early* stages; it matters less how, than whether to your mutual satisfaction. Or if this is impossible, "agree to disagree;" but settle on something.

A concessionary spirit is indispensable, and inheres in love. Neither should insist, but both concede, in all things; each making, not demanding sacrifices. The one who loves most will yield to oblige most. What course will make both happiest should overrule all your mutual relations.

Write down and file all. Your present decisions, subject to mutual changes and amendments, will become more and more important for future reference, as time rolls on, by enabling each to correct both for our own changes make us think others have changed. A mutual diary is desirable; for incidents now seemingly trivial, may yet become important.

Important Trifles.

See or correspond with each other often. Love will not bear neglect. Nothing kills it equally. In this it is most exacting. It will not, should not, be second in anything. "First or nothing," is its motto. Meet as often as possible. After its fires have once been lit, they must be perpetually resupplied with their natural fuel; else they die down, go out, or go elsewhere; and are harder to rekindle than to light at first.

A splendid young man, son of one of New England's most talented and pious divines, endowed with one of the very best of organisms, physical and phrenological, having selected his mate, and plighted their mutual vows, being the business manager of a large manufactory, and obliged to defend several consecutive lawsuits for patent-right infringements, neglected for weeks to write to his betrothed, presupposing, of course, that all was right. This offended her ladyship, and allowed evil-minded meddlers to sow seeds of alienation in her mind; persuade her to send him his dismissal, and accept a marriage proposal from another.

As he told his mournful story, he seemed like a sturdy oak riven by lightning and torn by whirlwinds; its foliage scorched, bark stripped, limbs tattered, even its very rootlets scathed; yet standing, a stern, proud, defiant, resolute wreck. A gushing tear he manfully tried but failed to suppress. His lips quivered and voice faltered. Perceiving his impending fate, he seemed to dread his future more than present; and hesitated between self-abandonment, and a merely mechanical, objectless, business life. In attempting his salvation, by proffering advice to the "broken-hearted," he respectfully but firmly declined; deliberately preferring old-bachelorship, with all its dearths, of which he seemed fully conscious. He felt as if he had been deeply wronged.

Yet was not he the *first* practically to repudiate? He suffered terribly, because he had sinned grievously, not by commission, but omission. He felt the deepest, fullest, manliest love, and revelled in anticipations of their future union, but did not *express* it; which was to her as if he had not felt it; whereas, had he saved but one minute per week to write lovingly, "I long to be with you, and love you still," or, "Business does not, cannot diminish my fondness," he would have saved her broken vows, and his broken heart.

Mingling other enjoyments with love, by going together to picnics and parties, sleigh-rides and Mayings, concerts, and lectures, marvellously cements the affections.

Love Feeds on Love.

Meet in your most attractive habiliments of mind and person. French ladies will see their affianced only when arrayed in their best toilet. Yet mental charms vastly surpass millinery. Neither can render yourselves too lovely.

Express affectionate fondness in your visits and letters; the more the better, so that you keep it a sentiment, not debase it by animal passion. It is still establishing its rootlets, like young corn, instead of growing. Allow no amatory excitement, no frenzied, delirious intoxication with it; for its violence, like every other, must react only to exhaust and paralyze itself by its own excesses.

Affianced young man, life has its epochs, which revolutionize it for good or bad. You are now in one. You have heretofore affiliated much with men; formed habits of smoking or chewing tobacco; indulged in late suppers; abused yourself in various ways; perhaps been on sprees. Now is your time to take a new departure from whatever is evil to all that is good and pure. Break up most of your masculine associations; and affiliate chiefly with your affianced. Be out no more nights. Let your new responsibilities and relations brace you up against their temptations; and, if these are not sufficient, your prospective spouse will help. No other aid in resisting temptation and inspiring to good equals that of a loving, loved woman.

Break off from your cronyisms, clubs, societies, all engagements except such as mean imperative, cold-blooded business. Your new ties furnish an excellent excuse. All your spare time and small change are wanted for *her*. To give to bad habits the time and money due to her and setting up in life, is outrageous. Bend everything to your new relations, them to nothing. Now's your time to turn over a new leaf, and turn all the angles, corners and right-about faces needed.

Affianced maiden, you have some departures to take and corners to turn. Your life has till now been frivolous, but has now become serious. You have no more need of toilet fineries; for "your market is made," and you have work on hand far more important, namely, fitting yourself for your new duties. Find out what they demand of you, and set right about making a premium wife and mother. Both begin life anew. Forgetting the past, plant and sow now what you would gather and become always.

The Best of all Possessions.

Woman is man's choicest treasure. That is the most precious which confers the most happiness. She is adapted to render him incomparably happier than any other terrestrial possession. He can enjoy luscious peaches, melting pears, crack horses, dollars and other things innumerable; but a well-sexed man can enjoy woman most of all. He is poor indeed, and takes little pleasure in this life, be his possessions and social position what they may, who takes no pleasure with her. All description utterly fails to express the varied and exultant enjoyments God has engrafted into a right sexual state. Only few experiences can attest how many and great, from infancy to death, and throughout eternity itself. All God could do He has done to render each sex superlatively happy in the other. Of all his beautiful and perfect work, this is the most beautiful and perfect. Of all his benignant devices, this is his most benign. All the divine attributes, all human happiness, converge in male and female adaptations to mutual enjoyments.

Each is correspondingly precious to the other. Man should prize many things, yet woman is his pearl of greatest price. He should preserve, cherish, husband many life possessions, but woman the most. He has many jewels in his crown of glory, but she is his gem-jewel, his diadem. What masculine luxury equals making women in general, and the loved one in particular, happy?

The Source of Miseries.

Beginning and conducting courtship as this chapter directs, avoiding the errors and following the directions it specifies, will just as surely render all superlatively happy as sun will rise to-morrow. Scan their sense. Do they not expound nature's love-initiating and consummating ordinances? Are they not worthy of being put into practice? Discordants, can you not trace many of your antagonisms and miseries to their ignorant violation? Parents, what are they worth to put into your children's hands, to forewarn them against carelessly, ignorantly, spoiling their marriage? Young ladies, what are they worth to you, as showing you how to so treat your admirers as to gain and redouble their heart's devotion? Young men, what are these warnings and teachings worth to you? God in his natural laws will bless all who practice, curse all who violate them.

The conduct during engagement on the part of the gentleman should be marked by the utmost courtesy toward and confidence in the woman of his choice; a state of feeling which she should fully reciprocate.

In public their behavior toward one another should not be markedly different from that displayed by them toward other men and women of their acquaintance; save that the bridegroom-elect should be on the watch that not the slightest wish of the lady be unfulfilled.

As for the lady, while she is not expected to debar herself from accepting the customary courtesies extended by the gentlemen of her acquaintance, a slight reserve should mark her conduct in accepting them. At all places of amusement or entertainment she should appear either in the company of her *fiance*, or that of some relative.

She should never captiously take offense at her *fiance's* showing the same attention to other ladies that she, in her turn, is willing to accept from other gentlemen, and she should take the same pains to please his taste in trifles that he does to gratify her slightest wish.

This does not mean, though, that in the selfishness and blindness of love—and love is very blind and selfish sometimes—she is to shut herself up to his companionship at all times, excluding him from the family circle of which he is so soon to become a member, and "pairing off" on all occasions, thus rendering both the mark for silly jestings.

How to Cherish Love.

But, in sober matter-of-fact, that little ring of gold does not mean utter blindness. It does not mean that she is to devote her evenings exclusively to the chosen one, ignoring her family entirely. It does not mean that she is to accept valuable presents of all kinds at his hands, to expect him to give up all his friends for her sake, nor to confide all the secrets of the household to his keeping, but, as one wise woman says, to "guard herself in word and deed; hold his love in the best way possible; tie it firmly with the blue ribbon of hope, and never let it be eaten away by the little fox who destroys so many loving ties, and who is called familiarity."

Neither is this counsel to be deemed over-cautious, since, alas! even "engagements" are sometimes broken in this uncertain world, and surely there is no womanly woman that would not in such an event reflect gladly, as she took up her life once more at the old point, that she had remembered these things.

A domineering, jealous disposition on either side before marriage is not the best possible guarantee for after happiness, and if these traits are clearly shown during an engagement, the individual who escapes from such thraldom before it is too late has shown conclusively that discretion which is, at times, the better part of valor.

Conduct Toward Parents.

The gentleman should exercise some tact in regard to his conduct toward the family of his betrothed. Marked attention should be shown toward the lady's mother. He should accommodate himself as much as possible to the wishes, habits and ways of the household, and not being, as yet, a member of the family, he should not presume to show an intrusive familiarity of conversation.

The lady, on her part, should strive to show consideration, friendliness, and a desire to please the parents of her husband-that-is-to-be. Thus both will unite in the endeavor to overcome that loving jealousy so natural on the part of those who see the claims of another grown paramount in the heart of one of their number, and feel that these new links are fast becoming stronger than ties of blood and relationship.

The respective families should meet these advances with all kindness, and should also endeavor, in view of the new union pending between them, to make, if this be necessary, one another's acquaintance as soon as convenient.

Length of Engagements.

Engagements should not be entered upon prematurely, a certain degree of acquaintanceship proving no mean preparation for an arrangement of this nature. But when an engagement is once formed it should not, in the majority of cases, be of an undue length. This is a matter to be settled by the wishes or the circumstances of the contracting parties.

It is oftimes the measure of wisdom, where the obstacle is lack of fortune, to risk some degree of deprivation, rather than submit to a long-protracted engagement; the man, as head of the new home, finding a fresh motive for ambitious striving, and both parties being preserved from that coolness of feeling too often attendant upon years of waiting. No homes are happier than those constructed on the principle of economy and patient effort.

Broken Engagements.

Not unfrequently does it occur that circumstances arise that render the dissolution of an engagement inevitable, and, as such a course, unless mutual, of necessity involves an injury to the feelings of one party, great care and delicacy should be employed in approaching the subject.

If the occasion should arise on the lady's side, it must be remembered that she is not bound to declare any other reason than her own sweet will. It is better, however, for reasons to be frankly given, that the step may not be attributed to mere caprice on her part. On the side of the man the reasons must be strong, indeed, that can justify him in breaking a solemn engagement sought of his own free will, and urged by him upon the object of his choice. By thus releasing himself he not unfrequently leaves the lady in an embarrassing position before the public, not to mention the possible injury that may be inflicted upon the deepest feelings of her heart.

If the cause should arise from any fault on the part of the lady, a man of honor will ever preserve the strictest silence on the subject. If from sudden failure in his own fortunes he should feel himself in duty bound to relinquish his hope of present happiness lest he selfishly drag another down to penury, let the reason be carefully and clearly explained.

At the conclusion of an engagement let every gift, including the engagement ring, and all photographs and letters that have been exchanged between the two, be promptly returned by each that as little as possible may remain to remind of the days that are done. It is especially a point of honor on the gentleman's part to retain nothing that the lady may have given, or written, him.

Etiquette of Married Life.

Marriage, to the elect, may be fitly termed a state of grace, but without a close observance of all the courtesies that tend to uplift everyday life in some degree above the narrowness of mere existence it may but too easily become what the old cynic declared it to be when he wrote, "Marriage is a feast in which the grace is sometimes better than the dinner."

Mutual confidence and mutual respect are the two principal factors in the case. Without these there can be none of that harmony so necessary to happiness in the state matrimonial. And not only this, but they should strive to be mutually entertaining.

The pains they took during their engagement to be agreeable to one another at a time when they were by no means entirely dependent upon themselves for companionship, would surely not be amiss in rendering pleasant the years, and it may be decades of years, during which they must be to a great extent dependent upon each other for entertainment. The young man who spent so much time at the home of a certain lady that he was finally asked why, if he was in love with her, he did not marry her, uttered a sad truth when he answered, "Ah, but where then should I pass my evenings?" A reflection upon the agreeableness of married life that might easily be avoided by the exercise of care and tact on both sides.

The Art of Agreeableness.

Philip Gilbert Hammerton, in his *Intellectual Life*, wisely suggests: "A married couple are clearly aware that, in the course of a few years, their society is sure to become mutually uninteresting unless something is done. What is that something? Every author who succeeds, takes the trouble to renew his mind by fresh knowledge, new thoughts. So, is it not at least worth while to do as much to preserve the interest of marriage?"

The wife who dresses for her husband's sake, who reads that she may qualify herself for conversation with him, who makes him the chief end of her cares, and the husband who brings home from the outside world some of its life and animation to share with her, who has a loving interest in all that she has done for his pleasure, and, if wealth be a stranger at their door, stands ready to lift the heaviest burdens from her shoulders, have solved for themselves the problem of married happiness, and found it to be a condition wherein every joy is doubled and every sorrow halved.

Duty Toward One Another.

Let the wife have no confidant as to the little shortcomings of her husband, over which love, as well as pride, should draw a sheltering veil. Never listen to an unkind tale of his past or present mistakes, and count all those who would seek thus to destroy your peace of mind as your bitterest enemies. Let the husband in his turn remember that an unkind or slighting word spoken of his wife, touches his own honor to the quick, and be instant in resenting the words that should never have been spoken in his presence.

Another point to be remembered in view of the duty of husband and wife toward one another, is with reference to attending church or entertainments. The wife has, in all probability, left a home where the different members of the household were ready to accompany each other whenever occasion served, and young friends were planning many a pleasant outing, and now she is wholly dependent upon her husband for all of these things. Let her beware, under these circumstances, of allowing herself to attend church, lecture, or any other evening entertainment, in the company of well-meaning friends. For the husband, once seeing that his wife can attend these places without his assistance, will soon, if such be his disposition, remain selfishly home at all times, or, if otherwise inclined, still more selfishly find his amusement in places widely foreign to his wife's happiness or peace of mind. The carelessness of many well-meaning men in this respect is the cause of very much unhappiness that might be wholly avoided by a little consideration as to the utter dependence of the wife upon her husband for all these recreations.

Home Attire.

This is a subject that it should be unnecessary to touch upon, but, unfortunately, too many bright, pretty, carefully-dressed girls degenerate into careless, fretful, untidy and illy-clad young wives, whose presence is anything but a joy forever to the individuals who must face them across the family board for three hundred and sixty-five days in every year. And it is this careless young woman who is first to complain that "John does not care for me in the least, now we are married," while John is very apt to think, "If Carrie would only take just a little of the pains to please me now that she did six months ago, how much happier we would be." And John is quite right about it. This very carelessness on the part of wives has marred the happiness of more than one new home. The ribbon, the flower, the color that "John likes" and the smile that crowns all are magical in their effects.

Then let John always remember to bring to this home a pleasant face, from which business cares are driven away, and a readiness to please and be pleased, that meets the wife's attempts half way, and the evening meal will be made delightful by pleasant chat, which should never consist of a *résumé* of the day's tribulations, but should turn on subjects calculated to remove from the mind all trace of their existence, and thus will they arise at its close better and happier for the hour that has passed.

Household and Personal Expenses.

One of the chief sources of unhappiness in married life is the strife arising from the vexed question of home and personal expenses. In the first place, the husband frequently fails in regard to openness with regard to his business concerns and profits; thus the wife, entirely ignorant as to what amount she may safely spend, errs too often on the side of extravagance, finding too late, when a storm of reproach descends upon her innocent head, where and how she has sinned.

Then, too, it is often a sore trial to the wife's pride to ask for the money necessary to keep her own wardrobe in repair. Especially is this the case when, before marriage, she was in receipt of her own money, earned by her own hands. It seems to her that her husband ought to see that she has need of certain articles, and the very fact that he does not, leads her to the false supposition that he has ceased to care for her, while he, if there was any thought about it in his mind, would say, "Why doesn't she ask for money if she wants it? She knows I will give it to her if I have it."

All these troubles would be avoided if married couples early came to a definite understanding on this subject, and a certain sum were set aside which the wife was to receive weekly for household expenses, her personal wants to be supplied from such surplus as she may be able to save from out this sum, or in some other way provided for by a stated amount, both of which sums should be under her exclusive, unquestioned control.

Some simple system of accounts should then be kept and regularly gone over together on every quarter. A mutual agreement thus established on the money question, much annoyance and much extravagance may be prevented. It is not too much to suggest that, perhaps, it might not be amiss to present an account of the husband's expenses also, at these quarterly reckonings.

Above all things, never let the wife, from a weak desire to gratify her own personal vanity, enter upon some extravagant purchase, the amount of which she must conceal from her husband, and (vainly often) strive to pay in small amounts saved or borrowed. The result is usually exposure, sometimes disgrace, pecuniary loss and loss of esteem in the husband's eyes. Perfect confidence is the only basis upon which happiness can be safely founded.

A Pleasant Disposition.

Cultivate, on both sides, a disposition to restrain all unseemly exhibitions of temper. Hysterics and prolonged and repeated fits of tears soon lose their effect, and, at the last, a half-pitying contempt is their only result. Let all conversation be refined in its tone. The force of example in this respect carries with it a silent, impressive power that is not easily resisted and lapses therefrom involve a loss of this influence that cannot be easily estimated.

Profanity, too, is a deadly foe in the household and any wife that permits her husband to swear in her presence, either to herself, or concerning others, lessens her own self-respect each time it occurs. That profanity can be repressed, has been shown her by the fact that, no matter how long the previous engagement may have lasted, no word of such import escaped the man's lips in her presence, and surely the woman chosen to be head of his home is no less worthy of his respect than was the girl he wooed.

The habit of indulging in cutting or harsh remarks is one to be guarded against. Mutual politeness should be exercised by both husband and wife, and in all cases watch should be set over the mouth, and the door of the lips well kept.

Boarding Versus Home Life.

The tendency in all large cities, at this present time, points toward fashionable boarding-houses, or expensive lodging-houses, as the nuclei round which the newly-married most do congregate.

It may be that the wife is utterly unused to the care of a house (in which case the sooner she learn the art, the happier for both parties) or, perhaps, the financial resources of the husband are unable to support the drain consequent upon furnishing a home that shall gratify the foolish pride of the wife. But, whatever the cause, the effects are the same, and are to be found in the utter unfitness of women adopting this manner of existence for any of the serious duties of life that, sooner or later, come upon all who wear this mortal garb.

Then, too, in the idle, censorious, gossiping, novel-reading life that flourishes in this hothouse existence, the seeds of lifelong misery are not unfrequently sown.

Let a home, then, however small, be one of the first considerations in beginning the married life, and let the adding to, and the beautifying of, this precious possession be the duty and the privilege of the years to come.

To the wife, in her housewifely *rôle*, belongs the care of overseeing or accomplishing with her own hands, the varied duties that go to secure the daily well-being of the home. She must see that the rooms are bright, neat, and cosily arranged; that the meals are appetizingly and punctually served, and be herself neatly and tastefully attired to preside at the table.

Due allowances are to be made for the amount of manual labor she has been obliged to perform with her own hands, still, by care and tact a woman can always maintain a certain degree of neatness.

Let the husband, on his part, bring into the home cheerfulness, with a quick remembrance of all those little attentions that go so far toward making up the sum of earthly happiness. Let him see that, to the best of his ability, the home wants are provided for, and be not forgetful to lend the help of his stronger hand wherever needed. (Read carefully other hints in department of Home Etiquette.)

Never demand of your wife more than you are willing to give. If you desire to be received with smiles, enter the house with a cheerful mien, and you will find there are few women who are not willing to give measure for measure, and even a little more than they receive of kindly attention. For a wife will usually shine, like the moon, by reflection, and her happiness will always reflect your own.

WEDDINGS AND WEDDING ANNIVERSARIES.

IN discussing the important subject of etiquette as connected with weddings and wedding anniversaries, it may be mentioned here that the forms for invitations to all occasions of this sort, and acceptances and regrets of the same, card-sending, etc., have been fully treated in their respective departments. The observances immediately preceding, during, and following the ceremony, are now to receive consideration.

Paying for the Cards.

The form, size and use of these important bits of pasteboard having been before stated, it only remains for us to say here that all the expenses relative to their purchase and distribution are to be borne solely by the parents or other guardians of the bride. To have it otherwise implies a lack of delicacy on the part of the bride, and lays upon her a certain amount of obligation which every right-minded girl would desire, above all things, to avoid. Hence when the parents are financially unable to incur the expense, good taste demands that all display be abandoned and the couple be quietly married in the presence of the family only.

The bride should always remember that until the fateful words are spoken that make the twain one flesh, she has no claim whatever on the purse of her future husband, and conduct herself accordingly.

Hence it is that a very plain *trousseau* is more commendable to the self-respect of the wearer, than the elaborate outfittings, toward the purchase of which the groom-expectant has largely contributed, and which, in case of the oft-recurring "slip twixt the cup and the lip," must weigh heavily upon the maiden's pride.

Even the "after cards" are usually ordered by the parents with the others, and paid for at the same time. If, however, they are ordered after marriage, they are paid for by the groom.

There is only one exception to the rule of the bride's parents paying for the wedding cards, and this occurs when the wedding ceremony is performed quietly in church and the reception, for some reason, is held at the home of the groom's parents, in which case they, as the entertainers, properly pay for, and issue, the cards of invitation.

The groom, in England, always pays for the carriage that conveys himself and bride to the station after the ceremony and reception are past, but in this country the fashionable father usually claims the privilege of sending them on this first stage of their married life in his own carriage. However, the groom buys the ring and a bouquet for the bride, furnishes dainty presents for the bridesmaids, remembers the best man and the ushers, pays the clergyman's fee, the size of which is to be regulated only by his inclination, or the length of his purse-strings, and furnishes the marriage license.

Naming the Day.

This privilege belongs by right to the lady herself, but, in reality, the business engagements of the groom, and the time when he can best leave for the bridal tour have much to do in settling the exact date for which the invitations shall be issued. In very fashionable circles it is the mother that names the day of her daughter's marriage.

Time was when during the two weeks, or longer, elapsing between the issuing of the invitations and the occurrence of the wedding, the bride-expectant was not to be seen in public, nor by chance callers at the house, a custom which still prevails to some extent, but is superseded in the most fashionable circles by a series of especial entertainments given during this interval.

It frequently happens that one, or each, of the bridemaids entertains the bride and other bridemaids at a lunch or dinner, either informally or on a large scale. Some married friend of the family may give a large farewell dinner to Miss —— and her bridemaids; and the bride herself, or her mother, may give a rehearsal dinner. Ordinary invitations, however, are not to be accepted.

If the presents are not to be exhibited at the wedding reception, the bride frequently gives an informal tea the day before to her lady friends for the purpose of displaying them. She should also, for her health's sake, take a daily drive.

Announcing the Engagement.

An engagement is now frequently announced in rather a formal manner. This, however, is not usually done until a short time previous to the marriage itself. Sometimes it comes out in the society papers immediately after it has been made known to the kinfolk and intimate friends. Felicitations follow as a matter of course.

Sometimes a dinner-party is given by the parents of the bride-elect and the announcement is made by the host just before leaving the table. Congratulations follow. Sometimes notes are written by the young lady or her mother in announcement.

If the families of the contracting parties have been strangers heretofore it is expected that the gentleman's family will make the first call. Any friends that choose may give entertainments in honor of the couple.

The lady does not make any ceremonious calls after this announcement has been made, it being supposed that before this occurs she shall have left cards upon all her friends. If no formal announcement is made the bride-to-be must, before invitations are issued, leave cards with her friends and acquaintances. In the city she need not enter to make a personal call, in the country she will probably find it necessary so to do.

Wedding Gifts.

There is much to be said for and against the custom of wedding presents. And while the fact remains that they too often become the vehicle for an expenditure so uncalled-for as to encroach upon vulgarity in its excess, another fact still exists, that the simple remembrances of friends are very grateful to the bride, who, perhaps, is bound for a distant home where every loving token will recall a well-known face.

Then remember your friends on their wedding day, wisely, and according to their tastes and your own resources, for:

"Policy counselleth a gift,

Given wisely and in season,

And policy afterward approveth it,

For great is the power of gifts."

By those so desiring, the words, "No presents," or "No presents received," may be engraved in the left hand corner of the card. This is often a relief to many of the guests, and, at the same time does not prevent the very intimate friends, as well as members of the family, from sending quietly such gifts as they may choose, which, of course, are not exhibited.

Where presents are to be given they are frequently sent some time in advance, and the bride often takes much pleasure in arranging them for exhibition in some upstairs room. Each article is accompanied by the card of the giver; these are removed or not, as may be desired before exhibition.

The bride acknowledges the reception of each gift by a graceful little note of thanks. Some of them doubtless will come from persons unknown to her, friends of the groom, and to these she must be especially prompt in returning her acknowledgments.

List of Invitations.

Making up the list of invitations should be attended to carefully. The engaged couple should carefully prepare their respective lists and the mother of the bride should attentively scan names, for from this is to be made up the future visiting list of her daughter, and she cannot but hesitate at burdening her at the outset of her new life with a host of calling acquaintances, hence is forced to exclude every ineligible name; a cutting painful but oftimes necessary.

Ushers.

The duties of the ushers in a church wedding are very important. At large weddings as many as half a dozen, or more, ushers are sometimes needed to manage the great number of guests. They usually appoint one of their number as head usher, and to him falls the duty of deciding on the space to be reserved for near relatives, which is to be divided from the remainder of the church by white ribbons. He makes sure that the organist is in place, indicates the approach of the bridal party that the Wedding March may greet them, and instructs the other ushers as to their respective duties.

Ushers must escort guests to their seats, and as relatives of the groom are seated on the right of the main aisle, or center of the church, and those of the bride on the left, it is proper for an usher to ask any one with whom he may be unacquainted whether their relationship is to the bride or groom.

In escorting guests to their seats an usher gives his right arm to a lady. A gentleman who may be in her company should follow after.

The guests assembled, part of the ushers should leave the church at once and drive to the bride's residence in order to be there to receive the bridal party upon their return.

"The Best Man."

The "best man" is usually an intimate friend or relative of the groom. He drives to the church with him, stands by his side at the altar-rails while he awaits the approach of the bride, and, stepping back, it is he that holds the groom's hat during the ceremony and hands it to him at its close. To him is confided the payment of the wedding fee, and if there is a marriage register he signs as a witness. He then drives by himself to the bride's home, reaching there in time to receive the bridal party and to assist the ushers in the presentation of guests to the newly-married couple. He also makes the necessary arrangements about their departure, secures the tickets, and, if their destination is to be kept a secret, to him alone is it confided.

It occasionally happens that there are as many groomsmen as there are bridemaids, but this is the exception and the "best man" takes their place.

The ushers frequently form, two and two, and precede the bridal party up the aisle.

Bridemaids.

The number of these is optional, from one to twelve being allowable. Four, six or eight are usually chosen. Unmarried sisters of the bride and groom are frequently selected. Custom emphatically declares that they must be younger than the bride. For an elder sister thus to officiate would be extremely inappropriate.

Indeed, the favored fashion of the present time is for little tots, all the way from three or four to eight, clad in bewitchingly quaint and picturesque costumes and crowned by the largest of Gainsboro' hats, to precede the bridal couple to the chancel. In addition to these, the bride is followed by a chosen number of bridesmaids as well, but often the children are all. Frequently they carry baskets of flowers, and, preceding the newly-made wife in her progress down the church aisle, they scatter the blossoms in her pathway.

Sometimes this order is changed, and children rise in groups from seats near the front, and, preceding the bridal *cortège* to the door, scatter flowers before them. Children selected for this purpose should be under ten. Young boys, selected from among relatives, are sometimes dressed as pages and accompany the bride as train-bearers.

Bridemaids usually consult the bride as to their toilets, and each other as well, that there may be no unfortunate combinations of color to mar the effect of the whole. They usually dress in colors, unless the bride choose some faint tint for her costume; then it is customary for them to wear pure white, and sometimes the whole group are clad in spotless purity.

AN UNSEASONABLE CALL.

A MOORISH BEAUTY

The bridemaids' gowns are walking length, as a rule, and they wear large, picturesque hats, overshadowed with plumes or adorned with flowers, and carry huge bunches, or baskets, of fragrant blossoms. Wealthy brides, who have some special fancy to carry out, often provide the gowns for their maids. Historic styles are frequently chosen, making every gown after the exact mode of the epoch selected, but adopting a different color for each.

Where there is but one bridemaid, if she be escorted at all, which is not always done, it should be by some friend, not the "best man," whose duties in attendance on the groom are all-sufficient.

Bridemaids should not refuse the proffered honor, if possible for them to accept. If, after acceptance, unforseen circumstances should occur to prevent participation in the festivities, no time should be lost in sending a regret and full explanation, so that her place may be supplied in time to prevent disarrangement of the entire plan.

A Church Wedding.

A church wedding is more picturesque and solemn than any other form of celebrating the marriage rite and the etiquette of all full-dress affairs of this nature is essentially the same.

The groom drives first to the church, accompanied by his "best man" and enters either vestry or church parlor. The relatives, the mother of the bride and the bridemaids now drive to the church in carriages, closely followed by the carriage of the bride and her father.

By this time it is supposed that the carpet and awning, if it is a city church, are in place, the invited guests assembled, and the bridal procession immediately forms, entering the church and passing up the aisle to the strains of the wedding march. In England a lovely innovation is made on this threadbare custom by having a chorus of boy-voices sing an epithalamium, or wedding ode, during their progress. This custom has found its way here in some ritualistic churches where the vested choir march, two and two, at the head of the bridal procession, singing as they march. Sometimes as high as forty, and even seventy, in number swell the *cortège*.

The order of progression is as follows: first the ushers, (unless there are choristers to take the lead) who march up the aisle by twos, keeping step with the music, then, if there are child-bridemaids, they follow in the same order. Some brides have two, some four or six of these dainty dots of maids. The children are followed by the grown bridemaids, also two by two. Sometimes children alone fill the place, there being no grown maids. The maids, both children and grown folk, are arranged according to their height and the harmony of color in their gowns.

THE MARRIAGE CEREMONY.

After them comes the bride leaning on the right arm of her father. It sometimes happens that she walks up the aisle alone, and again that she is accompanied by some male relative who is to take a father's place in giving her away. Occasionally young brothers, mere boys in age, are permitted to assume this touching duty.

At the altar steps the ushers separate and pass to the right and left, the bridemaids also separate in a similar manner, leaving space for the bridal couple. The groom, having come from the vestry, accompanied by the "best man," should be standing in readiness to advance, take the bride by her right hand and turn to the clergyman, who proceeds with the marriage formula sanctioned by his faith.

At that point in the service where the question is asked, "Who giveth this woman to be married to this man?" the father, or whoever takes his place, should bow, and then in a moment leave the group and seat himself beside the bride's mother in the front pew at the left.

In a ritualistic church the bride and groom at once kneel before the officiating clergyman, who will signify to them at what point of the service to rise. Hassocks should be provided for the occasion.

The first bridemaid, or maid of honor, takes her stand close to, and slightly back of, the bride, that she may be ready to take her bouquet, if she has one, remove her glove, or, as is the better custom in this day of many-buttoned gloves, to turn back the neatly-ripped glove-finger that the ring may be adjusted, and to hold her bouquet or prayer-book when necessary. In the meantime, it is the "best man" who hands the ring to the clergyman in readiness for use.

After the Ceremony.

The service over, which may or may not have been accompanied by low, slow music, the clergyman shakes hands with and congratulates the newly-wedded couple (kissing being no longer permissible), the groom draws the bride's right hand within his left arm and conducts her to the carriage, taking the center aisle if the church have one; if not, taking the opposite from that by which they entered, the bride, her veil over her face, neither recognizing nor paying the slightest apparent heed to any one in the church. The organ peals forth, the procession re-forms and follows to the door, first the bridemaids, next the ushers. If there have been choristers, they lead the line, chanting as before, until their voices die out of hearing in the vestibule. Often, too, the child-bridemaids precede the couple as they leave the church, scattering flowers before them, the whole forming a very pretty pageant to the eye. The church may have been richly decorated with flowers and potted plants.

Where there is but one bridemaid or maid of honor, as she is then called, she attends to all the duties necessary, but the bridal procession is shorn somewhat of its fair proportions.

The vestibule reached, certificate or church register signed, the bride is cloaked, and, entering a carriage with her husband, is quickly driven home, the guests remaining in their seats until the cessation of the wedding march, when they, too, enter their carriages. Meanwhile the "best man" takes the shortest route possible to the same destination in order to assist the head usher, who with, perhaps, some of the other ushers, is supposed to be already there, in receiving the bridal party and guests as they reach the house. The remaining ushers busy themselves in assisting the bridesmaids to their carriages and speeding them onward that they, if possible, may reach the house in time to receive the bride and groom.

If the church wedding be in the evening the same order will be observed, save that the gentlemen wear evening dress.

The Reception.

At the house the ushers introduce the guests to the newly-married couple who, together with the bridesmaids, form a group to receive the good wishes of the company. The parents of the bride stand a little apart from this party and receive the felicitations of their guests in behalf of their daughter's welfare. The parents of the groom, if present, form part of this group.

If the company is very large it is well to divide the centers of attractions by placing the young couple in one room and the parents in another, thus compelling a freer circulation of the guests, who else would crowd the bridal party to suffocation.

The house may be profusely decorated with flowers, and the rooms though daylight reign without, may have been carefully darkened only to be re-illuminated by the softer radiance of waxen candles or shaded gas jets.

Refreshments.

The banquet may be as elaborate as desired, but is usually served in the refreshment room from the *buffét*, guests repairing thither at any time where they are served by attendants, ushers seeing that ladies unattended by gentlemen are invited to partake and properly served.

Tea or coffee is not considered a necessity, though, in compliance with tastes that do not yield easily to fashion's decree, it is usually to be had, but in winter bouillon, in cups, is usually offered. Wine, of course, depends upon the scruples of the entertainers. Salads, lobster, salmon, etc., birds and dainty rolled sandwiches, do duty for meats. Fancy cakes, such as macaroons, kisses, etc., are always offered, together with ices. The variety of other cakes is always at the option of the hostess, save the regulation rich black fruit, or groom's cake, and the bride's snowy loaf. These are necessities, and if the bride so far conform to the old custom of "cutting the cake" as to make one incision therein with a wonderful silver knife, "ye ancient superstition" is satisfied, and the work of cutting it and packing in dainty boxes to be carried home, if this be wished, is deputed to attendants. These boxes are deposited in some convenient place within reach of the departing guests.

When there are a number of elderly guests it is generally thought best to set two or more small tables in the refreshment-room, or an ante-room, where they may be comfortably accommodated with seats, and one of the ushers should see that they are so seated and promptly served.

Rehearsals.

In view of the complicated arrangements made necessary for the proper carrying out of a fashionable church wedding, and in consideration of the large number of people involved in the ceremony and the necessity of each one being in the right place at the right moment, in order to prevent confusion, it will be seen that some preparation is necessary before all can act in concert.

The needed drill is usually given by an exact rehearsal of the entire affair, to give which, the whole party meet at the church and rehearse, so to speak, their respective parts; the forming into procession, the parting right and left at the chancel and the re-forming to return to the vestibule, being all gone through with to the sound of music, until every part of the long procession moves like clockwork.

The grouping of the bridesmaids, the appointed duties of maid of honor and "best man," even to the smallest details, are all made perfect, until even the principal actors in the scene can retire without fear of any disaster to come.

This rehearsal is frequently made the occasion of a rehearsal dinner, given by the mother of the bride, at which the intimate participants of the wedding-to-come entertain and refresh themselves.

The Wedding Breakfast.

Wedding breakfasts are an exclusively English fashion, but are gradually creeping into favor here. The breakfast does not differ from the ordinary reception, save that it is usually at an earlier hour and is more frequently a "sit-down affair."

The guests all go into the refreshment room at the same time, even though it sometimes happens that the assembly is so large that no one but the bridal party and immediate relatives are provided with seats at small tables. In this case, the gentlemen help the ladies and themselves from a long table in the center of the room, the whole affair, under these circumstances, being simply a cold collation. Gentlemen leave their hats in the hall; ladies retain bonnet and gloves.

After the usual greetings to the bridal pair and a few minutes general conversation, the repast is announced and the guests proceed to the appointed room in the usual fashion—bride and groom, bride's father and groom's mother, groom's father and bride's mother, "best man" and maid of honor, other bridesmaids and gentlemen appointed, usually ushers, etc.

A "stand-up" breakfast has many things in its favor. It is more easily served than one where all the guests are seated at a table that, in everything but name, is a dinner table; it is less formal and therefore pleasanter, and far more guests can be accommodated. The refreshments are the same as for a reception.

Departure.

After mingling with the guests for a short time the bride quietly withdraws to don her traveling garb, and soon descends the stairway. She is met at the foot by her bridesmaids, who part and form in line on either hand, through which dainty pathway she passes to join the groom.

Quick good-byes are said, the carriage is entered and whirls rapidly away, followed by showers of rice and cast-off slippers, and the pretty scene is ended.

Home Weddings.

Home weddings are attended with much less trouble, fatigue and expense than fashionable church weddings. The clergyman enters the room and stands facing the people; the bridal couple follow and stand facing him. Hassocks are provided for kneeling, if desired. The father, or some near male relative, stands ready, in sight of the clergyman, to give away the bride. He should simply bow his affirmation when the question is asked.

There are many additions that may be made to this simple ceremony, such as a troop of pretty children holding white ribbons each side to mark the path the bridal pair must walk to reach the minister, while the sweet strains of a hidden band of musicians may accompany their footsteps.

Floral decorations, within limits, are beautiful and appropriate, but where they are so lavishly displayed as to remind more of the florist's bill than the beauty of the blossoms, their effect is lost in a certain vulgarity that attends all too-visible evidences of outlay.

One pretty idea is to carry out the fancy of having one kind of flower, massed according to the chosen design, serve for the decorations, at flower weddings; for example, rose weddings, lily weddings, daffodil weddings, etc. The design itself is according to the taste of the florist or the family, and is a subject changing so easily with the season or the fashion as to merit no mention here.

The supper may be as elegant an affair as one chooses to make it. If served by caterers, all care is removed from the hostess as to possible accidents, and she is left free to entertain her guests.

At evening weddings the company remains late or not, according to the hour of the bride's departure. Sometimes dancing is arranged as one of the evening's amusements. If so, the bride may, if she choose, open the first quadrille with the "best man." Should she do this, the groom is expected to dance with the first bridemaid.

The bride can slip away at any time, to reappear in traveling costume, and bidding a quick farewell, disappear from the company, who, after this, begin to disperse.

One most pleasant custom, English in its origin, should not be forgotten; it is that of remembering all the servants with some little gift as a souvenir of the occasion.

Invitations to Church Weddings.

There is a good deal of dispute in regard to the etiquette of acknowledgment of a card for a church wedding. Some high authorities assert that the invitation is so general and means so little particular attention that no notice need be taken of it except in the regular line of future visits to the bride and to the bride's mother. But one of our American social oracles declares that a card is obligatory at the hour of the wedding, if one cannot attend, and that if the house address is unknown, this card should be sent to the church. If this is necessary, most people err woefully, for few non-attendants send the card.

For church weddings everything pertains to formality, and the invitation as well as the ceremony is impressive in all details. The names of the parents heading the invitation are now more often written in full, thus insuring a good-looking line at the top of the note. The line, "request the honor of your presence," almost invariably appears on a church invitation with "honor" spelled with a "u."

The names of bride and groom are separated by the little word "to," although some consider "and" quite as proper.

The omission of the prefix "Miss" from the daughter's name is customary on an invitation but should never occur when the bride is a sister, cousin or niece of the people issuing the invitations. If a widow is re-marrying, she uses the prefix "Mrs." with her Christian names and the surname of her deceased husband. If the bride is an orphan, with no one to issue the invitations for her, the heading reads, "The honor of your presence is requested," etc. When the bride has more names than one it is customary to use all.

THE PRINCESS OF WALES.

A SOCIETY BELLE—"CALL AGAIN."

The address of a well-known church is generally omitted, although it is frequently a convenience for out-of-town friends to know it. Names of churches ending with "s," as Saint Thomas, are written with an apostrophe "s"—thus, Saint Thomas's.

Dress for the Occasion.

The Bride's Dress may be as elegant as desired, or as simple, but it is to be hoped that the custom of using pure white in the composition of the toilet will not be superseded by any passing freak of Dame Fashion's for softly tinted bridal robes. This innovation should be stoutly resisted by all brides-to-be. If the white robe is simple in material, a simple style should be chosen for the making; richer goods allow of more elaboration. The bride wears no jewels, and the typical orange-blossoms and myrtle are supposed to crown her brow. As a fact, however, other white flowers, such as roses, lilacs, lilies-of-the-valley, are more frequently chosen.

Where the wedding decorations are of one flower exclusively, that blossom alone figures in the bridal wreath and bouquet. Some High Church brides carry an ivory or silver-bound prayer-book in preference to flowers; thus associating it with the most sacred vows of their life and hoping to preserve it as an heirloom in the family.

White shoes and gloves are to be worn with this toilet. The best taste prescribes a high corsage for the bridal costume, and sleeves either to the elbow or longer, in either case to be met by the long kid gloves. This gives a certain modesty to the toilet that is in keeping with the occasion. By many brides who expect to wear their bridal costume to after evening entertainments, the wedding gown is frequently supplied with two corsages; the high for the wedding day and the low for evening wear.

The Veil is usually of thin, sheer tulle, as this is most becoming to the face, but those brides who can display fine old point on this occasion will be very apt so to do. If the bridal costume is to be worn on any other occasion, it must be divested of orange-blossoms and worn without the veil.

The above-described costume is appropriate for either a morning or evening wedding. Brides, who are married in traveling costume, should wear a bonnet rather than a hat.

The Groom's Dress is decided by the hour at which the wedding takes place. If it is in the evening, the conventional evening dress is imperative. Black suit, dress coat, low-cut waistcoat, white tie, white or pale pearl-colored gloves, thin patent leather shoes and possibly a white flower in the button-hole, constitute proper costume.

Morning Costume.

At a morning wedding, that is, one taking place at any hour between ten and seven (before which time a dress suit can by no possibility appear) full morning costume is worn by the groom. This consists of a dark frock coat, dark waistcoat and lighter trousers; a stiff hat, a light scarf and gloves if desired. The gloves should be light but not evening tints; pale tan or gray being suitable. The Groomsmen's Dress is decided by the hour and by the dress of the groom, of which it is a faithful copy.

The Usher's Dress follows the same law as that of the groomsmen, save that if wedding favors are worn it is by the ushers only. The other gentlemen present will find it well to copy the same styles, save that those only who are immediately connected with the ceremony are expected to wear white gloves.

The Bridemaid's Dress has been already described.

Friends in Mourning are expected to lay aside their somber robings for this hour. Even the widowed mother is bound to don either a pale gray, or a deep purple, costume for the occasion, the presence of black at so joyous a moment always casting a certain shadow over the party.

The Traveling Dress. This is occasionally worn by brides who do not wish to incur the haste and annoyance of changing their costume before leaving for the bridal tour. This is done at times even when the ceremony is performed in church, but is almost always resorted to where the wedding is quiet. Sometimes this dress is as elaborate as is at all consistent with good taste for traveling, and when this is the case it is usually exchanged for the regulation traveling gown at the first stopping place in their journey. More frequently, and more appropriately, the plain tailor-made suit, with gloves and hat in harmony, is made to do duty. In any case where the bride chooses to wear a traveling costume, even should the ceremony be performed in the evening, the groom will wear a morning costume.

A Quiet Wedding.

To many people the idea of so much splendor and ceremony on the occasion of their marriage has in it something distasteful, and to others the physical weariness thereby incurred is almost an impossibility. In this case the quietest of ceremonies may be chosen. It may take place in church if the bride desire this further seal of solemnity set upon the service, with parents and one or two friends for witnesses; or at home with the family and clergyman only present, the bridal couple being driven from thence directly to the depot if the stereotyped wedding tour is to follow.

Re-marriage.

A widow, re-marrying, no matter how youthful she may be, is prohibited from wearing the white gown, veil and orange-blossoms of the bride. Neither may she surround herself with a bevy of bridesmaids. Her wedding, to be absolutely correct, should be quietly solemnized and her garb a traveling dress.

Still, if she should wish, she may wear the most elegant of tinted silks, the most elaborate in make-up, and have a large and elegant assembly to witness her marriage and participate in its festivities, but no bridesmaids are allowable.

At a church wedding she should be attended by her father, brother, other male relative, or some friend. She should always remove the first wedding ring from her finger before the service and not again assume it. Invitations to the marriage of a widow are engraved with her whole name, maiden and married, thus: ELIZABETH STUART FIELDING.

If she have sons or unmarried daughters at the time of her second marriage she should prefix their last name to her new one on all ceremonious occasions in which they also are interested, thus: MRS. STUART FIELDING GRANT and MISS FIELDING, At Home. 20 Grosvenor Square.

The Ring.

The fourth finger of the left hand, counting from the thumb, is the finger upon which the engagement and wedding rings are worn. The engagement ring varies in extravagance according to the means of the groom, and has almost always a set of some description; the wedding ring is always the same, a plain, round-edged band of gold. Initials and dates may be engraved in both.

The engagement ring is usually worn afterward as a guard for the wedding ring. As to its setting there is a wide latitude given wherein all the pretty conceits and superstitions attached to precious stones may be exercised at will. The German consider pearls unlucky for brides, as significant of tears. Birth-month stones may be used, even the fateful opal losing its power for harm when worn by an October maiden. The turquoise is perhaps the favored of precious stones for this purpose. The old Persian proverb says that "He that hath a turquoise hath a friend." Its known power of turning pale under certain climatic influences has invested it in story with the power of not only warding off evil influences, rendering its wearer constant and assuring success in love, but still more of revealing by a certain pallor of coloring, coming danger or the existence of inconstancy in its wearer. It is also said that in case of a fall the turquoise takes all injury upon itself; the stone being fractured and the owner being uninjured. Add to this the item that the stone must be a gift, not a purchase, to possess these marvelous powers, and it will be seen that it is admirably suited to adorn an engagement ring. The diamond is another very appropriate stone for this purpose, either *solitaire* or in cluster.

A TOKEN OF FRIENDSHIP.

Reception Days.

It is necessary for the bride to include her new address with her wedding invitations, unless, as is still more "chic," cards for several reception days are issued after her return. These dates being fixed, it is then that first calls may be made upon her at her new residence with the happy certainty of finding her at home.

At these quiet, informal receptions, she receives simply as a member of society, wearing usually a rich, dark silk without any reminders of her recent bridehood.

WEDDING ANNIVERSARIES.

The wedding anniversaries are numerous, but only a few of these are habitually observed. Paper, wooden, tin, crystal, silver and golden are the favorite ones, the others being so rare as to hardly merit being included in the list.

The following complete list of the anniversaries, with the respective dates of their occurrence, may be useful for reference:

First Anniversary	Paper Wedding.
Second Anniversary	Cotton Wedding.
Third Anniversary	Leather Wedding.
Fifth Anniversary	Wooden Wedding.
Seventh Anniversary	Woolen Wedding.
Tenth Anniversary	Tin Wedding.
Twelfth Anniversary	Silk and Linen Wedding.
Fifteenth Anniversary	Crystal Wedding.
Twentieth Anniversary	China (sometimes Floral) Wedding.
Twenty-fifth Anniversary	Silver Wedding.
Thirtieth Anniversary	Pearl Wedding.
Thirty-fifth Anniversary	Coral Wedding.
Fortieth Anniversary	Ruby Wedding.
Forty-fifth Anniversary	Bronze Wedding.
Fiftieth Anniversary	Golden Wedding.
Sixty-Fifth Anniversary	Crown-Diamond Wedding.
Seventy-fifth Anniversary	Diamond Wedding.

It may be well to mention here that the twentieth anniversary is considered unlucky to celebrate, or even to mention.

The manner of sending out invitations and accepting and refusing the same has been fully described in the proper department, and a few words only will be necessary as to the gifts and entertainment suitable on such occasions.

Tin and Paper Weddings and some other of the earlier anniversaries are usually occasions for happy frolics, and merry jests as to the form the gifts will take, though the paper wedding gives place for the presentation of elegant books, and a supply of fashionable stationery that is sufficient to fill the family needs for a long space of time.

Suitable Presents.

The Wooden Wedding is a little more expensive in its demands, and the gifts range from elegant *suites* of carved furniture down to dainty bits of hand-carving in the shape of panels and placques; and from rolling-pin and potato-masher all the way up to oaken mantles, rich with all manner of ingenious fret-work of design.

The Crystal Wedding may also show forth a glittering array of gifts both ornamental and useful.

The Silver Wedding is, perhaps, the most important of all the wedding anniversaries. This arises partly from the fact that it is most generally observed, partly because of the value of its gifts, and, more than aught else, because the date of its observance finds the happy pair still in the enjoyment of comparative youth and with length of days still before them. In the matter of presents it is almost impossible to go amiss, since there is scarcely an article of use or ornament from dining-room to reception-room and from the library desk to my lady's toilet table, that has not been made a thing of beauty and a joy forever by the silversmith's art.

The Golden Wedding, from the advanced age at which it occurs, has an element of sadness in its celebration. The aged couple who stand so near the brink of separation can have little of bridal joy as they look back to the day when they stood before the altar in the first flush of youth, with life before them, or as they look forward to the shortened span of years that links them to their loved ones here. The gifts that are laid before them should be fitly wrought of gold, since their love has been as gold tried in the furnace of life.

If the family means are insufficient for numerous valuable gifts, let all the friends "club" together and purchase some fitting souvenir for the occasion. Golden-rod forms an appropriate floral decoration.

But, after all, the chief idea and the pleasure of this anniversary is the gathering together of as many as possible of the relatives that yet remain to greet the pair at this, the golden milestone of their life's journey.

Speeches and Congratulations.

The Diamond Wedding occurs so seldom, and is so much like the others in the manner, if not the matter of its gifts, as to scarcely require mention here.

The entertainment at these anniversary celebrations is very much the same as at weddings or other gatherings. The refreshments may be served at tables, or a "stand up" collation given. In this latter case, there should be one or two tables set for the elders of the party.

At Silver and Golden Weddings presentation speeches are frequently made by some friend, and at golden anniversaries a regular program is oftentimes carried out. Anniversary poems are read, "The Hanging of the Crane" recited, congratulatory telegrams from absent friends are announced, and any old acquaintances present that can be persuaded to say a few words of "ye olden times" are pressed into service. Good taste, however, would seem to prevent any repetition of the marriage service on such an occasion.

Cards in acknowledgment of bridal presents are worded in the following fashion: MR. and MRS. GEORGE H. BRANDON express sincere thanks to — — for the beautiful wedding gift. June 18th. 62 West 126th street.

An ultra-fashionable bride, supplying herself with several packages of these stereotyped acknowledgments, has nothing to do but fill in the name of the sender and thus avoid infinite labor.

HOME ETIQUETTE

GOOD manners are a plant of slow growth, and one that should be cultivated in the home circle.

"Give a boy address, and it opens palaces to him," says Emerson, and nowhere is this address, "this habit of encounter," so easily gained as within the walls of home. There his character is formed for life.

Good breeding, in reality, is but the outcome of "much good sense, some good nature, and a little self-denial exercised for the sake of others, with a view to obtain the same indulgence from them."

These words of the scholar, Chesterfield, learned as he was in worldly lore, and satisfied of the expediency of such observances from a selfish standpoint, are but another, and more selfish, rendering of the Golden Rule, whose value as a rule of action in life is apparent.

Courtesy, it must be conceded, is not only pleasant, but profitable in all places, and at all times, but more especially in the home circle are its virtues most brilliantly set forth.

Courtesies of Married Life.

"Marriage very rarely mends a man's manners," is a sadly true statement of the playwright Congreve, and one whose truth touches women also as concerning the marriage state.

If the slight formalities that are the bulwarks of love as well as friendship, many forbearances, and more of the small, sweet courtesies of life, were but permitted to blossom forth like unexpected flowers beneath the family rooftree, fewer unhappy marriages would catalogue their miseries in the divorce court.

The man who takes off his hat as politely to his wife when he parts from her on the street as he would to his lady acquaintance of yesterday; who opens the door for her to enter; who would no more speak harshly to her than to any other lady, is very likely to retain her first affection and to add to it that sweeter, closer love that comes of knowledge and companionship.

What Women Admire.

Women admire fine manners and graceful attentions. The man who never forgets their tastes; who remembers wedding anniversaries and birthdays; is interested in their pursuits, and ready with an appreciative word of praise, is the man that claims their admiration by virtue of thoughtfulness and consideration.

This man, too, would be far more apt to hold a woman's affection than the best and most upright of his sex, who is thoughtless and indifferent, not of her physical comfort, but of all her pet fancies and sentiments, who never saw her new gowns, and is profoundly neglectful of all those trifles, light as air, which go far toward making up the sum of woman's happiness or misery.

What Men Desire.

Hepworth Dixon, on being asked what men most desire in a wife, and what quality held them longest, unhesitatingly replied, "That she should be a pillow." Then, noting the inquiry thus suggested, he went on to say: "What a man most needs is that he should find in his wife a pillow whereon to rest his heart. He longs to find a moment's rest from the outer whirl of life, to win a ready listener that sympathizes where others wound." And she whose eyes are flattering mirrors, whose lips console and soothe, will find that she has secured a hold upon the heart of her husband, that the embodiment of all the virtues of her sex could not secure, were she wanting in this sympathetic tact.

Sweet-tempered people are the joy of the world. Their civilities, their self-sacrifice, their thoughtfulness for others it is that oils the wheels of domestic life. People who, according to the old phrase, have "tempers of their own," are not, at the best, agreeable companions. We may respect their good qualities, but we are apt to give them a wide berth where possible. But when they are inmates of our own households, the evil spirit must be confronted and exorcised if possible.

Many a wife has, by exercising her own self-control, subdued and shamed a tyrannical, evil-tempered husband into a better disposition, but never by argument, dispute, or anger on her part.

Many a husband, too, has by the firmness and sweetness of his own temper, won his young, impatient wife, tried by the half-understood cares of her new existence, to evenness of spirit and control of temper. "It is impossible to be cross where Charlie is," said one young wife, taken from a home where self-control had never been taught. "I am always ashamed of it afterward."

Fault-Finding.

"Take us the foxes, the little foxes that spoil our vines," and of the insidious foxes that spoil the tender fruitage of the household vine, a fault-finding disposition is most dangerous.

A quick, ungovernable temper is not as destructive to household peace and comfort as the nagging, carping, fault-finding spirit that sees good in nothing. A temper that is like a tornado in its violence at least clears the air as it passes, and is usually followed by quick repentance and ready reparation. But the fault-finding, nagging, suspicious temperament is a veritable foe in a man's own household.

Where no word of praise is heard, no commendation follows the best-intentioned efforts, but the ceaseless nagging, the ever recurring criticism meets one at every turn, it is not strange if the ties of affection are too often strained even to breaking.

Temper proceeds from, and is an indication of the character. It is inherited, even as features are; but, like features, it may be modified by culture and training, and a temper thus conquered becomes a very desirable possession.

Home Conversation.

Educate yourself, as a wife, to keep up with the times sufficiently to be at least a companionable conversationalist. Read the papers, read late books; endeavor to be as entertaining to your husband as you were to your husband-elect.

ETIQUETTE OF THE DRAWING-ROOM.

As a husband, share your knowledge of the activities of life with your wife, who, from the very nature of her occupation is excluded from much of its exciting whirl. Read together, talk together of art, of music, of literature, of the stirring events of the outer world, and put afar the evil day when topics of mutual interest shall have been worn so threadbare that the average man and woman must feel a strange desire to fall asleep directly dinner is over.

Then, too, the children hunger for new ideas, and one of the greatest educational advantages they can enjoy is to listen daily to the conversation of intelligent people. Too many parents who are bright and entertaining abroad are dull and uninteresting in their own households, to the great detriment of their children and to their own loss of intelligent companionship in one another.

"What little Jack learneth not, the same neither learneth great John." There is a truth in this old saying that the parents and guardians of children would do well to ponder in their hearts, for it is a well substantiated statement that the first ten years of a child's life stamp upon his character the imprint for good or ill-breeding. Thus is spared the after struggle on their part to attain the grace and self-possession that should have been theirs by birthright.

SUNSHINE AT HOME.

Children are naturally imitative, hence the value of example over precept. The children of courteous parents will imbibe courtesy as naturally and unconsciously as the growing plant absorbs oxygen from the air and sunlight that bathes its leaves and petals.

Softly modulated tones should mark the words spoken to a child, and reproof carries an added weight when lowered tones convey the rebuke. Even a baby before it can speak recognizes shades of meaning in the tones the mother utters, and is soothed by the one and startled by the other.

Kindliness, politeness of the parents one towards another, are the first steps toward training children in the acquirement of good manners. Gentleness and sweetness of manner can be taught at the cradle far more surely than from the schoolroom desk, and when baby has learned to preface its little wants with "please," and Master Four Years-old to run and open the door for mamma, or mamma's visitors, or to give up the easiest chair without being asked, the firm foundation has been laid for courteous behavior in after life.

And so on, all through the school years, boys and girls may be so taught to respect one another's possessions, letters, feelings, and to discriminate closely between *meum* and *tuum* after such wise that they will be made better husbands, better wives, better citizens, for all their days.

Slang and Exaggerations.

By our own speech it is that we are sure to be judged, for,—

"'Tis only man can words create,

And cut the air to sounds articulate

By nature's special charter. Nay, speech can

Make a shrewd discrepance 'twixt man and man.

It doth the gentleman from the clown discover;

And from a fool the great philosopher.

As Solon said to one in judgment weak:—

'I thought thee wise until I heard thee speak.'"

And if we talk with flippancy and exaggeration, load our sentences with slang phrases, and preface and punctuate them with oft-repeated expressions of "Say!" "Well!" "You know," "Do tell," and so on, *ad infinitum*, all wisdom, or propriety of speech will be lost.

It is difficult to believe in the refinement of a girl who permits her fresh young lips to utter the slang of the bar-room hanger-on, the gambler and the street gamin.

Equally difficult is it to believe in the absolute truthfulness of one who declares to you that the heat of a lovely June day is "simply awful" or "perfectly terrible," from sheer wonder as to what terms she would use to characterize the intense heat of some sweeping fire.

THE INDUSTRIOUS HOUSEWIFE.

Again, it is hard to understand the taste of one who informs you gravely that "the chicken salad was too lovely for anything!" or the last evening's sunset was "perfectly elegant!" The Websterian definition of "elegant" being "polished, stylish, refined, etc.," it is to be wished that all perpetrators of like sins could meet the punishment a young lady once dealt to a gentleman who remarked with great effusion: "This moonlight is perfectly elegant!" To this observation she answered with gravity, "Yes, it really *is* very stylish!"

Let, therefore, all who strive for the grace of good breeding, men and women, boys and girls alike, "set a watch over their lips and keep the door of their mouth," for "words have wings, and so soon as their cage, the mouth, is opened, out they fly and mount beyond our reach, and past recovery."

Some Do's for Girls.

The following hints for girls, each prefaced by the auxiliary "Do," will prove a safe guide, not only for the girls but for any of their elders who may choose to follow them.

Do answer your letters soon after they are received, and do try to reply to them with some relation to their contents; a rambling, ill-considered letter is a satire upon your education.

Do, when you talk, keep your hands still.

Do observe; the faculty of observation, well cultivated, makes practical men and women.

Do attach as much importance to your mind as to your body.

Do be natural; a poor diamond is better than a good imitation.

Do try to remember where you put your gloves and cardcase; keep the former mended and the latter filled.

Do recollect that your health is more important than your amusements; you can live without one, but you'll die early without the other.

Do try to be sensible; it is not a particular sign of superiority to talk like a fool.

A CALL FROM BABY'S ADMIRERS.

Do be ready in time for church; if you do not respect yourself sufficiently to be punctual, respect the feelings of other people.

Do get up in time for breakfast.

Do avoid causes of irritation in your family circle; do reflect that home is the place in which to be agreeable.

Do be reticent; the world at large has no interest in your private affairs.

Do cultivate the habit of listening to others; it will make you an invaluable member of society, to say nothing of the advantage it will be to you.

Do be truthful; do avoid exaggeration; if you mean a mile say a mile, not a mile and a half; if you mean one say one, and not a dozen.

Young Ladies, Take Heed.

Do, sometimes, at least, allow your mother to know better than you do; she was educated before you were born.

Do sign your full name to your letters.

Do learn to say "No."

Do, if you have brothers, try to gain their confidence, to be interested in their sports, to cultivate their manners, not by censure, but by the force of your own example.

Do laugh, girls, not boisterously, not constantly, but clearly and pleasantly, but *don't* giggle. If girls from fourteen to eighteen could only understand the vulgarity of continually putting their heads together and giggling, as if the whole world was a supremely ridiculous affair, about which they must chuckle, and whisper, when in truth their own actions are the one thing ridiculous, they would refrain from such unmitigated nonsense.

Do be exquisitely neat in your attire. Beware of the lawn dress, the light kids, the collar, the laces that are worn once too often.

Do be careful about giving away your photographs, especially to men. You would hardly like to hear the comments that are sometimes passed upon them. If you cannot learn to say "No," refrain from displaying them to your gentleman friends.

Some Do's for Boys.

As for boys, there are a few "Do's" for them to consider if they would become that noblest work of God, a true man, a gentleman.

Do respect your father and mother and give them their proper titles at all times. To call them "the Governor" and "the old lady," does not in the least add to your supposed manliness, but rather displays a very unmanly fear on your part that people might suppose you were in some degree under their authority; not only an unmanly, but a foolish fear, since no one is fit for authority until he has first learned obedience.

Do learn to respect women. Never speak slightingly of their worth, nor trifle with their name. Learn the lesson now, and you will find its value in your manhood.

Do treat your sisters and your girl schoolmates in a gentlemanly manner. You have no idea how much it will add to your own appearance.

Do guard against a profusion of slang that would do credit to a pickpocket.

Do be determined not to use profane expressions in the presence of ladies, children, or ministers, or anywhere else.

Do keep your lips from uttering coarse and unclean things that you would blush to have overheard by mother or sister. More than this, do not listen to them from the lips of others. A pure-minded boy will be a pure-minded man.

Do take care of your various belongings; do not expect mother or sisters to pick up your necktie, your gloves, your schoolbooks, your hat, from as many different places as there are articles, and put them properly away. It is quite as necessary for boys or men to have some neatness in their habits as for girls or women. Do learn to help yourself occasionally. It is quite possible that you should be able to arrange a necktie, comb your hair, or get the articles together for a fresh toilet without calling some one to your assistance. Quite possible and vastly convenient for other members of the household.

Do close the doors without slamming; don't tear the house down.

Do lower your voice sometimes; everyone is not deaf.

Do be neat in personal appearance; collars, handkerchiefs and cuffs, should be spotlessly clean, and hands and finger nails receive careful attention.

Do not fail to use three brushes every day—the tooth-brush, the clothes-brush and the blacking-brush.

Do break yourself of disagreeable personal habits. Do not yawn in people's faces, lounge in your chair, scratch head or person, or clean finger-nails when others are present.

Do not forget to use your handkerchief, and that quietly as possible.

Do decide that temperate habits are more manly than intemperate ones, and don't think that it is one of your "rights" to smoke cigarettes.

Do learn to say "No," to lead sometimes instead of always following.

Do be careful of your manners. Remember that as the twig is bent, so the tree is inclined, and that the polished boy will be the polished man. Polish, it is to be understood, is not inconsistent with strength, but rather adds to it. The strongest machinery is of the finest polish, and the Damascus blade is of the surest mettle.

Do be sure to give up your seat in omnibus or car to a lady. Even if she be not sufficiently grateful, you have shown your good breeding.

Do remember to remove your hat when you enter a house, private office, hotel elevator (if ladies are present), when you bow to a lady or when you offer to assist a lady.

Do lay these "do's" up in your memory and practice them in your lives.

Guard the Voice.

A harsh voice, or shrill, high-pitched tones, are a source of discomfort to all who hear them. Nothing gives a more favorable impression of good breeding than a voice, musical, clear, low in its key, and careful in its articulation.

George Eliot, who had a face of extreme plainness, possessed a low musical voice that had a perfect fascination for the listener. At times such a voice is the gift of nature, but usually it requires careful cultivation, and the earlier the age at which this cultivation begins, the surer and the simpler is the price of success.

Children can be early taught not to raise their voices shrilly to demand attention, but to speak softly and gently at home, and then their "company voice" will possess a natural quality. Train the tones softly and sweetly now, and they will keep in tune through life.

Those whose early education in this respect has been neglected will win success only at the price of eternal vigilance. A few lessons in voice culture will work wonders in training the ear to appreciate the different keys, the voice to acquire lower and richer tones, and the articulation to become clear and distinct.

Even where there are serious vocal defects, such as stammering, lisping, etc., they can be relieved by some good teacher of voice-culture. Indeed, some attention to the culture of voices ought to become a necessary part of education. A low, sweet voice is like a lark's song in heart and home, and the self-control necessary to always keep it at this harmonious level, exercises a most salutary influence over mind and temper.

How to Treat Servants.

A large proportion of the domestic economy in many households is left entirely in the hands of servants, and on the good or ill behavior of these servants depends the comfort of the home, and the behavior of the servants depends very greatly upon the behavior of their employers toward them. The manner even of addressing servants in this country is rather important, offense being so readily taken at what is deemed disrespect.

Men servants may be addressed by their last name without any prefix. If they have been in the family a long time the first name may be used, if desired. In addressing servants that are perfect strangers it can be generally managed without the use of any name. In writing to them address without prefix, as, Robert Johnson.

Do not be insolent towards, or demand too much of, servants. They have very much the same feelings of pride that the house-mistress has, and the less those feelings are wounded the better help they will render.

Do not reprimand them before guests. Nothing so injures their self-respect or so tends to make them careless. Whatever the blunder, be apparently unmoved in the presence of your guests. Save all reproof until their departure. Have a perfect understanding of the work you would have them perform, if you would have them accomplish it satisfactorily. Ignorance never yet made a good master or mistress, and always puts a premium on incompetency on the part of employés.

Have Rules and Enforce Them.

Require all house servants to be quiet in their movements, not to slam doors or rattle china. Impress upon them the importance of dressing neatly. Teach them to treat all comers with politeness; to answer the door-bell promptly and to thoroughly understand whatever rules you may have about being "engaged" or "not at home."

If reproof is to be administered or orders given, it is much better that the servant be called upstairs to receive them, than for the house mistress to descend to the kitchen. This will insure an opportunity should dispute arise of dismissing the employé to the kitchen with but loss of dignity on her part; while, if it is in the kitchen that the difference of opinion may arise, the house-mistress must herself leave the field.

Insist upon systematic arrangement of the week's work, and punctuality in carrying out its details. Explain carefully to all newly-engaged servants the routine of the house and expect them to conform to it. Be mild but firm in exercising authority, and servants will respect you and your rules.

If there is a housekeeper, all these details will be committed to her hands, and she has need to be competent, compelling respect, to be fitted for the position. Teach servants not to expect fees from your visitors.

Respect all their privileges. See that their evenings out, and their precious Sunday afternoons are not encroached upon. Give them all the needed opportunity to attend their own place of worship. See that children of the family are respectful toward them, not disturbing them at their work; prefacing their requests with "please," and thanking them for any favor.

Rights of Others.

Respect the rights of all members of the household. Remember that each one has a perfect right to open his or her own correspondence. No difference if one is ready to confide the contents of the letter the moment it is read, there is still a pleasure in opening one's own correspondence.

Respect the belongings of another, no matter how close the relationship. The careful member of the family suffers at seeing his belongings misused and destroyed by the careless one. Discourage borrowing among the members of a family. Teach each one to have all necessary articles of their own and to care for them properly.

Guests in a family should also be very careful in this respect. Boxes, drawers, or any repositories of any kind, should be scrupulously respected. Private papers, even if not protected by lock and key, should not be glanced at. A due observance of these rules, while making home life pleasanter, might in after years lead to a little less tampering with the larger rights of law and property, for "manners are but the shadows of great virtues."

ETIQUETTE FOR CHILDREN.

JEAN PAUL RICHTER, in his great work on education (*Levana*), intimates that we scarcely realize the momentous possibilities that lie all about us folded up in the heart of childhood, as the blushing petals of the beauteous blossom yet to be lie folded close within the sheltering calyx.

"Do you know," he queries, "whether the little boy who plucks flowers at your side may not one day, from his island of Corsica, descend as a war-god into a stormy universe to play with hurricanes for destruction, or to purify and plant the world with harvests?" And just because we do not know the extent of these possibilities, children must be carefully trained to fill whatever post or province may be theirs in the time to come.

Now, they are in our hands to mold as we will; then, they will be the masters, and much of the character of their sway will depend upon the guidance of the present. Viewed in this light, the manners and the morals of children, closely associated as they are, become of the greatest importance to the world.

Power of Example.

Teach the embryo man or woman, in the nursery, the traits, the habits, the customs of the best etiquette, and you have stamped upon them, at an age when the character is impressible as wax, not only the outer semblance, but, in a great degree, the inner reality, of a true man or woman.

Let the children grow up in a home where rude gestures, or ill-tempered words are unknown, where truthfulness, kindliness, forgetfulness of self and careful consideration of others, permeates the very atmosphere, and they will go forth into the world armed with the integrity in which all men may trust, the polish that will win them admiration, and the true refinement that will render their friendship elevating.

See, also, that there is perfect unanimity between the parents as to the government and instruction of the children in the household, and, if any difference should arise, it should be settled in private. Children, being strongly imitative, are best taught by example. Never reprove unless absolutely necessary, and never let the voice rise excitedly to ensure obedience. By keeping your own voice low and calm, you do much toward lowering the key of their high-pitched, childish treble, and soothing the troubled waters of their souls.

Keeping Promises.

Never permit yourself to threaten where you do not perform; children are quick to learn the value of your promises, and place very accurate estimates, in their own minds, as to what their parents will, or will not do under given circumstances. Absolute truthfulness can never be taught a child by precept, when by constant example he is taught that the word of his parents has little or no value in his own case, so far as threats and punishments, or even rewards, extend. If a punishment is the penalty for a broken law, see that it is inflicted; if a reward is promised, be sure that it is given.

Enjoin upon children strict justice in their dealings one with another, even in their games, never allowing the stronger to impose upon the weak, but teaching forbearance and tenderness in all their actions.

Talebearing.

Discourage, as far as possible, all talebearing in the home, and, as a rule, do not listen to complaints, and long recitals of injuries received from little playfellows. Care in this respect will nip in the bud the tendency toward exaggeration and talebearing that so early develops in a child, and so soon matures into the "gossip" of riper years. This demand for exactitude in childish statements will pave the way for strictly truthful declarations in the more important affairs of later life, redounding thus to the lasting benefit of the individual and the community.

Truthfulness.

The least approach toward prevarication, or concealment of their childish misdemeanors, should be treated as a grave fault. To prevent, as far as possible, all attempts at disguising the truth, penalties for faults should rarely be of so severe a nature that the little transgressor resorts to evasion through fear of the consequences.

Respectfulness.

Children should be taught to be respectful toward their parents and others older than themselves, to be polite towards those of their own age, and very thoughtful for the comfort of the sick and weak. Respect must also be shown toward servants and dependants, and no unnecessary demands made upon their time or services.

Obedience.

Prompt obedience should always be demanded of a child, and the spirit of murmuring and questioning firmly repressed. None can command except they have first learned to obey.

Do not allow children to tease, nor, having once refused on good and sufficient ground, suffer your consent to be gained by siege. Make your refusal final, but do not refuse thoughtlessly, or for mere caprice. The wishes of a child are as real to him as those of grown people are to them.

Manner of Address.

Rudeness and abruptness must never be tolerated in the manners of a child. "Yes," and "no," in reply, and "what?" in interrogatory, are uncouth and disagreeable in sound. "Yes, sir," "Yes, ma'am," and "What, ma'am," are much better substituted, but even these are open to criticism. English etiquette relegates "Sir" and "Ma'am" to the use of servants, save in case of addressing the higher nobility when "Sir" is sometimes used.

THE NURSERY.

The better and more graceful etiquette of the day would teach a child to say, "Yes, mamma," "No, papa;" or a student at school to address the teachers as, "Yes, Prof. Stanley," "No, Miss Livingstone." If they fail to understand a remark, a quick, "Beg pardon," or, "I beg your pardon," or even, "I did not understand," can soon be taught to even childish lips and never be forgotten as they advance to maturity. The use of "Please," and "Thank you," or, "I thank you," (never the thankless "Thanks,") should be early impressed upon their minds.

Teach them never to speak of grown people without prefixing "Mr.", "Mrs.", or "Miss," to their name. It is very objectionable for a child to fall into the habit of saying "Brown did so and so," instead of, "Mr. Brown, etc." Insist, too, that at school they shall never say "Teacher," but address their preceptor by his proper name.

Impress upon children that they must answer politely when spoken to, but strictly repress any tendency on their part toward questioning visitors at the house. Here let it be added, for the benefit of their elders, that nothing can be a surer evidence of ill-breeding than for a grown person to question a child in regard to his family affairs.

Interrupting Conversation.

Never permit children to interrupt the conversation of their elders, and see, as a preparation for this, that among the little ones themselves, one who has a story to tell is permitted to finish without an impatient brother or sister breaking in with his, or her, version of the same tale. See that each has his turn and many of the noisy disagreements of the playroom will thus be done away with.

Insist, too, upon the lowering of each eager little voice, and a long step will have been taken toward doing away with the high-keyed voices and the all-talking-together habits that afflict so many of their elders.

See, too, that the children, while not allowed to interrupt the conversation of grown persons, receive in some degree the same consideration from them. In other words, let the children talk sometimes, and listen to them sincerely and respectfully. There is no better way to train a child in courtesy than to observe toward it the most scrupulous politeness, and a child whose own conversation is respected can be easily taught to respect the conversation of others, and to know when to talk and when to be silent.

This habit of listening, inculcated in childhood, will do much toward forming agreeable members of society in after years. If a guest should converse with a child for a moment, watch that it does not make itself tiresome by engaging his or her entire attention.

"Showing Off."

Never "show off" children to visitors. It fosters in them a feeling of vanity, and is often very tedious to the persons upon whom it is inflicted, it being barely possible that your own estimate of their brilliancy is not shared by outsiders.

Neither should strangers be allowed, under any circumstances, at home or abroad, to tease a child "just for fun." Its angry answers may be amusing, but the practice is one that works irreparable injury to the child. As soon as this tendency is discovered in a visitor, send the child quietly, but firmly, from the room, remarking casually, when it is gone, "that children are apt to be troublesome when they talk too much."

Reproof Before Others.

Never, unless it is absolutely unavoidable, reprove a child in the presence of strangers. To do this injures their feeling of self-respect. It is an annoyance to the visitor also. While it frequently happens that a word of timely admonition is necessary, all extended reproof should be left until alone with the child.

Cleanliness and Order.

Insist upon cleanliness in dress, and teach the children early that their hair should be combed, their teeth and finger-nails clean, and their clothing fresh and neat upon all occasions.

Teach the boys that their shoes should be polished and free from dust, and their clothes thoroughly brushed. Slippers should be furnished boys for house wear, and the importance of using a doormat before entering should be early impressed upon both girls and boys. Teach them also order and care as to their personal belongings, and the lessons of neatness thus early inculcated will be of untold value in their after life.

Home Hints.

Cultivate in children the habit of assuming pleasing attitudes. Do not let them constantly lounge about over chairs, couches and tables, and their company manners will not then be a terror in the house. Teach them the proper use of a handkerchief, and insist that they observe it.

Instruct them what to do with their hands and feet, never twisting the former, or swinging the latter. Never permit them to scratch the head or person, to clean ears or finger nails, or to use a toothpick in public. Teach them to suppress a yawn or to conceal the mouth with the hand.

Do not let them pass in front of people in a room, or, if from the arrangement of the furniture it is impossible to avoid so doing, let them ask to be excused.

If they should accidently tread upon the toes, or otherwise disturb a guest, teach them at once to apologize with an "Excuse me," or, "I beg your pardon." Do not permit them to slam doors, or to shout up and down stairs. Never allow requests or messages to be called from one end of the house to the other; insist upon a child coming into the room with whatever he or she may have to say.

Impress upon boys and girls not to stare at others, nor to take any apparent notice of personal peculiarities, deformities, or oddities of dress or demeanor.

Teach the children always to play a fair game upon the playground, and not to lose their tempers over any little difference of opinion that may arise during its course.

Do not allow them to be cruel in their treatment of animals; to do so, is to deliberately teach them habits of cruelty for a lifetime and render them brutal in disposition.

"Visiting."

Children should not be allowed to "visit" other children solely upon the request of the children. The invitation should come from the parents. Otherwise great annoyance may result from such unconsidered calls.

Do not take children while making formal visits. They are often an annoyance, and always a check upon conversation. If they must be taken, do not allow them to meddle with anything in the room, nor to interrupt the conversation. Neither should they be permitted to handle the belongings, or finger the attire, of callers at the house. Do not take them to art galleries, artist's or sculptor's studios, and never allow them to meddle with goods in stores.

Slang, Profanity, Intemperance.

Slang should be eliminated, as much as possible, from the household vocabulary. Boys should be taught that profanity, or vulgarity in expression, far from being manly, only lowers them in the estimation of all sensible people.

It should also be early impressed upon them that there is danger in the use of liquor in any form, as well as folly in falling into the tobacco habit.

At Table.

Punctuality at the table should be taught first of all. The little table observances so necessary to refinement of manner should be early inculcated. Table manners (see proper department) should be taught at the earliest age that the child is capable of appearing at the table. The proper use of knife, fork, spoon and napkin should be impressed upon their minds from the first, and much after annoyance will be saved.

Teach them to eat quietly without any noise of mastication, swallowing or drinking being audible. Insist upon their sitting still while waiting to be served and not to play with knife, napkin ring or other small articles on the table.

Insist upon their breaking bread, instead of cutting it, and never to pick up one piece of bread or cake from the plate and then exchange it for another.

Teach them to eat fruit properly, to use finger bowls, if such are provided, and to keep their lips closed as much as possible while eating. Teach them to pass a pitcher with the handle toward the one served, and not to eat with one hand and pass some article with the other.

See that they do not eat too fast—both health and appearances being considered in this item—and that they do not talk with their mouths full. Teach them to turn away their heads and cover their mouth with their hand, if obliged to cough, sneeze or yawn at table, and, as soon as possible, require them to suppress these exhibitions. Never let them pick their teeth at the table, or lounge upon it with their elbows while eating.

Leaving the Table.

If children must leave the table before the meal is over, they should ask to be excused, and should never rise with their mouth full. When they have once left the table, do not, as a rule, permit them to return, for a child soon falls into the habit, if permitted, of leaving the table to play, and returning to complete his meal.

Teach children not to complain of the food set before them; but, at the same time, if a child has known likes or dislikes, they should be, to a certain extent, gratified, since, to some delicately constituted temperaments, a compelled partaking of some obnoxious dish is a real torture. Teach them also to acquire a liking for as large a variety of food as possible. In after life, on many occasions, this may be a great convenience.

In conclusion, let it be added that the Department on Home Etiquette should be read in connection with this, especially the section devoted to children. See to it carefully that children are not taught one code of manners for company use, and permitted to exercise no manners for home use.

DINNER GIVING

"MAN is essentially a dining animal. Creatures of the inferior races eat and drink; only man dines!" And he should do it properly.

"To invite a friend to dinner," says Brillat Savarin, "is to become responsible for his happiness so long as he is under your roof."

If, therefore, any lady would entertain her friends in the best manner that her means permit, it will be well for her to understand the routine of the table herself, and never trust entirely to the skill of an ordinary cook. It is hardly to be expected that she should understand the preparation of each dish, but she must be capable of judging it when served. If she distrusts her own power of arranging a *menu*, and seeing it properly carried out, the dinner should be ordered from the best of caterers. Then, with full assurance of perfect cookery, and faultless service, one may prepare one's list of favored guests with a peaceful conscience and a mind free from care.

Invitations.

Forms of invitations suited to all classes of dinners, have been given at length in the department devoted to that subject, and acceptances and regrets for the same carefully explained, together with the obligation upon every one to answer all such invitations at once, either in the affirmative or negative. Since a dinner is, in all respects, so important a social event that the least one can do is to signify immediately one's course of action, Sidney Smith was not so far out of the way when he burlesqued the solemnity of the occasion, and the aversion that all dinner-givers have to an empty chair, when he wittily wrote: "A man should, if he die after having accepted an invitation to dinner, leave his executors a solemn charge to fill his place."

Host and Hostess.

The hostess is expected to put her guests, as much as possible, at their ease. She must encourage the timid, and watch the requirements of all. No accident must ruffle her temper. In short, she must, for the time, be that perfect woman who is—

"Mistress of herself though china fall."

She must not seem to watch her servants; she must not scold them. Her brow must remain smooth through all embarrassing hitches, her smile be bright and quick, her attentions close and complimentary to her guests.

On the host devolves the duty of drawing out any of the guests with whose particular specialties he is acquainted, and his manners, too, must at least simulate ease, if he have it not. Let host and hostess refrain from boasting of the price of any article of food upon the table.

Whom to Invite.

All the tact and good breeding at the command of the hostess should be exercised, first in choosing, then in arranging, the guests to be present. Not too many are to be bidden to the ordinary dinner; six, eight and twelve are desirable numbers, and four frequently forms the cosiest party imaginable.

The reason of thus arranging for even numbers arises from the fact that, in a mixed dinner party, it is well to have as many ladies as gentlemen. The conversation will then be prevented from dropping into long, or heated, discussions, both of which are destructive of pleasure. It will also be found pleasant to invite the young, and those of more advanced years, together for an occasion of this sort.

Large parties may be made very enjoyable, but where there are more than eight or ten at table general conversation becomes impracticable. Twenty-four, and even thirty, guests, however, when well selected, may make a very brilliant and successful gathering. Too brilliant a conversationalist is not always a desirable acquisition, since he may silence and put in the shade the remainder of the company to an extent that is hardly agreeable even to the meekest among them.

A small dinner of one's most intimate friends is easily arranged. An eminent artist, author, musician, to pose as chief guest, renders it always easy to select among one's other acquaintances a sufficient number who would be pleased with, and pleasing to, this bright, particular star. Or, if it be a bride, or a woman of fashion, to whom the courtesy is to be extended, it is equally easy to find a sufficient number of guests of similar social standing and aspirations to make the occasion a success.

There is also the satisfaction of knowing that, as one cannot possibly invite all of one's dear five hundred friends to a little dinner, no one can be offended at being left out, thus rendering it easy to choose one's list to fit the circumstances.

Do not invite more guests than there is room to comfortably seat. Nothing so spoils a dinner as crowding the guests.

Seating the Guests.

Since, at no social entertainment are the guests so dependent upon one another for mutual entertainment as at a dinner, both by reason of its smallness and the compactness of arrangement, it will be seen that an equal care devolves upon the hostess in seating as in inviting her guests.

The most tedious of one's friends can be tolerated at a party where it is possible to turn to others for relief, but to be chained for two or three hours, with the necessity upon you of talking, or trying to talk, to the same dull or conceited individual that the fates have unkindly awarded as your companion, is a severe social strain upon equanimity of soul.

Hence, each hostess should strive to so arrange her guests that like-minded people should be seated together, and people with hobbies should either be handed over to those likewise possessed, or into the hands of some sympathetic listener, thus securing the pleasure of all.

Known enemies should be seated as far apart as possible, and, in reality, should never be invited to the same dinner. If this should inadvertently happen, they must remember that common respect for their hostess demands that they recognize one another with ordinary politeness.

Laying the Table.

Much has been said upon this subject in the department of "Table Etiquette," and as laying the table formally for a state affair approaches so nearly the proper setting of the home table, much will be found there that is available upon this important topic.

The table, which, since the introduction of the extension, is no longer the cosy round form which brought the guests so comfortably near one another, should be first covered with heavy felting, or double Canton flannel. Over this is to be laid the heaviest, snowiest damask cloth that the linen closet affords. This should have been faultlessly laundried, and is accompanied by large, fine napkins matching the cloth in design. These should be very simply folded, and without starch, and are laid just beyond the plate toward the center of the table. Square is the best form for folding, and each should contain a small thick piece of bread in its folds. This should be about three inches long and at least an inch thick. This is to be eaten with the soup, not crumbed into it. A roll sometimes takes its place. Some hostesses have the bread passed in a silver basket.

A plate is furnished each place, large enough to contain the Majolica plate for raw oysters. Of course a small plain plate may be used for these, but those designed for the purpose are much more elegant. A tiny, fancy salt is provided for each place (see farther in "Table Etiquette").

Two knives, three forks, and a soup spoon, all of silver, are placed at each plate. Some dinner-givers place the knives, forks, and spoon, all on the right side of the plate, excepting the small, peculiarlyshaped oyster fork, which is placed at the left, it having been decided that raw oysters shall be eaten with the fork in the left hand, prongs down.

Still other hostesses place the knives and spoon at the right hand, the forks at the left, the oyster fork diagonally, with the prongs crossing the handles of the others, the law of their arrangement being nowise immutable in its nature.

Silver, glass, and china, should all be of the brightest. At the right hand of each guest should be placed an engraved glass for water. To make certain that these are in line all around, it is well to measure with the hand from the edge of the table to the tip of the middle finger and there place the glass; following this rule around the entire circumference. This glass, if wine is used, gives a center, round which the vari-colored wineglasses may be grouped.

A Well-Furnished Sideboard.

The sideboard should contain relays of knives, forks, and spoons, in rows; glasses, dinner plates, finger bowls standing on the fruit plates, as well as any other accessories that may be needed. At another sideboard, or table, the head waiter, or the butler, does the carving. If the room is small, this last may be relegated to hall or pantry.

In luxurious houses the sideboards are often devoted to bewildering displays of rare china, and cut glass, but in more modest domiciles they are used simply for the needs of the hour.

Water carafes (water bottles) are placed between every two or three guests. The table should be laid in time,—thus, if the dinner is to be at seven, all things should be in readiness on table and sideboard at six o'clock; this course preventing the slightest confusion. If the dinner napkins are to be changed for smaller ones, these also should be laid in readiness. All the cold dishes, salads, relishes, condiments, etc., should also be on hand.

The most elegant tables frequently have a long mat, or scarf, of ruby, or some other colored plush, with fringed and embroidered ends, laid the entire length down through the center of the table. This affords a charming contrast to the snowy napery, and sets the keynote of color for the floral decorations. The center decorative pieces are now no longer high, thus rendering a glimpse of the person opposite almost impossible, but are low and long.

A mirror, framed in silver, may be set in the center of one of these plush mats; and upon this artistically arranged floral decorations are placed to be reflected in its polished depths. Where massive silver table-wares are heirlooms in the family, they are used, despite their height. Center pieces that are recent purchases, are usually of glass, cut and jewelled, until their brilliancy is a marvel in the lamplight.

Table Decorations.

Where the resources of the dinner-giver are limited, the simple decoration of a few flowers arranged in a fanciful basket, or a rare old bowl filled with roses, is sufficient, and is far more indicative of taste and breeding than many of the set floral pieces fresh from the florist's hand, and speaking more eloquently of the size of his bill, than of taste or appropriateness.

The fancy of the hour, and a pretty one it is, is for massing one variety of flower for decorative purposes. Banks of crimson roses down the center of the snowy cloth, or great clusters of vivid red flowers, can be very effectively employed. Shells may be filled with flowers and used as a table decoration. A large one in the middle, and a smaller one on each side, has a pleasing effect. At each plate a small bouquet of flowers may be laid, those for the gentlemen arranged as buttonholes.

In choosing the flowers for decorations, avoid those blossoms having a heavy fragrance, such as the tuberose, jasmines, syringas, as their penetrating odor is productive of faintness in some, and is disagreeable to many, while roses, lilies, lilacs, and many other delicately-scented blossoms, are pleasant to all.

Naturalness is to be aimed at in these decorations, and set floral pieces are in bad taste at a private dinner. Though hundreds of dollars may have been spent in the fleeting loveliness of flowers, the effect to be aimed at is naturalness rather than display. A border of holly, or ivy leaves freshly gathered, may be sewed around the plush scarf through the center of the table, and is a beautiful decoration, far outshining gold embroidery and lace.

Harmonize the color of this scarf with the decorations of the dining-room. Blue, however, or green, does not light up well, while ruby, or some other red, brings out the effect of glass, china, and silver to the best advantage. Old gold, or olive-brown, is also very pretty. The dining-room should be carpeted to deaden the sound of footsteps.

Lighting the Table.

Gas is, perforce, the most common, but not by any means the most æsthetic means of table illumination, because of its heating and glaring qualities. Wax candles are extremely pretty with tissue shades to match the prevailing tint of the other decorations, besides giving an opportunity for displaying all manner of pretty conceits in candelabra. About twenty-six candles will, all other conditions being favorable, light a table for twelve guests. Much depends, however, on whether the dining-room is finished in light or dark woods as to the number of candles required. Very carefully filled and carefully cared-for lamps of pretty designs are also, especially in country places, an admirable method of lighting the table.

Serving the Dinner.

There are two methods of performing this most important function of the entire dinner, namely, service *a la Russe*, and the American service. The first named, the Russian service, is universally adopted in all countries at dinners where the requisite number of sufficiently well-trained servants are to be had.

This service, which consists in having all articles of food carved, and otherwise prepared, and brought to the guests separately by waiters, or footmen, as they are called in England at private tables, has the advantage of leaving the host and hostess free to converse with their guests. It also has another advantage of presenting the table, as the guests enter the room, free from dishes, save the oyster plates, glass, silver, flowers, and perhaps at the two ends of the board, Bohemian glass flagons, of ruby-red, containing such decanted wines as do not need icing.

The table also, being so carefully cleared at the end of each course, should present about the same faultless appearance at the close of the feast as at its beginning. The guests being seated at their respective places, Majolica plates containing raw oysters on the half-shell, or otherwise, with a piece of lemon in the center are, if not already in place, immediately put before each guest. The roll, or piece of bread, should be at once removed from the folds of the napkin, and the servants, when all are seated, pass red and black pepper. The oyster plates are then removed and plates of soup follow, dished from a side table by the head waiter, and served by two others, who pass down opposite sides of the table carrying each two dishes. Where two kinds of soup are provided, each guest is given the choice.

How the Dishes are to be Passed.

The servants, in passing the dishes, begin with the guest upon the right hand of the master on one side of the table, ending with the mistress of the house. Upon the other side they begin with the guest upon her right and end with the host. As one servant passes the meat or fish, another should follow, bearing the appropriate sauce or vegetable that accompanies it.

The servants should wear thin-soled shoes, step lightly, be ungloved, and always have a small-sized damask napkin wrapped around the thumb of the right hand, as dexterity in handling the dishes requires that they should extend the thumb over the edge of the dish.

They should pass all dishes at the left of the guests, that their right hand may be free to take them. Wines only are excepted, these being always poured at the right. Servants should never lean across any guest at table in order to reach or pass an article.

In passing an *entrée* (ongtray), which is simply a dish served in the first course after fish, the dish should be supplied with a silver spoon and fork and held low enough so that the guests can help themselves easily. *Entrées* follow the roasts sometimes, as well as, or instead of, coming after fish. Sweetbreads and croquettes come under this head. These require hot plates.

The soup removed, which should be done quickly as possible, fish should be immediately served, together with whatever vegetables form the accompaniment. When these plates are removed the roast meats are served on hot plates. One vegetable is usually served with each meat course, and occasionally some vegetable forms a course by itself. This, however, only lengthens out the repast, and is not to be recommended.

A fresh plate is served with each course, it being the rule that no two meals should be eaten from the same plate.

Serving the Different Courses.

Game forms the next course, with such sauces and accompaniments as are desired. The salad follows and usually forms a course by itself, accompanied by crackers, or thinly buttered half slices of brown bread. These are usually passed in a silver breadbasket.

Roman punch, when it is served, comes between the roasts and the game, thus preparing the palate for the new flavor. Cheese follows the salad sometimes, and sometimes accompanies it. Then the ices and sweets. When the ices are removed, the desert plates, overlaid with a dainty doily, upon which is set a finger-bowl, are passed, and the fruits appear. Confections are then served, to be followed with black coffee in tiny after-dinner coffee-cups, which are passed on a salver, together with lump sugar, and small gold or silver spoons; no cream. The strong, French *Café et noir*, or black coffee, is always used.

If liquors are served they come in here, a decanter of Cognac being frequently handed around with the coffee.

Jellies for the meats, relishes such as olives, celery and radishes, all the sharp sauces and condiments which are to be used during the meal, are on a sideboard, together with a silver breadbasket containing a reserve of bread.

The butler should have some means of signalling for anything wanted by means of a bell that rings in the kitchen, also of letting the cook know when it is time to send up another course.

Guests, while not expected to ask for second helpings of any course, are always permitted to ask for renewed supplies of bread, water or champagne when wished.

All dishes are to be removed quietly, and either placed in a dumb-waiter or given in charge of a maidservant just outside the door. If it is necessary to have any dishes or silver used again, they must be cleansed out of sight and hearing of the guests, as also no odor of cookery must reach the dining-room. Large, flat baskets must be in readiness to transport the china and silver to the kitchen.

To wait at a large dinner the attendants should average one to every three people: hence, it will be well for the small household to engage outside attendance. Very skilful servants have been known to successfully attend to as many as six guests, but one must be sure of this beforehand.

The Menu.

It will be seen after a perusal of this that the order of the formal, modern dinner *à la Russe*, is very much as follows: Oysters, soup, fish, roast, entrées, Roman punch, game, salad and cheese, dessert, fruits, sweets, coffee. To make this clearer, one bill of fare will be given as an example, always remembering that the number of courses may be lessened in order to suit the taste or purse of the host. Many courses are not a necessity, but the finest quality and the best of cookery should mark each dish served.

Every dinner should begin with soup, to be followed by fish, and include some kind of game. To this order there is no repeal, since "soup is to the dinner," says De la Regnier, "what the portico is to the building or the overture is to an opera." From this there is never any deviation.

A standard bill of fare for a well-regulated dinner is as follows;

Oysters on the Half-shell. Mock Turtle Soup.
Salmon with Lobster Sauce. Cucumbers. Chicken Croquettes.
Tomato Sauce. Roast Lamb with Spinach.
Canvas-back Duck. Celery. String Beans served on Toast.
Lettuce Salad. Cheese Omelet.
Pineapple Bavarian Cream. Charlotte Russe.
Ices. Fruits. Coffee.

Each course may be served on dishes different from the other courses; also fancy dishes, unlike any of the rest, may be used to pass relishes, such as olives, and add greatly to the beauty of the table service. Suitable sets for fish and game, decorated in accordance, are greatly to be admired.

Menu holders are frequently very pretty, and upon the menu card itself much taste and expense are sometimes lavished. Still it is not considered good taste to have them at every plate, for the reason that it savors too much of hotel style. The guests are expected to allow their glasses to be filled at every course. If it is something for which they do not care, they may content themselves with a few morsels of bread and a sip or two of water until the next course is served. The host should always have a menu at his plate, that he may see if the dinner is moving properly in its appointed course.

Favors.

Very pretty favors besides flowers are frequently laid at the ladies' plates to serve as souvenirs of the occasion. The location card or name card may be very beautifully painted. Other articles, such as decorated Easter eggs of plush, velvet, or satin handkerchief holders, fans, painted satin bags, etc., are all in good taste. Each of them, if possible, is made to open and disclose some choice confection. They may be ordered in quantity from some house dealing in such articles, or many of them can be prettily and inexpensively devised at home by any one having sufficient time and taste. Baskets of flowers, with bows of broad satin ribbon tied on one side the handle, are also suitable for both ladies and gentlemen.

Gentlemen's favors are usually useful, such as scarf pins, sleeve buttons, small purses, etc.

Wines, and How to Serve Them.

Fortunately, since more than once the first lady in our land, for the time being, has proven to us by example that the stateliest of dinners may be wineless, it is far from necessary that wine should be served. Still, if wines are to be used, they should be brought on correctly, each wine having its proper place in the varied courses of a dinner, as each note has its fit position in a chord of music.

By long-established custom certain wines have come to be taken with certain dishes. "Sherry and Sauterne," as given by a very good authority, "go with soup and fish; Hock and Claret with roast meats; Punch with turtle; Champagne with sweet breads or cutlets; Port with venison; Port or Burgundy with other game; sparkling wines between the meats and the confectionery; Madeira with sweets; Port with cheese; Sherry and Claret, Port, Tokay and Madeira with dessert."

Red wines should never be iced, even in summer; Claret and Burgundy should always be slightly warmed (left in a warm room is sufficient). Claret-cup and Champagne are iced (some epicures object to this). Cool the wines in the bottles. To put clear ice in the glasses is simply to weaken the quality and flavor of the wine, and, as a matter of fact, to serve wine and water.

The glasses for the various wines are usually grouped at the right of the plate, and as different styles and sizes are used for different wines, it is well for the novice to be accustomed to these in order to avoid the awkwardness of putting forward the wrong glass. High and narrow, also very broad and shallow glasses, are used for Champagne; large, goblet-shaped glasses for Burgundy and a ruby-red glass for Claret; ordinary wine glasses for Sherry and Madeira; green Bohemian glasses for Hock; and large, bell-shaped glasses for Port.

Port, Sherry and Madeira are decanted. Hock and Champagne appear in their native bottles. Claret and Burgundy are handed around in a claret jug. In handing a bottle fresh from the ice-chest the waiter wraps a napkin around it to absorb the moisture.

Coffee and liquors should be handed around when the dessert has been about a quarter of an hour on the table. After this the ladies usually retire, a custom that has happily fallen into disrepute, the coffee being served without the liquors, and ladies and gentlemen partaking of it together. Roman punch is served in all manner of dainty conceits as to glass, imitations of flowers, etc.

Never allow servants to overfill the wine glasses. Ladies never empty their glasses, and usually take but one kind of wine. This is especially true of young ladies, who, very often, do not taste their one glass.

Gracefully Declined.

If wine is not desired from principle, merely touching the brim of the glass with the finger-tip is all the refusal a well-trained servant needs. A still better plan is to permit one glass to be filled and allow it to stand untasted at your plate. In responding to a health, it is ungracious not to, at least, lift the glass and lets its contents touch the lips.

Never make your refusal of wine conspicuous. Your position as guest in no wise appoints you a censor of your host's conduct in offering wine at his table, and any marked feeling displayed on the subject would simply show a want of consideration and good breeding.

A dinner given to a person of known temperance principles is often marked, in compliment, by an entire absence of wine.

If there is but one wine served with a simple dinner, it should be Sherry or Claret, and should be in glass decanters on the table. The guests can help themselves; the hostess can offer it immediately after soup.

The announcement of dinner is given as quietly as possible. The butler, or head waiter, who should be in full evening dress, minus gloves, quietly says, "Dinner is served," or, as in France, "Madame is served." Better still, he catches the eye of the hostess and simply bows, whereupon she immediately rises, and the guests following her example, the order of the procession to the dining-room is formed at once. The waiters, aside from the head one, are usually in livery.

Order of Precedence.

In the matter of going out to dinner the host takes precedence, giving his right arm to the most honored lady guest. If the dinner is given in honor of any particular guest, she is the one chosen, if not, any bride that may be present, or the oldest lady, or some visitor from abroad. The other guests then fall in line, gentlemen having had their partners pointed out to them, and wherever necessary, introductions are given. The hostess comes last of all, having taken the arm of the gentleman most to be honored. In the dining-room no precedence is observed after the host, save that the younger couples draw back and allow their elders to be seated. Precedence of rank is not as common here as in Europe.

On entering the door, if it is not wide enough to permit of two entering abreast, the gentleman falls back a step and permits the lady to enter first. All remain standing until the hostess seats herself, when the guests find their places, either by means of name cards at their plates, or by a few quiet directions, the gentlemen being seated last. The highest place of honor for gentlemen is at the right of the hostess, the next, at her left, and for ladies at the right and left of their host.

The hostess should never eclipse her guests in her toilet, and neither host nor hostess should endeavor to shine in conversation. To draw out the guests, to lead the conversation in pleasant channels, to break up long discussions, and to discover all possibilities of brilliancy in the company around their board, should be their aim.

The hostess must never press dishes upon her guests, but they are permitted, if they wish, to praise any viand that has pleased them. The hostess must appear to be eating until all the company have finished, and her watchful eye must see that every want is supplied. At the close of the repast the hostess slightly bows to the lady at the right of the host, when all the guests rise and return in order to the drawing-room.

Where gentlemen remain around the table for that fraction of an hour,—

>"Across the walnuts and the wine,"

all rise, and the gentlemen remain standing until the ladies leave the room. The gentleman who had the honor of escorting the hostess into the table, walks with her to the door; here she pauses to allow the host's companion to pass through, when the host, who has escorted her thither, returns to the table, the other gentlemen following his example. The hostess is the last lady to leave the room, whereupon her escort closes the door and returns to the table, where the gentlemen group themselves carelessly at one end of the table, for that half hour of conversation and cigars. Where wine is not used the gentlemen frequently remain behind for smoking, and some hosts immediately withdraw with them to the smoking-room. Coffee is frequently served in the drawing-room, where the ladies have had their little chat after the return thither of the gentlemen.

Informal and Easy.

The hostess, assisted by a daughter, or a young lady friend, usually pours the beverage, and the gentlemen pass it around to the ladies, thus forming the most delightfully informal groups for conversation. Sugar is passed by a servant, or else the hostess drops two or three lumps of it in each saucer, a sugar bowl, with sugar tongs, standing beside her. Cream is not the correct thing for after-dinner coffee.

Very many hostesses, however, prefer to have coffee and fruits finish the table menu, after which the entire party retire to the drawing-room, where, for the half or three-quarters of an hour preceding their departure, soft music from some hidden orchestra may be permitted to fill the air with harmony. Occasionally, a little programme is arranged of music and song, to fill this interval. But, in many cases, and wisely, conversation is the preferred entertainment.

French Terms.

Good taste now dictates that the bill of fare, where one is printed or written, should be couched in the "King's English," yet, one is so frequently thrown in positions where a knowledge of the French terms so often used in such cases is somewhat of necessity, that a short glossary of the same may be useful:

Menu	Bill of fare.
Café et noir	Black coffee.
Café au lait	Coffee with milk.
A dinner begins with,	
Huitres	Oysters.
Followed by,	
Potage	Soup,
Hors d'œuvres	Dainty dishes,
Poisson	Fish,
Entremets	Vegetables,
Roti	Roast,
Entrées	Dishes after roast,

Gibier	Game,
Salades	Salads,
Fruits et dessert	Fruits and dessert,
Fromage	Cheese,
Café	Coffee.

Right or Left Arm?

This is a disputed question, for the solution of which each party gives valid reasons. Most gentlemen prefer to give the right arm, since the seating of the lady is at the right side always; but many, to preserve the feudal significance of the custom that bade the good knight keep his sword arm free for defence, if need be, offer the left. Since, too, dinner gowns have usually a train to be managed as best it may, ladies also prefer the tender of the left arm, as that leaves their own left arm free to manage the trailing, silken folds. The right arm, however, has the balance of favor, though gentlemen are bound to follow the example of their host as he precedes them to the dining-room.

Further Hints.

Members of families should never be seated together. This rule has no exceptions. A gentleman should never forget the wants of the lady under his charge, but the lady should remember not to monopolize his attention exclusively. The gentleman is supposed to be particularly attentive to the lady at his right, to pass the lady on his left anything with which she may be unsupplied, and to be agreeable to the lady opposite.

He will, even if a young man, feel it a mark of respect when he is invited to take an elderly lady down, but if the hostess is careful for the happiness of her guests, he will probably find a young lady at his left hand. In selecting the number of guests, care should be taken that it is not such as shall bring two ladies or two gentlemen together. Odd numbers will do this, while even will not.

American Dinner Services.

The American dinner service is much more simple, and is the one usually adopted in modest establishments in this country. One well-trained maid should be able to render all the assistance required at the table. Given the before-mentioned maid, a lady can, with previous management, give a dinner as elegantly, and perhaps with more perfect hospitality, than where the whole affair is relegated to the hands of an experienced caterer.

In laying the table the same manner of arrangement is to be observed as for dinner *a la Russe*, save that there are more dishes on the board and the decorations are placed with a view to leaving all the space possible.

Celery is now served in low, flat dishes, and these, together with olives and various relishes, may be placed on the table in all manner of dainty, ornamental dishes. Large spoons for the next course are also supplied.

Oysters are in place when the guests enter the room, and the servant sometimes passes brown bread to eat with them; this is cut thin, buttered and folded. After passing this it is replaced on the sideboard; water is then poured, when, beginning with the oyster plate of the guest at the right of the host, she removes it, and the others, as rapidly as possible, leaving the under plate.

Soup tureen, ladle, and plates, or bowls, are then placed before the hostess and the maid, standing at her left hand, takes the plates one by one, and passes them at the left hand of guests. This accomplished, the tureen is removed, and the host, having finished his soup, is ready for the fish, which is placed before him together with hot plates, and potatoes in some form, accompanied or not by a salad.

Directions to Waiters.

The servant then proceeds to remove the soup-plates and the plates beneath. By this time the host has divided the fish, and, standing at his left hand, the maid takes the plates as he fills them, and passes them, serving first the guest at his right. A piece of fish, a potato, and a little fish sauce, are placed on each plate. If both salad and potato are served at the same course, place the salad dish before the hostess and let her serve it upon small, extra plates or dishes. If salad alone is served, it is usually placed upon the plate with the fish.

The fish-platter should now be removed. The plates may also be taken when it is seen there is no more need of them, beginning with those first served, as it is presumed they will have first finished, since it is etiquette for each guest to begin eating so soon as the plate is placed before him.

The next course is the roast. While the host is carving this, one or more varieties of vegetables are set at hand. Portions of the meat and the accompanying vegetable are placed on the same plate, and the servant passes them in the same order as before, and immediately follows them with the second or third vegetable dish, if two kinds have been placed on the plate. This is where the gentleman sitting next the lady on the host's right can help her and then himself, afterwards moving it as she passes the plates, so that the other gentlemen can do likewise.

If a double course is served, which is hardly advisable, save at very large dinners, the lighter dish is placed before the hostess, and the servant presents each plate to her for a portion before passing it. After this the courses do not move so rapidly and the maid remains standing a little back at the left of the hostess' chair where she can easily observe the slightest signal. The hostess signs when the plates are to be removed, and the principal dishes are allowed to remain until the course is finished.

In removing courses no piling up of dishes should be allowed. One plate in each hand is all that can be conveniently managed. After the fish, if other forks are not on the table, they must be supplied for the next course. After the plates are removed, the roast and smaller dishes follow.

Salads and Desserts.

Sherbet, or wines, are served here, if at all. The game, or poultry, comes next, salads or jelly accompanying it. The salad is placed before the hostess. If salad is served in a separate course, it is usually accompanied by cheese, and sometimes by small pieces of brown bread, thinly buttered and folded.

This course finished, everything is removed from the table—plates, dishes, relishes, etc.—crumbs brushed, and the principal dessert-dish placed before the hostess together with every requisite for serving it. The maid then passes the tart or pudding same as the other dishes, taking two plates at a time, and beginning with the two ladies on right and left of host, taking the others in order.

Each person, on receiving a plate in any course, begins to eat, since this facilitates the serving of the dinner and gives warm dishes to all. The maid, during this course, quietly arranges the fruit-plates, finger-bowls, and the after-dinner coffees and tiny spoons upon the sideboard, when she is ready to remove the dishes, and place the fruit-plates in position. The coffees are then put at each guest's right, unless they are to be served afterward in the drawing-room, and the dinner service is virtually ended.

If wine is offered, it is served between the courses, the host helping the lady at his right, and asking the gentleman next to do the same, and so on around the table.

Both host and hostess should have been able to keep up an interest in the conversation at table, and not to betray the slightest anxiety as to the success of the affair. Host or hostess should never make disparaging remarks as to the quality of dishes; and still less should they refer to their costliness, and should know beforehand as to the edge of the carving-knife, as the use of a steel is not permissible.

The foregoing rules will be found to embody the simplest and most correct method of serving a dinner *a la American.*

Dinner Dress.

Ladies dress elegantly, and in any manner, or color, that fancy or becomingness may dictate. Corsages, however, while open at the neck in either square, or heart-shaped fashion, are not as low-cut as for a ball-dress, while the sleeves are usually of demi-length. Gloves are always worn, and not removed until seated at the table. They are not resumed afterward unless dancing follows.

Very young ladies wear less expensive toilets of white or delicately tinted wools, or light-weight silks.

Gentlemen are expected to wear the conventional evening dress. To be gloved or not to be gloved is a vexed question with them. It is well to be provided with a pair of light gloves, and let your own self-possession and the example of others decide for you at the moment. A gentleman faultlessly gloved cannot go far wrong.

Coming and Going.

Promptness in arriving is a virtue, but remember that you have no claim upon the time of your host or hostess, until ten or fifteen minutes before the hour appointed, and, if you inadvertently arrive too soon you should remain in the dressing-room until very near the hour.

Departure is from half to three-quarters of an hour after the repast, and no matter what the entertainment, eleven o'clock should find every dinner guest departed.

Functions.

The practice of calling the ordinary reception, ball, party or dinner a "function" is simply a bad habit. It comes to us from England, where a confusion of ideas has made this word the popular synonym for any social happening. The error in England is perhaps pardonable, for the reason that very many of the society performances there are actually functions, and in course of time the unlearned and the careless have come to call every society performance a function. The royal "drawing-rooms" (so-called) are functions, and the Lord Mayor's dinner is a function—in fine, that is a function which is "a course of action peculiarly pertaining to any public office in church or state."

The receptions and dinners which, in his official capacity as President of the World's Fair, Mr. Higinbotham gave were functions. But the receptions, dinners, high teas, given by people holding no official position whatsoever, do not partake of the nature of "functions."

Dinner Favors.

Favors may be simple or elaborate, as the purse of the giver may dictate. Appropriateness and simplicity, however, show better taste than the extraordinary vagaries in which some indulge.

Among the really admirable selections which are offered by dealers of many sorts, nothing is better than the bonbonnieres shown by confectioners of the higher grade. They are delightful in color, exquisite in design, and while they are made into receptacles for sweets for the time being, they can later be turned to a dozen more permanent uses. One design which is, perhaps, the most elegant of all, takes the form of an opera bag. It is made of the heaviest cream-white silk and has embroidered on it in dainty ribbon work forget-me-nots, tiny rosebuds, or jessamine. At the top it is finished with the popular extension clasp of fine burnished gilt, and when in use as a favor is lined with tinted paper and filled with the finest chocolates or with candied violets.

Slippers, too, are seen, and, while not of glass, are suggestive of Cinderella's tiny foot. They are crocheted of fine colored cord, are stiffened and molded over a form, then fitted with a bag of silk and tied with ribbons of the same shade. Like the bags, they are made the excuse of sweets, and, like them, they add to the decorative effect, for they stand in coquettish fashion before each cover and challenge the admiration inspired in the prince of fairy legend.

Books and "booklets" are much in vogue and make as acceptable favors as any that can be desired if only selected with judgment and with care. Small volumes of verse bound in vellum are always good. Single poems from any one of the recognized poets put up in artistic booklet form are as nearly perfect as favors can be. Book covers, too, are good, and some bookmarks are shown that are excellent both in color and in their evident ability to withstand the usage they are sure to get if they are allowed to do any service at all.

One clever hostess who gave a dinner, and who handles her brush unusually well, devised a book cover and leaflet combined that proved a great success. She had the covers made in the regulation size of pale sage chamois skin and added the decoration herself. She painted each in the flower that the guest loved best, for her feminine friends, and each in some convenient design for the men, and across the corner was the name of each in quaint gold letters. She folded heavy parchment paper in booklet form, and with her brush wrote in silver bronze selections from the wit and wisdom of the ages. Then she slipped the miniature books within the covers and left the brilliant thoughts that they contained to start the conversational ball. Her dinner was pronounced a great success, and it was remarked by many that there was none of that awkward silence which so often precedes the soup.

TABLE ETIQUETTE

THE minutiæ of table etiquette offers to onlookers the best evidence of good or ill-breeding, and in the graceful observance thereof is displayed all the "difference between dining elegantly and merely consuming food," for it is at the table that the ill-bred and the well-bred man are most strongly contrasted.

How to eat soup, or partake of grapes, and what to do with a cherry stone, though apparently trivial in themselves, are weighty matters when taken as an index of social standing. And it is safe to say that the young man who drank from his saucer, or the young woman who ate peas with her knife, would court the risk of banishment from good society.

In regard to the first essentials of table manners we are bound to consider the laying of the table, the manner of being seated thereat, the use of the napkin, the proper handling of those most invaluable implements, knife, fork and spoon, together with a short dissertation on those older implements, "Adam's knives and forks."

The Breakfast Table.

This first repast of the day should always be daintily and appetizingly spread, and the etiquette there observed, as at all other meals of the day, should be of a nature to render the observance on more stately occasions second nature to the members of the family. Children so trained will find little difficulty in after days as to their table etiquette.

The table itself should be spread with clean linen, first overlaying the surface with a sub-cloth of double canton flannel, felting, or a white blanket that has seen its best days of usefulness. This is done for the better appearance of the table linen, for the deadening of sound, and the protection of the table from the heated dishes. The table linen for home use need not be of the finest; cleanliness being, after all, the chief requisite.

ETIQUETTE OF THE TABLE.

Before the mistress of the house stands the tray covered with a large napkin, or a prettily etched tray-cloth. This is filled with cups and saucers. The coffee-urn is at her right hand with cream, sugar, spoons, and waste-bowl convenient. In front of the master of the house is spread a large napkin with the corner to the center of the table. An ornamental carving cloth may be used in its place. On this is placed whatever dish of meat it is his province to serve. On the opposite side of the table dishes of bread and any hot breakfast rolls or gems balance one another. The dish of potatoes stands close to, and at the right of, the platter, ready to be served with the meat. Any other vegetable served at the same meal should be placed at the left of the platter.

Mats are wholly a style of the past. Where the dish is very hot, or liable to soil the cloth, fringed squares of heavy linen, etched or embroidered, take their place.

The castor, too, is banished from tables polite, and its place may be taken by a few flowers, or bits of vine, in a simple vase. The butter dish and the individual butters should be placed by the side of the one who is to serve it. Fancy sauce and vinegar cruets, and salts and peppers are grouped at each end of the table, sometimes on small trays of hammered brass.

Knives, Forks and Napkins.

Heated plates are placed before the carver, and the carving knife (well sharpened) and fork are placed, with their rest at his right. On any occasion when plates are laid at each place, turn them face up. To the right of the plate is the knife with edge turned from the person to use it. As to the fork, authorities differ, some contending that it should be placed on the right hand, and the knife next, with sharp edge turned from the user. This latter fashion is best at simple meals where but one knife and fork are used. Others contend that the fork should be laid at the left. This latter fashion should be followed where several knives and forks are necessary for an elaborate dinner.

The simply-folded napkin is at the left hand. The glass and individual butter plate are placed near the point of the knife. To avoid waiting where there is any haste, the butters may be filled before the family are seated.

If oatmeal, or any porridge, is to be served, the dish should be placed upon the table before the house mistress, together with the requisite number of small bowls, or saucers, in which she serves it, adding sugar and cream, or passing these, as seems best to her. Afterwards these plates and the dish itself should be removed, when the hot plates and the remainder of the breakfast should be brought in.

Where there is fruit, as is the case in very nice homes, it is to form a third course; all other dishes are to be removed before the fruit is placed upon the table, and each person provided with a small plate with a doily, or fruit napkin, laid upon it, a silver fruit knife, and possibly a finger-bowl set upon the doily; also a teaspoon or orange-spoon when oranges are on the table. If berries are served fruit saucers will be required. In busy homes the fruit is frequently placed upon the table at the beginning of the repast and served at its end without change of plates. Many persons prefer to begin their breakfast with fruit. The napery at breakfast may be colored if so desired.

The Dinner Table.

The dinner table for home meals is laid very much after the fashion of the breakfast table with the omission of the server. If there is to be more than one course, such as a salad, another fork must be added, in which case it will be best to place the forks at the left of the plate. If there is fish, another extra fork, or else the appropriate little fish knife and fork, is demanded. If a fork only is used, the flakes of fish may be pushed upon the fork by means of a bit of bread.

A half slice of bread should lie in, or beside, the folded napkin. The soup tureen is placed before the mistress of the house, together with the soup dishes. Into each of these she puts a ladle full of soup and passes it along. Where there is a servant to wait, he, or she, takes each dish from her hand

and serves those at table, always passing to their left hand in so doing. When the soup is removed, the under plates should also be taken and hot plates brought in for the next course.

The meat is placed before the carver, dishes of vegetables flanking either side. The plates are filled and passed, or else handed around by a servant. Sometimes the meat only is put on the plates and the dishes of vegetables are passed from one to another at the table or handed around by a servant. Do not place a quantity of small vegetable dishes at each plate; it is too suggestive of hotel and restaurant life; peas and some other similarly cooked vegetables are an exception to this rule. Side dishes, such as pickles, etc., are placed on the table when it is first laid.

If a salad is to form the next course, all the dishes should be carried out, the meat being taken first, then the dishes of vegetables, after that, plates and butter plates. A tray is much better to transfer all articles except large platters. Never permit a maid to scrape the contents of one plate into another, with a clatter of knives and forks, and then triumphantly bear off the entire pile at once. The salad is to be eaten with a silver fork, and is served with rolls or biscuit. Where the home dinner is simple the salad is frequently served in small dishes and passed during the progress of the repast.

Before dessert is brought on, all table furniture should be removed save glasses and water bottle, and the cloth brushed free from crumbs with crumb-tray and napkin, or scraper, in preference to a brush, which is apt to soil the cloth. The dessert is then to be placed on the table and the mistress serves the pastry or pudding on small plates or saucers which are placed before her. Tea, coffee, or chocolate, may now be handed around, but never sooner. At a very ceremonious dinner they appear last of all.

If fruit is to follow the pastry, fruit plates, arranged as for breakfast, must be substituted for the dessert plates, as soon as the guests are done with these.

It is to be expected that each family will adapt the above outline to suit their own needs, omitting such features as they have neither time to devote to nor servants to accomplish. The ideas here given, however, are suitable as the nucleus of the most elaborate dinner, or may be simplified to fit the plainest repast.

The Supper Table.

The table for supper is laid very much after the general plan given for breakfast, with the exception of the oatmeal. If the tea is made at the table, which is the daintiest way, the other adjuncts of the tray must be supplemented by a dainty brass or bronze hot-water kettle swung over an alcohol lamp, and a pretty tea caddy. Lovely silver caddies, with lock and key, are to be had and make an appropriate wedding gift. A "cosy" or thick wadded cap for setting over the teapot, to keep the heat in, is another pretty essential, which may be made as ornamental as is liked. At supper cold meats are usually served, and cake is taken with the fruit, while vegetables, unless those served in salad form, are omitted.

The Lunch Table.

In cities, the lunch takes the place of the twelve o'clock dinner, just as the late city dinner replaces the supper, dear to country hearts.

The table for lunch is laid much like that for supper, the dishes being all placed at the table at one time, and the ladies of the family, for to them it is usually devoted, gathering around it without the formality of a servant.

Signs of Ill-Breeding.

The order of laying the table, and serving the dishes having been given, it now remains to give some information as to the conduct of those at the table. This is rendered more necessary from the fact that many well-dressed, and apparently well-bred people, sin so grievously against the simplest laws of table etiquette, as not only to display their own want of breeding, but to actually annoy those about them by their sins of omission and commission.

The most important table implements are knife, fork, and spoon, and with these we begin, in the order of their prominence.

The Fork.

The fork having, as one writer happily suggests, "subjugated the knife," demands our first attention. The subjugation of the knife is so complete in this country, England, France and Austria that any attempt to give the knife undue prominence at table is looked upon as a glaring offense against good taste. This aversion to the use of the knife probably arose first from the more agreeable sensation to the lips that is produced by the delicate tines of a fork in contrast to the broad blade of a knife. Also the fact that the steel of which knives were, and are still, to some extent, made, imparts, by contact, a disagreeable flavor to many articles of food.

In the use of the knife and fork daintiness should be cultivated. They should be held with the handles resting in the palms of the hands when cutting, or separating food; but, in conveying food to the mouth, the handle of the fork should not be kept against the palm, as to do so would give it an awkward appearance in lifting to the lips. Fork and knife should be held firmly but without any apparent exertion of strength.

Never strive to load the fork with meat and vegetables at the same time. To do so is to commit an offence against manners and digestion, and never push the food from the fork with the knife. Take upon the fork what it will easily carry and no more.

Oyster forks are usually provided when oysters on the shell are served. Either the right or the left hand may be employed in lifting them to the lips. The shell should be steadied with the other hand. The fork may be handled with either hand, the right being more generally used. It is well, however, to be trained in the use of both hands, thus avoiding the slight awkwardness attending the constant changing of the fork from one hand to the other.

THE CORRECT POSITION FOR HOLDING KNIFE AND FORK.

In using the fork in the left hand it should be lifted to the lips, tines pointing downward. The fork, which should convey but a very moderate amount of food, should always be carried to the mouth in a position as nearly parallel to it as possible. This does away with the thrusting motion and the awkward sweep of the elbow that is so annoying to the onlooker.

The fork is also used to convey back to the plate bits of bone or other substances unfit to swallow. Eject them quietly upon the fork and quickly deposit them upon the edge of the plate.

The softer cheeses are eaten with a fork. As to the harder varieties, some use the fork and others break with the fork and convey to the mouth with the fingers.

Use the fork to break up a potato on your plate; do not touch it with the knife. Ices, stiffly preserved fruits, etc., are all eaten with a fork. In fact, the fork is to convey all food to the mouth that is not so liquid in its nature as to require the use of a spoon.

The Spoon.

The spoon comes next as an article of importance at the table. Soups, all thinly cooked vegetables, canned and stewed fruits, peaches and cream, melons, oranges by some, very thick chocolate, Roman punch, and other dishes that common sense will dictate at the moment, are to be partaken of by its aid. One should *drink* tea and coffee, however, and not spoonful it. Use the teaspoon to gently stir up and dissolve the sugar in the cup, then lay it in the saucer and lift the cup to the lips by the handle. Never be guilty of leaving the spoon in the cup and compassing it with one or more fingers in carrying it to the lips.

In partaking of soup the spoon should be swept through the liquid away from the person, lifted to the mouth, and the soup taken noiselessly from the side of the spoon. In thus lifting any liquids from the further side of the dish, or cup, there is time for any drop adhering to the outside to fall in the dish before carrying to the lips.

Only to gentlemen possessed of a luxuriant mustache is it permitted to take soup from the point of the spoon, always providing they can do so skilfully and without an awkward use of the arm. The gold or silver spoons for after-dinner coffee are very small, as befits the dainty cups of egg-shell china.

The Knife.

Properly, the knife may be said to have no use at the table save to assist the fork in separating food into morsels fit for mastication. Never, no, *never*, permit it to be introduced into the mouth upon any occasion whatever. To do so is the height of ill-breeding.

Adam's Knives and Forks.

There are a number of things that the most fashionable and well-bred people now eat at the dinner table with their fingers. They are: Olives, to which a fork should never be applied; asparagus, whether hot or cold, when served whole, as it should be; lettuce, which, when served in whole leaves, should be dipped in the dressing or in a little salt; celery, which may be properly placed upon the tablecloth beside the plate.

To these may be added strawberries, when served with the stems on, as they are in most elegant houses. Dip them in cream and then in sugar (sometimes sugar only is served), holding by the stem end and eating in one or more bites, according to size.

Bread, toast, and all tarts and small cakes; fruit of all kinds, except melons and preserves, which are eaten with a spoon; cheese, except the softer varieties; all these are eaten with the fingers, even by the most fastidious people. Even the leg, or other small piece of a bird is taken up daintily in the fingers of one hand at fashionable dinners.

Water cress is taken in the fingers. It is usually served upon a shallow dish or a basket, a fringed napkin covering bottom and sides. Artichokes, also, are eaten with the fingers. Lump sugar may be taken with the fingers, if no tongs are provided. If a plate of hot, unbroken biscuit is passed, one may be broken off with the fingers.

Napkin and Finger-Bowl.

Napkins vary in size, from the diminutive, fancy doily, for ornament rather than use, through all gradations, up to the largest sized dinner napkin. In using these do not spread over the entire lap, nor fasten under the chin bib-fashion, nor in the button-hole, and, if a man, do not tuck in the vest pockets. All these are fashions which should have been outgrown in the nursery. Simply unfold and lay carelessly in the lap on one knee, use to wipe the lips lightly, or the finger tips when necessary.

Some very exquisite people manage to eject fruit seeds, or skins, or anything unfit to swallow, from the lips into the napkin, by pressing it against the mouth, then dropping them skilfully from its folds upon the plate. All such careful observances tend to remove, as much as possible, from the modern repast, the prosaic, and unromantic ideas suggested by the idea of eating.

Finger-bowls are brought on the table after the dessert is removed and before the fruit is served. They are usually placed before each individual on the fancy glass or china plate that is to be used for the fruit, a fancy doily being laid between the bowl and plate. Remove bowl and doily at once to the right hand side, leaving plate free for the fruit. This doily is frequently an elaborate article of fancy work, not for use but ornament. Hence, unless its place is taken by a fruit napkin or smaller napkin, as is sometimes done, passed around before dessert, the dinner napkin is used.

Avoiding Fruit Stains.

Some hostesses dislike to have fruit stains upon their elegant dinner napkins; hence, the custom of supplying smaller napkins at the beginning of dessert. This, however, cumbers the dinner with much serving and is not to be recommended. If done, the smaller napkins are to be passed around, and the large ones permitted to remain.

At the close of the dinner the napkin is not to be folded, but left lying loosely at the side of the plate. If a guest in the house, however, unless fresh napkins are supplied at every meal, they should be folded and placed in the napkin ring.

The rule for using napkins is that they be touched gently to the lips, and the finger-tips wiped daintily upon them, but as "nice customs courtesy to great kings," so, to those gentlemen possessing luxuriant mustaches, a greater freedom is permitted in its use.

The finger-bowls are to be two-thirds full of slightly warmed water, and a rose geranium leaf or a slice of lemon should float upon the surface of each.

The fingers of one hand at a time are to be dipped in the water, rubbing the leaf or lemon between them to remove any odor of food, and then dried upon the napkin.

Sometimes, after partaking of meats, one may dip a corner of the napkin in the finger-bowl, and, allowing it to drop back of the dry portion of the napkin, wipe the lips with it. A gentleman is permitted to moisten and wipe his mustache in the same manner. Remember, always to exercise the greatest care not to have the operation a very visible one, as it is not particularly attractive to the onlooker.

A small glass of perfumed water is sometimes placed in the center of the finger-bowl for this purpose. Lift it to the lips and sip slightly, being careful not to have the appearance of taking it for a beverage, and immediately dry the lips upon the napkin.

While eating meats, etc., use the napkin before touching the lips to a glass, else the crystal edge may present a very disagreeable spectacle to one's neighbors.

General Table Etiquette.

In seating one's self at table, assume a comfortable position, neither so close as to be awkward, nor so far away as to endanger the clothing by dropping food in its passage from table to lips. Sit upright, and do not bend over to take each mouthful of food.

If a gentleman is accompanied by a lady, he should draw her chair out from the table, and, when she is seated, assist her in putting it back in position, unless in some public dining place, where this office will be assumed by a waiter.

On being seated, remove the roll, or piece of bread, from the napkin (the best form for this bread is in blocks four inches thick and about three inches long), unfold the napkin, lay it upon the knee, and quietly wait your turn to be served. Never handle, or play with, any articles on the table; it bespeaks ill-breeding. Never drum on the table with the fingers.

As soon as a bowl of soup, or a plate of oysters is offered you, begin, without any appearance of haste, to eat. This facilitates serving, as, by the time the last are served, the first will have finished their half-ladleful of soup (which is all that society allows) and the waiter may begin to remove the first course. The old custom of waiting until everyone was served before beginning is no long countenanced, since "soup is nothing, if not hot," and by waiting it is decidedly cooled.

Never, unless requested so to do, pass a plate on to a neighbor that has been handed to you. It is supposed that the carver knows what he intends for each guest. When dishes are passed, help yourself as quickly as possible, and never insist upon some one having it first. If a gentleman, you may help the lady next you from its contents, if she so desire.

Always take the food offered in a course. Quietly wait and talk while others eat, rather than call the attention of the table to your likes and dislikes, and disarrange the whole order of serving. If a gentleman, see that the lady you have brought down wants for nothing, and let the lady, on her side, take care not to entirely monopolize the attention of her escort.

How to Treat Waiters.

If, for any cause, the services of a waiter are desired, catch his eye quietly, and on his approach, state your own or the lady's wishes, in a low tone of voice. This same rule of conduct will apply to public places, where the knocking of spoons against cups, and other noisy attempts to gain the attention of a waiter cannot be too greatly discouraged.

Never thank a servant for passing any of the dishes or wines; that is his business; but for any personal service, such as picking up a fallen napkin, or replacing a dropped knife by another, it is proper to return a murmured "Thank you," not "Thanks."

A lady should never look up in a waiter's face while giving an order, refusing wine, or thanking him for any special service. This savors of familiarity, and should be avoided. A man, however, that is attentive will see that a lady has none of these things to do.

At table one may talk to one's neighbor on either side, or to those directly opposite, if the center decorations are not too high; but it is absolutely ill-bred to lean across an individual to converse with some one on the other side. Of course, at a small dinner, or at the family table, conversation is expected to be general. Never attempt to converse while the mouth is filled with food, and never *have* the mouth filled with food; it is bad both for manners and digestion.

Decline any dish passed that you do not wish with "Thank you, not any;" if by a waiter, "Not any," is sufficient. Do not enter into any explanations as to your tastes, nor the whys and wherefores of your refusal. That interests no one but yourself.

If wine is served, do not call the attention of everyone to the fact that you do not drink it. The table of a friend, to which you have had the honor of an invitation, is no place for a temperance lecture. Do not reverse the glass; it is a needlessly conspicuous act; simply motion the waiter away with your finger on the edge of the glass, or shake your head. Some, still more careful, allow a glass to be filled for them at first, and, by letting it stand untasted, show to the waiter that further offers are useless. If a lady does not wish more wine than remains in her glass, let her make a little motion of dissent when the waiter is about to replenish it, otherwise a good glass of wine is wasted. In drinking wine, lift the glass by the stem, instead of by the bowl. Young ladies, if they drink wine, had best content themselves with one glassful. "Rosebuds" should not indulge. The latest dictum declares that sparkling wines should be drunk at once and not sipped.

Sundry Rules and Hints.

Never display any hesitation in selecting food. If your host asks what part of a fowl you prefer, at once give your choice. To say you have none is an annoyance. Never tip the plate in order to dip up the last spoonful of soup. In partaking of soup, or imbibing any liquid, do so noiselessly. Be sure not to spread the elbows while using knife and fork. Keep them close to your side while cutting meats.

Never try to dispose of the last mouthful of soup, the last morsel of food. "It is not expected," says one writer, "that your plate should be sent away cleansed by your gastronomic exertions." On no account cool any drink or soup with the breath. Never pour tea or coffee into the saucer to cool it. Never drink from the saucer; it is an unpardonable sin.

With salads small knifes and forks are often furnished, where the salad is served uncut with dressing. Again, the uncut leaves are taken in the fingers and dipped in the salt or dressing. The roll is to be eaten with the salad.

Individual salts are an American fashion. If used, it is proper to take salt from them with the knife, if they are the open salts. In the most stylish circles great favor is shown to ample silver *salieres* with their accompanying salt spoons or shovels. Salt, thus taken, should be deposited upon the left hand rim of the plate. The custom followed by so many of depositing little piles of salt on the tablecloth is very annoying to the hostess, as giving her table a shabby look during the removal of courses. Salt is the only condiment placed upon the table at a dinner; the others are passed with the course demanding their use. Neither is butter put upon the table at an elaborate dinner; the small square of bread or the roll furnished, are to be eaten without.

Use of Knife and Fork.

Peppers and salts are to be shaken with one hand. Never use the other to in any wise expedite the distribution of their contents.

Never cut up all the meat on your plate at once, in morsels fit for eating; to do so savors of the nursery. But, on the other hand, do not seem to be perpetually using your knife and fork at table. Be sure not to insert fork or spoon too far into the mouth. Never turn the spoon over in the mouth in the effort to free it entirely from its contents. Do not let the most adhesive of food betray you into this most disagreeable of habits. Take small mouthfuls and there will be less danger of this occurring. Handle knife and fork carefully, so as not to cause any unnecessary clatter at table.

Waiters pass all food to the left, and all dishes are removed at the left. Wine is passed at the right. All dishes that are being passed must be held low enough so that the guests can help themselves without difficulty.

When there is a waiter to remove the dishes from the table, the guests should never assist in the work by piling small dishes, etc., upon their plate. Simply place knife and fork upon the plate.

In passing the plate for a second helping, remove knife and fork and hold easily by the handles. Never ask for a second helping of soup, or of anything at a course dinner. At an informal repast, where there is but one principal dish, it is proper to pass the plate for more. A second helping of fish chowder is allowable, but not of soup.

Food should be masticated quietly, and with the lips closed. Drink all liquids without the slightest sound.

Never butter bread that is to be eaten with soup. To do this is only less vulgar than to thicken the soup with the crumbs of bread. Simply eat the bit of bread with the soup. Take the soup that is brought you, even if you do not care for it, so as not to interrupt the order of the dinner by a refusal.

Disgusting Habits.

Lift cups by the handles, and wineglasses by the stem, and do not tip them up, until almost reversed upon the face, in order to drain the last drop. It is not necessary, and really bad form to completely empty a wineglass.

Never pick the teeth at the table. Such habits are well calculated to disgust sensitive people, and should be performed in private as much as any other portion of our daily toilet.

Never rinse the mouth with the last mouthful of coffee, tea or water; nothing can be more disagreeable.

Bread should be broken by the fingers in pieces sufficient for mouthfuls, as it is needed. Never butter a slice and cut with a knife; butter each piece as needed. Butter should never be eaten in large quantities.

Cake is broken in bits and eaten from the fingers. Very rich, crumbly, or filled cake may be eaten with a fork; tarts also, unless they are of a nature to permit the use of the fingers, and pastry of all kinds, as well as puddings not too liquid in form.

Muffins can be eaten from the plate with a fork, or they can be torn apart, buttered, and eaten while held in the fingers, like toasted bread. Hot gems can be torn apart and partaken of in the same way. Never take one piece of bread or cake and then reject it for another.

If any little accident should occur at table, do not apologize for it; let it pass without note, and it will be apt to escape observation. If there should be anything accidently spilled upon the cloth, the waiter should quickly remove the traces, and spread a fresh napkin over the soiled spot.

Fruits.

Apples are pared with a silver knife at table, and eaten in small sections from the fingers. There is often much time devoted to paring fruit by holding it on a fork, not touching it with the fingers. This is unnecessary, unless when a gentleman is preparing the fruit for a lady, or where the peach or pear is too juicy to do otherwise.

Grapes are plucked from their stems and the pulp squeezed into the mouth, while the fingers hold the skin which is then laid on one side the plate. This is far daintier than to put the fruit in the mouth and then eject the skin into the hand or upon the plate. Bananas are peeled and eaten from the plate with a fork. Oranges are skinned, divided into sections, and eaten from the fingers, rejecting the seeds into the hand. Some prefer, however, to cut the end of the orange and eat the pulp with a spoon. Pineapple is the only fruit that must be eaten with a knife and fork.

Silver knives and forks must always be used with fruits, as steel becomes colored by contact with the fruit juices and imparts a disagreeable flavor.

Green corn, in ear, is a stumbling-block, and perhaps one's best plan would be to conform to the custom of the table where you may be. In eating it directly from the ear hold it in one hand only. Some hostesses provide small doilies with which to hold the ear.

If a guest is pleased with any particular dish on the table, a delicate compliment upon its unusual excellence is always pleasing to the hostess.

EVENING PARTIES, RECEPTIONS AND SUPPERS.

THE evening party may be as elaborate or as simple an affair as the hostess may desire. In its elaborate form it only differs from the ball in the one respect that dancing may, or may not, be introduced as a feature of the entertainment, while a ball is given for the express purpose of dancing, and is always so understood.

Invitations.

Invitations for an elaborate evening party are sent out ten days or two weeks in advance and are issued in the name of the hostess alone. Husband and wife may be invited together, addressing the envelope to "Mr. and Mrs. John Doe;" and daughters, if there are several, may be included in one invitation as "The Misses Doe." Sons, if there be more than one, receive separate invitations, though they can be included in one as "Messrs. Doe." But friends, even though sheltered by the same rooftree, must receive separate invitations. To invite "The Misses Doe and Roe," or "Messrs. Brown and Green," or even "Mrs. Doe and Family," would be in bad form. To invite the husband to any entertainment where there are ladies without including the wife would be a direct insult. Invitations may be sent by post or carried by messengers. (For forms see Department of "Invitations, Formal and Informal.")

Society is so complex, and there is so much ground to cover in picking up its relations that many ladies are tempted to pay off all social debts at once by giving one great crush of an entertainment and inviting all those to whom they are socially indebted. To all these one is tempted to say, "Don't." The labor is less and the pleasure greater where two or more smaller entertainments are given at different times.

A hostess is at liberty to invite only those to whom she is socially indebted, and members of a large social circle from whom she has not received recent hospitalities must not feel hurt at being left out. Where the family is large she may invite some members and not others, but should she courteously invite the entire group, it is a rule of society that never more than three members of the same family should accept an invitation to the same entertainment. Either accept or decline such invitations at once. (For proper forms see department of "Acceptances and Regrets.")

Receiving.

At a large evening party the arrangements for receiving guests, the dressing rooms, etc., and duties of the hostess in receiving, are the same as at a ball, and the supper served in the same fashion.

Ladies invited to help receive are not simply asked as a compliment to their friendship. It is not their sole duty to stand beside the hostess for the hour of coming and smile and shake hands with each guest and then see no more of them that evening. When a lady issues invitations for a large evening gathering she usually decides to ask some intimate friends "to receive with her."

If she expressed what she really meant, and what she supposes her friends understand, she will say: "Will you come and help me in the actual entertaining of the guests, for I shall have only time to stand at the door and say, 'How do you do;' 'Good-by.'" But no, she phrases it conventionally: "Will you come and receive with me?" And so they come in a flock and do nothing but "receive."

Should Make Every One Happy.

A woman who is invited "to receive" should arrive at the hour of the invitation, not one minute before, unless for some especial reason she is requested to do so by her hostess. She should remove her wraps and quietly join her hostess in the rooms below, where, probably, she will have a cup of hot bouillon brought to her at once and maybe a glass of wine. For a half hour or so she should stand with the hostess and only take upon herself the task of greeting, but, as the rooms begin to fill, she should leave her place and go slowly about the rooms, not talking and visiting with friends, and having a good time herself, but passing by the groups of gay and lively ones, who know every one and seek out the solitary and alone. To these is her especial mission, to make them known to some of her own intimates, whose friendship is so certain and so warm that it will stand this demand of introducing a stranger.

An acquaintance is not necessary for this giving of attention. A member of the receiving party may speak to any one in the room without even the form of introducing herself, although, if she sees after a few words that she is unknown she will bring her own name casually into the conversation, making no effort to do so. Any guest will feel flattered on being addressed by the ladies receiving.

Making Things Easy for the Hostess.

Another duty she owes is keeping her eyes on the hostess and seeing that she is never left alone for one single moment in her position by the door. One of the receiving party ought to be beside her constantly ready to execute any wish she may express, as, for instance, if she say: "I see Mrs. K. coming down the stairs; she is a perfect stranger; see that she meets a few—Mrs. Blank, especially." She will greet Mrs. K., chat a second, and quietly draw her to one side continuing the conversation all the time. Then seeing somebody near she will say: "I want you to know Mrs. So-and-So; come over here and let me introduce you." Then she may leave Mrs. K. and look after some other awkward one near, and, after a few minutes, taking some one else up to where Mrs. K. and Mrs. So-and-So still stand, make them known. If Mrs. So-and-So has a kind heart, by this time she will have made Mrs. K. acquainted with some one else. The lady receiving should keep an eye on Mrs. K., particularly if she seems to be afraid to move from one spot, as strangers sometimes are.

Meantime, another member of the receiving party notices that the hostess is alone, and she leaves her acts of mercy and returns to her post, ready to assist in any way. To have such a little group of friends transform themselves into willing slaves for the moment makes the art of entertaining no trouble or fatigue at all.

Think of the utter loneliness to the stranger of entering the drawing-room to be greeted by the hostess and handed down a long line of the receiving party and then left to "that bath of loneliness amidst the multitude," which has its terrors for us all. It is over such strays as this that the receiving party is supposed to have most careful oversight, since to the hostess comes small leisure for this duty.

Entertainment.

Before supper, cards, conversation, music are made use of to entertain the guests. When dancing is a feature, it does not begin until after supper, and while this amusement is in progress opportunity for conversation, games, etc., should be provided in other rooms for those who do not dance. Rules for going out to supper at a large party are the same as those at a ball.

Duties of the Guests.

If music is one of the features, try and suit its character to the company. Do not play classical music where it cannot possibly be appreciated, and, above all, attempt nothing that cannot be executed perfectly. In singing, let gentlemen remember that if it is an amusing song they are to render, it must be perfectly unexceptional in character. Ladies should bear in mind in singing that it is much better taste in large assemblies to avoid the purely sentimental order of songs, which, with the large number of beautiful compositions at our disposal, is easily done.

ENTERTAINING THE GUESTS WITH A SONG.

Observe scrupulous silence while others are playing and singing. If you possess any musical accomplishments, and are asked to contribute your share toward the entertainment of others, do so without waiting to be urged; or, if you decline, decline absolutely. Urging should not be resorted to by the hostess, which custom would soon cure a certain class of performers from the disagreeable habit of holding back for repeated solicitations. If you consent to play or sing, do not weary your audience. Two or three stanzas of a song, or four or five pages from a long instrumental piece are sufficient. If more is greatly desired it will always be called for.

Remember, it is only the lady of the house who has the right to ask you to play or sing, and to all other requests give a smiling refusal.

Beware of too Much Reserve.

Remember also, that, for the time being, owing to your mutual acquaintance with the host and hostess, you stand on a perfect equality with all the guests present and should, therefore, without further preliminaries, converse freely with any.

Never commit the blunder of stealing away to a side table, and there affecting to be absorbed in some volume of engravings, or finding some unlucky acquaintance in the room, fasten upon him or her for the entire evening. These are social crimes that no shyness can or should excuse.

Where the party is a small social gathering and various parlor games are resorted to for amusement, one should always join in when asked, even while not caring so to do. Exercise skill, appear pleased, and while, perhaps, not enjoying the evening greatly one's self, there will be at least the consciousness of having contributed to the happiness of others. In reality, there is no better field for employing the Golden Rule than in the whirl of social life—no wider field for unselfishness.

A superficial knowledge of the etiquette and rules that govern the various social games of cards will be found a great advantage in society, since, if one does not dance or play cards, he will be forced to content himself with other wall-flowers like himself. A gentleman should never let even urgent solicitation induce him to play for stakes at a party. There is a code of right and wrong beside which the code of society has no weight.

Hours of Arrival and Departure.

An evening party usually begins about nine P. M. It is supposed to end about midnight unless the devotees prefer to remain later. Some who do not care for this amusement retire immediately after supper.

When to leave at a ball is a very elastic rule which varies to suit the circumstances of the case. To leave as soon after supper as may be or to stay until the ball is actually over, are equally correct courses to follow. Half past one is a very good time to depart. Here in this busy country where the gallants of the evening will be the business men of the morrow, earlier hours are usual than among the leisure classes of the Old World.

In retiring from a large party it is sufficient to bow politely when expressing the pleasure you have received. And if the hostess or host offer the hand, shake it cordially, but not too roughly.

An after call is required the same as after a ball or dinner party.

RECEPTIONS.

For informal receptions, invitations are most frequently written on the left hand corner of the hostess's visiting card: MRS. CHARLES GREY, Thursday, from five to eight o'clock.

At an evening reception, the lady should be dressed in handsome home toilet, and receive standing. If several ladies receive together, their cards should be enclosed with the invitation. The simplicity of the occasion leaves the hostess the more time to devote to the enjoyment of her guests. Music, both vocal and instrumental, is a great addition to an evening reception.

Refreshments are generally served informally. The table should be set tastily in the dining-room, and supplied with coffee or chocolate at one end and a tea service at the other. Besides these, daintily prepared sandwiches, buns, cakes, ices and fruits are served. If the reception is very select, and the number of guests small, a servant presents a tray with tea, sugar and cream, while another follows with the simple refreshments that should accompany it.

A wedding reception, or a very elaborate evening reception, of course admits of much more ceremony, as well as more substantial refreshments, than small entertainments.

Ladies attend evening receptions in *demi-toillette*, with or without bonnets, and gentlemen in full morning dress.

THE CENTRE OF ATTRACTION.

Invitations to evening receptions, lawn or musical parties are informal, but require an answer, as it is agreeable to every hostess to know the number of her expected guests.

> To meet their Royal Highnesses,
> The Infanta Eulalia
> And
> Antoine of Spain.
> The Spanish Consul
> And
> Mrs. Chatfield-Taylor
> At Home.
> Monday, June twelfth, at nine o'clock.
> 21 Pearson Street.

If the reception is given in honor of some individual or celebrity the name of the honored guest should appear at the top of the invitation, as above *facsimile* of cards issued by the Spanish Consul in honor of the Infanta of Spain during the Columbian Exposition.

Evening Receptions.

Evening receptions being simpler in detail and less expensive than parties, are becoming more fashionable every year, especially among people of literary and artistic tastes.

Guests calling, meet a select circle, among whom are usually poets, artists, and persons of elegant leisure, formality is readily broken, and the occasion is always one of pleasure.

The hour for leaving a reception is varied (anywhere from eleven P. M. to one A. M. being usual). Early hours are usual among those who have other engagements and who go on to other parties, remaining about half an hour at each one: thus, at crowded receptions the departures commence before the arrivals have ceased to be announced.

Morning Receptions or Matinées.

Of all the entertainments given during the daytime, luncheons, breakfasts, afternoon teas, kettledrums, etc., the morning reception, so-called, although it is given in the afternoon, is perhaps the most formal. Some hostesses adopt the French fashion of calling it a matinée, meaning any social gathering that is held before dinner, as any party is called in France a *soirée*.

There are many advantages in a morning party. It affords ladies who do not attend evening receptions the pleasure of meeting on a semi-formal occasion, and is also a well chosen occasion for introducing a new pianist or singer. For a busy woman of fashion a matinée, beginning at two and ending at four or half-past, which are the usual hours for these entertainments, is a most convenient time. It does not interfere with a five o'clock tea, or a drive, nor unfit her for a dinner party or evening entertainment. Convenient, however, as this hour is for ladies, it is quite the reverse for gentlemen, since the majority of them in America do not belong to the leisure class. Hence to avoid this inequality of the sexes, ladies often give these matinées on some of our national holidays.

When, as often happens, some great celebrity is to be presented to a large circle of friends, there is no more satisfactory form of entertainment to be afforded him than a morning reception. To this we may draw to meet him many men who could not be brought together at a late-hour, full-dress, evening entertainment. Authors, artists, clergymen, lawyers, statesmen, editors, doctors and capitalists, as well as cultivated society women, financiers and philosophers, can all be brought together in easy and friendly social intercourse.

But, if we hope to gather about us men of mind and distinction, we must not expect to be amused only, we must be amusing, we must offer some tempting equivalent; something that has the ring of pure gold, rather than the glamour of fashionable dress, dancing or music. So, with an Archbishop to entertain, we may hope to attract the distinguished clergy of the city; with a great author, other celebrities of the pen and pencil who will gladly come to greet him; and once drawn to a successful and brilliant assembly, they will be easily induced to return. Therefore, any lady who would make her home attractive to the best society must offer some higher stimulant than the glitter of fashion. For good society we need men and women who can talk. We need relaxation, and it is best sought in intercourse of abiding value with those whose lives differ from those of our own.

Correct Dress.

The invitations are written in the same form as those given for an evening entertainment, and although given by daylight, the rooms are frequently darkened and artificial illumination gives to the whole a festive air. The hostess may be dressed in demi-toilet, somewhat low at the throat if wished, and of the richest materials, but not in full evening dress, laces or conspicuous jewels. She may have friends to receive with her who will dress in the same demi-toilets. The guests wear reception dresses or handsome street dresses. Wraps are laid aside, but hats and gloves are kept on. Gentlemen wear full morning dress on all these occasions. Overcoats and umbrellas are left in the hall or dressing-room, but hats, if the stay is to be short, may be carried into the drawing-room.

Visitors do not usually remain more than half an hour, though, if the occasion is especially interesting, an hour or more is often spent. Conversation is indulged in, and guests listen to music, or whatever is provided for their entertainment. At an ordinary morning reception the refreshments are light, and served the same as at an evening reception. If, however, the occasion is unusually important, the collation is more abundant, and the service more formal.

Visitors leave cards to serve instead of the after call. Those who were invited but unable to attend, call within a few days. (For general forms of invitations see Department of "Invitations.")

Introductions are not expected to be general, except where the reception is given in honor of some one person, when, of course, all comers are presented to this guest. Morning parties given in small country towns are attended with less formality than in large cities, and introductions are general.

SUPPER PARTIES.

Some lover of this social repast says, "Suppers have always been invested with a peculiar charm. They are the most conversational, the most intimate and the most poetical of all entertainments. They are the favorite repast of men of letters, the inspiration of poets, and a form of hospitality eminent in history. Who has not heard of the *petite soupers* of the Regency and the brilliant minds there assembled?"

Suppers are the popular entertainment of gentlemen, and usually take some distinctive name, such as fish suppers, game suppers, wine suppers, and each has suitable supplies for the table.

Invitations to suppers may be given in person, by a friendly note, or writing on the card of the host or hostess: "Supper at 10 o'clock, Thursday, December 18th."

The very late city dinners have prevented supper parties from keeping their popularity, but there is no reason why in towns these should not be favorite entertainments.

The same service is proper at a supper as at a dinner, with the exception of soup plates. Oysters on the half-shell and bouillon served in cups are the first two courses. Then follows the usual order of dishes, such as sweetbreads and green peas, whatever game may be in season, salads of all kinds, then ices, fruits and coffee. It is not quite so heavy a repast as the elaborate dinner party. Games and salads are served together. If wine is used it is found on the table in handsome decanters. Three sorts may be served, such as Sherry or Madeira and Burgundy. Bread and napkin are beside each plate, or else the bread is passed after the guests are seated. Next, plain plates and cups of bouillon are served, with gold teaspoons. Then follow the other courses. The dishes are removed after each course as at a formal dinner. At the close of the supper a tiny glass of cordial is served to the gentlemen. Wines may be entirely omitted if against the principles, and mineral waters may be substituted. The table may be decorated as for a dinner party.

There is perhaps no entertainment where so much brilliant conversation and repartee is indulged in as at the "sit-down" supper.

Residents of large cities, possessing abundant means, can avoid trouble by ordering supplies from the professional caterer, but in the country home, where economy is an object, it devolves on the housekeeper to prepare the appetizing dainties for her entertainments. For the benefit of such, we give a few items that may be useful in arranging the menu. Any reliable work on cookery will give the directions for their preparation: Boned turkey, boned ham, deviled ham sandwiches, salmon salad, chicken salad, potted fish, fish salad, etc., etc.

A Simple Supper.

There is a much simpler supper possible to be offered by a hostess after the opera or theatre which may be made very charming and inexpensive. This is a desirable little "spread," since there are few people who can undergo the excitement of an evening at the opera, play, concert, or card party, without a feeling of hunger; and with many, unless this hunger is appeased a sleepless night will be the result; and as the excitement is usually so good an aid to digestion, no evil consequences may be feared.

This little supper is well set out with a few oysters, a pair of cold roast chickens, a boned turkey, or boned ham, and a dish of some kind of salad, and perhaps one sort of ice cream or ice and coffee. Oysters are invaluable for a supper. Scalloped or broiled, they can be used in place of chicken or turkey.

A Game Supper.

A game supper consists of wild fowls and fish, with jellies, ices and bon-bons, while a wine supper admits of almost every variety of luscious dishes, differing very little from dinner, except that the delicacies are all cold, and of course no vegetables are served. Fillets of game, boned turkey, cold ham, fish, salads, ices, jellies and creams, are suitable to this style of entertainment.

A Fish Supper.

When a fish supper is given, dishes are generally composed of the products of the sea or river. This is a fashionable mode of entertainment for the season of Lent. Salads, olives, pickles and sauces are served as relishes. Sweet desserts never accompany a fish supper, but fruits are an appropriate addition. Coffee must be given with all suppers.

BALLS, DANCING AND MASQUERADES

BALLS, to distinguish them from other evening gatherings where dancing is one of the features of the evening, may be designated as parties given for the express purpose of dancing.

Balls should begin at about nine o'clock in the evening, and terminate at two or three in the morning. A private ball may be a very elaborate affair, from fifty to seventy-five guests being necessary to make the occasion enjoyable. Where the size of the ball-room will permit, many more are frequently bidden. Over-crowding should be guarded against, as ruinous to the toilets of the ladies, and the pleasure of all concerned. The invitations to very elaborate affairs are sometimes sent out from three weeks to one month in advance.

It is always proper for an invited guest to solicit an invitation for a young lady visitor, or some stranger of distinction, or for a young gentleman known to be a dancing man, and it is always permissible for the hostess, if she wish, to refuse such solicitations on the ground that her list is full, and no one should feel offended at such refusal. Should the request, however, be for the admission of an eligible, dancing man, it is rarely refused.

Never more than three from one family (the mother or chaperon excepted) should accept an invitation to a ball, or party, unless in the case of a ball, where two brothers, if they dance, may be accompanied by two sisters from the same family. Those who do not dance should refuse invitations to balls (chaperons excepted). The most brilliant man who does not dance is usually out of place in an entertainment given for that sole purpose.

The ball-room should be large; the floor well waxed, or covered with drugget, and an abundance of palms and potted plants set about to make cosy nooks just lighted by a shaded lamp. Cut flowers may be massed upon the mantels with gorgeous effect. If the stairway be of sufficient breadth, it should be bravely furnished forth with plants in bloom. If it should be a first-floor room and open into the cool dusk of a faintly lighted conservatory, then it is everything to be desired for the occasion. Good ventilation is an absolute necessity.

Invite at least one quarter more guests than can be comfortably accommodated, since about that number will fail, from different causes, to accept. If it is impossible to entertain with comfort all those to whom one is socially indebted, then it is better to divide the entertainment into two or three smaller gatherings, always leaving space for as many mothers of daughters, or other appointed chaperons, as may choose to attend and who should always be included in the invitations.

Sitting accommodations should be furnished for them, as well as for those who may not be dancing. All other furniture should be removed from the rooms.

Full-dress toilets are demanded for the occasion; flowers, jewels,

"The gloss of satin and the glimmer of pearls,"

should mingle in this festivity, the gayest of our social gatherings.

The ball-room should be brilliantly, and at the same time, softly illuminated, the lights coming chiefly from the sides.

General Arrangements.

In a large city it is necessary to provide an awning to extend from the carriage to the front entrance, thus screening guests from the crowd that usually gathers on such an occasion. A carpet should also cover the steps and walk to protect the ladies' gowns. A manservant in evening dress and white lisle gloves should be at the curbstone to assist ladies, who may have come unattended, in alighting, (providing they have no footman). He also provides each party with the number of their carriage, giving the same to the driver, in order that he may be ready when called. This same attendant also calls for the carriages upon the departure of the guests.

Another manservant, or a white-capped maid, waits at the door, which is opened without the bell being touched. This functionary receives the cards of the guests, and directs them to their respective dressing-rooms. These should be large and convenient as possible. Assistants should be provided with thread, needles and pins to rectify any accidents that may occur to the ladies' toilets, and to render every possible aid to them in making ready for the drawing-rooms. Duplicate tickets should also be in readiness; one to attach to each wrap and one to hand its owner. These precautions lessen the confusion and add to the comfort of all concerned.

Combs, brushes, and hairpins should be in abundance, while a powder-box and puff is not amiss. Cologne, camphor and ammonia should also be in the rooms for use in cases of sudden faintness. A couch in the room is also useful, and low chairs or ottomans, in case any of the ladies should wish to change their shoes.

The gentlemens' dressing-room should also be presided over by an attendant supplied with the same duplicate system of tickets and ready to render any called-for assistance.

Programs with the order of the dances and blanks for recording engagements for each, should be distributed to the guests as they enter the ball-room. To each card should be attached a small pencil.

Concerning the Music.

Good music is a prime necessity. An orchestra, even if it must be a small one, is needful for a ball. Four pieces are enough: violin, piano, violincello, or harp, and cornet. If more are desired, leave the choice to the leader, with whom the selections will have been carefully talked over beforehand, and who must be furnished with a copy of the dancing program.

The musicians should be concealed back of a group of flowering shrubs at the end of the hallway, or some other convenient nook or corner. If there should be a balcony, a shady bower can be constructed for them there, and by taking out the window frame they will be heard to perfection.

Never, even at a "small and early," depend, for the pianist, upon volunteer service from among the guests. In the first place, it is a tiresome and unwillingly performed service, and in the second, there are few amateurs who play dance-music with sufficient correctness to render dancing after their music a pleasure.

Refreshments.

At a ball elaborate refreshments are to be expected, and are usually served all the evening from a long table loaded with silver and glass and softly but brilliantly illuminated. No one is expected to sit down at such a supper, but the guests as they come in, a few at a time, are served by waiters in attendance.

Both hot and cold dishes are to be had; and substantial food, as well as all manner of sweets, should be furnished for an amusement that begets a most unromantic hunger. Small game birds may be served cold; the larger fowl hot. Boned turkey (cold) is especially liked. Game *patés*, oysters, cooked or raw, all manner of truffled dishes, and a variety of salads are served, while fruits, ices, confections, cakes, and so on, *ad infinitum*, do fitly furnish forth the feast.

If the German is to finish the evening, a separate, hot supper should be served at its close, and the all-night supper confined more exclusively to cold dishes, with the exception of hot drinks.

In case of a very spacious mansion, the hostess may, if she prefer, keep the supper-room closed until half-past twelve, or one, when she will give the word. Her husband should lead the way to supper with some lady to be especially honored. The hostess should not go out herself until she sees that every lady has been properly escorted, save in cases where she is to accompany some very distinguished gentleman who is present. In this case she delegates her authority either to a grown son, some other relative, or to some gentleman especially appointed, who takes her place in seeing that there are no forgotten wall-flowers left to blush unseen.

No gentleman should presume to offer the hostess his escort to the supper-room, this being an honor she confers at pleasure.

A small tea-room on an upper floor is very desirable at a large gathering. Here guests, ladies especially, can, unattended, seek the refreshment of a cup of tea, coffee, cocoa, or bouillon before descending to the drawing-rooms. Gentlemen, too, may escort their wearied partners to this haven for a moment's light refection and rest after dancing. Iced lemonade should also be served here, and the room never left without an attendant.

Many who do not care for a heavy supper, are wont to resort to this room, where tiny sandwiches, maccaroons, etc., should also be in readiness.

A smoking-room is frequently provided at large entertainments where the gentlemen may retire. Cigars, effervescent waters, and lemonade are furnished here, and sometimes stronger drinks. This last, however, is a question which every hostess must settle according to her own convictions. If wines are furnished, champagne and claret punch are the usual choice, and a trusted attendant should be at hand to serve them. Those who patronize this room will, if they wish to lay any claim to the name of "gentlemen," carefully refrain from the slightest over-indulgence in these cooling, but deceptive drinks.

If there should be no smoking-room set aside, gentlemen must never smoke in their dressing-room. To do so is especially thoughtless and impolite.

Host and Hostess.

In giving a ball the hostess, upon whom the greatest strain will fall, must be sure of her own physical and mental strength. To stand for two consecutive hours in one spot and receive each comer with the same sweet courtesy is a severe strain upon both.

Daughters, young lady relatives or ladies invited to receive, are usually at hand to support her. The host, if there be one, does not stand beside his wife to receive, but is usually not far away and should assist in making the occasion an agreeable one.

Sons of the house do not seek their own pleasure at such a time, but quietly endeavor, aided by the daughters or receiving ladies, to provide dancing and supper partners for all present. Sometimes two or three young men are appointed beforehand to attend to this duty.

The hostess, while richly dressed, should never show any desire by the elaborateness of her costume to outshine her guests.

Should an obtuse cabman, misled by some similarity of name or error in number (as may occur in large cities), permit a perplexed guest, perhaps a stranger, to drift across the wrong threshold, let it be a hospitable one. The hostess, though she may not be able to unravel the mystery, should be gracious and attentive.

Arrival and Departure.

The first move after leaving the dressing-rooms is for ladies to join their escorts and proceed to the drawing-rooms.

In going up or down stairs the gentleman always precedes the lady by several steps, unless they walk side by side. This rule holds good on every occasion. A lady, if she wishes the gentleman's assistance should take his right arm, thus leaving her right hand free to carry her train. Her bouquet or fan may be carried in the hand upon his arm.

Gentlemen and ladies never enter the room arm in arm, no matter what their relationship may be. A lady enters somewhat in advance of a gentleman accompanying her, but at the side of a maiden whom she chaperons. A mother precedes her daughter.

Do not offer to shake hands with the hostess as you bow, unless she makes the initiatory move, since where the number invited is large the process becomes somewhat wearisome. Many hostesses prefer to sweep a graceful courtesy as they receive their guests.

Do not remain chatting with the receiving party. A bow, and a simple exchange of kindly inquiries, is sufficient, when you should pass on immediately to leave room for others. A gentleman's next duty is to search out his host and exchange the courtesies of the evening with him. Any who may arrive late should at once search out both host and hostess to offer a belated greeting.

A stranger who has received an invitation through friends, should be introduced to both host and hostess and to any daughters of the house. If a gentleman, he should be sure to invite the ladies to dance.

At a large ball any formal leave-taking is unnecessary. To

"Fold your tents like the Arabs,

And as silently steal away,"

is quite the thing. Do not make such a stir by your going as to call attention to your departure, apparently wishing others to take notice of it.

The Escort.

The escort of a young lady owes her attention beyond all others he may meet in the ball-room. He should assist her from the carriage, accompany her to the dressing-room door, and after due time return to escort her to the reception-room. He must be her partner in the opening dance and should also put his name down for the one immediately preceding supper, since it is expected that the gentleman dancing with a lady then will take her out to supper, and there see that all her wants are anticipated. If, for any reason, he cannot do this, he must see that she is suitably attended; a gentleman taking a lady into the supper-room must also escort her back to the ball-room and leave her wherever she may desire.

If there should be any seeming neglect he must see that she is provided with partners for as many dances as she may desire; never dancing himself unless she, too, is on the floor, or, if she prefer, sitting out the dance with some pleasant companion. He may introduce other gentlemen to her, after asking her permission.

It is his privilege to send her a bouquet for the occasion, and he first asks what the lady's costume is to be, in order to harmonize the color of the flowers with the shade of the dress, since it would be most annoying to send blue violets to be worn with a sea-green gown.

It is the lady's privilege to suggest the hour of departure. After seeing her safely within her own door he should leave; even if she asks him to enter he should politely refuse, remembering, however, to call upon her within two days.

A FRIENDLY GREETING

Receiving Ladies.

Ladies called upon to assist in receiving are not to consider their duties ended when they have supported the hostess through the trying hours of standing to greet her guests, but are supposed (though they too often fail in this) to mingle with the company, seeing that strangers and timid or non-attractive girls are not allowed to remain wall-flowers for any length of time. Bashful men, too, must not be left without partners, and all should be provided with escorts to supper.

These things are a part of the hostess' duty, but in a large entertainment it is quite beyond her power to attend to all the claims upon her time.

The sons of the house, and sometimes a few other especially deputized young men, must sacrifice their own preferences in order to give pleasure to others. If the number of ladies exceed that of gentlemen, these aids frequently take two out to supper.

Daughters of the house, together with receiving ladies and the hostess, do not go out to supper until the last guests are supplied with partners. However, should the hostess be expected to accompany some distinguished gentleman to the table, she will delegate her duties to another.

General Rules for Observance.

Gentlemen may introduce other men to ladies of their own family or to friends, first asking their permission or the permission of their chaperons. In case of a chaperon, the introduction is made first to her and then to the young lady, and the gentleman at close of the dance returns his partner to her chaperon.

Where the gentleman is well acquainted with the lady, a short promenade is often indulged in; but if the gentleman be a stranger to her, she should not expect this, for he may have another engagement, and will return her immediately to the side of her chaperon or some lady friend she may designate. In Europe this promenading is not allowed, the young lady being at once escorted back to her chaperon after dancing.

Supper being announced, a gentleman, having no other engagement, offers his arm to the lady with whom he may be talking or dancing and escorts her out, unless some previous partner arrives to claim her before his invitation is given. Once given, a lady is not free (unusual circumstances excepted) to decline it, even though she may have expected another to offer her the same attention. If she be accompanied by a chaperon, the elder lady is invited at the same time, and it is to her that his arm is offered, the younger lady walking by her side. For two ladies to each take an arm is not good form.

A gentleman requesting a lady for a certain dance, should never ask if she is engaged for it. He may request the pleasure or honor of her company for the next dance, and he will learn from her answer whether she be free, without compelling her to acknowledge at the last moment that she has been hitherto unsought.

Formality of Introductions.

The request for a dance should be accompanied by a bow on the part of the gentlemen. At its close he should thank her for the pleasure, and she should return this courtesy with a smile and bow, and a murmured "Thank you."

An introduction to a lady in the ball-room pre-supposes that the gentleman will dance with her or walk with her through one dance.

In England, where introductions are rarely given to those invited to an entertainment, a gentleman may ask any lady for a dance. She will probably accept, but he must not take this as the prelude to an after acquaintance. In America, however, it is necessary to ask some mutual friend to first request the favor of the lady, and then, if granted, give the introduction.

However, in case of any little accident, or sudden faintness, gentlemen should be quick to assist, bringing an iced drink, aiding to the dressing-room, or calling a carriage, as the case may be, without the formality of an introduction. A gentleman may also ask an older lady who seems left unattended at supper-time, if he may bring her some refreshments, and this without an introduction.

It is very bad form for gentlemen to stand about the ball-room, especially if there be a scarcity of dancing men present. Even if there is no one in the room for whom they particularly care, they should be unselfish enough to remember that dancing is almost the only active form of amusement in which the majority of ladies may participate.

A young man should ask the young ladies, daughters or relatives of the hostess, for their company in the dance early in the evening. A married gentleman should be general in his attentions in the ball-room. He should not dance more than once or twice with his wife, nor should he take her out to supper; but he must keep a quiet outlook over her comfort, and see that she is no wise lonely or neglected.

Attentions Paid to Ladies.

Neither should he confine his attentions in a marked manner to any one lady. It is ill-breeding to excite the comment sure to follow such a course. It is also bad form for any gentleman to confine his attentions to any one lady, or, as a rule, to ask her for more than two dances. Even engaged couples are not exempt from this law.

Gentlemen may put down their name on a lady's program for certain dances, and the engagement should never be forgotten. If, however, this lapse should occur, the humblest apology should follow, which the young lady, no matter how annoyed, should gracefully accept. Ill-humor is out of place in the ball-room.

If a lady from weariness, or any other cause, should wish to stop at any time in the dance, the gentleman must, without any comment, at once lead her to a seat, and remain with her until the set is finished, notwithstanding that she may, from a spirit of kindness, request him to seek another partner. Should she show symptoms of weariness, and be either too timid or too thoughtful for his enjoyment to ask him to take her from the floor, he should be quick to see, and to suggest that she rest for a moment.

Gloves form an important adjunct to a gentleman's toilet for a dancing party. Light colored gloves are always good form. Gentlemen are expected to wear gloves while dancing, since their ungloved hands would not only soil the delicate tints of the lady's gloves, but the slightest pressure of a warm, uncovered hand is liable to discolor the frail gauzes, or pale silks of their ball-room toilet.

It is not amiss to be provided with an extra pair of gloves which will be very useful should the first pair come to grief. Upon the same principle, two fresh handkerchiefs should be carried.

If dancing is not formally announced in the invitation, gentlemen will do well to provide themselves with gloves to be donned if that amusement is introduced in the course of the evening. Notwithstanding the royal indolence or whim of the Prince of Wales led him some time back to discard the use of gloves at evening parties, an example which many ultra-fashionables have followed, it still remains that gloves are both proper and necessary. If a gentleman attempts to dance without them he must hold his handkerchief in his hand in such a manner as to prevent its contact with the bodice of the lady's gown.

Loud talking and boisterous laughter are not to be tolerated. Scrupulously avoid stepping upon the train of a lady's gown. Apologize if it accidentally occurs, and if serious damage ensue from the awkwardness, beg the privilege of taking her to the dressing-room to have the damage repaired.

For Ladies.

Young ladies must never refuse to dance with one gentleman, and afterward give the same dance to a more favored suitor. Nothing so quickly speaks of ill-breeding as this course. Ball-room engagements should not be forgotten. Young ladies should never be so unwise as to appear on the floor at every dance.

Daughters of the hostess should not repeatedly appear upon the floor while other lady guests are neglected. Not their own pleasure, but the pleasure of the company should be their first care.

Ladies should not cross the ball-room alone. It invites attention. Ladies must not burden gentlemen (unless husband or near relative) with bouquet or fan to hold while they dance. Young ladies should not refuse a ball-room introduction to a gentleman without a sufficient reason, since to do so is always an embarrassment to the one asking it. Still a lady has the privilege of refusal and may not be pressed for a reason. Young chaperons should never dance while their *protégés* are unprovided with partners.

A lady removes at least one glove while partaking of supper. But when a cup of tea, or an ice, only is taken this is not necessary.

DANCING.

Pope says: "They move easiest who have learned to dance," and while the opinions of society are greatly divided on the subject of this amusement, it cannot be denied that there is much truth in the assurance that Locke gives us in his treatise on "Education:"

"Since nothing appears to me to give children so much becoming confidence and behavior as dancing, I think they should be taught to dance as soon as they are capable of learning it. For though this consists only in outward gracefulness of motion, ... yet it gives children manly thoughts and courage more than anything."

For the many, however, to whom these early advantages have not been given, while the dowry of a quick ear and natural grace has enabled them to "pick up" this social accomplishment, a few hints may be of use.

Dancing is really an art, and one that the gentleman especially should understand (since he takes the lead) before he ventures to ask a lady out upon the floor.

The gentleman should be very careful in the manner of holding his partner. He should give her proper support by putting his arm firmly around her, but not drawing her too close. Her right hand should be held in his left, the lady turning the right palm downward and almost straightening her right arm. The gentleman should bend his left arm slightly backward. The joined hands should be held steadily but kept away from the gentleman's body. To rest them upon his hip, is actual vulgarity. The gentleman's right shoulder and the lady's left, should be kept as far apart as the other shoulders, hence his right elbow must not be too much bent. The upper part of the body should be kept quiet, and the head held naturally, not turned one side, while the eyes are neither thrown up nor cast down in an affected style. Their steps should be in harmony and the gentleman must be very careful not to permit a collision with other couples.

At every slightest pause in the dance the gentleman should instantly drop his arm from the lady's waist. In these intervals it is proper to fan her if she desire it, and to enter into chatty conversation.

Gentlemen avoid all boisterous conduct in the dance, such as swinging a partner too rapidly, or lifting her too much from the floor. She, on her part, should dance lightly, never permitting her partner to carry her around, but performing her share well, or not dance at all.

The Most Desirable Dances.

In making up a dancing program, quadrilles should always find a place, since many can walk through its measures that will not undertake the more active dances. It also gives opportunity for the graceful curtsey which no lady should fail to learn, and can be enlivened with conversation.

To the alluring round dances, polka, schottische, waltz, etc., there are many who strongly object, but, danced in private homes and in most cases under the eye of the young girl's mother, there can be found nothing dangerously objectionable in this favorite amusement. The minuet is a stately, beautiful old dance that is sometimes introduced, enabling both old and young to join in its slow and gracious measure.

New steps, new changes and new dances, with the technical features of which it is not the province of this book to deal, are continually coming into vogue with each season. A few words, however, with regard to the general etiquette of that justly popular dance, the German, will be in place here. The German, called the "Cotillion" in France and in Germany, where it originated, is the most fascinating dance in social use. Balls at which it is to appear, signifying that fact in the invitations sent out are more elaborate in their arrangements, and are held to a later hour, since the earlier portion of the night is devoted to waltzing and other dances, and the German is not commenced until after supper.

Many leave before it begins, especially those who expect to make the tour of several balls and receptions during the night. A second and hot supper is usually served at its close, to those who participate in its measures. Be certain when the German is to be introduced that a sufficient number of men are invited to make the affair a success.

The leader of the cotillion is chosen by the hostess, and should be thoroughly familiar with all its figures, new and old; skilled to command, and prompt to bring order out of confusion; at the same time energetic and good tempered. As there will always be some in a German who do not understand it, the leader must be ready to help them out. Such parties should take their places near the end, and, in this way, will become familiar with a figure before it is their turn to dance.

No Favorites to be Allowed.

The leader will also see that gentlemen do not neglect some ladies for the pleasure of dancing frequently with more favored partners. In this he should be assisted by the hostess, and gentlemen should never disregard her quiet suggestion on this score. After all, "the ball-room is a more fitting field for a display of the Christian graces than most Evangelical people are willing to admit."

All those dancing the German must consider themselves as introduced, and each lady or gentleman is free to call "up" any participant for his or her partner. In fact it is desirable that they should do so, since by devoting themselves entirely to their acquaintance there is danger of some being debarred from the amusement. For these reasons the German is unsuited for a public ball, and fitted only for a private house where the invitation is expected to certify the character of the guest.

Varied and beautiful are the figures that may be adopted, but the scope of this book will not permit full instructions for its elaborate changes. One suggestion, however, is in point; do not choose those "romping" figures where the fun is liable to become too fast and furious for ball-room decorum. The figures requiring "properties," such as ribbons, flags, Japanese lanterns, aprons, mirrors, etc., should have all the necessary articles carefully provided beforehand.

During most of the figures, "favors" are distributed; flowers, amusing trinkets, or sometimes pretty little souvenirs are given. Rosettes, scarf pins, bangles, tiny flags, artificial butterflies, bon-bons in embroidered satin bags, badges, painted silk sachets, etc., are all appropriate. Tiny lanterns filled with perfume, and sometimes amusing toys will add to the fun of the occasion. It is better taste to give simple articles than to resort to the gifts of great value that some hostesses have bestowed, since such giving always suggests ostentation. Flowers alone are sometimes used and it is not necessary to make the favors a source of undue expense.

Regrets must be sent one's hostess if unable to attend a German, that the place may be filled. If a gentleman invites a lady especially as his partner for a German, he should send her a bouquet and if some unforseen occurrence should prevent his attendance, he must at once send her an explanatory regret to that effect.

Private Balls Given in Public.

Many hostesses, feeling the inadequacy of their parlors to accommodate all the guests that they wish to invite at one time, without disagreeable overcrowding, have adopted the custom of giving their large entertainments at public assembly rooms. This custom, while it frees the hostess from much care, must also be deplored as depriving the gathering of that home atmosphere which is ever a safeguard.

The etiquette is the same as that of a private ball, and after calls are demanded within the same length of time. The decorations and arrangements resemble closely as possible those of a private house.

Public Balls.

Much of the etiquette given for Private Balls governs the conduct of those attending public entertainments of the same nature. Introductions, however, must be sought before any attentions are offered a lady, and there is much more care exercised in granting them than under a private roof. Gentlemen, too, use their own pleasure in the choice of partners, not having the courtesy of their hostess to regard in this respect.

THE MASQUERADE ASSEMBLY.

Of course, Military, Charity and Civic Balls are under the charge of trustees and committees, who not only take charge of the convenience of the guests, but endeavor by all means within their power to regulate the social standing of those obtaining *entrée* to the assembly. In many of the large cities a board of lady patronesses add prestige and a certain home protection to the successful carrying out of a public ball of the highest order. It seems to supply the protection of a hostess to the *fête*.

A young girl, even if the omission be excused at a private ball, does not attend a public affair of this nature without a chaperon. Late hours are more especially objectionable at public balls than at a private house. One, or half-past, should find the adieux made.

A young lady, in refusing to dance with a gentleman, is not obliged to sit the dance out as she would be at the house of a mutual friend. She may, however, if she wish, do it in deference to his feelings.

MASQUERADES.

A few words with regard to masquerades will not be out of place here, with the one proviso added that they refer exclusively to private entertainments. Public gatherings of this nature should be shunned as questionable amusements, excepting, of course, any case where, from want of room, a lady may choose to give the entertainment in some public assembly-room instead of her own parlors. This course lends the protection of home to the charm of its veiled mysteries.

A masquerade is an entertainment giving much trouble to both hostess and guests. Elaborate decorations are necessary in the ball-room. Invitations for it should be issued from three weeks to a month in advance, in order to give the guest time to choose and prepare the costume to be worn.

Some hostesses give their invitations for a fancy dress party only, omitting the feature of masks. In this they may act their own pleasure. In event of permitting masks they must be laid aside at supper hour.

THE MASQUERADE.

Occasionally the hostess arranges a costume scheme for the entire *fête* beforehand, signifying to each guest the character, historical or imaginary, that it is her pleasure he shall, for the time being, personify. In this way the perfection and beauty of the ball-room are assured beforehand, and repetitions of time-worn characters prevented from appearing upon the floor.

Choice of Costumes.

Again, the hostess may content herself by selecting the costumes that she wishes a few particular friends to don, sufficient in number to form one or more quadrilles to open the ball. Each set must be carefully arranged as for instance, a court party, costumed after the time of Louis XIV. A group of Watteau Shepherds and shepherdesses, or a hunting party garbed after any chosen period, etc.

The remainder of the guests may be permitted to use their own taste in the selection of costumes. A full dress rehearsal of these especially arranged quadrilles should be held beforehand to ascertain the most satisfactory method of grouping the characters in each set.

Invitations to an entertainment of this nature are issued like those for ordinary balls, adding "*Bal-masqué*" or "Fancy Dress Ball," down in the left hand corner. When the entertainment is to be very elaborate these words are given an entire line, extending through the center of the invitation. Occasionally the words, "Ordinary ball dress permitted," find a place upon the card, to the relief of those who prefer to appear in their own proper character.

The host and hostess in fancy dress, assisted by daughters or friends, all costumed, receive as in other balls, and the etiquette is in all ways similar. Some ladies, and gentlemen also, wear mask and domino over the regulation party dress, removing this when the others unmask.

Guests, as far as in them lies, should seek for originality in their costumes. Historical and mythological characters, personification of the powers and attributes of nature—as ice, snow, stars, planets, etc.—are always suitable. Standard works of fiction whose characters are familiar to all, as well as Mother Goose and Kate Greenaway, are always fruitful sources for characters. Accurateness should be sought after in carrying the costumes out.

[Etiquette of Ball Dress, Invitations, etc., may be found in their appropriate departments.]

SOIRÉES MUSICALES AND LAWN PARTIES.

IN France almost any social gathering that occurs in the evening is called a *soirée*. Here in this country the term *soirée* is applied to an evening entertainment that partakes of the nature of an evening party, but is not quite so elaborate and means earlier hours both of arrival and departure.

Soirées, as a rule, offer some particular form of amusement, such as music, dancing, a reading; an interchange of bright ideas, such as a *conversazione*. It means also pretty evening dress, not elaborate, ball costume, and a supper. It attracts gentlemen, who appreciate the easy-going, early-houred *soirée*. That is, gentlemen who do not particularly care for the ball-room, and it is here we are sure to find wits and the aristocracy of intellect. In short, the very best elements of society are found in the elegant unpretentious *soirée*, where the intelligent woman of fashion has the tact to welcome and make at home the artist, the author, the professional man, and the man of business. The *soirée* has still another advantage: a lady can give one in a small house and with very little expenditure, and if she has the gift of entertaining, her gathering will always be sought after.

Suitable Dress.

Women, as before mentioned, wear pretty evening dress (not ball costume), and remove their bonnets, and in this way differing from *matinées* and from morning receptions, at both of which entertainments bonnets are worn. Men wear morning dress. (See Department of Dress.)

Receiving Guests.

For small evening parties, the host and hostess during the early part of the evening remain near the door to receive guests. Later they must mingle with the company to assist in entertaining. A late arrival, however, should be noted, though it is their place to search out their hostess and offer the greetings of the evening.

As guests enter the room the hostess should advance a step to meet them. Her words of greeting should be first addressed to the elder ladies of an incoming group, then the young ladies, lastly the gentlemen. The hostess should be perfectly at her ease, having apparently no thought beyond the reception rooms.

The Entertainment.

Where the entertainment is mixed, a little music is appropriate, a little dancing and a little card-playing. It is well to engage some one to play for the dancing, since guests usually do not care to preside at the instrument. A violin is a great addition.

If, however, the dancing is an afterthought, any gentleman who is a good pianist may offer his services to relieve any lady at the instrument.

The hostess should see that conversation does not lag. She must not interrupt an entertaining *tête-à-tête*, unless it last too long; but, if conversation languish between a couple thrown together, she should bring in a third person, or draw away one, while substituting another.

Invitations.

If invitations are issued a week or ten days in advance, the hostess has a right to expect that her guests should arrive on time, and carefully attired.

The form of the invitation is similar to an "At Home," as: MRS. EMMONS VAN ZANT, At Home, Thursday, June sixteenth, at eight o'clock. 2040 Westmoreland Street.

Duty of Guests.

The hostess may ask her guests to sing or play; but, if they refuse, it is bad taste to urge them. The hostess, if she plays or sings, may favor the guests with a single selection after others have been heard. It is well for amateurs to master a few pieces that they can render without the notes. This relieves one of that time-worn excuse—"I haven't my notes." This is also the case with those who sing. By ceasing to urge performers, the company will be freed from much of that repeated, coy refusal that only needs sufficient coaxing to comply.

When a lady is asked to play or sing, the gentleman nearest her should at once escort her to the piano, remaining near her while she plays, and turning the music, if he be competent. He will also take charge of her fan, bouquet and gloves, and when the music is finished, he will again offer his arm for her return to her seat. At the same time he will thank her for the pleasure she has given himself and the company. Other guests, together with the hostess, should also express their gratification. Never comment on the quality of the instrument. Never offer to turn the sheets of instrumental music unless familiar with the notes.

When any one is playing or singing, let the company preserve silence, and if they should converse, let it be in the lowest tones. To interrupt a performer is the worst possible taste. Instrumental performers have as much right to expect the courtesy of silence as vocalists. The hostess has the privilege of indicating, to a noisy group, by a gesture, her desire for silence. Those who will talk should at least withdraw from the immediate vicinity of the instrument. If asked to play an accompaniment, do so, not to display your own accomplishments, but so as to afford the best possible support for the singer.

MUSICALES.

A musicale, or a musical reception, is a difficult entertainment. A program must be arranged, and sufficient amateur performers secured to make a success of the affair. Herein comes the difficulty, amateurs, after a very unwilling consent has been wrung from them and their name and selection placed upon the program, are so little to be depended upon. Would that there could be found some way of oiling the machinery at a musical entertainment and of soothing the ruffled feelings of a hostess when those most depended upon to render assistance withdraw at the last moment for some vague reason. When one firmly refuses at the first to appear upon the program, no offence can be taken, but to withdraw for any but the most urgent reason is an actual breach of etiquette.

For this reason, those hostesses whose purses are of sufficient length, are driven to employ professional assistance upon these occasions. Another objection to amateur performers is the semi-professional jealousy existing between them as to precedence on the program.

Performers should arrive punctually, and while the order of the program should be followed as far as possible, no one should be offended at being asked, when it is necessary to play or sing out of the order agreed upon.

Arranging the Program.

If the musicale is to be entirely professional, much trouble will be saved by seeking some prominent musician, and with him arrange the program, and letting him act for the hostess in the matter.

A professional artist should not be kept beyond the time agreed for, neither should he be urged to render selections entirely different, or largely in excess of those arranged for. The hostess should express her pleasure, and may request some little favor. Applause is allowable, but it must be within limits.

A courteous reception must be accorded to all performers by those who desire their talents. The hostess should see that the piano is carefully tuned and not keyed too high.

It is customary to commence with a piece of instrumental music, followed by solos, duets, quartets, etc., with instrumental music between.

A successful musicale can be held with the piano alone for music, an accompanist, and a tenor and soprano of note, but very often a violin is added, and sometimes a mandolin orchestra and four or more singers vary the program. Professional singers and musicians usually leave when their numbers are over, in order to protect their throats from night air and the strain of conversing.

Guests should arrive early so that the confusion of entrance and taking seats will be over before the music begins. If late, they should wait until the number then in progress is finished before taking their places. The singular impression, so common everywhere, that at all society gatherings it is much more genteel to appear late upon the scene than at the time appointed, has less reason to justify it when a musicale is the entertainment than at any other entertainment or society event, except a dinner. Music, interrupted by noise, is a failure. The cards of invitation are after this fashion:

> Mrs. Chandos Miller,
>
> At Home,
>
> Thursday, June fifth, at eight o'clock.
>
> 25 Westmoreland Street
>
> Music.

The programs are usually written instead of printed, and are sometimes hand-painted and ribbon-bedecked, and again they are engraved on dainty cards. They are frequently enclosed with the invitations.

If dancing is included, this is the formula:

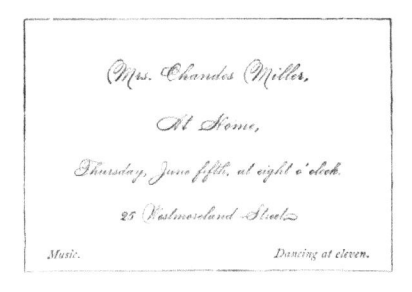

> Mrs. Chandos Miller,
>
> At Home,
>
> Thursday, June fifth, at eight o'clock.
>
> 25 Westmoreland Street
>
> Music.   Dancing at eleven.

If the musicale is for afternoon, it partakes of the nature of the matinée. Bonnets are to be worn. Refreshments are not necessarily served. The afternoon is often selected when noted stars are to sing, since their time is taken up in the evening. The evening musicale, however, is a more brilliant affair.

Replies are to be sent to these invitations, since for any entertainment when all are to be seated, it is a convenience to know the number of the guests.

The drawing-room is cleared of the greater part of its furniture, and, if dancing is to follow, the carpet is covered with canvas, or removed, if there is a hard wood floor. Camp chairs are provided for the guests.

Arrangement of Performers and Guests.

The seating arrangements should present a clear space for the performers. Too close proximity is not conducive to tranquility on the part of the singer, and also spoils the tone effect. Professional singers insist upon sufficient space. Remove all ornaments of breakable china and *bric-a-brac* from the vicinity of the piano, which should be bare of cover, and admit of the lid being easily raised and lowered. A bowl of cracked ice, some tumblers, and a pretty jug of water should be placed upon a table near the piano. Good ventilation should be ensured. A reading or recitation can be introduced into a musical program with good effect, and a long program should be divided by a recess for conversation, and to permit those to retire who do not wish to remain to the end.

If dancing follows, the camp chairs are removed, or placed where they can be used. Supper is also served before the dancing. Cigars, matches and ash trays are usually found in the library by the gentlemen, or the cigars are placed in the cloak room to be smoked on the journey home. Either plan, or their omission altogether, is eminently proper.

A day musicale calls for morning dress for men, and a visiting or walking toilet for women. An evening affair, with dancing, calls for evening dress for both.

LAWN PARTIES.

"A green lawn, a few trees, a fine day, and something to eat are really all the absolute requirements of a garden party." If true, this places the pleasant mode of entertaining our friends in the power of many people of moderate means. In remote country localities these parties are very delightful, particularly if city friends are guests for the Summer.

When properly conducted, a garden party may be given with very little trouble, and made very simple and informal, but if desired may be made elaborate and ceremonious.

When only neighbors are to be entertained, a hasty invitation, so as to be sure of fine weather, may be sent two or three days in advance, but when guests are expected from any distance it is customary to send invitations eight or ten days in advance, as suitable preparations must be made.

These invitations are usually engraved on handsome, plain note paper, and may be in this form.

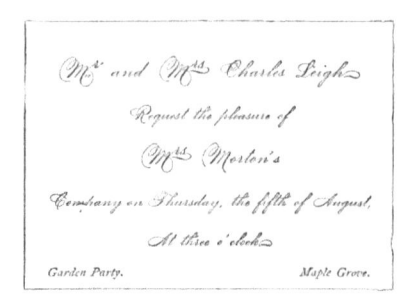

> Mr. and Mrs. Charles Leigh
> Request the pleasure of
> Miss Morton's
> Company on Thursday, the fifth of August,
> At three o'clock
> Garden Party.   Maple Grove.

When guests are to come by rail it is well to send a card stating the hours at which trains arrive and leave the station. Then if carriages are to meet the train, on a card enclosed might be printed: *Carriages will meet the 3.30 train from Union Depot.*

A lady, also, may invite her friends to a garden party by sending her visiting card with "Tennis" or "Garden Party" written in the lower left hand corner, and day and hour in the lower right hand corner, or under her name. It is well sometimes to specify the time of closing.

At a garden party the hostess receives her guests on the lawn, or in the garden, wearing her hat and gloves. But guests should always be invited to the house to take off their wraps, or arrange their toilet if desired. Of course, a maid servant should be in the dressing-room to attend their wants.

The thoughtful hostess will take care to have everything in readiness for the comfort and entertainment of the company. Rugs should be laid on the grass for the accommodation of those not accustomed to standing on the ground, and easy chairs provided for delicate or aged ladies who may be present, so all may enjoy the party without fear of the consequence.

Amusements to be Provided.

Much tact is required to properly entertain guests at a garden party, and prevent them from wandering aimlessly about the grounds. Ample amusements must, therefore, be provided.

The lawn tennis ground must be in perfect order, croquet sets in readiness, archery tools supplied, as well as arrangements for all kinds of suitable games made. Music is a very delightful addition to the pleasure of such an occasion, and should always be had, when practicable.

Ladies wear hats or bonnets at a garden party, and should dress otherwise appropriately. If a plain, informal affair, the dress should be simple and becoming, and if games like lawn tennis or archery are among the amusements, light flannel dresses are suitable. But if invited to a ceremonious lawn party, where style will prevail, handsome though simple toilets are required. Picturesque costumes may be made very effective on the grass and under the trees, and ladies of taste have a fine field for displaying it upon such occasions.

Many very fashionable people conduct the garden party in the style of an afternoon tea, receiving and entertaining their guests in the open air until ready to serve refreshments, when all are invited to the dining-room to partake of them. This mode is very convenient and quite pleasant, though it divests the occasion of much of the novelty and charm belonging to it.

When the refreshments are to be served in the garden or lawn, of course the dishes must all be cold, and may consist of salads, *patés*, pressed meats, Charlottes, jellies, ices, cakes, lemonade and iced tea. A cup of hot tea should always be in readiness in the kitchen for those ladies desiring it.

A LAWN PARTY.

Servants should be well trained when in attendance to prevent confusion. Dishes, knives, forks and spoons should be removed when used, and put in baskets or trays in readiness for them, and a fresh supply brought to replace them.

Tables and Refreshments.

Numbers of small tables, with pretty, fancy covers, and colored napkins, should be set around under trees, near fountains and other suitable places, with camp-stools for the accommodation of guests when partaking of refreshments.

Servants should be very careful in going from place to place with dishes to be served never to spill or drop the contents on ladies' dresses.

Gentlemen may help the ladies, if they prefer, and wait on themselves, requiring the servants only to remove the dishes and replenish the pitchers with lemonade, milk or water.

Fruits, pineapples, strawberries, raspberries, peaches and grapes are served at garden parties, and should be of the finest quality.

Ices are a very acceptable addition to an outdoor entertainment, being light and refreshing for warm weather; they are served in fancy paper cups, laid on ice plates.

For ladies desiring to give garden parties, the following bill of fare will be found sufficient:

>Cold Rolls. Mixed Sandwiches. Brown Bread. Pickled Tongue.
>Pate de foie gras. Jellied Chicken. Cold Birds.
>Lobster Salad. Charlotte Russe. Biscuit. Glaces. Fancy Cakes.
>Fruits.   Lemonade.   Iced Tea.   Strawberry Acid.

In England the refreshments are always served in a *marquee* (large tent) on the lawn.

For such outdoor entertainments foods that require little use of knife and fork should be chosen; sandwiches should never be made of sliced meats as they are awkward to handle. Crusts should be trimmed off, and the filling shredded or grated to a paste, and highly seasoned. For the same reason hot drinks should be dispensed with as far as possible. Glasses are to be filled but two-thirds full. None of these precautions are necessary when the refreshments are served indoors.

For the out-of-doors feast a number of small tables should be provided; cover with fancy cloths and on them place piles of plates alternating with folded napkins, breadbaskets, or trays heaped with sandwiches and buttered tea biscuit, baskets of fancy cakes, and plenty of reserve napkins. Have some of the assistants pass these, beginning with the plates, and to the maidservants leave the service of tea, coffee, cream and sugar (when these are given) and other drinkables.

By this time the gentlemen who first assisted will have been served and the maids can turn their attention to the ices. Ice cream can be served as above, and ices in glass cups; after this the maids can gather up the dishes in baskets. A caterer may be called upon to furnish the feast, in which event all trouble will be spared the hostess. Do not use the best glass and china at these entertainments; the danger of breakage is too great.

At many gatherings a special table is supplied for the gentlemen, where soda-water, claret cup, and sometimes wines are served. The men help themselves, but a manservant is present to supply fresh glasses, etc. This table depends entirely upon the principles of the hostess. If no hours are mentioned, the guests usually disperse about dusk, unless dancing is provided for those who wish to stay and enjoy it.

Seats.

The business of providing seats is a comparatively trifling affair when there are to be young people present, who prefer clean turf or the piazza steps to any more luxurious lounging place. For the older guests, less unconventional accommodations may be devised. Light rockers, camp chairs, wooden or wicker settees are pretty, and in harmony with the rustic nature of the reception. It is well, also, to have rugs or strips of carpet laid about, for the benefit of those who dread the dampness that some imagine rises from the ground even in the midst of the most obstinate drought. Cushions are invaluable at such times, whether used as footstools for the more delicate guests, to soften porch steps, or to convert stumps and grassy knolls into divans, for those who like low seats, but yet have a due regard for their bones or dresses.

A charming, and thoroughly rustic style of seat, can be formed of dry, sweet hay. Tossed up in generous piles, to make couches, or heaped against the trunks of trees to simulate arm chairs, they provide resting places that are not only luxurious, but uncommon. The costliest upholsterer can furnish no chairs or sofas more softly padded or more deliciously perfumed than these. With rugs or shawls thrown over them, to guard the garments of their occupants from any possible injury from moisture or from crushed insects, they are all that the most fastidious could demand.

Hammocks, also furnished with cushions, are always comfortable and picturesque, while screens are valuable additions to the furniture of this open-air drawing-room. Covered with cretonne, felt or paper of any shape and size, these are almost indispensable for shielding from draughts in breezy weather, or sheltering from obtrusive sunlight on a sultry day.

Lawn Parties for Charity.

In case of a charitable object, the refreshments are disposed of at reasonable prices. In this case the menu should be restricted to a few articles. Berries, ice cream and cake are frequently sufficient; coffee can be added. Dainty buttonhole bouquets should also be provided and sold to the gentlemen for prices in advance of their value. Afterward, with the piazza for a stage, a little program of music, singing and recitations can be carried out.

At any garden party, music and singing are in order, and at very grand affairs, paid musicians of note are engaged. Orchestras also are frequently somewhere on the grounds.

BREAKFASTS, LUNCHEONS AND TEAS.

A BREAKFAST or a luncheon is somewhat less formal than a dinner and, hence, so much the more delightful.

The breakfast party includes both gentlemen and ladies while, as a rule, the luncheon is an entertainment given to ladies. The invitations to a breakfast may be written, engraved or verbal. If a large number of guests are invited to meet some distinguished stranger, engraved invitations are issued.

Five days or a week's notice is usually considered sufficient, but if distinguished wits and scholars are to be secured, it is well to give a longer period, since their time, always in demand, should be bespoken well in advance. A reply to the invitation is a necessity, because the hostess wishes time, in case of non-acceptance, to secure another guest.

Where the breakfast is less stately in character, an informal note, written by the hostess, in the first person, is a pleasant method, or simply written on the lady's visiting cards under the name in this form: Breakfast, Tuesday, ten o'clock, February fifteenth.

Artificial light is out of place, and sunshine should flood the apartment, while a certain airiness and daintiness should pervade the table appointments, quite the opposite of the elaborate display that characterizes the dinner party. Flowers should form the decorations of the table. Breakfast parties are a very convenient mode of social entertainment for those whose limited means will not admit of a more extensive display of hospitality.

Ten o'clock is the usual hour, though it may be as late as twelve, thus differing from the luncheon, which is never earlier than one.

Breakfast parties are a favorite reunion with literary people, who generally take the morning hours for leisure, leaving brain work until later in the day. Sidney Smith said he liked breakfasts, "because no man was conceited before one o'clock in the day."

In serving breakfast the bill of fare, unless for special occasions, should never be elaborate, but rather dainty and attractive, as the appetite usually needs tempting at this early hour; fewer courses of a more delicate variety should be served than at other meals. The hostess dispenses the coffee, tea and chocolate from the head of the table; the substantials are set in front of the host, who may help the plates and hand them to the waiter to serve; the vegetables and other dishes may be handed from the side table.

Concerning the Viands.

It is well-bred to serve the breakfast with as little formality as possible, and with as few attendants; one servant, a maid, or man servant is sufficient unless the party is unusually large.

If grape-fruit be used for a first course, or orange skins filled with juice, a wreath of smilax on each plate makes a pretty decoration.

A breakfast should invariably begin with fruit, followed by a course of eggs. This latter is one of the essentials, and offers a greater variety than is perhaps known outside of France. A Spanish omelette, if properly made, is a thing to be treasured among the "pleasures of memory." Stuffed eggs, or hard boiled eggs cut in slices, with a bechamel or white sauce, are appropriate and generally liked. A fish course, an entrée, one meat, a salad and a sweet course should follow next in order, concluding with coffee. The entrée and the meat may form one course, if a slice of duck with olives, fried chicken or some such dish be selected.

Ices of all kinds are entirely out of place at a breakfast. An omelette soufflée, peaches with cream, or best of all a fruit salad, are within the proprieties. This last never fails to call forth enthusiastic appreciation. It is simply made, and keeps perfectly for two or three days. Half a dozen oranges should be peeled, leaving no particle of the white adhering, and then cut in small pieces. Half a ripe pineapple, broken with a fork into bits and sugared to taste, and four bananas sliced, are mixed with the oranges, and the whole put on ice for three or four hours. This will be found a dish rivalling the ambrosia of high Olympus.

With the first course of fruit, finger-bowls are in readiness, but are removed at its close. Hot breads and breakfast cakes are always suitable, and oatmeal, carefully cooked and served with thick cream and powdered sugar, often follows the fruit. The closing course should be hot cakes served with honey or maple syrup.

If there are ladies present, or the hostess presides, the coffee, chocolate, etc., are poured by her, and after the first course she asks the guests when they will have it served.

The following will be found an acceptable bill of fare for an ordinary breakfast party. It can of course be varied to suit the convenience and taste of housekeepers.

Bill of Fare for Breakfast.

Melons. Grapes. Oranges. Fried Perch with Sauce Tartare.
Young Chickens with Cream Gravy. Saratoga Potatoes.
Poached Eggs on Toast. Broiled Quails. Baked Mushrooms.

Tomatoes or Celery. Bread and Butter.
Crackers. Hot Cakes. Coffee. Tea. Chocolate.

If a butler serves at a breakfast he does not wear full dress as at a dinner.

Wedding Breakfast Menu.

A menu that would be easy to prepare for a wedding breakfast would be two hot dishes consisting of chicken croquettes, lobster cutlets, oyster patties or creamed oysters. Everything else might be cold and as follows: salad, either chicken or lobster, pickled oysters, a small wedding cake, little cakes for the bridesmaids, Charlotte russe and coffee. The table decorations should either be all white, or the colors used in the bridesmaids' costumes. Let the waitresses be dressed in white.

The simplest costume is in good taste for breakfast parties. Men wear morning dress, and ladies handsome but plain street costumes. Gloves are removed before going to the table. Bonnets are kept on.

Each gentleman is given the escort of a lady. The host conducts the lady who is the most distinguished guest to the table, and the hostess follows last with the gentleman whom it is desired to honor particularly.

Upon entering the dining-room the ladies are assisted to their seats, and the gentlemen then follow, and the meal is served. The signal for rising from the table is given by the hostess, with a smile and simple bow, and all proceed to the parlor, exchange a few pleasant remarks, and take their leave.

For informal breakfasts no after-call is expected, but for ceremonious entertainments of this kind the same observance of the rules of etiquette are required as for dinners and large parties.

Guests should not remain more than half an hour after leaving the table, and many do not even return to the drawing-room.

A Bachelor Breakfast.

If a breakfast has been given by a gentleman to ladies and gentlemen, the lady who chaperones it and presides as hostess, receives all the attentions of a lady in her own home. The host calls upon her soon after the event, and also calls upon his lady guests. Gentlemen usually give their breakfasts at fashionable hotels or restaurants.

A Golden-Rod Breakfast.

This is a pretty country entertainment. It can be given out of doors under wide-spreading trees. For the one in mind, great roots of golden-rod were dug up and transplanted into jardinieres (stone jars in this case) and a hedge of the nodding yellow plumes placed all about.

The carpet was of checkered sunshine and shade, and the green canopy of the leaves made the scene a perfect one. The guests, arriving at ten o'clock, were ushered into the rustic breakfast room. Four tables were used. On one pure white damask napery was enlivened by low baskets of maidenhair fern, and sprays of the same delicate plant tied with baby ribbon of green gave a cool look to the whole. The largest table was resplendent with cut glass vases filled with golden-rod. White asters gave a hint of autumn's snow to the third table, and the ingenuity of the hostess found pleasure in decorating the remaining one with the delicate grasses and rich-colored small fruits of autumn. Gold-banded china, cut glass and silver, which had been in the family for three generations, supplemented the floral charms of the tables.

Choice Blending of Colors.

Autumn and yellow were the main ideas which guided the selection of the menu for this golden-rod breakfast. Everything possible was in the yellow tint or rich golden brown. With plenty of cream and fresh eggs and the fresh fruits of the farm to work with the menu was an easy one to furnish. Ices served in the shape of tiny melons and cakes decorated with frosted sugar. As a memento of the feast each guest retained her name card which bore a spray of pressed golden-rod fastened with narrow yellow ribbon, and on it in golden script a verse with some thought suggested by autumn or the flower.

Tiny garden hats of yellow straw, filled with golden-rod, accompanied the name cards. The golden-rod in itself proved a veritable gold mine as a help to conversation. Discussions as to whether or not it should be chosen as the national flower; descriptions by travelers of where they had seen it growing best, bright quotations of favorite authors leading to discussions of poems or books by these authors, anecdotes of travel all followed each other and naturally, led by the clever hostess who, in her quaint gown of yellow, with golden rod in her belt and a spray tucked close to the wide tortoise shell comb which held her golden hair, looked like the personification of the flower she had honored at her breakfast.

Wine at a breakfast is optional. If used, two varieties are enough, and should be in keeping with the principal dishes; claret, sherry, Burgundy are suitable.

LUNCHEONS.

A luncheon is usually an entertainment given by a woman to women. From whatever cause, luncheon parties are rapidly gaining popularity among us. Macaulay wrote, "Dinner parties are mere formalities, but you invite a man to breakfast because you want to see him," and the same may apply to luncheon parties for ladies, these being almost exclusively their affair.

Invitations to small luncheons are usually very informal, and may be written in the style of a familiar note of friendship; or a visiting card may be used, underneath the name of which is simply written: Luncheon at one o'clock, Thursday, January eight.

The repast may be elaborately made up of salads, oysters, small game, chocolate, ices and a variety of dishes which will destroy the appetite for dinner, or it may simply consist of a cup of tea or chocolate, thin sliced bread and butter, chip beef or cold tongue, but there is the same opportunity to display good taste and a well-appointed table as at a grander entertainment.

Ladies attend formal luncheons in very elegant street or carriage costumes. They wear rich and becoming bonnets, which they do not take off. They appear with gloves, removing them when seated at the table.

The toilet of the hostess may be as elegant as she wishes, anything, in fact, short of an actual evening costume.

Luncheons of ceremony are sometimes given in honor of distinguished guests, or upon special occasions, instead of dinners, and may then be very stylish affairs. Flowers should be artistically arranged, both for the adornment of the parlor and dining-room and the table more sumptuous, though always dainty; broiled delicacies, such as do not require carving, take the place of joints, and too rich dishes, with salads, oysters, croquettes and ices; bouillon is very generally served at large or small lunches, as is also chocolate with whipped cream.

Tea is not expected to be present on these occasions. Coffee, served without cream after luncheon in the prettiest little cups the hostess can muster, is generally at hand.

The table may be decorated with flowers and fruit as a centerpiece, around which should be placed glass dishes of fancy cakes, and bon-bons.

At very formal luncheons each dish is served as a separate course. Instead of coffee being served in the drawing-room, as after dinner, the hostess dispenses it at the luncheon table.

The invitations to fashionable, elaborate luncheons should be handsomely engraved after the following style:

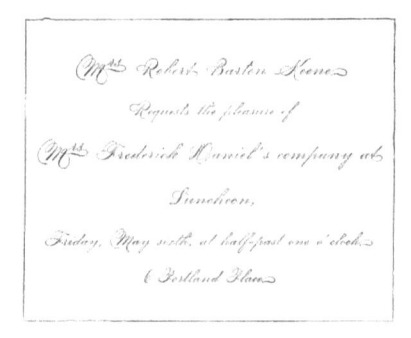

> Mrs. Robert Barton Keene
> Requests the pleasure of
> Mrs. Frederick Daniel's company at
> Luncheon,
> Friday, May sixth, at half-past one o'clock.
> 1 Portland Place

The toilets of the ladies attending should be elegant, and always appropriate to the occasion.

The hostess usually leads the way to the table, keeping the most distinguished guest at her right, the others following and seating themselves as they choose. Guests are not expected to remain longer than half an hour after they return to the parlors.

Calls are a polite acknowledgment after receiving hospitalities, and should be made within a few days after the entertainment.

If gentlemen are invited, and the master of the house is present, the guests proceed to the dining-room in the same order as at a formal dinner party. If the luncheon is given in honor of some particular individual, this fact should appear upon the invitation. The following is a good form:

> Mrs. Vincent
> Requests the pleasure of your company at luncheon,
> On Tuesday, February fifth,
> To meet
> Genevieve Gallatin.
> One o'clock.   1807 Chestnut Street.

The rooms are usually darkened for an elaborate luncheon, and artificial lighting resorted to. Wax candles are the most pleasing, their radiance having a softening effect.

Nowadays there are candles in the market warranted not to drip, and made not wholly of wax, but of some composition which burns brilliantly and slowly. They average eight to the pound, and cost something like twenty-five or thirty cents a pound. No light is so satisfactory or so becoming as candlelight. When the great question of illumination and flowers is settled, there remains one more opportunity for individual taste, for bon-bons, salted almonds and olives may be disposed here and there in small dishes of cut glass or silver.

The usual hour at which to take leave after luncheon is three o'clock, and, unless pressed to do so, luncheon guests should not remain beyond this hour, thus avoiding any inconvenience to a hostess in the matter of her afternoon engagements. Of course, the hour of leaving depends on the hour at which the luncheon is given.

Luncheon Refreshments.

The refreshments must not be heavy, for the reason that many of the guests may be expecting to attend a dinner or evening party that same day. If a butler serves at a luncheon he does not wear full dress, as at a dinner party.

Only light wines are offered at a ladies' luncheon, and more frequently none at all. Mineral waters and pure water are supplied.

Entering the Dining-Room.

Ladies who are intimate with the hostess often arrive half an hour before the time set for the luncheon and chat with the hostess. Usually there is no formality in entering the dining-room. The hostess leads the way with the honored guest, if there be one, on her right. The ladies go down together, talking as they go. If there are gentlemen present, they follow. Once there, they seat themselves at random, with the exception of the host and hostess, who seat themselves at the head and foot of the table.

Again, it may happen that the guests, when they reach the table, find name cards at each plate to designate the place to occupy. These often are simple bits of pasteboard with a gilded edge which the hostess buys and writes thereon her guests' names. This is especially the case if other favors are given.

Where the luncheon is very informal the entire menu frequently consists of cold dishes, such as boned turkey, boned ham, raw oysters, salads of all kinds, chickens, fruits, fruit salad, Bavarian cream, or other creams, fancy cakes, *pate de foie gras*, etc. The coffee is hot. Let the hand of the caterer be kept as much as possible out of luncheon.

Lunch or Luncheon.

There has been much questioning as to the distinction between the words "lunch" and "luncheon," which are often used interchangeably. The latest and best definition would be, that a lunch is a meal to be partaken of informally by the members of a household, at midday or before going on some pleasure excursion. Luncheon, on the contrary, signifies a form of entertainment given after breakfast and before the evening dinner hour. It is a meal of compliment and more frequently extended to ladies alone.

The invitations given for a luncheon are issued on the same principle as those for a breakfast. A young performer, vocalist or elocutionist, is often introduced at a luncheon.

Luncheon Favors.

Favors for a luncheon may be very elegant, or only simple and pretty. A single rose laid at each plate is frequently all that is given. Name cards are often made to serve as souvenirs. A very new and pretty design for a name card is made of a plain white or cream square envelope, painted with a dainty design of violets.

Where the name is to be seen, an opening like that of a picture frame is cut through the face of the envelope, a line of narrow gilding finishing the edge. The name of the guest is written on a plain card and put inside the envelope so as to show through the opening.

Some other small graceful flower in place of the violet is sometimes painted on it with good effect; and if one color, as yellow, for instance, predominates in the table decoration, a design of jonquils or buttercups is chosen.

A cardboard rest is tied in at the top of these envelope cards by a narrow ribbon caught through two little slits in the envelope over the one in the rest itself. They are then stood around the table like dainty little picture frames, which in reality they are, making the most charming souvenirs when taken home and a small photograph substituted for the card with the name on it.

Some quaint and pretty conceit is always sought after for favors. Too expensive articles suggest a desire for display. Painted satin bags or other fancy receptacles, filled with choice confectionery, are always acceptable, especially at a ladies' luncheon. If the satin bag can be turned into an opera bag, so much the better. Tiny baskets, purchased for a trifle, and metamorphosed by means of a little gold paint, and a bow of ribbon on the handle, into dainty flower-holders, are also pretty. Hand-painted book covers are suitable, and, again, fans are much admired. Those of Japanese style can be bought reasonably.

Favors for gentlemen, such as fancy pocket pincushions, small coin purses, scarfpins, sleeve-buttons, etc., are more useful than ladies' favors, but not so ornamental on the table. A pair of oars, artistically carved, are appropriate for the athletic-minded. Silk handkerchiefs with initials are also proper. Little silver *bonbonnieres* are nice for women, and silver matchboxes for men.

Some Betrothal Luncheons.

The bride-elect entertains her girl friends at luncheon, and revives all the old innocent superstitions to add merriment and interest to the occasion, notable among them the ring baked in the cake, the chance recipient of which will be first to wear the orange blossoms.

One of the prettiest of these luncheons was given on occasion of the announcement of the betrothal of the young hostess, and a veritable "feast of roses" was the result. As was proper, everything was *couleur de rose*—even the light in which the guests saw each other shone through dainty candle shades formed wholly of pink silk rose petals.

The central *epergne*, holding a luscious mass of bridemaids' roses, was laid on a circle of filmy, transparent "bolting cloth," the edge of which was embroidered with a wreath of pink roses of natural size and varied shades. Even the salt was contained "in the heart of a rose"— tiny little porcelain affairs—originally intended for candlesticks, but now appropriately used for the symbol of hospitality.

Dresden cupids, in pretty and artistic poses, held dishes filled with candied rose leaves and heart-shaped cakes covered with pink icing.

A wreath of paper roses surrounded the drop-light above the table; the ladies' names were written on rose-petals (of cardboard), the sorbet was in the form of pink roses and flavored with the cordial *parfait amour*, while the ice cream repeated the design, and was served in a garden hat of straw-colored candy wreathed with natural roses. The human flowers around the table against such a background of "sweetness and light" made the scene one to be remembered.

Blue and White Tableware.

A contrast to the foregoing (which was, perhaps, rather suggestive of languors and luxury) was a dainty, prim little luncheon, where the table decorations were all of the soft delf, blue and white.

The centerpiece held bluets and "marguerites," that carried one's thoughts far afield, and brought memories of flower-scented breezes and of joys, healthful, pure and vivifying.

The service was entirely of blue and white delf china, and the quaint candelabra, of like material, were decorated with crimped paper candle shades repeating the same colors. Under the dish holding the flowers was a square of linen embroidered in blue. The design was an exact copy of that on the china.

The candlelight merely illuminated the little shades and added to the effectiveness of the decorations, but its pale beams were lost in the sunshine that streamed into the room and lighted up the intelligent faces of the women about the table.

Each guest read on the reverse side of her name card a little rhyming assurance of her welcome. For instance:

"If wishes were dishes,

These should be so rare,

You would vow that you never

Had tasted such fare!

"If wishes were riches,

A feast should be spread

That would tempt old Lucullus

To rise from the dead.

"But, since wishing is vain,

Take the will for the deed,

And the warmest of welcomes

I offer instead."

A Dresden Luncheon.

A Dresden luncheon is a dainty and flowery style of entertainment for springtime, that is considered a more perfect combination of the exquisite and the elegant than any artistic gathering yet seen. The keynote is the blending everywhere upon the table of the delicate Dresden china colors, blue, pink, yellow and violet.

The fine flowers seen upon the royal china are scattered in embroidery over the linen centerpiece; on this stands a Dresden bowl holding an old-fashioned nosegay of pink rosebuds, hothouse daisies with their yellow centers, pansies and heliotrope. These are tied loosely together with a bow of blue ribbon, which gives the needed touch of that color, unless one is able to get natural forget-me-nots or some other fine blue flowers, like scillas. A few airy and smaller bunches of the same flowers, in little cut-glass stands, are placed about the table. The candelabra have pink rose shades.

The finger-bowl mats are embroidered to match the Dresden flower centerpiece, and floating in the water of the bowls are the different flowers—a few rose petals in one, a daisy in another and a pansy in another until each has one. Every cup, saucer, plate or dish used is of Dresden china, the greater the variety of their shapes the prettier.

The ice cream is served in small satin cases, in the different pale colors, blue, pink, violet and yellow. When boxes in these colors cannot be procured plain white is used. On the top of each is tied a little bunch of satin flowers composed of tiny pink rosebuds, blue forget-me-nots, a daisy, a bit of heliotrope, or a few violets.

At the place of each guest is a name card, done in the Dresden design. The cards are made of water-colors paper and the design painted in water-color. The color of the painted ribbon bows in the designs given varies in the different cards in blue, pink, yellow and violet, and where the loop ends extend over the edge they are cut out, making the ribbon look more realistic.

The sign of all Dresdenware from the royal factories is the tiny blue crossed swords on the reverse or bottom of the dish, without which no piece is genuine; so on the back of the cards one must be sure to paint the sword sign in just the right shade of old blue, thus making complete the idea of a veritable feast of royal Dresden.

CONCERNING TEAS.

The distinction between five o'clock teas, kettledrums, afternoon receptions and high tea, is not very clearly drawn. Strictly speaking, the afternoon or morning reception is the most formal, and has been dwelt upon in a former chapter.

High Tea.

This is really the evening supper, which has also been described in detail, although sometimes the "high tea" is spread for an earlier hour than the supper, say seven or eight o'clock. The ladies come in visiting costume, and the gentlemen in morning dress in country towns. In cities, sometimes, dress coats and light gowns are considered essential. Guests are expected to spend the evening.

Where there are two rooms, such as dining-room and parlor, or two parlors, the tables can be laid in one room, while the guests are assembling in the other. Often, however, the hostess can command but one large room in which to entertain her friends. In this case, the little tables can be brought in by a servant and spread in the presence of the guests without the least breach of propriety. After the meal is over, the dishes are quickly carried out on trays and the tables either taken from the room or left where they stand for cards or any of the many pencil-and-paper games that are pleasant at such gatherings.

One waitress, if quick and deft, can readily wait on a dozen people, especially if all the necessary articles for changing the courses, plates, silver, etc., are arranged on a side table in the room or outside the door.

There are many attractive menus that can be suggested for teas, but the following seems to demand as little home labor for satisfactory results as any other. The word *tea*, by the way, is something of a misnomer, as at these entertainments the beverages are almost invariably coffee or chocolate, or both, tea being left entirely out of the question.

Menu.

Bouillon. Bread. Crackers. Celery. Pickled Oysters.
Chicken Salad. Peanut Sandwiches. Olives. Salted Almonds.
Chocolate. Coffee. Ice Cream. Fancy Cakes. Fruit.

Serve the bouillon in cups, and be sure that it is *very* hot. Have a thin slice of lemon floating on the surface of each cup. Pass crackers (the Zephyr or Snowflake brands are best,) with this, and choice blanched celery. If the tables are set before the guests arrive, it is well to have a couple of short stalks of celery laid at each plate and spare that amount of waiting. Have each cup and saucer set in a plate, and take all three pieces off at once. Either tea or coffee cups may be used, and it is, of course, unnecessary to have them match.

The pickled oysters, with not too much liquor, may either be served on the same plate with the salad or separately. Glass or china dishes may hold the salad and oysters. Forks should be used with this course. The sandwiches must be neatly piled on fringed napkins on bread plates, and must be passed several times, and the olives and salted almonds may fill small glass dishes. The olives may be helped with a fork or spoon or with the fingers, the almonds may be served with spoons. The coffee and chocolate should be poured out at a side table, and sugar and cream passed with them to each person.

The ice cream should also be served off the table and passed in the plate or saucer from which it is to be eaten. The cakes should be prettily arranged in a cake dish with a doily under them. The fruit should be placed on a flat salver, as high piled dishes are apt to be top-heavy and difficult to pass. Oranges, bananas, grapes, the last cut into rather small bunches, make a pretty array. Each guest must be supplied with a fruit plate, doily, finger-bowl, fruit-knife and fork or spoon. Souvenirs are sometimes given, or attractive menu cards are used.

Five O'clock Teas, or "At Homes."

Some ladies make it a point to be "at home" almost every day at a certain hour, and serve tea or coffee in their drawing-rooms, accompanied by either wafers, maccaroons, fancy cakes, or small delicate sandwiches, and perhaps bouillon for masculine callers.

Such a lady who is bright and interesting, who gives a warm welcome, yet does not bind any one to a longer stay than the conventional ten minutes, is sure of drawing about her a delightful circle of acquaintances, men and women alike being pleased to drop in on their way home from the city, or from more pretentious gatherings.

This is the afternoon tea in its simplest form. In London afternoon tea is universal. If you are calling anywhere in the latter part of the afternoon, tea and thin bread and butter will be offered you as a matter of course, or if it has already been handed round, you will be asked if you have had your tea, and if not a fresh supply will be immediately brought.

If bread is thin enough, butter fresh, cake good, and tea and coffee perfection, you have provided all that is necessary. In warm weather ices or strawberries could be added. In England you will very seldom be given more than this at the best houses, and in Italy, where the afternoon receptions are the most agreeable entertainments imaginable, you will never be offered anything more than dainty little cakes, chocolate and tea. These slight refreshments are usually served in the simplest way. The hostess herself, or if the guests are numerous a white-capped *bonne* or two, pours out the tea and chocolate and the men of the party hand it to the ladies. Often the children of the house flit to and fro, carrying cups of tea or plates of cake, and everybody talks to everybody else. There will be the best pictures on the walls or the easels, often the best music from people the world knows well, and a reception thus simple in point of refreshment, but rich in the pleasures of art, is a memorable delight.

Still other ladies are at home on some one afternoon in each week, and announce that fact on their cards under their names as follows: Thursdays in February. Tea at Four O'clock. Or, if for a single occasion, it may read thus: Four O'clock Tea. Tuesday, February Fifth. Or, MRS. GEORGE GREEN, Five O'clock Tea. Tuesday, January Fifth. 47 Sussex Place. Or, MRS. GEORGE GREEN. Thursdays. Four to Seven. 47 Sussex Place. The year, or P. M., should not appear on the card.

These invitations require no answer, and no after calls, since really it is nothing more than a grand calling day. Those who cannot attend, call as soon as convenient, and those who come leave cards in the hall. Walking or carriage costumes are worn. Men wear morning dress. The hostess dons a handsome reception gown, never an evening dress. The young ladies who assist her are prettily clad in fabrics that suit the season, but which must not suggest ball toilet.

The simple refreshments served must be the very best of their kind. This style of afternoon tea is suitable for city or suburban life.

The Five O'clock Tea Table.

Beginning with the table itself, it may be a small oval, circular or hexagon shape. Any one of these is preferable to a square one. If the surface of the table is highly polished and it is preferred not to cover it entirely, a handsome square or round centerpiece doily, which is only a dinner centerpiece, is used, or a teacloth a yard square may prettily and wholly veil it.

For the actual furnishing of the table there are required a tea caddy, teapot, a hot water kettle, a cosy, a wafer or cracker dish, two or three pretty cups and saucers, cream jug and sugar bowl.

To measure the tea with a spoon is not considered quite so correct, and so redolent of the old-time flavor as to use the cup-cover of the caddy, "one fill to a brew." A glass mat may be provided to set the hot teapot upon, and the spoons are laid loose upon the table.

Cups should hold more than an actual thimbleful, though they need not hold a pint, and should bear some relation to the laws of gravitation in their poise upon the saucer. They should have a smooth rim. A fluted edge is a most uncomfortable finish for a drinking vessel. The wafer-basket may be silver, china or cut glass.

For the winter months many hostesses have introduced a variety on the menu of the five o'clock tea table. Tea is a doubtful beverage in many hands, and is wholly abjured by many women as injurious to the complexion, hence a big, egg-shaped urn, beneath which a tiny alcohol jet burns, is set up in the corner of the drawing-room. The urn is filled with chicken bouillon, served piping hot in small silver cups, and with an invigorating dash of sherry for those who prefer it so. With the bouillon are served platters of toasted water biscuit that have been sparingly buttered and lightly sprinkled with salt. Sometimes, in place of salt, a powdering of cheese is grated over the hot cracker, and for a relish at five o'clock nothing could be preferable to this light, warm repast. Men, it is well to remark, heartily advocate the change from insipid tea to the invigorating hot bouillon.

Pages.

The special innovation for the benefit of women are two drawing-room pages. These are small, well-trained little boys in buttons, livery or done up in slippers, white linen and turbans, who at intervals of fifteen minutes carry about among the callers large lacquer trays, on which are spread violets and rose leaves, crystallized and salted nuts with ginger. One is supposed to scoop up a few of the confections or nuts as the pages pass.

Receiving Friends.

Those friends invited to pour tea or chocolate also come at the hour named, and after removing their wraps seat themselves at their particular tables, or at their end of the one long table. It is their duty to dispense, besides the cups that cheer, words and smiles that cheer also to every one who comes, no matter whether they know them or not. Usually they can do much to make it lively for all in their immediate vicinity. If the afternoon is a long one and guests numerous several of the receiving party volunteer to relieve those at the urns, and they spend an hour pleasantly about the rooms and beside the hostess.

These are the kindly things expected of a woman who accepts an invitation "to receive," and when she has done them gracefully and prettily she is a social "sister of mercy."

If the number of guests is small the hostess herself frequently serves, with perhaps her daughter or some friend, to assist.

The Eatables.

The tea, with its pretty equipage, is placed on the table by her side; sometimes chocolate is provided, and occasionally a crystal pitcher of milk for any who may desire it. Some very thin sandwiches (rolled ones are better), a silver basket of sweet biscuit and one of mixed fancy cakes, form an all-sufficient menu. A small cluster of flowers in a slender vase and the table is complete.

Friends greet one another, drink a social cup of tea, chat a little, and that is all. Formal leave-taking is not expected.

Sliced lemon should be at hand for any who prefer the creamless, sugarless Russian tea with a slice of lemon floating on its ambertide.

Some ladies invite several young girls to help serve and entertain, and, in the eyes of the masculine half of creation, this adds greatly to the beauty of the picture; for ever since tea became famous in our society, men have found much to admire in a girl who can serve it gracefully.

A kettledrum and an elaborate five o'clock tea are precisely the same form of entertainment. The term "kettledrum" is not very frequently used.

Some of the guests at "at homes" have so little judgment in the matter of departure that experience never serves them in good stead. They are nervous and vacillating when they should be neither; they linger and know not how to get themselves gracefully away, and usually succeed in making an abrupt exit. They know the right moment at which to leave, but fail to put this knowledge into practice. "Almost think it is time to go now," or "I wonder whether I ought to say good-bye or wait until some one else comes in."

The regulation conventional time for a call on an "at home" day is about twenty minutes, but this can be lengthened out to half an hour or forty minutes, circumstances being favorable, or shortened to ten minutes when the position is distinctly unfavorable to a longer stay.

"Bringing Out" a Debutante.

The "bringing out" of a *débutante* at an afternoon tea has become, because of its simplicity, a favorite method. It affords opportunity to invite a number of young "rosebuds" to cluster about her, and it does not subject the "bud" to the ordeal of a ceremonious, or large, ball.

The *débutante's* name will be engraved below that of her mother, on at "At Home" card.

If she be the eldest daughter, her name is written MISS MANNING. If she have elder sisters, it is MISS AMY MAY MANNING.

No answer is expected to these cards, but each recipient will note the especial significance of the occasion by leaving cards in the hall for her as well as her mother, and, if the invitation be not accepted, they will send or leave cards within a few days, for both her and her mother.

An elaborate afternoon tea is often given in honor of some stranger, when the cards will read as follows: MRS. JAMES LADD, At Home, Tuesday, March Tenth, from Four until Seven o'clock, to meet MRS. GORDON BENNET. 5 South Fiftieth street.

This would indicate a daytime, but not usually a day-lighted assembly, and means flowers, gaslight and music; elaborate costumes as may be without infringing on actual evening dress, and refreshments, all too abundant for those who expect a dinner to follow.

Ladies leave outer wraps in hall, or dressing-room, but do not remove their bonnets. Gentlemen who expect to spend but a few moments, carry their hats with them into the drawing-room.

The table is made attractive with beautiful linen, china, and silver, and salads and oysters, ices and cake turn this entertainment from a simple afternoon tea into a "high tea." The tea-room is never deserted, and, although servants are in attendance, there are young girls to pour the tea and add the charm of their presence to the hour.

Dancing even is suggested by the enchanting waltz music that floats from some hidden nook, and a hostess with a sufficiently spacious home often provides a room for this amusement, gentlemen and ladies who wish to participate, disposing of their wraps in the dressing-room.

Gentlemen Visitors.

These occasions usually capture more men than any other daytime gathering. They attend in Prince Albert (frock) coat, neat scarf, faultless gloves, perfect-fitting shoes, and unexceptionable hat. They need not remain long, they need not talk much, and they are sure to find some few that they recognize; and besides, in the best society, the theory of non-introduction gives each person the privilege of conversing with anyone present. Yet, hostesses who are strong in their social positions are not afraid to introduce people who meet under their roof, or to express pleasure that you took the time to call. Such a hostess brightens and warms the atmosphere, and the busy, tired man, who does not usually enjoy such affairs, will enjoy coming to her house and will come again.

How to Leave.

When the drawing-room is crowded it is possible to leave without saying adieu to the hostess, and good form does nor necessitate the hostess to ask anyone to call again.

An Afternoon Tea-Saucer.

A convenience that any victim of the afternoon tea will appreciate is a tray or elongated saucer, oval in shape. At one end is a rest made of gold wire, in which the cup stands. The other is quite large enough to allow of serving sandwiches, biscuit, or even a bit of salad without burdening the guest with a second object to hold. The cup stands firm in its place. Not even the jostling common in a crowded room will displace it or endanger that breakage which so often follows a crush. The tray is easily held in one hand, and the other is free to handle fork or spoon without inconvenience of the smallest sort.

Pretty teapots for the five o'clock tea table are of rosewood in a pinkish brown and in the usual olive coloring. The handles of the lids are butterflies, and a butterfly is on the handle used for pouring. Some of these elegant little pots are overlaid with a tracery of silver. Teapots intended for Easter favors are of brown porcelain in the form of a chicken with the mouth doing duty for the spout.

"Pink and Blue Teas."

These have been a great "fad," and while not quite so popular, are pretty enough to deserve mention. A table is too often confused in its arrangement of color on account of its changes of courses. This can be entirely done away with by adopting some simple color scheme. A luncheon, or tea, is easier to serve in this fashion because of its simpler menu.

Amber and white will harmonize with celery, salads, ices and other articles needed at a luncheon. The yellowish white, full of sunlight, harmonizes with amber and can be followed up to deepest bronze. Amber glasses, creamy damask, all the tints from white to bronze, can be used in the dishes. Apricots heaped on amber dishes, ices tinted in harmony, and a great mass of white roses for a center ornament, are appropriate.

Another beautiful effect is to do away with the cloth and let the polished wood of the table set the keynote of color. An oak table, with its rich yellows and browns and its lurking suggestions of green, would afford a color scheme with which all shades of amber, bronze and yellow would blend. *Bon Silène* or *Malmaison* roses would also be in harmony with the other decorations.

MISCELLANEOUS ENTERTAINMENTS.

COFFEES are so exactly like teas, with the exception that coffee is the reigning beverage, that extended description is unnecessary. The invitations are precisely the same as for teas, simply substituting the word, "Coffee," or "Kaffee Klatsch" in the corner of the card instead of "Tea." The German term, "Kaffee Klatsch," is frequently used. This, literally translated, would be "Coffee Chat" or "Gossip." The entertainment is of German origin, and was adopted to fit the fiction that the stronger sex, of whom the lateness of the hour captures many a willing or unwilling victim, do not revel in tea.

Chocolataire.

This is rather a new entertainment. Its novelty lies in the fact that the beverage served is chocolate, and that chocolate enters into all the refreshments served, such as chocolate wafers, etc. A chocolate lemonade will be a nice addition in hot weather, chocolate bon-bons being passed in dainty silver bon-bon baskets.

The cards are the same as for "Teas" and "Coffees," simply substituting the word "Chocolataire" or "Chocolate" in the left hand corner.

If this is used, as it sometimes is, for a church or charitable entertainment, cards are not issued, but it is simply announced through the usual channels as a "Chocolataire," and numerous other refreshments all containing chocolate in some form can be dispensed, chocolate ice cream, chocolate cake, etc.

Theater parties may be made into very elaborate entertainments, or they may be simple and quietly arranged. Ladies and families often give these parties as an easy method of repaying their social debts.

But the theater party is the entertainment, par excellence, dear to bachelor hosts, especially those who have no homes of their own to which they may invite guests, and wish to return some of the many courteous hospitalities of which they have been the recipients.

In one of these elaborate affairs the host first secures some popular lady to chaperon the party. Then he calls upon his florist, makes arrangements with some famous restaurant and pays a visit to the box-office of some theater where a new play is to be brought out in ten days or two weeks.

Invitations for Theater Parties.

He then gives the invitations in person to the selected number of his lady friends, not less than six, not more than fifteen, explaining to the mothers who will chaperon the party and what gentlemen he has invited. These must number the same as his lady guests and will have been chosen from among the most eligible of his friends.

The rendezvous will be at the restaurant where dinner will be served at six o'clock. The young ladies attended by father, brother or a maid, come in carriages and the coachman is told at what hour to return. This is usually half past twelve or one o'clock.

The dinner will be served in a sumptuously decorated, private dining-room, and by eight o'clock the party are *en route* in carriages for the play. Each lady is first supplied with exquisite corsage and hand bouquets by an attentive maid.

Boxes are engaged at the theater, or in case of large parties, the front row of the balcony. Programs printed on scented satin are frequently placed in front of each chair and serve as souvenirs of the occasion. When the play is over the party returns in carriages to the same restaurant where an elegant supper is laid.

Frequently each lady finds costly souvenirs at her plate. Each gentleman acts as escort through the evening to whatever lady he has been assigned by the host. At the appointed hour carriages call for the ladies and the gentlemen escort them thereto. If some male relative comes, he does not accompany her home, but if it is the maid only, he is expected so to do.

The young ladies and gentlemen must call upon the chaperon within a few days and the host calls upon the mothers to express thanks for the pleasure of the daughter's attendance. The men invited must each call within three days upon the especial lady to whom they devoted their time during the evening, or if this is impossible, leave a card.

A simpler form of this entertainment is where the host calls upon each proposed guest, and if the invitation is accepted, leaves two entrance tickets, and one for some male relative who must accompany her. The party meet in the box, where the host and a lady chaperon greet them. After the theater supper is served at some fashionable resort, or perhaps at the home of some friend, where dancing occasionally follows the supper. After calls are expected.

These parties are sometimes given by a lady, when the invitations are sent by informal notes in her own name, and a six o'clock dinner laid in her own home precedes the opera. After the entertainment the guests return in carriages to the house where a little supper is served, and perhaps some dancing varies the program.

Occasionally this entertainment takes the form of a matinée party of ladies only, who adjourn at its close to the hostess's home for a supper.

Dress for the Opera.

When a gentleman invites a lady to the opera, he should tell her what part of the house they are to occupy. If it is a box she must at least wear a light opera cloak, even if she does not array herself in full evening dress. However, evening toilet, no bonnet and beautifully dressed hair, are the correct thing. At an opera matinée, elegant visiting dress and dainty bonnets are always worn. If a gentleman is to escort a lady to the opera in any of the public conveyances she must wear street toilet.

Picnic Parties.

Picnics and excursions are delightful summer entertainments. But it is essential that whoever goes on a picnic should possess the power to find "sermons in stones, books in the running brooks, and good in everything;" know how to dress, know where to go, and above all, know what to carry to eat.

A very great variety of food should be avoided, also soft puddings and creamy mixtures of any sort, which persistently "leak out." Plain, substantial food, simple and well-cooked, should ever be chosen, with a few sweet and simple dainties to top off with. This can be divided up among the party by the one who is most executive, with the ladies to furnish the substantials and the gentlemen the beverages. The men assume the expenses of the boats or other conveyances.

Paraffine paper is indispensable in wrapping up the viands, which are much more wisely carried in boxes, than baskets, as the former can be thrown away, and the fewer the burdens on the home-coming the better. A rubber coat or mackintosh is also a necessity, for no matter how warm the day, there is a risk of sitting out in the woods on the bare ground. This can be easily managed in a shawl strap. It is best not to carry a tablecloth, but if something is preferred to spread upon the ground, a strip of enameled cloth is the most satisfactory thing, and whatever is spilled upon it can be easily cleaned off. Japanese napkins take the place of linen, and wooden plates, which can be thrown away, are most desirable, like those which the bakers use for pies.

There are several important items which must not be forgotten, and among them are hand-towels and soap, combs, hand-mirror, thread, needle and thimble, a corkscrew and a can opener.

What to Eat.

There should be a clear understanding at the outset what eatables each one is to bring. One girl may promise to furnish a certain proportion of the rolls or sandwiches, and another, part of the cake. Others may promise cold or potted meats, sardines, stuffed eggs, Saratoga potatoes, olives, pickles, fruit, lemonade and cold coffee. Salad may easily be carried if the lettuce and chicken or lobster are arranged in a dish set in a basket, and the dressing contained in a wide-mouthed bottle or pickle jar. The best way to transport lemonade, if fresh water can be readily procured at the picnic grounds, is to take the lemon juice and sugar in a jar, adding the water after the party reach their destination. Apollinaris water is excellent for lemonade. The coffee and milk should have been put together before leaving home, but the sugar is carried separately.

Tongue and Sandwiches.

To begin with the substantials, a cold roast, a boiled tongue, deviled eggs, are simple and tasty. The roast may be sliced off before going, and carefully wrapped up, but the tongue should be carried whole and cut up when required, or it is apt to become dry. The eggs are easily prepared, being hard boiled, cut lengthwise, the yolks taken out, mixed in a bowl with pepper, salt and mustard, and a few drops of Worcester and put back again in the whites.

Different kinds of sandwiches may be served. For one time there may be finger-rolls, split, the inside hollowed out and filled with chopped chicken or tongue, and the two sides tied together with the narrowest of ribbon. Again, bread and butter, cut wafer thin and rolled, may appear. Sweetbread sandwiches, sardine sandwiches, egg sandwiches, are delicious and easily prepared variations upon the everlasting ham and tongue. Very dainty sandwiches are made of two thicknesses of thin bread and butter, with a layer between of cream cheese and chopped water cress. The fruit should be heaped in a basket or arranged as a centerpiece with the flowers.

Ice cream may be taken to a picnic without much additional trouble. The brick molds can be so packed by a confectioner in a pail of ice that there will be no danger of the cream melting. For this, of course, wooden plates are not available, but china saucers will have to be transported. For the sweets some plain cake and bon-bons, and a box of crystallized ginger are all-sufficient. Cold tea, with lemon and ice, is certainly the most refreshing and satisfactory.

If more side dishes are preferred, there are olives, salted peanuts or pecans, gherkins, radishes or club-house cheese and wafers to choose from, and if berries in season are desired, they are best carried in a glass preserve jar.

If one person gives a picnic, she should expect to furnish all the food, the means of transportation for her guests, the plates, glasses, knives, forks and napkins—in short, to defray all the expenses of the trip. This is apt to prove a rather expensive proceeding, if there are many guests invited, but it is a very pretty style of entertaining for those whose means permit them to indulge in it. A "Basket Picnic" is a more general affair, where each member of the party supplies a quota of the provisions. Some one person undertakes the charge of the party, and invites such people to join it as she thinks would make it a success. The girls usually provide the refreshments.

Chaperons.

It might seem needless to say that there should always be a chaperon on picnic parties if it were not that even in this day there appears, in some places, to be a lack of proper understanding of this subject. Dwellers in large cities see matters in a clearer light, and a young man who is thoroughly versed in points of etiquette will not think of inviting a young lady to accompany him to the theater without also requesting her mother or a married friend to join them. In the same manner he asks a chaperon to go with them when he escorts a young lady to a ball or party.

When a number of young people get off together, they are apt, without the least intention of impropriety, to let their spirits carry them away and lead them into absurdities they would never commit in a graver moment. If a chaperon is bright and cheery, sympathizing in the enjoyment of the young people, and avoiding making her presence a bar upon innocent gayety, she need be no drawback to the pleasure of the expedition. On the contrary, most young men and women will feel a security and sense of comfort from having some one along to take the responsibility of the conduct of the party that they could never know were there no chaperon present.

It is a good rule, if possible, to have an equal number of persons of each sex on a picnic. This is especially desirable if the party is to be on the water, in rowboats, where each boatload must be evenly divided. The hostess or projector of the party may arrange in whose escort each girl is to go, or this may be left to the young people themselves.

A Marshmallow Toast.

This is exclusively a girl's entertainment. A very pretty one was given to about twenty girl friends. The guests were invited in the afternoon from two until six o'clock. A large room had its furniture removed and in its stead were placed small tables, which contained trays holding marshmallow candies, skewers and lamps. The mallows were toasted and eaten after a little supper. Tables were spread prettily with white linen and decorated with flowers. The supper was arranged as follows:

Oyster Patties. Buttered Bread. Sandwiches.
Salad with French Dressing. Assorted Cakes. Chocolate.
Toasted Marshmallows.

The young girls had a delightful time and the entertainment was simple and inexpensive.

Roof Parties.

Roof parties are the very latest diversion which the girl who stays in town is enjoying. They are the very jolliest entertainments imaginable, and the best part of them is that one can go in any sort of an outing suit without feeling *de trop*. Even the dwellers in the big apartment houses are able to give these high-in-the-air festivals, and they have become very popular from the fact that they are so informal and delightfully novel.

If your roof is spacious and walled in by a high parapet so much the better, for, of course, one can always imagine danger if there be only a narrow coping about the edge.

Pick out a night when the clerk of the weather will be polite enough to give moon and stars and soft southern breezes. Then cover the surface of the roof with rugs or else stretch a matting over the tin. Improvise couches upon boxes covered with rugs, or bring up a couple of cots and pile cushions upon them.

Palms and plants placed about always add to the effect, and if you wish the place to look like a little bit of fairy land hang Chinese lanterns on strings stretched about the edge, and when they are lit they will look remarkably pretty. If the roof be provided with ledges between your own and your neighbors, the bricks can be spread with napkins and refreshments arranged thereon.

Almost any sort of menu is permissible, but salads, sandwiches, olives, ice cream and liquid refreshments of all kinds are always in order.

Bachelor's Parties.

Bachelors who live in apartments are giving "Dutch" parties on roofs, and in those cases the refreshments consist of beer and ale served from the wood, rye bread and cheese sandwiches, sausages cooked in a chafing-dish and Rhine wine in the cup.

Roof parties can be so elaborate that they will cost quite as much as a more pretentious function, but they are more enjoyable when they are simply gotten up. One was given in a fashionable part of the city, and the aid of the caterer and the decorator had been utilized in such a manner as to produce the effect of a gorgeous *al fresco* reception. A gaily striped awning was stretched across the part of the roof where the edibles were spread upon a table loaded with flowers. A carpet was spread for a dance at one side with only the stars for a canopy. About the entire roof and reaching far up in a pyramid of light there were lanterns lit by electric lamps fastened within. There was a pleasant breeze blowing, and these many swaying colored lights produced a beautiful effect. Rich rugs carpeted the roof surface, and flags were draped about the high coping.

This party was given on the roof of a large hotel and was such a success that a number of similar ones were arranged for.

A Flower Party.

Another young girls' entertainment is a "flower party"—an appropriate name, as the writer once attended one where all the young ladies wore snowy gowns, each beautifully adorned with the wearer's favorite flower. A large silver salver filled with sprigs of flowers awaited the young men in the reception-hall, and upon his entrance each selected according to his fancy a flower from the waiter and sent it up the decorated staircase to find its mate and the young lady wearing the matching one met him on the landing, pinned his chosen flower to the lapel of his coat and became his partner for the evening.

Bicycle Teas.

With the bicycle comes the bicycle tea. In the large cities these teas have been given for charity and have been great successes. But there is no reason why any girl may not give an attractive bicycle tea and make it very original. Sandwiches in the shape of tennis rackets, with an olive steak in the center for a ball, are among the novelties. Sandwiches in the shape of a wheel and a saddle might easily be cut. Bicycle lanterns, which resemble glowworms, should furnish decoration. If possible, a bicycle tea should be given out of doors, where outing costumes would not be incongruous.

A Barn Party.

There is a big, red barn on a fine old farm, that is easily reached by city friends, and there, every year, is given an autumn revel in the shape of a genuine "barn dance." The mow is filled with sweet smelling hay and the cattle, stalled, are below. The big center floor is cleared and swept and reswept and chalked to make it fit for dancing feet. The decorations for the dance consume much time, and into them the hostess throws many a loving thought. Pumpkins form the chief theme. In flower-like or hideous forms as jack-o'-lanterns they hold posts of honor on rafter and beam.

The lanterns used are the regular farm lanterns, though the walk through the old-fashioned garden to the barn is outlined by the fancy Japanese lanterns. Ears of corn tied by fluttering ribbons, the husks turned back to show the golden ears, cornstalks, golden-rod, milkweed, woodbine and clusters of purple grapes are all worked into the decorations.

The young folks learn by previous experiences not to wear perishable finery at the barn dance, and the girls all come in pretty wash-dresses that will stand a good romp. Music is furnished by an old darkey fiddler, not violinist, who plays "Money Musk," "Fisher's Hornpipe," "Ole Dan Tucker" and any number of plantation melodies.

The supper, of course, is the best part of the dance to hungry city-bred people. Hot coffee is served in bright new tin-cups, for these young people mimic harvesters; there is fried chicken, cold ham, potato salad, rolls with golden country butter that melts in one's mouth, plenty of fresh milk, pumpkin and apple pie, with cottage cheese, ginger cakes and doughnuts, and even cider for those who wish.

The dance is always given during the full harvest moon and the stone wall which bounds the orchard, the old farm wagons, the grain bins and even the low apple trees furnish flirtation nooks for lovers. One year the barn dance was also a potato roast. Huge fires were built on the lawn, and during the intermission the crowd gathered around the fires and roasted potatoes. This time, too, the dance was made a house party, and the girls were stowed away in the farmhouse while the boys enjoyed tents and the big haymow. Is it any wonder that the pretty hostess' friends call her barn dance the big event of the year?

Bachelor Women and their Entertainments.

The bachelor women in their cosy little city apartments, or even their one apartment, refuse to be debarred from the pleasure and privilege of giving the little entertainments so dear to the heart feminine. They not only give the most charming little "teas" and "coffees," but they are past masters in the use of the chafing dish and those who have feasted with them will no longer deem that liveried service and stately rooms are necessary to the proper receiving of one's friends.

After all, "the highest hospitality is in giving what one has." Hawthorne and his wife never forgot the little American studying art in Rome, who, in her tower room, reached by many flights of stairs, made tea before their eyes, and took from a cupboard the cake and crackers that made her feast. Neither will the world forget her, since she it was, who, in the "Marble Faun," is the Hilda who fed the doves from the tower.

A Sandwich Spread.

A sandwich spread is another entertainment easily given by a "bachelor maid." This is a meal at which everything, barring the tea and coffee, is served in the form of a sandwich. Not until one has tried does one realize to what excellence and variety this form of viand lends itself. Deviled ham sandwiches, egg sandwiches, cheese sandwiches, lettuce sandwiches, potted ham, potted fish, potted cheese sandwiches, pineapple sandwiches, peanut sandwiches, cucumber sandwiches, tomato sandwiches, walnut sandwiches, oyster sandwiches and so on indefinitely. Any modern cookbook will furnish the formulas for all these and more.

"He or she," says one writer, "who partakes, forgets the presence of the folding bed and gas stove; of the curtained china cupboard in friendly proximity to the writing desk or easel. There is no paint on the artist's fingers, and the newspaper woman wears as pretty a gown as any woman could wish."

Private Theatricals.

The etiquette of invitations is the same for Private Theatricals, as for musicales. Simply substituting the word, "Theatricals," "Charades," or "Tableaux," whichever it is to be, in the left hand corner of the card. The same observances as to arranging the seats, toilettes of the guests, etc., are requisite, and performers should be equally careful not to fail at the last moment in taking their part. In reality they should be more so, since the failure of one performer might ruin the entire play.

A drama entails more expense and care than characters and tableaux. A host or hostess should never take leading part unless it be especially urged upon them by the others, and even then it is not best, first, because the entertainers should never eclipse their guests, and, second, they should be free for a general oversight of the whole affair, ready to settle disputed points and find missing stage "properties." An effort should be made to assign, as nearly as possible, acceptable and suitable parts to all.

Those invited should display willingness to take parts assigned them, even if not the most important in the cast. All cannot be Romeos or Juliets. There are minor parts to play on all stages. Learn the part given you thoroughly, and do your best to make the play a success. If sickness or unavoidable accident intervene, inform the hostess at once that she may be able to supply a substitute for the part.

Guests indulge in conversation between the acts, and the music of an orchestra often fills the pause.

A carpenter is usually called in to build the temporary stage, or a curtain is fitted to rise and fall in the archway between two parlors; the first parlor being used for the audience room and the second one for stage, with dressing-room in the rear. A private billiard-room, also, can be used to good advantage. At the conclusion of the play, supper is served, and social conversation and dancing follow.

A Social Evening.

There are many ways of making pleasant entertainments out of these informal gatherings. Such an evening may last from nine to twelve o'clock. Where impromptu dancing is resorted to, as it so often is, another hour is sometimes added. If dancing be excluded, games, music, cards, or recitations should take its place. If neither card-playing, nor dancing is permitted, the supper usually becomes the feature of the evening.

When friends are invited to pass an evening socially with cards and music, refreshments are always served. They can be placed upon the dining-room table, and the company invited to partake of them. They should consist of sandwiches or cold meats and rolls, and cakes and coffee or chocolate, or only cakes, ices and lemonade can be served. The best dishes the china closet affords should be used.

Or, the supper can be made an elaborate "sit-down" banquet. If the long table is not sufficient for all, the guests can be served in relays. The table should be prettily decorated. There are different forms of home parties, such as birthday celebrations, where gifts and toasts are in order, house-warmings, or a church party.

When the supper is served in relays the hostess had better wait until the last table, and circulate about among those guests who have not yet been served. Some appointed lady can serve as hostess at each table. The elder guests should be seated at the first. Sometimes small tables are scattered about the rooms to accommodate those who cannot find place at the large table, thus all are served at once.

Where neither card-playing nor dancing are indulged in, it becomes necessary to find some other amusement. Impromptu charades are sure to break the ice. A shadow party also, where any amount of sport can be had with a darkened room and a tightly stretched sheet illuminated from the rear, whereon shadows can be cast for guessing. There are also a great many interesting games of which enough can be furnished for an entire company.

Authors' Parties

Are also amusing entertainments, but they must be arranged for beforehand. It is usual to take the works of one author and give out the characters to be represented to each one, that repetitions may be prevented. Then the guessing that will follow when the company are all together, and the conversation that naturally ensues on literary subjects, ensures the success of the party.

Firelight Parties

Are pleasurable affairs. There is no light furnished except by an open fire. The guests sit around in a circle and tell stories. Each one is provided with a bunch of twigs, or fagot to be thrown on the fire, the guest being expected to sing a song, tell a story, give a recitation, or otherwise amuse the company while his fagot burns.

Conversaziones.

These gatherings, as the name signifies, are devoted entirely to conversation, and are supposed to be chiefly gatherings of literary and scientific people. Where one especially fine conversationalist is the star of the evening, one or two lesser lights should be invited to share with him the honors of the occasion.

A Country Dinner.

A summer dinner in the country has many pleasant features peculiar to itself. Chief among these is its lack of formality, and city guests are always pleasurably entertained at the country dinner table. A good cook and a competent waitress are necessities.

The flowers that ornament the table must partake of the field and forest rather than suggest the city hothouse. Slender, light, glass vases and rose-bowls are best for the light grasses, field flowers and garden blossoms. Pretty, modern, inexpensive china is sufficient for a country dinner, and not too much silverware should be used.

Light, clear soups should form the first course (mock turtle or ox-tail soup is not in order). The roast should be carved away from the table. Plenty of fresh vegetables should be prepared, that being one of the privileges of country life. Delightfully fresh salads are also at command of the suburban householder; and if the dining-room be cool and large, and therewith the grace be given of a beautiful view, what greater gift can the gods grant!

Let the housekeeper forbear to serve hot puddings or heavy pastries. Fruit tarts, the freshest of fruits with great glass pitchers of country cream, cold custards, gelatine creams of all kinds and ice cream are always satisfactory; and many substitute for the heavy roast the lighter dishes of broiled fish, chicken, or chops. A cold boiled ham on the sideboard adds another dish to the board.

Etiquette of Card Playing and Games.

There is a certain etiquette to be observed in playing all social games. In card-playing especially this is a necessity. In the first place, it is the hostess who proposes the game. In the second, no one who refuses should be urged to join in the amusement. They may have conscientious scruples, and respect should be shown their principles. Unless, however, this be the reason, no one should refuse to play from mere caprice when their presence is required to make up a table.

New packs of cards should be provided by the hostess. Playing for money, even the smallest amount, should be strictly avoided. It is unfit for the home parlor.

Those who do not understand playing should not join a set unless especially urged, as their ignorance is apt to spoil the pleasure of the others. The fingers should not be wet to deal the cards. Partners should never exchange signs. Let every one play his best and not act indifferent to the game.

Do not talk on all manner of topics; it disturbs those who enjoy the game.

Do not criticise, nor hurry other players.

Never lose temper over a game.

To cheat is extremely ill-bred.

If you have a poor partner manifest no annoyance.

Never reflect upon the playing of your opponents.

Those who have played together so much that they understand one another's play should not be partners in general company.

Never manifest anger at defeat, nor undue exultation at winning.

These rules, many of them, apply to all other social games, both outdoors and in.

Outdoor Amusements.

Coaching parties are delightful. They give much latitude for gay, pretty costumes, and there are few brighter pictures than that of a tally-ho coach as it dashes along the city boulevards and over the country roads to the music of jingling chains and winding horns.

OUTDOOR SPORTS.

Appetites are sharpened by the long drive, and hampers must be well packed with substantial viands. Potted meats, all manner of sandwiches, game pies, cold birds, and substantial beef and tongue, will be sure of appreciation.

(See "Dress," etc., for suitable attire.)

Hunting Parties.

Hunting is very little favored by ladies on this side the water, though it is occasionally indulged in by a few. The enthusiasm, however, of a ride to hounds is much dampened by the knowledge that an anise-seed bag, instead of a fox, furnishes the scent over which the hounds give eager tongue. Those who attempt to hunt must be at home in the saddle.

(See "Dress," etc., for appropriate attire.)

Archery, Lawn Tennis and Croquet.

These popular games have their own etiquette, rules, dress, etc., so thoroughly established that all devotees of these sports understand the routine without giving it place here.

Never dispute, or show any temper over the outcome of any game.

Boating and Yachting.

Many ladies are quite expert with the oars, and boating, when not overdone, is a healthful and pleasant amusement. When gentlemen are with a party of ladies, one of them should step in the boat to steady it, while another "assists" the ladies in. See that their dress is so arranged that they will not get wet. Inexperienced rowers should learn before joining a party.

The stroke oar is the seat of honor. It may be offered to a guest. Ladies should wear short dresses, free from encumbering draperies, heavy shoes, and a hat with a broad brim. Heavy gloves, if they intend rowing, should be worn.

Yachting is a delightful and rather dangerous amusement. Ladies wear warm wool dresses that water will not injure, made short in the skirt, and jaunty of cut, with sailor-like emblems for adornment. No young lady should go out alone with a gentleman either yachting or rowing. In yachting especially a boat is sometimes becalmed for hours and even all night. A party composed entirely of young people should have a chaperon.

Children's Parties.

The celebration of children's birthdays and other little anniversaries by means of parties, is a pleasant custom and one worthy of observance. Such red-letter days are long remembered by the little ones.

The invitations are issued in the children's own names, and may be written or engraved. Usually they are written upon small note sheets and enclosed in small envelopes. If the invitation is for a Christmas-tree, or an Easter-egg hunt, a tiny tree, or a colored egg, may ornament one corner of the sheet.

The form varies hardly at all: Miss GERTRUDE HALL requests the pleasure of Miss CLARA WINSHIP'S company, on Wednesday, June twentieth. From three until five o'clock. 3 Madison Avenue.

These invitations should be carefully and promptly answered in the same form as given and in the third person. (See "Invitations," etc.)

This teaches the little host or hostess the gravity of their position as entertainers, and impresses the little guests with the importance of their behavior. Also giving them an early lesson in the etiquette of social life.

If it is a birthday party, a birthday cake will be the chief feature, and it is a pretty fancy to have it decorated with as many tiny wax candles as there are years in the child's life in whose honor the party is given. These tapers may be placed around the cake, or put in tin tubes and sunk into the top of the cake. Light them just before the little guests are called out to the table.

At the close of the supper the child whose birthday it is, blows out the candles, and, if old enough, cuts the cake and passes it.

Presents are sometimes brought by the guests, but it is not best to encourage this fashion.

Dancing or games may follow the supper, and older persons should constantly superintend the amusements to see that the merriment does not flag, nor the little folks become too boisterous.

At an Easter party, dainty little egg-shaped boxes, filled with bon-bons, may be placed at each plate, or else hidden in a room from which the lighter articles of furniture have been removed, and the children permitted to search for them. The hunt is the chief pleasure.

If it is a Christmas party the tree is the source of interest, and often a make-believe Santa Claus adds to the merriment of the occasion. The refreshments should be simple but fanciful. Make the table bright as possible—snowballs, cornucopias, lady-fingers, assorted cakes, love-knots, sandwiches (fancy), crystalized fruits, tarts, sliced tongue, pressed veal, thin bread and butter, rolled and tied, ice cream in molds, and one large heavily-frosted cake. A host of flowers, and the table is complete. Lemonade for a drink, or perhaps hot chocolate.

The good breeding learned, the opportunities of impressing upon children the beauty of self-denial and politeness, and of teaching them to dispense, and to receive hospitalities, and to restrain that tendency toward favoring certain playmates, so strong in childhood, will more than repay for the trouble of preparing the feast. Never permit the party to extend to late hours, and never overdress the little folks. White is always suitable for girls, and jacket suits for boys under the age for long trousers.

CHRISTENINGS CONFIRMATIONS AND GRADUATIONS

ANNOUNCEMENT Cards are frequently sent out to all friends immediately upon the arrival of a little heir or heiress. These cards are variously worded. One seen by the writer was as follows:

ARRIVED: In Los Gatos, Sunday morning, November third, eighteen hundred and ninety-five, FLORENCE WESCOTT. Weight, ten pounds; blue eyes and sound lungs. She sends greeting to all her friends.

A simpler one would be: GREETING: EDITH MAY TOUCEY, November 1, 1895. Weight, 9-1/2 pounds.

These cards received (or even if they are omitted), the lady friends and acquaintances call and leave cards with kind inquires or send them by a servant. Gentlemen do not call, but they are expected to see the happy father and inquire after mother and child.

When the mother is ready to receive friends she sends out cards to all that have called "with thanks for kind inquiries," written beneath her name, or issues invitations for a candle or christening party.

The Christening.

The baptism or christening is performed according to the rites of whatever church the parents may be members of. If the ceremony is performed in church, personal fancy has very little play, though it is almost a law that flowers shall cluster about the place where little ones are brought for dedication.

If the occasion is to be further celebrated by festivities at the house they may take whatever form is most agreeable. When the christening is held at the house and guests are invited, it is customary to defer the ceremony until the mother is ready to take the part of hostess; usually until the child is a month or six weeks old.

Invitations are issued for an afternoon or early evening reception. They may be written or engraved, and are issued in the name of both parents, thus: MR. and MRS. JAMES GRAY request the pleasure of your presence at the Christening of their son at half-past four o'clock, Wednesday, May tenth. 12 Madison Avenue.

Or: MR. and MRS. JOHN THURSTON request the honor of MR. and MRS. BROWN'S presence at the Christening of their daughter on Thursday, May

11th, at three o'clock. Reception from two to five, 150 Delaware Place. Sometimes the words, "No presents expected," are added to the invitation.

Attendance at the Ceremony.

These invitations are promptly answered, and those who attend should wear a reception dress. The solemnity of the occasion should be recognized by the appearance, previous to the hour named, of all who expect to be present. Those who cannot be in time to witness the ceremony should defer their arrival until a sufficient time has elapsed to allow of its completion.

A temporary font is placed in a central position. This is best arranged by banking up the top of a small round table with mosses, smilax and delicate ferns, while the top, outside the rim of the bowl holding the china basin containing the water, is a mass of white flowers.

The drawing-room may be decorated with blossoms, and vocal or instrumental music is usually provided. Hired musicians are sometimes engaged. See that the selections are suitable to the sacred character of the occasion. Friends are sometimes asked to give two or three vocal selections.

At the appointed time the father and mother stand before the clergyman at the font and receive their child from the nurse or some friend; the godparents range themselves on either side, and the clergyman proceeds with the service. If the parents are able, the clergyman is usually given a handsome fee on these occasions.

Congratulations are offered the father and mother, and the baby, robed elaborately, then becomes the center of attraction for a few moments, until the host leads the way to the refreshment table which is bountifully spread as for a reception.

A toast in the child's honor is often given at this time by one of the sponsors. Guests shortly disperse. After calls are made, or cards left, within ten days. Sometimes relatives only are invited to these parties. When the christening is held in church, the party is set for some hour of the same day.

Godfathers and Godmothers.

In selecting godparents or sponsors, relatives are often given precedence and very close friends come next. Be careful in the choice, as from these godparents is to be expected much good counsel and kindly aid in the future. In all old countries this relationship is expected to last for a lifetime, and the godparents are supposed to watch over the religious growth of the child and see that in due time he is brought forward for confirmation, or for union with the church in some other manner.

A boy is expected to have two godfathers and one godmother; a girl one godfather and two godmothers. A note is sent to each person selected as sponsor asking him to assume that friendly office. This request should never be refused except for good and sufficient reason.

Godparents usually make a present to the child, generally in the form of some suitable silver article. Among the very wealthy, especially if the child bears the godfather's name, very valuable presents are often made, these generally taking the form of checks for large amounts.

Caudle Party.

The modern caudle party is given when the child is about six weeks old, and is quite a separate affair from the christening, the church having objected in some cases to having the two celebrated at the same time. Caudle parties, simply in the nature of a name-festival, are frequently given when the christening is not observed.

Invitations are sent out one week in advance, and are in the following form: MR. and MRS. BROWN request your company, Wednesday afternoon, at three. CAUDLE. 125 Vancouver Street. No presents expected.

The words, "no presents," need not prevent any who wish from making a gift, but relieves those who may not be prepared.

The phrase, "Caudle Party," is somewhat difficult to define, but the name and the custom have come down from olden times. It used then to be the habit to serve all who called with inquiries and congratulations on the arrival of a little stranger, with a kind of spiced gruel, flavored with rum or Madeira, and known as "caudle." This was served in china cups having two handles, so they could be passed from one to another. These were called "caudle cups," and are much prized heirlooms in more than one old family. This ceremony was then observed when the child was three days old; now the "caudle party" is celebrated when it is at least six weeks old.

The mother receives her guests in some elaborate house gown, the baby in robes of state is on exhibition for a short time, and the guests are served with "caudle" in the form of an oatmeal gruel, long and slowly boiled with raisins and spices, and fine old Madeira or rum added at the last until the beverage is "to the Queen's taste."

Christening Gifts.

When the announcement cards of a baby's birth are sent out, very many friends of the family interpret this as an opportunity for making a present to the new arrival. This is not a new social custom, for its origin goes back to the time of the Chaldean shepherds, when wise men of the East journeyed to the stable cradle to present their gifts of frankincense and myrrh.

The most sensible plan in this case, and, in fact, in all gift making, is to consult the condition of the recipient as well as the purse of the giver. If the parental purse is a little slim, gifts that are useful are generally the best to give. Dainty gowns, embroidered flannels, coach rugs, things that every baby needs.

The least expensive and simplest gifts and always of use, are the lace pin, shoulder pin and chained buttons in gold. Three pins connected by delicate gold chains are very much in demand, and a studding of turquoise of pearl adds much to their beauty. The dear little silver-backed brushes and powder boxes have always been favorites.

One exquisite present from a point of sentiment and value was recently presented to a girl. Each of her father's groomsmen sent a five-dollar gold piece to the goldsmith, who melted them down and transformed them into a gold chain and locket. The locket bore the monogram of the baby and the initial letter of each groomsman's name.

Dainty Presents for the Newcomer.

Another tiny new woman received from her grandmother a spoon which was made of little bits of silver melted down. A silver piece taken from the pocket of a dead aunt, two or three bits left in the purse of the grandfather, who had died; a bit of a broken spoon used by the baby's own mamma—these and other souvenirs of the family history made the gift spoon something far out of the ordinary.

One of the most magnificent and costly gifts in silver that is given to the baby is the entire food set, consisting of plate, bowl, pitcher, knife and fork, spoon and napkin ring. These sets come in cases and range in prices ordinarily from $50 to $150, though some very elaborate ones may be ordered which go far into the hundreds.

A very pretty and surely most interesting gift that could be sent to a baby is a baby diary in which the principal events of the little one's life can be entered by the mother and kept in after years as a record of those marvelously interesting days of babyhood.

A certain very sensible woman usually deposits a small sum of money in bank and presents the bank book to her little new friend, thus laying the foundation for future habits of economy and thrift.

Some Birthday Superstitions.

Monday's child is fair of face.

Tuesday's child is full of grace.

Wednesday's child is born for woe.

Thursday's child has far to go.

Friday's child is loving and giving.

Saturday's child must work for a living.

But the child that is born on the Sabbath Day,

Is bonny and happy and wealthy and gay.

CONFIRMATION.

In the Episcopal, Lutheran and Roman Catholic churches, "Confirmation is the sequel of baptism." Here comes in one of the duties of the godparents, and should the child become orphaned, or should its parents by reason of carelessness, or irreligion, neglect this important matter, the church holds the godparents in a large measure responsible that these children be brought before the Bishop for confirmation.

Some weeks prior to the arrival of the Bishop, persons desirous of admission to the church present their names to the clergymen, and classes are formed of instruction and preparation for the solemn event.

The ceremony of the confirmation service is in accordance with the forms of the church in which it is observed. The only uniformity being in the garb of the young candidates. This for the girls is always gowns of purest white, with gloves and shoes to match. White bound prayer-books should be carried, and in the Roman Catholic and the Lutheran churches white veils and wreaths crown the young heads. For the youths, black suits, black ties and gloves are the proper thing.

GRADUATION.

With the important event of graduation ends the three great ceremonies of youth. The church and the school have both set their seal upon the young man and maiden, and the business world and the social world are waiting to receive them.

In the matter of dress for this important event, the young man is supposed to confine himself to conventional black with white tie. The young girl is usually in white, with gloves, shoes, hose and fan to match.

This, however, depends upon the taste of the class, as they expect to dress alike, and often select some other delicate shade of color for the class costume.

Avoid all Extravagance.

There is one thing to be remembered—that is, that too much extravagance should not be displayed in the selection and adornments of the gown for the occasion. In the first place, simplicity is the prerogative of youth. In the second, it is bad taste to overload a young schoolgirl with expensive materials and lavish ornaments. In the third, there will always be found in every graduating class one or more students to whose purse the expenses incident upon the school course have been a heavy drain, and to whom compliance with the style of dress worn by other members of the class will mean a serious strain upon the home exchequer, or the incurring of a debt for the future, while to dress as their purse affords requires more self-denial than an outsider realizes. The slights, the sneers of insolent classmates have driven more than one sensitive soul to solitude and tears, and clouded what should have been the bright beginning of life with sorrow and anger.

Directors of schools have more than once striven to do away with this abuse of the occasion by prescribing the dress to be worn, but with poor success, since sumptuary laws are not kindly received in this free country.

Now, the remedy lies in the hands of the girls themselves, and with their parents. Let it be once understood that such a display is the mark of social *parvénus*, of the newly-rich, and the custom will cease to exist.

Friends bring flowers to the place of graduation which are sent up, either by the ushers, who are chosen among intimates of the classmates, or by tiny boys dressed as pages. These floral offerings have come to be so extensive that the stage is often banked with the beautiful blossoms. Here, too, is another abuse. To those who have few friends, and less money, the absence of these remembrances is often so marked as to cause many a heartache.

Cards with the donor's name and the words, "Congratulations," or "Graduation Congratulations," penned in one corner, are tied with narrow ribbons to these gifts. Presents of a more substantial nature are also sent up; books, watches, jewels, etc., and have a more lasting remembrance than the fleeting blossoms. One of the prettiest floral gifts seen on an occasion of graduation was a graceful ship, white sailed, and lovely, all of fragrant flowers, and full freighted with the hopes and prayers for the young legal graduate, who was sole son of the house.

Carriages convey the graduates to and from the hall, and a class reception is supposed to finish the long round of the gaieties of "Class Week."

ETIQUETTE OF FUNERALS AND MOURNING

THE great sorrow brought upon a family by the death of a loved one renders the immediate members of the family incapable of attending to the necessary arrangements for the funeral. The services of an intimate friend, or a relative, should, therefore, be sought. He should receive general instructions from the family, after which he should take entire charge of the arrangements, and relieve them from all care on the subject. If such a person cannot be had, the arrangements may be placed in the hands of the sexton of the church the deceased attended in life, or of some responsible undertaker.

The expenses of the funeral should be in accordance with the means of the family. No false pride should permit the relatives to incur undue expense in order to make a showy funeral. At the same time, affection will dictate that all the marks of respect which you can provide should be paid to the memory of your beloved dead.

Funeral Invitations.

In some parts of the country it is customary to send notes of invitation to the funeral to the friends of the deceased and of the family. These invitations should be printed, neatly and simply, on mourning paper, with envelopes to match, and should be delivered by a private messenger. The following is a correct form, the names and dates to be changed to suit the occasion:

"Yourself and family are respectfully invited to attend the funeral of DAVID B. JONES, on Tuesday, March 18, 189-, at 11 o'clock A. M., from his late residence, 1926 Amber Street, to proceed to Laurel Hill Cemetery."

Where the funeral is from a church, the invitation should read:

"Yourself and family are respectfully invited to attend the funeral of DAVID B. JONES, from the Church of the Holy Trinity, on Tuesday, March 18, 189-, at 11 o'clock A. M., to proceed to Laurel Hill Cemetery."

Where such invitations are sent, a list of persons so invited must be given to the person in charge of the funeral, in order that he may provide a sufficient number of carriages. No one to whom an invitation has not been sent should attend such a funeral, nor should those invited permit anything but an important duty to prevent their attendance.

When the funeral is at the house, some near relative or intimate friend should act as usher, and show the company to their seats.

Showing Respect for the Dead.

Preserve a decorous silence in the chamber of death—speak as little as possible, and then only in low, subdued tones.

The members of the family are not obliged to recognize their acquaintances. The latter show their sympathy by their presence and considerate silence.

As the coffin is borne from the house to the hearse, gentlemen who may be standing at the door or in the street remove their hats, and remain uncovered until it is placed in the hearse.

The pall-bearers should be chosen from among the intimate friends of the deceased, and should correspond to him in age and general character.

With regard to sending flowers, the wishes of the family should be considered. If you are uncertain upon this point, it is safe to send them. They should be simple and tasteful.

Letters of condolence are sent to those in bereavement by their intimate friends. We append a few forms that will be helpful to all persons who wish to express their sympathy with the bereaved.

To a Lady on the Death of her Husband.

CLEVELAND, O., June 6, 189—.

DEAR MRS. WALROD:

Though I know that no words of mine can bring comfort to your sorely tried heart, yet I can not refrain from writing to you to express my deep and heartfelt sympathy in your affliction.

Knowing your husband as intimately as I did, I can understand what a blow his death is to you. He was a man whose place will not be easily filled in the world; how impossible to fill it in his home!

You are, even in your loss, fortunate in this. He left behind him a name unsullied, and which should be a priceless legacy to his children and to you. His life was so pure and his Christian faith so undoubted, that we may feel the blessed assurance that he has gone to the home prepared for those who love and faithfully serve the Lord Jesus.

This should comfort you. You have the hope of meeting him one day in a better and a happier union than the ties that bound you here on earth. He waits for you, and reunited there, you will know no more parting.

I pray God to temper your affliction and give you strength to endure it. May He, in His own good time, give you the peace that will enable you to wait with patience until He shall call you to meet your loved one in heaven.

Sincerely yours,
WALTER BAILEY.

MRS. LYDIA WALROD, New York.

To a Friend on the Death of Her Sister.

GENEVA, N.Y. May 4, 189—.

MY DEAR NELLIE:

The melancholy intelligence of your sister's death has grieved me more than I can express, and I beg to render you my heartfelt sympathy. Truly we live in a world where solemn shadows are continually falling upon our path—shadows that teach us the insecurity of all temporal blessings, and warn us that here "there is no abiding place." We have, however, the blessed satisfaction of knowing that death cannot enter that sphere to which the departed are removed. Let hope and faith, my dear friend, mingle with your natural sorrow. Look to that future where the sundered ties of earth are reunited.

Very sincerely yours,
SARAH CLARK.

To MISS NELLIE BARTON,
No. 4 Beacon Place, Boston.

To a Friend on the Death of His Brother.

CHICAGO, July 12, 189—,

DEAR MR. AMES:

In the death of your brother, you have sustained a misfortune which all who had the pleasure of knowing him can feelingly estimate. I condole with you most sincerely on the sad event, and if the sympathy of friends can be any consolation under the trying circumstance, be assured that all who knew him share in your sorrow for his loss. There is, however, a higher source of consolation than earthly friendship, and, commending you to that, I remain,

Yours sincerely,
JEROME C. HOOVER.

G. H. AMES, St. Louis.

To a Friend on the Death of Her Child.

ATLANTA, GA., November 17, 189—.

MY DEAR BLANCHE:

I feel that a mother's sorrow for the loss of a beloved child cannot be assuaged by the commonplaces of condolence, yet I must write a few lines to assure you of my heartfelt sympathy in your grief. There is one thing, however, that should soften the sharpness of a mother's agony under such a bereavement. It is the reflection that "little children" are pure and guileless, and that of such is the kingdom of heaven. "It is well with the child." Much sin and woe has it escaped. It is treasure laid up in a better world, and the gate through which it has passed to peace and joy unspeakable is left open so that you, in due time, may follow. Let this be your consolation.

Affectionately yours,
MAUD TROWBRIDGE.

To MRS. BLANCHE NORTON,
New Haven, Conn.

To a Friend on a Sudden Reverse of Fortune.

LOUISVILLE, KY., June 5, 189—.

MY DEAR FRIEND:

Hackneyed phrases of condolence never yet comforted a man in the hour of trouble, and I am not going to try their effect in your case. And yet let me say, in heartfelt earnest, that I was deeply pained to hear of your sudden and unexpected reverse of fortune. Misfortune is very hard to bear, when it falls upon one, like a flash of lightning from a clear sky, without any warning. But do not be discouraged. When Senator Benton saw the work of many years consumed in ten minutes, he took the matter coolly, went to work again, and lived long enough to repair the damage. So I hope will you. There is no motto like "try again," for those whom fate has stricken down. Besides, there are better things than wealth even in this world, to say nothing of the next, where we shall neither buy nor sell.

If I can be of any assistance to you, let me know it, and I will help you as far as I am able.

In the meantime, cheer up, and believe me as ever,

Yours sincerely,
JAMES STERLING.

H. R. DRAYTON,
Covington, Ky.

"SHE ENTERED ON UNTROUBLED REST."

ETIQUETTE OF PUBLIC PLACES

THERE is no surer mark of a well-bred man or woman than proper and dignified conduct in public. The truly polite are always quiet, unobtrusive, considerate of others, and careful to avoid all manifestations of superiority or elegance.

Loud and boisterous talking, immoderate laughing and forward and pushing conduct are always marks of bad breeding. They inevitably subject a person to the satirical remarks of the persons with whom he is thrown, and are perhaps the surest means of proclaiming that such a person is not used to the ways of polite society.

Etiquette in Church.

It is the duty of a well-bred person to attend church regularly on Sunday.

In entering the church you should pass quietly and deliberately to your pew or seat. Walking rapidly up the aisle is sure to disturb the congregation.

If you are a stranger, wait in the lower part of the aisle until the sexton or ushers show you a seat, or you are invited to enter some pew.

A gentleman should remove his hat as soon as he enters the inner doors of the church, and should not replace it on his head after service until he has reached the outer vestibule.

In accompanying a lady to church, pass up the aisle by her side, open the pew door for her, allow her to enter first, and then enter and seat yourself beside her.

Should a lady desire to enter a pew in which you are sitting next the door, rise, step out into the aisle, and allow her to enter.

Once in church, observe the most respectful silence except when joining in the worship. Whispering or laughing before the service begins, or during service, is highly improper. When the worship is over, leave the sacred edifice quietly and deliberately. You may chat with your friends in the vestibule, but not in the hall of worship. Remember, the church is the house of God.

Should you see a stranger standing in the aisle, unnoticed by the sexton or usher, quietly invite him into your pew.

You should see that a stranger in your pew is provided with the books necessary to enable him to join in the service. If he does not know how to use them, assist him as quietly as possible. Where there are not books enough for the separate use of each person, you may share yours with an occupant of your pew.

In attending a church of a different denomination from your own you should carefully observe the outward forms of worship. Stand up when the congregation do, and kneel with them. A Protestant attending a Roman Catholic church should be careful to do this. It involves no sacrifice of principle, and a failure to do so is a mark of bad breeding. Whatever the denomination, the church is devoted to the worship of God. Your reverence is to Him—not to the ministers who conduct the worship.

To be late at church is an offence against good manners.

Gentlemen will not congregate in groups in front of a church, and stare at the ladies as they pass out.

In receiving the Holy Communion both hands should be ungloved.

Etiquette of Fairs.

Fairs are generally given in aid of a church or some charitable purpose. At such fairs ladies serve the tables at which articles are offered for sale.

Ladies should not use unfair or unladylike means to sell their wares. Do not importune a gentleman to buy of you; and do not charge an extortionate price for a trifling article. A young man may not have the courage to refuse to buy of a lady acquaintance; but his purchase may be beyond his means, and may involve him in serious embarrassment.

Visitors to a fair should make no comments upon the character or quality of the articles offered, unless they can offer sincere praise.

Do not dispute the price of an article offered for sale. If you cannot afford to buy it, decline it frankly. If you can, pay the sum asked, although you may think it exorbitant, and make no comment.

A gentleman must remove his hat upon entering the room in which a fair is held, although it be a public hall, and remain uncovered while in the room.

Flirting, loud or boisterous talking or laughing, and conspicuous conduct, are marks of bad breeding.

When a purchaser offers a sum larger than the price asked for the article, return the change promptly. Some thoughtless young ladies consider it "a stroke of business" to retain the whole amount, knowing that a gentleman will not insist upon the return of the change. To do this is simply to be guilty of an act of gross ill-breeding.

A lady may accept any donation of money a gentleman may wish to make at her table. The gift is to the charity, not to her; and the gentleman pays her a delicate compliment in making her the means of increasing the receipts of the fair.

Etiquette of Shopping.

In visiting a store for the purpose of examining the goods or making purchases, conduct yourself with courtesy and amiability.

Speak to the clerks and employés of the store with courtesy and kindness. Do not order them to show you anything. Request them to do so in a polite and ladylike or gentlemanly manner. Give them no more trouble than is necessary, and express your thanks for the attentions they may show you. In leaving their counter, say pleasantly, "Good-morning," or "Good-day." By treating the employés of a store with courtesy, you will render your presence there, welcome, and will receive all the attention such conduct merits.

Should you find another person examining a piece of goods, do not take hold of it. Wait until it is laid down, and then make your examination.

To attempt to "beat down" the price of an article is rude. In the best conducted stores the price of the goods is "fixed," and the salesmen are not allowed to change it. If the price does not suit you, you are not obliged to buy, but can go elsewhere.

Pushing or crowding at a counter, or the indulgence in personal remarks, handling the goods in a careless manner, or so roughly as to injure them, lounging upon the counter, or talking in a loud voice, are marks of bad breeding.

Never express your opinion about an article another is purchasing, unless asked to do so. To say to a customer about to make a purchase that the article can be bought cheaper at another store, is to offer a gratuitous insult to the clerk making the sale.

You should never ask or expect a clerk engaged in waiting upon a customer to leave that person and attend to you. Wait patiently for your turn.

It is rude to make unfavorable comparisons between the goods you are examining and those of another store.

Have your parcels sent, and so avoid the fatigue of carrying them.

It is best to buy for cash. You can always buy cheaper in this way. If you make bills, however, pay them promptly. Make no bill you are not sure of paying at the time promised by you. Avoid debt as the greatest curse of life.

Etiquette of the Theatre, Opera and Concert.

A gentleman, desiring a lady to accompany him to the opera, theatre, or other place of amusement, must send her a written invitation not later than the day previous to the entertainment. It must be written in the third person, upon white note-paper of the best quality, with an envelope to match. The lady must send her reply immediately, so that should she be unable to accept, the gentleman may secure another companion.

Should the lady accept the invitation, the gentleman must secure the best seats within his means. To ask a lady to accompany you to a place of amusement, and incur the risk of being obliged to stand during the performance, is to be inexcusably rude to her. Should the demand for seats be so great that you cannot secure them, inform her at once, and propose another occasion when you can make this provision for her comfort.

In entering the hall in which the entertainment is given, a gentleman should walk by the side of the lady until the seat is reached. If the width of the aisle is not sufficient to allow this, he should precede her. As a rule, he should take the outer seat; but if this is the best for seeing or hearing, it belongs to the lady.

The habit of leaving ladies alone during the "waits," and going out to "get a drink," or "to speak to a friend," is indicative of bad manners. A gentleman escorting a lady to a place of amusement is bound to remain by her side to the end of the entertainment.

Between the Acts.

At the opera it is customary for ladies and gentlemen to leave their seats, and promenade in the lobbies or *foyer* of the house during the intervals between the acts. The gentleman should always invite the lady to do so. Should she decline, he is bound to remain with her.

A gentleman accompanying a lady is not bound to give up his seat to another lady. His duty is solely to the lady he accompanies. He cannot tell at what moment she may need his services, and must remain where she can command them.

It is rude to whisper or talk during a performance. It is discourteous to the performers, and annoying to those of the audience around you, who desire to enjoy the entertainment.

To seek to draw attention to yourself at a place of amusement is simply vulgar.

It is in especial bad taste for lovers to indulge in any affectionate demonstrations at such places.

A gentleman must see that the lady accompanying him is provided with a programme. If at the opera, he must also provide her with a libretto.

Applause is the just due of the deserving actor, and should be given liberally. Applaud by clapping the hands, and not by stamping or kicking with the feet.

Upon escorting the lady back to her home, the gentleman should ask permission to call upon her the next day, which request she should grant. She should, in her own sweet way, cause him to feel that he has conferred a genuine pleasure upon her by his invitation.

A gentleman who can afford it should always provide a carriage on such occasions. If his means do not permit this, he should not embarrass himself by assuming the expense. If the evening be stormy, he should not expect the lady to venture out without a carriage.

A gentleman should call at the lady's house in full time to allow them to reach their destination before the commencement of the entertainment.

WALKING RIDING BOATING DRIVING

YOUR conduct on the street should always be modest and dignified. Loud and boisterous conversation or laughter and all undue liveliness are improper in public, especially in a lady.

When walking on the street do not permit yourself to be so absent-minded as to fail to recognize your friends. Walk erect and with dignity, and do not go along reading a book or a newspaper.

Should you stop to speak to a friend, withdraw to the side of the walk with him, that you may not interrupt the passing of others. Should your friend have a stranger with him, apologize to the stranger for the interruption. You must never leave your friend with whom you are walking to speak to another without first asking him to excuse you.

In walking with a lady on the street, give her the inner side of the walk, unless the outside is the safer part, in which case she is entitled to it. Your arm should not be given to any lady except your wife or a near relative, or a very old lady, during the day, unless her comfort or safety require it. At night the arm should always be offered; also in ascending the steps of a public building. A gentleman should accommodate his walk to that of a lady, or an elderly or delicate person.

When a lady with whom a gentleman is walking wishes to enter a store, he should open the door, permit her to pass in first, if practicable, follow her, and close the door. He should always ring door bells or rap at a door for her. A gentleman should never pass in front of a lady, unless absolutely necessary, and should then apologize for so doing.

Should a lady ask information of a gentleman on the street, he must raise his hat, bow, and give the desired information. If unable to do so, he must bow and courteously express his regrets.

In crossing the street, a lady should gracefully raise her dress a little above her ankle with one hand. To raise the dress with both hands is vulgar, except in places where the mud is very deep.

A gentleman meeting a lady acquaintance on the street should not presume to join her in her walk without first asking her permission. It may not be agreeable to her, or convenient that her most intimate friend should join her. She has the right, after granting such permission, to excuse herself and leave the gentleman whenever she may see fit; and a gentleman will never take offense at the exercise of such a right. If it is inconvenient for a lady to accept the gentleman's company, she should frankly say so, mentioning some reason, and excusing herself with friendly courtesy. Gentlemen give place to ladies, and to gentlemen accompanying ladies, in crossing the street.

If you have anything to say to a lady whom you may happen to meet in the street, however intimate you may be, do not stop her, but turn round and walk in company; you can take leave at the end of the street.

Etiquette of the Street.

When you are passing in the street, and see coming toward you a person of your acquaintance, whether a lady or an elderly person, you should offer them the wall—that is to say, the side next the houses. If a carriage should happen to stop in such a manner as to leave only a narrow passage between it and the houses, beware of elbowing and rudely crowding the passengers, with a view to get by more expeditiously. Wait your turn, and, if any of the persons before mentioned come up, you should edge up to the wall, in order to give them the place. They also, as they pass, should bow politely to you.

When two gentlemen accompany a lady in a walk, she should place herself between them, and not unduly favor either. A gentleman meeting a lady friend accompanied by another gentleman should not join her unless satisfied that his presence is agreeable to both parties.

A lady should not venture out upon the street alone after dark. By so doing she compromises her dignity, and exposes herself to indignity at the hands of the rougher class. When a lady passes the evening with a friend, she should make arrangements beforehand for some one to come for her at a stated hour. If this cannot be done, or if the escort fails to come, she should courteously ask the host to permit a servant to accompany her home. A married lady may, if circumstances render it necessary, return home alone. An unmarried lady should never do so.

Should your host offer to accompany you himself, decline his offer, politely stating that you do not wish to give him so much trouble; but should he insist upon it, accept his escort. In the case of a married lady, the husband should always come for her. He is an ill-bred fellow who refuses to render his wife such attention. A lady, upon arriving at her home, should always dismiss her escort with thanks. A gentleman should not enter the house, although invited by the lady to do so, unless for some especial reason.

Evading a Long Talk.

Never offer to shake hands with a lady in the street if you have on dark gloves as you may soil her white ones.

If, when on your way to fulfil an engagement, a friend stops you in the street, you may, without committing any breach of etiquette, tell him of your appointment, and release yourself from a long talk; but do so in a courteous manner, expressing regret for the necessity.

A lady does not form acquaintances upon the street, or seek to attract the attention of the other sex, or of persons of her own sex. Her conduct is always modest and unassuming. Neither does a lady demand services or favors from gentlemen. She accepts them graciously, always expressing her thanks.

A gentleman will not stand on the street corners, or in hotel doorways, or club windows, and gaze impertinently at ladies as they pass by. This is the exclusive business of loafers, upon which well-bred men will not trespass.

Do not shout to your acquaintances from the opposite side of the street. Bow, or wave your hand, or make any courteous motion; but do it quietly and with dignity. If you wish to speak to them, cross the street, signalling to them your desire.

A lady walking with two gentlemen should not take an arm of each; neither should a gentleman walk with a lady on each arm, unless at night, in coming from a place of amusement or passing through a crowd.

In walking with a lady who has your arm, should you have to cross the street, do not disengage your arm and go around upon the outside unless the lady's comfort renders it necessary.

In walking with a lady, where it is necessary for you to proceed singly, always go before her.

ETIQUETTE OF RIDING.

The etiquette of riding is very exact and important. Remember that your left when in the saddle is called the *near*-side, and your right the *off*-side, and that you always mount on the *near*-side. In doing this, put your left foot in the stirrup; your left hand on the saddle; then, as you take a spring, throw your right leg over the animal's back. Remember, also, that the rule of the road, both in riding and driving, is, that you keep to the *right*.

Never appear in public on horseback unless you have mastered the inelegancies attending a first appearance in the saddle, which you should do at a riding-school. A novice makes an exhibition of himself, and brings ridicule on his friends. Having got a "seat" by a little practice, bear in mind the advice conveyed in the old rhyme—

"Keep up your head and your heart,

Your hands and your heels keep down,

Press your knees close to your horse's sides

And your elbows close to your own."

In riding with ladies, recollect that it is your duty to see them in their saddles before you mount. And the assistance they require must not be rendered by a groom; you must assist them yourself.

The lady will place herself on the near side of the horse, her skirt gathered up in her left hand, her right on the pommel, keeping her face toward the horse's head. You stand at its shoulder, facing her, and stooping, hold your hand so that she may place her left foot in it; then lift it as she springs, so as to aid her, but not to give such an impetus that, like "vaulting ambition," she loses her balance, and "falls o' the other side." Next, put her foot in the stirrup and smooth the skirt of her habit—then you are at liberty to mount yourself.

THE PROPER POSITION OF A LADY AND GENTLEMAN IN RIDING.

Keep to the right of the lady or any ladies riding with you.

Open all gates and pay all tolls on the road. Never, under any circumstances, allow a lady to attend to any duty of this kind while under your escort. You must anticipate her every need, and provide for it; making her comfort your first thought.

If you meet friends on horseback, do not turn back with them; if you overtake them, do not thrust your company upon them unless you feel assured that it is agreeable to them for you to do so.

If you are on horseback and meet a lady who is walking, and with whom you wish to speak, dismount for that purpose, and lead your horse. To put her to the inconvenience of straining after and shouting to you, would be a gross breach of manners.

MODE OF ASSISTING A LADY INTO A CARRIAGE.

If you enter a carriage with a lady, let her first take her place on the seat facing the horses. Enter a carriage so that your back is toward the seat you are to occupy; you will thus avoid turning round in the carriage, which is awkward. Take care that you do not trample on the ladies' dresses, or shut them in as you close the door.

The rule in all cases is this: you quit the carriage first and hand the lady out.

You may properly speed your horse in driving with a lady, but remember that it is vulgar to drive too fast; it suggests the idea of your having hired the "trap" from a livery stable, and is in every respect ungentlemanly.

The carriage or buggy should be driven close to the sidewalk, and the horses turned from the sidewalk, so as to spread the wheels away from the step. The gentleman should then alight, quiet the horses, and hold the reins in his right hand as a guard against accidents. The lady should, in leaving the carriage, place her hands on the gentleman's shoulders, while he should place his under her elbows. Then, with his assistance, she should spring lightly to the pavement, passing him on his left side to avoid the reins which he holds in his right. In driving, the gentleman must place a lady on his left. This leaves his right arm free to manage his horses.

A gentleman should not drive fast if the lady accompanying him is timid, or objects to it. He should consult her wishes in all things, and take no risks, as he is responsible for her safety. Above all, he should never race with another team. Such conduct is disrespectful to the lady who accompanies him.

THE ETIQUETTE OF BOATING.

There are certain customs and usages in connection with this interesting pastime that deserve to be noted and observed.

Gentlemen unaccustomed to the management of a boat should never venture out with ladies. To do so is foolhardy, if not criminal. Great care should be taken not to overload a boat. The frequent boating accidents that happen are in most instances due either to overloading, or to the inexperience of the man at the oars. Men who cannot swim should never take ladies upon the water.

Assisting Ladies to Their Seats.

When the gentlemen are going out with the ladies, one of them steps into the boat and helps the ladies in and seats them, the other handing them down from the bank or pier. When the ladies have comfortably disposed themselves, and not before, the boat may be shoved off. Great care must be taken not to splash the ladies, either in first dipping the oars or subsequently. Neither should anything be done to cause them fright.

A BOATING PARTY.

Who Should Row.

If a friend is with you, he must be given the preference of seats. You must ask him to row "stroke," as that is the place of honor.

If you cannot row, do not pretend you can. Say right out that you can't, and thus settle it, consoling yourself with the pleasant reflection that your confession entitles you to a seat by the side of the ladies and relieves you from the possibility of drowning the whole party.

A Popular Exercise.

Rowing has become a great fad among the ladies in recent years, and it is to be commended as a wholesome and vigorous exercise. But it should be indulged only on quiet rivers or on private lakes. If ladies venture into more frequented waters, they must at least have the protection of a gentleman. And in all cases they must wear costumes proper for the exercise, which requires freedom of movement in every part. Corsets should be left at home, and a good pair of stout boots should complete an equipment in which a skirt barely touching the ground, a flannel shirt and a sailor hat are the leading features. Rowing gloves should protect the hands.

The ordinary rowing costume for gentlemen is white flannel trousers, white rowing jersey and a straw hat. Peajackets are worn when their owners are not absolutely employed in pulling the oar.

BICYCLE: ETIQUETTE

CYCLING having taken such a mighty grasp upon the land, it has naturally followed that an etiquette of cycling should be established, and that it should be well established and rigidly regarded by society.

There are the details of meeting, mounting, right of way and various other points which are carefully observed and give the desired air of fashionable righteousness, without which, for many people, the pleasure of meeting in a social way on one's wheel would be but legendary.

It is distinctly understood in the first place that "cycling" is the correct word; the up-to-date woman dares not speak of bicycling nor of wheeling.

A Cycler's Guide.

If in town, the early hours of the morning are chosen for a ride through the park. This is on the same principle that it is considered good form for a young woman to drive only in the morning, that is, when she herself is the whip. In the country the rules, both as regards cycling and driving, are not as rigid. The maiden, however, who is a stickler for form, does all her cycling in the hours which come before noon—unless there be a special meet, a bicycle tea, for instance, or a spin by moonlight.

Neither is it correct for a young woman to ride unaccompanied. In the matter of chaperons we are becoming almost as rigid as the French, who scarcely allow a young girl to cross the street, to say nothing of shopping or calling, without being accompanied by an elder woman, her mother, relative, or a friend, as a chaperon.

During the past few years there has been a tendency in America toward a closer imitation of all French etiquette which has brought in its train a strict construction of the duties of a chaperon.

Maids Do Duty.

The unmarried woman who cycles must be chaperoned by a married lady—as every one rides nowadays, this is an affair easily managed. Neither must the married woman ride alone; failing a male escort, she is followed by a groom or a maid.

A woman is very fortunate if among her men or women servants, one knows how to ride a bicycle. Ladies occasionally go to the expense of having a servant trained in the art.

A Man's Duty.

If one possesses such a commodity as a brother or a husband, he can always be made useful on a cycling excursion. Never is a man better able to show for what purpose he was made than upon such occasions.

The man's duty to the woman who rides might be made the text for a long sermon; but long sermons are never popular; therefore, it may be better to state briefly that he must always be on the alert to assist his fair companion in every way in his power—he must be clever enough to repair any slight damage to her machine which may occur *en route*, he must assist her in mounting and dismounting, pick her up if she has a tumble, and make himself generally useful and incidentally ornamental and agreeable.

He rides at her left in order to give her the more guarded place, as the rule of the road in meeting other cyclers is the same as that for a carriage, to turn to the right. In England, the reverse is the case.

Assisting the Lady.

In mounting, the gentleman who is accompanying a lady holds her wheel; she stands on the left side of the machine and puts her right foot across the frame to the right pedal, which at the time must be up; pushing the right pedal causes the machine to start and then with the left foot in place, the rider starts ahead—slowly at first, in order to give her cavalier time to mount his wheel, which he will do in the briefest time possible.

When the end of the ride is reached, the man quickly dismounts and is at his companion's side to assist her, she, in the meantime, assisting herself as much as possible. This is done—that is, dismounting in the most approved style—by riding slowly, and when the left pedal is on the rise, the weight of the body is thrown on it, the right foot is crossed over the frame of the machine, and, with an assisting hand, the rider easily steps to the ground.

In meeting a party of cyclists who are known to each other and desire to stop for a parley, it is considered the proper thing for the men of the party to dismount while in conversation with the ladies.

As to the furnishings of the bicycle, to be really complete, it must be fitted out with a clock and a bell, luggage carrier and a cyclometer, the latter being an absolute *sine qua non* to the woman who cares for records. From five to six lessons are always considered necessary before one can master even the details of riding.

On the Road.

On the road the woman who wishes to ride *a la mode* has to know a number of little things that are overlooked by another woman, just as the smart set have a code for riding and driving that is as inexorable as that they should not eat with their knives or put sugar on oysters. Society insists on an upright position, with, of course, no attempt at racing pace. It also frowns upon constant ringing of the bell—that will do for the vulgar herd who delight in noise. The well-informed wheelwoman keeps eye and ear alert and touches her bell rarely. She dresses daintily and inconspicuously—effaces herself, in fact, as much in this exercise as she does in all public places.

Very gallant escorts use a towrope when accompanying a lady on a wheeling spin. These are managed in various ways; one consists of an India-rubber door-spring just strong enough to stretch a little with the strain, and about six feet of shade cord. One end is attached to the lady's wheel at the lamp bracket or brake rod by a spring swivel, and the other end is hooked to the escort's handle bar in such a way that he can set it free in a moment, if necessary. When he has finished towing he drops back to the lady's side, hanging the loose end of the cord over her shoulder, to be ready for the next hill. A gentle pull that is a bagatelle to a strong rider is of great assistance to a weak one up hill or against a strong wind.

For Protection Against Dogs.

Every bicyclist in the land will rise up and call the inventor of the ammonia gun for dogs blessed. Nothing is more annoying to the rider than to have a mongrel dog barking at his pedals and scurrying across his pathway in such close proximity to the front wheel as to be a constant reminder of a possible "header." The gun is calculated to make an annoying dog sneeze and sniff away all future ambitions to investigate the pace of a rider. It is said to be a perfect instrument in every way. The advantages enumerated for it are: Positively will not leak; has no spring to press or caps to remove, and will shoot from five to twelve times from fifteen to thirty feet with one loading.

A Few Don'ts for Cyclers.

Don't try to raise your hat to the passing "bloomer" until you become an expert in guiding your wheel.

Don't buy a bicycle with down-curve handles. It is impossible to sit erect and hold that kind of a handle.

Don't go out on a bicycle wearing a tail coat unless you enjoy making a ridiculous show of yourself.

Don't travel without a jacket or loose wrap, to be worn while resting. A summer cold is a stubborn thing.

Don't allow a taste for a bit of color in your make-up to tempt you to wearing a red or other gay-colored cap.

Don't get off the old gag about "that tired feeling" every time you stop by the roadside for a little breathing spell.

Don't absent yourself from church to go wheeling, as you and your bicycle are welcome at most houses of worship.

Don't leave your bicycle in the lower hallway of your flat-house for the other tenants to fall over in the dark.

Don't believe the farmer boy who says that it is "two miles to the next town." It may be two, four, six or twelve.

Don't be more than an hour passing a given point, although wheeling on a dusty road is honestly conducive to thirst.

Don't smile at the figure others cut astride their wheels, as it is not given you to see yourself as others see you.

Don't coast down a strange hill with a curve at its bottom. There is no telling what you will meet when it is too late.

Don't ride ten miles at a scorching pace, then drink cold water and lie around on the grass, unless you are tired of life.

Don't try to carry your bike downstairs under your arm. Put it on your shoulder, or you will come to distress.

Don't laugh the watchful copper to scorn because your lamp is burning brightly. He can afford to wait his time to laugh.

Don't dress immodestly or in the costume of a track sprinter. Sweaters worn like a Chinaman's blouse are almost indecent.

Don't forget that the modern law of the road requires you to turn out to the right in passing another bicycle or other vehicle.

Women's Bicycle Rides.

"Women who ride bicycles should make it a law with themselves never to ride after a feeling of weariness comes over them," said a well-known physician. "I just came from visiting a woman who tried to ride around the city last Sunday. It was the fourth time she had ever ridden a wheel out of doors. She got half way around, came home in street cars and a carriage, and has been sick in bed ever since. She ought to be an example to all women who ride. For those who are beginning, especially, and in a measure for all women, there is a great danger in overdoing. Some women ride centuries, it is true, but they are men in strength. No ordinary woman should start out before knowing how far she is going. Ordinarily, though, they ride twice as far as they ought. They start out and ride away from home until they get tired.

"Then they have to ride back, getting more and more exhausted with every turn of the wheels. No ordinary woman who rides once or twice a week should go more than ten miles at a trip. That is perhaps an hour's ride, that may be easily extended to an hour and a quarter before that distance is covered, and if she does not feel fresh and in a glow when she stops, she may be certain that she has ridden too long. Naturally there is that healthy tired feeling which any one recognizes after athletic exercise, but it is quite different from and never to be mistaken for the weariness which comes from too much exertion and straining of the nerves and muscles. Very few women have ever been injured on a bicycle who kept to this rule and limited their riding to nominal distances."

Length of the Ride.

"This limit of distance, which is designated by the feeling of weariness, is only a little more important than the limit of speed which the female frame is capable of undergoing under healthy exercising rules. Whether a man can ride at full speed for a long distance and still retain his good health is a doubtful question. It is certain, however, that no woman can keep up a high rate of speed for even a generous portion of a mile and not create the beginning of injuries. The added strength required to increase speed even a little after a certain amount of power has been expended is out of all proportion to the results. There is no relaxation of the muscles between revolutions of the pedals, nor any let up on the nervous and muscular strain while the speed lasts. The heart is far more taxed than one realizes at the moment, and that species of tingling or numbness in the nerves and muscles which often results is only a sign that they have both been overtaxed."

Properly used, a wheel is certainly a promoter of health. It develops muscles that are seldom, if ever, otherwise used. It gains for women that ideal condition of the flesh so prized by sculptors and artists, namely, a firm, solid tissue when the muscles are flexed, and a softness of an infant with muscular relaxation. It develops the entire torso and limbs, it renders one's nerves like steel and is a splendid antidote for headaches.

An exceedingly smart and yet thoroughly practical cycling costume is known as the "Londonderry," and is made in gray-green hopsack, a soft fabric which lends itself admirably to the full folds of the ample knickerbockers, which form a most important part of this costume. The "Londonderry" coat is made with long and very full basques, which form a kind of skirt when on the machine, and which, nevertheless, do not interfere in the least with the rider's freedom of action. This coat is prettily braided with black, and fastened with big black buttons. It is so arranged in front that it can be worn either with a shirt or over a double-breasted vest of cloth or leather.

Skirts are an Abomination.

A renowned lady writer says: "In the first place let me condemn the skirt—not from prejudice, but from experience. Skirts, no matter how light, how trim, how heavy, are both a nuisance and a danger. A nuisance because they are always subject to entanglement in the wheel; because they fly up with every breeze and motion; because they have not the chic appearance of the properly made bloomer, and because, if they are weighted, like a riding habit, they make so much more to carry against the wind. And breeze makes weight.

"They are a danger because with the constant pumping of the pedals the knee is required to raise too great a weight; this bears upon the body just below the back of the hips, giving backache; often more serious troubles. I wouldn't wear a skirt. I had one torn off me by the wheel; but I rode with them long enough to give a just comparison of the merits of skirts *versus* bloomers.

"Riding suits should be of fine, light weight, navy blue or black material, made with bloomers, and the blouse with tailor-made jacket. I wear the sweater myself in preference, because it is not so apt to leave one subject to changes of temperature. The Alpine hat of Tam O'Shanter is *au fait* for street, with leggings to match the bloomers and jacket, and low shoes made broad on the ball of the foot. All bicycle shoes should be broad on the ball, because the pedaling is done with the ball, not with the under curve, as so many think. Doeskin gloves are best for ordinary riding. Bloomers should be made to fasten at the left side of the back, which leaves room for a pocket on the right side. Tinted leggings should always match the hat and gloves.

"Tell the ladies to have their saddles built high and wide in the back, sloping away and downwards in front; and that if they pedal properly there is no reason why bicycling should not be a healthful, moral, modest and permanent form of exercise. For, mark it," she added, as a parting sally, "the wheel has come to stay."

A Pace Indicator.

A man who rides for health and pleasure and not to race or score centuries says that his plan is never to go so fast that he must breathe through his mouth. As long as his nostrils can supply sufficient air he knows that he is not over-exerting himself. As soon as he feels an inclination to breathe through his mouth he slackens his pace.

Don't Dodge a Bicycle.

Before bicycling will ever become a success a meeting must be called for the purpose of allowing the wheelmen and the pedestrian to arrive at some understanding. "I am in favor of a convention or something of that sort," said a prominent wheelman to a reporter.

As it is now, a rider comes down the street and sees ahead of him at a crossing a man or woman who is supposed to be endowed with reasonable intelligence. This person is in the act of crossing the street. He looks up, sees the rider coming and stands still right in the middle of the street. Of course, he is mentally calculating his chances for getting across safely.

In the meantime, the rider is getting closer and closer and is in a study equally as profound as to what the person is going to do. The pedestrian takes a step forward, takes another glance up the street, stops, starts back, makes an effort to reach the pavement, stops again, starts forward, stops.

Of course, by this time the cyclist is almost at a standstill and is also zigzagging from one side to the other, waiting and muttering. The pedestrian seems to give up all possibility of escape, faces the rider, both arms extended, jumps from one foot to the other, and the two collide. The cyclist is thrown to the ground, his wheel twisted, and he gets the blame.

And how easily all this can be avoided! Let the pedestrian, instead of performing all these trying evolutions, merely walk along as though there was nothing behind him, keep his course, and the cyclist will know what to do. He will turn his wheel to one side and slide past with perfect ease and safety. On the crossings let a man walk along as though there were not a bicycle in the state, and the wheelman will judge his course accordingly. He has control of his wheel and is as anxious not to collide as the other fellow.

CLUB ETIQUETTE

CLUB life in all large cities is becoming so important a factor of social life that no book on etiquette would be complete without some notice of its varied features.

The membership of the smaller social clubs is chosen solely for the purpose of social enjoyment, and they frequently blackball names that are brought up for membership simply from the standpoint of some member to whom the one proposed may not be personally agreeable. If an applicant is blackballed once, his friends should not persist in introducing his name again.

In the larger clubs, where the members are never all thrown together at any one time, no one should blackball a name from a personal standpoint.

If any one, however, is aware of some blemish in the character of the candidate for admission, he has good grounds for objection.

Observing the Rules.

A new member of a club should at once acquaint himself with the rules and regulations that govern the organization and govern himself accordingly. The courtesy that obtains in the home is to be observed in the club-rooms.

Opinions of others should be respected, and exciting discussions, or disturbing topics of conversation, are to be avoided there, as they should be in the home circle. Remember that every one has the same right to his preconceived opinions as you have to yours.

Treat all books, papers and other club property with due care. Never take any article away from the club-house. Never monopolize any one article to the exclusion of others.

When there are certain rooms appointed for smoking, confine yourself to them when indulging in the weed. In the reading-room observe the same respect for the readers that you would wish observed toward yourself, only another rendering of the Golden Rule which is at the foundation of all good manners. While there converse very little, and that in a low tone of voice.

Do not look upon the servants of the club as your private property, and never send them on personal errands without first obtaining the consent of the manager. Never expect undue attention from the waiters. Do not take dogs into club-rooms; they are liable to destroy furniture, and everyone may not appreciate them as much as you do.

Morning dress is worn at the club. In the evening a dress suit may be worn if desired, but morning costume is equally appropriate. Hats should be removed at luncheon or dinner.

Gentlemen will refrain from much mentioning of the names of ladies while in the club-rooms, or from indulging in scandal. Serious ill-feeling is often aroused in this manner. Many men refuse to listen to anything of the kind, and will retire if any such subject is brought up.

Introduction of Friends.

Some clubs have cards for introducing visitors, as:

VISITING CARD.

COLUMBIA CLUB, 420 Madison Square.

Admit Mr. ....

Introduced by Mr. ....

Club members are at liberty to introduce friends at their respective clubs, but care should be exercised in this respect, since they must vouch for their friends' behavior, and in many cases are held responsible for the debts they may contract. It is not at all necessary that such a guest should be formally presented to any of the officials, nor to many of the members, unless in the case of some guest whom the club would delight to honor.

RECEPTION AT THE CLUB.

The guest of a club is expected to conform to all rules of the association while enjoying its hospitalities, but he may also avail himself of all its privileges, with the exception that he is not permitted to introduce another stranger. A gentleman about to leave town, and who has been entertained at a club, leaves his card in a sealed envelope for the gentleman who introduced him.

Ladies' clubs are now coming to the front in such profusion as to make it necessary to give them some notice. The same general rules of etiquette apply to them as to a club of men. As a rule, women's clubs have some especial feature, some object to call them into being.

The most usual form that the club activities assume is that of literary work of some kind, either as a gathering of literary women, or simply a gathering of women for some particular form of literary study. They usually give club banquets and club luncheons, but rarely attain to the dignity of a café.

Barring Out Disputed Questions.

The temper of the meetings depends very largely on the kind of organization that holds them, whether, for instance, as in the case of Sorosis, it is a club of refined and educated women, of literary and artistic pursuits and tastes, or whether it is one for reform, as temperance, suffrage, social purity, or religious development and work. The members of Sorosis, when in session, are well-bred, if not always clearheaded and reasonable. Religious gatherings of women are seldom other than of good temper, and quiet in their tone.

Political meetings and sectarian meetings are apt to be turbulent. This fact has been recognized by some women's clubs, Sorosis, for example, and they will not permit the subjects to be discussed or introduced in any way at meetings.

The various business womens and working girls' clubs are instituted for the sole purpose usually of furnishing good lunches at the noon hour at reasonable rates, and combine this feature with pleasant reception and lounging rooms, and often with various literary and business courses of study.

There is one Ladies' Suburban Club—the Alexandra—the most exclusive of London's women clubs. It is also the most successful. No individual of the other sex above the age of twelve is admitted beyond the doormat. Husbands, fathers, and brothers, are all ruthlessly excluded from within its sacred precincts. It furnishes an admirable center for shopping operations, and for lunches, teas, etc. It possesses the advantages of bedrooms, let at the most reasonable rate, so that girls and young married women can spend a night or two in town without any trouble to chaperons or maids. Women friends, of course, may be admitted into the club, and servants and tradespeople interviewed. It is named for the Princess of Wales, and no one who has not been presented to the Queen is eligible to membership.

There is also a Ladies' Suburban Club in Chicago that partakes of the same features, save that it is not founded upon quite so aristocratic a basis, and the suburban woman heartily appreciates its benefits. No more does she wander aimlessly up and down the streets while awaiting a home-bound train. She has a resting place of her own within easy reach of the shopping district, one where she can be made presentable for matinée or theater. Here, on one floor, she finds hairdressers, manicurists, a café, a woman ready to repair damaged garments; and should she miss the last train, comfortable sleeping-rooms, where she can spend the night quietly. There, the club-shopper is ready to attend sales and do all manner of purchasing—from ordering funeral flowers to selecting a good seat at the theater, while the club nursery is responsible for all children left there. Their membership hails from many states.

Presiding at a Woman's Club.

The average woman is not so well qualified to preside over meetings in which continual interruptions are occurring, through the members rising to points of order, and other questions of privilege, because, unlike the average man, she has not given much attention to the study of parliamentary law.

The rules for conducting a meeting do not admit of any personal feeling or individual taste on the part of the presiding officer. On the contrary, there is a code of rules expressly laid down to guide and regulate such matters.

The presiding officer is not supposed to control the opinions of the members, but merely to direct them. She should be in entire sympathy with the objects of the meeting, and have a full and complete understanding of all its aims, objects and purposes. This latter is a very important consideration. Members, and especially new ones, are constantly asking for information, and unless the presiding officer can furnish it briefly and at once, delays are sure to occur, and the meeting be anything but pleasant or satisfactory to the other members present.

Order of Business.

Having been chosen to preside, the first duty is to call the meeting to order. If it is a first meeting, the objects for which it is called should then be stated clearly, but in as few words as possible. If it is not a first meeting, but a regular or constituted one, the presiding officer should have the roll of members called by the secretary. The minutes of the last meeting should then be read. Next, the presiding officer should appoint her committees for the session; or, if it is a regular meeting, the reports of the various committees appointed at the previous session should be heard. Next, the regular business should be taken up, and having been disposed of, the presiding officer should allow the introduction of any new business that may properly come before the meeting.

It is of the utmost importance that a presiding officer should be possessed of good eyesight, so as to be able to perceive a member as soon as she rises. There must be no hesitation or nervousness about a presiding officer. She must be ever on the alert, with all her faculties about her. She must be broad-minded, liberal, and clear-visioned, with a readiness to instruct the members when any mistakes are made, and always willing to grant the full liberty of debate to all; for out of the widest differences will come the very best conclusions after full and fair discussion.

SOCIETY

WOMEN are our only leisure class. This has been so often repeated that it scarcely matters to whom the credit of the saying must be given.

In this country the burden of social work rests upon women, while in all European countries, men, young and old, statesmen, officials, princes, ambassadors, make it one of the duties of life to visit, leave cards and take up all the numerous burdens of the social world.

Here it is the lady of the house that does all this. Husbands, fathers, sons, are all too much engrossed in the pursuit of business or pleasure to spend time in these multifarious cares. Mrs. John Sherwood says: "They cannot even spend time to make their dinner calls. 'Mamma, please leave my cards,' is the legend written on their banners."

Influence of Women.

The wonderful influence of women of culture and fashion, with their "happy ways of doing things" in the political, as well as the social world, is as great now in Washington as it ever was in Paris, in the palmiest days of the Imperial *Salon*.

The graces and the courtesies of life are in their hands. It is women who create society. It is women from whom etiquette is learned, not from association with men. The height of a stage of civilization can always be measured by the amount of deference paid to woman. The culture of a particular man can be gauged by his manner when in the company of ladies.

Primitive man made women do all the hard work of life, bear all the burdens, eat of the leavings, and be the servants of the tribe.

Civilized man, on the other hand, gives precedence to woman in every particular. He serves her first, he gives her places of comfort and safety, he rises to assist her at every opportunity, and we measure his culture by sins of omission, or commission, along this line.

Thus, all these small observances not only conduce to the comfort of woman, but they refine and do away with the rough and selfish side of man's nature, for without this refining contact with gentle womanhood, a man will never lose the innate roughness with which nature has endowed him.

It is women, as before said, who create etiquette, and Burke tells us that "manners are of more importance than laws." A fine manner is the "open sesame" that admits us to the audience chamber of the world. It is the magic wand at whose touch all barriers dissolve.

Effect of Cultured Manners.

"Give a boy address and accomplishments and you give him the mastery of palaces and fortunes wherever he goes. He has not the trouble of earning or owning them; they solicit him to enter and possess."

Whatever enjoyment we obtain from our daily intercourse with others is through our obedience to the laws of etiquette, which govern the whole machinery of society, and it is largely to women with their leisure, and their tact, that we must look to create and sustain the social fabric.

"To know her is a liberal education," was the stately compliment once paid a woman, and there are women left to whom it still applies.

As Emerson says in his essay upon "Manners:" "Are there not women who inspire us with courtesy; who unloose our tongues, and we speak; who anoint our eyes, and we see? We say things we never thought to have said. For once, our walls of habitual reserve vanished and left us at large; we were children playing with children in a wide field of flowers. Steep us, we cried, in these influences for days, for weeks, and we shall be sunny poets and write out in many-colored words the romance that you are."

The successful society woman has a genius for leadership. She molds and makes what she will of her surroundings. She undervalues the talents of no one; she rather draws out and makes the most of every one with whom she comes in contact.

She is quiet, she is reposeful, she has the tact that puts every one with whom she meets at ease, and, above all, she is sympathetic. A judiciously expressed sympathy with our fellow-beings is one of the highest attributes of our nature.

"Unite sympathy to observation and the dead spring to life." It is tact to so express that sympathy as not to seem aware of the weakness that we would support and conceal from others. Madame Récamier had this gift of hidden sympathy, this power of drawing out the best that was in those who approached her. To this gift it was that she owed that power over all men which survived her wonderful beauty.

A Sympathetic Nature.

It was not her wit, for with this she was not so greatly endowed; it was not alone her beauty, for the eminent men and women of the day followed her when, blind and poor, she sought the solitude of the abbey; but it was the delicate tendrils of her sympathy and the steadfastness of her friendship that drew towards her all hearts, and molded and welded her company of followers into one of the most perfect and powerful social circles that has ever surrounded any society leader.

Many an awkward situation has been saved by feminine tact. There was the cabinet-member's wife who drank out of her finger-bowl because her guest, a senator, had done so. And the general's wife who, when a clumsy tea drinker smashed a priceless cup, picked up another of the fragile affairs and crushed it between her fingers with a "They do break easily, don't they?" And the woman who, when M. Blanc was mistaken at an English garden party for a page, replied, "Well, M. Blanc is a page—of history."

This tact is in great measure a natural gift, but it can be cultivated, and is well worth the trouble. Nothing can be so utterly painful in society as the tactless person who is perpetually "doing those things which he ought not to have done, and leaving undone those things which he ought to have done."

The art of conversation, too, is worth cultivating. A woman, noted among her friends for her delightful letters and as delightful gifts of conversation, was asked how she managed it.

"Frankly," was the reply, "I strive for it. When I see in a book or hear anywhere a happy phrase, or a telling sentence, I make a mental note of it, and watch for an opportunity to incorporate it in my own speech or written word. I don't mean I appropriate other folks' ideas in wholesale fashion, but I do steal or utilize their knack of expression. Another point I make is never to permit myself to speak carelessly, that is, slovenly, any more than I let my hair be untidy or my gowns mud-stained. It does not seem to me frivolous or bestowing too much care on trifles to take this small pains for my betterment. I pin a flower on my dress for a bit of color, or adjust a bow where I know it is becoming; why should I not apply the decorative idea to my speech?"

Power through Repose.

Cultivate repose of manner. Be calm and restful. Do not fidget. Command of the tongue is a valuable accomplishment to cultivate. Many a young girl is actually fidgety, because she thinks to be a success she must be "full of life" and always "on the go." She wants to be bright and vivacious. If such is her temperament and her vivaciousness comes spontaneously it is perhaps attractive, though it is very likely to get tiresome.

Nine out of ten women would be twice as attractive if they would learn to keep still and thus gain the full social value of this ability. Especially is this true of young girls. When a young man is introduced, why plunge at him with a volley of phrases? An effect is made twice as quickly if his look is met with steady, quiet eyes, a few words spoken in a gentle, sincere voice, and a chance given him. Presumably, he requested the introduction, and so, probably, he has something to say. Anyway, he is likely to have, if you are serene and quiet.

A habit of repose will save from many a blunder. When a man, one does not remember, plunges into a conversation, the habit of repose enables one to keep an unmoved and quiet demeanor until something is said that will "place" him. To be in a hurry to speak is to betray oneself, and embarrassment ensues on both sides.

This command of quiet is also a protection against tiresome, talkative, people. It enables one to preserve an air of kindly attention, while one's thoughts, free and untrammeled, roam at their own sweet will, drifting back just in time to utter an appreciative affirmative, or negative.

A Good Listener.

This repose of manner is a boon to the shy and awkward man, who, under its influence, actually acquires some confidence in himself, which is simply impossible when he is bombarded with a volley of vivacious conversation.

Learn to be a good listener, a sympathetic and interested listener, and the majority of people will pronounce you "interesting." If the partner assigned you at a dinner party seems to have no topic in common with your thought, strive to find out what does interest him; a few skillful questions, and he is launched on a tide of talk, at his ease, even brilliant, and all that is needed on your part is to appear interested. Whether you understand the subject, or care for it, is another question; you have established your place in that man's estimation, and he will ever thereafter have a word of praise when your name is mentioned.

There are women who are themselves not fluent, and who enjoy being talked to, to be spared the trouble of "making conversation." With these women it is the ready talker who finds favor. But there is another class of women quite as large who love to talk, and to them the good listener is welcome; therefore, let the man who wishes to talk choose his audience with discretion.

Madame Récamier liked to be talked to, and was so sympathetic a listener that the careful student of her times is forced to conclude that was one of the chiefest of her charms, but he would have been a bold man who would have interrupted the flow of Madame de Staël's eloquence.

Men are less inclined to certain forms of etiquette than women. Not that they would be less polite, but, as a rule, they do not attach so much importance to the little niceties of life, and they are too prone to lack in certain courtesies which a society man should practice.

How Men are Spoiled.

This process of spoiling begins with the mothers, and ends with the young women. Women pride themselves upon being independent, and the result is that the men naturally fall back and let them wait upon themselves. Women take the lead, women plan entertainments and excursions, women tolerate neglect, and all of this spoils the men. Be a woman first and last, and exact all these little courtesies for the sake of your sex.

Says a well-known lady: "I remember a thing that impressed me very much, and made me ashamed of my own sons whom I have always waited upon, I am sorry to say. We had as guests a gentleman, wife and son, the latter about thirteen. In the morning there was a parade; the gentleman and his wife went, while I stayed at home with another relative. The boys came in to luncheon, and then as I was going up-town, Harry, our visitor, put up his wheel, brushed his clothes, and announced that he was ready to escort me. I assured him that we did not need him, to run along with the other boys, but he would not hear of it. He opened the gates, carried my umbrella, and stayed with me until he saw me safe at home. I complimented him to his mother, but she assured me that he would never have thought of doing anything else, for when the father could not accompany her, Harry had been taught to do so. I had always assured my boys that I could take care of myself, but I wish now I had made them take care of me."

GENERAL ETIQUETTE

THIS chapter is devoted to the gathering up of the fragments that remain from all the other departments that cannot be rigidly classified, and yet are useful to remember.

There are many minute points of etiquette which, although not extremely important, often serve as a source of embarrassment to uninitiated persons, and upon which information that can be relied upon is desired.

Who Bows First?

Whether the lady or gentleman should bow first is a point where many differ. That the lady should bow first, most authorities agree in declaring. This acts as a safeguard to a lady, permitting her to drop an undesirable acquaintance, as a failure to bow would be considered the "cut direct." But some ladies are forgetful of faces, and some are near-sighted, thus preventing ready recognition of others; so that, while this custom might apply to introductions given at a ball, still, a bow hurts no one, and an undesirable acquaintance is easily dropped without this rudeness. Hence it would seem that, whichever one recognizes first, the other ought to have the privilege of bowing without breaking this social law, which is better observed in the spirit than in the letter.

"Lady" or "Gentleman?"

These terms have come to be used so continuously, and sometimes so meaninglessly that they bid fair to crowd out the sweet, strong words, "man" and "woman," and a revulsion of taste has swept in that goes nigh in some "sets" to utterly swamp the "lady" and "gentleman." Either extreme is a mistake.

There is a right and wrong use of these terms; for example, one says to one's servants, or to one's children, "I expect some ladies to visit me to-morrow," while later, referring to them in conversation with a friend, one may say, "they are women of exquisite culture." A matron may speak of young ladies as "girls," but if she be not intimate, "young ladies," is more usual, or she may address them collectively as "young women."

Misuse of the Term "Lady."

The term "lady" has been more abused than that of "gentleman." The words "fore-lady," "sales-lady," "wash-lady," have rendered it ludicrous when one thinks of contrasting it with the terms, happily never used, of "fore-gentleman," "sales-gentleman," etc.

Formal consideration asks "if the ladies are at home," and refined custom requires it. But to express the graces and endowments of a woman, it is her womanliness that is emphasized. "She is a gracious, sweet-tempered, kindly woman." The same distinction applies to the use of the term "gentleman," or "man."

Says one writer, giving some examples of the use of these words: "A polite host would say, 'The men are looking for some ladies who would enjoy a game of tennis,' or, 'I can promise the young ladies a pleasant time, for there will be a great many dancing men present.' One gentleman says to another, in expressing his admiration, 'Miss Blank is my ideal of a lovely and lovable woman' (he does not say 'lady'), but in the same breath he may add, 'Let us join the ladies (not 'women') on the balcony.'"

One should always say "she is such a sweet old lady," rather than "she is such a sweet old woman."

Much might be said in this regard, but after all, exact discrimination of the proper term at the proper time must be left somewhat to the personal judgment of each man and woman.

The leading business and professional men owe their success, in great measure, to their graciousness in business manners. It is well, from many points of view, to form the habit of treating all, rich and poor, men and women, with uniform courtesy. The pleasant business man draws the largest custom. The polite professional man secures the best clientage.

Pay bills and drafts promptly, or else explain satisfactorily to your creditor when you will be able to meet the obligation. If your word has always been as good as your bond, in nine cases out of ten he will grant the extension of time desired.

Keep appointments to the moment. If unable to do so, send a messenger to explain. Finish your business promptly and then leave. Time is money. Never misrepresent goods, nor allow others in your employ so to do.

Enclose a stamped envelope for reply when asking for information that is to benefit yourself solely. Answer letters of inquiry promptly. Do not display curiosity in regard to business matters that do not concern you, nor try to examine the books or private papers of another. Be polite to all employés. They will give much better service.

Business Forms are always useful, hence we furnish some that are in constant use:

A Promissory Note.

$300. CHICAGO, Ill., November 5, 189-.

Ninety days after date I promise to pay to Charles Chapman, or order, at the Second National Bank, Three Hundred Dollars, value received.

MARTIN VOORHEES.

If it is intended to draw interest that should be added, thus, "with interest at six per cent."

A Joint Note.

$200. SALIDA, Col., December 2, 189-.

Three months after date we jointly promise to pay Howard Crosby, or orders, Two Hundred Dollars, value received.

GRACE HARDING.
GEORGE HARDING.

A Receipt on Account.

$500. SAN MATEO, Cal., November 1, 189-.

Received of George Woods, Five Hundred Dollars, on account.

FRANK JAMES.

A Receipt in Full.

$200. LOUISANA, Mo., October 31, 189-.

Received of John Jenkins, Two Hundred Dollars, in full for all demands up to date.

JAMES HIGGINS.

Form for a Bill.

NEW YORK, December 3, 189-.

MR. JOHN HENSON.

To JAMES CARROLL, DR.

To 10 pounds coffee, @ 30c	$3.00
To 20 pounds sugar, @ 5c	1.00
To 2 pounds lard, @ 18c	.36
To 1 pound tea, @ 60c	.60
	$4.96

What and What Not to Say.

Don't say "I feel good," for "I feel well."

Don't say "these kind," but "this kind."

Don't say "not so good as," for "not as good as."

Don't say "between three," but "among three."

Don't describe an unusual occurrence as "funny," unless something comic is meant. Strange, peculiar, unique, odd, are better expressions.

Don't say a garment "sets good," but it "fits well."

Don't say "had rather," "had better," for "would rather," "would better."

Don't speak of articles of diet as "healthy," but as "healthful" or "wholesome."

Don't say "fix my gown," "fix this room," but "arrange my gown," "the room." The best authorities rarely use fix, except to indicate stability or permanence. You don't fix the house, you repair it.

Say money is "plentiful," not "plenty."

Say "between you and me."

Say "If he should live," "If he should come," instead of "If he comes," "If he live."

Don't say "I have saw" for "I have seen."

Don't say "dress;" if a lady, say "gown." The word dress applies to the entire toilet. Gown, to the one article.

Various Hints on Etiquette.

Enter a room as if you felt yourself entitled to a welcome, but wished to take no undue advantage of it.

Do not press a favor where you see it will be unwelcome.

Treat all the guests you meet at your friend's table, for the time being, as your equals.

A very trifling and yet important thing that every woman should know is that it is exceedingly inelegant in rising from a chair to raise herself by pressure on the arms. Unless she is old or infirm she should rise without assistance.

Do not rush into a friendship with everybody you meet. Friendships so quickly made are quickly broken.

In another man's house do not take upon yourself to play the host—not even at the host's request.

In making gifts let them be in proportion to your means. A rich man does not thank a poor man for making him a present which he knows the giver cannot afford.

Do not claim the acquaintance of a man of rank on the ground that you once met him at a house to which you had been invited.

Let it be said of you as it was said of Macaulay, that he remembered everything, "except an injury."

In making calls, do your best to lighten the infliction to your hostess. Do not stay long; and do not enter upon a subject of conversation which may terrify her with the apprehension that you intend to remain until you have exhausted it.

Do not give another, even if it be a better, version of a story already told by one of your companions.

The touchstone of good manners is the way in which a man behaves to his superiors or inferiors.

It is not proper for a gentleman to call upon a lady unless he has first received permission to do so.

It is not proper for a gentleman to wear his overshoes in the drawing-room.

HOME DELIGHTS.

Children or young people should never monopolize the most desirable positions and most comfortable chairs.

No gentleman will smoke while walking, riding or driving with a lady, or while speaking to her in the street. Sometimes, at informal summer resorts, there is a little latitude allowed here.

If a dinner party is given in honor of a lady, it is the host's place to go in to dinner first, taking in the lady in whose honor the dinner is given. Furthermore, it is proper, under some circumstances, for the hostess to go in to dinner last with the husband of the lady whom the host is escorting.

It is proper to help all the ladies, including those of the household, before any gentleman is helped, no matter how distinguished a person he may be.

First Attentions for Ladies.

When the visitors are gentlemen, and only a mother and daughter are at the table, the maid ought first to serve the mother, then the daughter and last the gentlemen. If the mother serves tea at luncheon she helps the daughter first, and after her the men guests. The rule is always that a lady takes precedence.

On leaving the table at a public place, such as a restaurant or hotel dining-room, the lady precedes the gentleman.

Apples are pared, and eaten in small quarters, at dessert. Grapes are plucked from their stems, and the pulp squeezed out in the mouth, while the fingers hold the skins, which are laid at one side of the plate. Bananas are peeled, cut in thin slices, and eaten with a fork. Peaches are eaten after paring, with a silver knife and fork. Oranges are skinned by cutting in quarters, or left whole, and the sections are then pulled apart, and eaten, rejecting the seeds into the hand.

Celery is usually dipped into the salt-cellar, and eaten from the stalk, or it can be cut on the plate, in small bits, and eaten with a fork. When dining at a hotel you can partake of the side dishes on the same plate that meat and potato have been served, or ask the waiter to change your plate, as you prefer.

When fried eggs are used for a breakfast dish, they are put upon your plate, from the side dish; but in many homes, eggs are baked in small dishes, each person being served with a dish, which should be well buttered before putting in the egg to be cooked.

It does not matter upon which side of her escort a lady sits at table. The gentleman will draw out a chair for the lady, if a waiter is not in attendance to do it, and take the next seat himself.

When passing your plate to be helped a second time, lay the knife and fork at the left-hand side.

Do not, if talking to a friend, drop all conversation so soon as a child requires attention, or has some childish remark to make.

When in parlor, or drawing-room, if a woman, standing, hands a cup, a book, a flower, or any article to a man who is seated, he should rise to receive it. This rule is without exception.

Minor Usages of the Best Society.

When a man offers a lady any civility, a stranger or an acquaintance, opens a door, hands her a parcel she has dropped, or offers her a seat, he should lift his hat at the same moment.

If a young lady accepts the escort of a gentleman to an entertainment, she should never accompany him, at its close, to a restaurant for refreshments unless she is chaperoned by a lady much older than herself.

"Good-evening" is a proper salutation upon entering a room for a call. "Good-night" upon retiring at its close.

A man on horseback, who sees a lady wishes to stop him, will dismount and walk by her side, leading his horse, for there are few occasions on which it is permissible to stand talking on the street.

A lady may permit a man walking with her to carry any small parcel that she has, but never more than one.

A lady wishing to avoid bowing to an undesirable acquaintance, must look aside, or drop the eyes, for if the eyes meet a bow is absolutely necessary.

If a lady asks a man to accompany her to a place of amusement, she must provide the conveyance.

If a lady invites a man to drive with her, he should walk to her house, unless the distance is too great, when she should offer to call for him. If this is the case, he should watch, and, if possible, meet her on the way.

Do not refuse to accept an apology; even if friendship is not restored, an open quarrel will be averted.

Do not be familiar with a new acquaintance. One can be courteous without familiarity.

Breaches of Etiquette.

It is a breach of etiquette to remove the gloves when making a formal call.

It is a breach of etiquette to stare around the room.

It is a breach of etiquette for a caller who is waiting the entrance of the hostess to open the piano or touch it if it is open.

It is a breach of etiquette to go to the room of an invalid unless invited.

It is a breach of etiquette to look at your watch when calling.

It is a breach of etiquette to walk around the room when waiting for the hostess.

It is a breach of etiquette for the caller to open or shut a door, raise or lower a window curtain, or in any other way alter the arrangement of a room.

It is a breach of etiquette to turn your chair so as to bring your back to some one near you.

It is a breach of etiquette when making a call to play with any ornament in the room, or to seem to be aware of anything but the company present.

It is a breach of etiquette to remain when you find the host or hostess dressed to go out.

It is a breach of etiquette during a call to draw near the fire to warm your hands or feet, unless you are invited by the mistress of the house to do so.

It is a breach of etiquette to make remarks upon a caller who has just left the room, whether by the hostess or visitors.

It is a breach of etiquette and a positive unkindness to call upon a friend who is in reduced circumstances with any parade of wealth in equipage or dress.

It is a breach of etiquette for the hostess to leave the room when visitors are present.

It is a breach of etiquette to assume any ungraceful or uncouth position, such as standing with the arms akimbo, sitting astride a chair, smoking in the presence of ladies, wearing your hat, leaning back in the chair, standing with legs crossed or feet on the chairs, leaning forward in the chair with elbows on the knees. All these acts stamp you as ill-bred and unpolished.

WASHINGTON ETIQUETTE

IN addition to the ordinary rules of etiquette, official society in Washington City is governed by a code of fixed laws. The social observances of the White House are prescribed with great exactness, and constitute the Court Etiquette of the Republic. At the very commencement of the Government under the Constitution the social question became one of great magnitude, and in order to adjust it upon a proper basis, President Washington caused a definite *Code* to be drawn up; but the rules were too arbitrary and exacting to give satisfaction, and society was not disposed to acknowledge so genuine an equality as the code required among its members. Frequent and bitter quarrels arose in consequence of the clashing of social claims, and at last a code was agreed upon, which may be stated as follows:

The Recognized Head.

The President and his family are recognized as the head and front of the social structure. The President, as such, must not be invited to dinner by any one, and accepts no such invitations, and pays no calls or visits of ceremony. He may visit in his private capacity at pleasure.

An invitation to dine at the White House takes precedence of all others, and a previous engagement must not be pleaded as an excuse for declining it. Such an invitation must be promptly accepted in writing.

During the winter season, a public reception or levee is held at stated times, at which guests are expected to appear in full dress. They are presented by the usher to the President, and have the honor of shaking hands with him. They then pass on, and are presented by another usher to the wife of the President, to whom they bow, and pass on. These receptions last from eight until ten o'clock P. M.

On the first of January and the Fourth of July the President holds public receptions, commencing at noon, at which the Foreign Ministers present in Washington appear in full court dress, and the officers of the army and navy in full uniform. On such occasions, the President receives first the Heads of Departments, Governors of States, Justices of the Supreme Court and Members of the two Houses of Congress, in the order named; then the Members of the Diplomatic Corps, who are followed by the officers of the army and navy. The doors are then thrown open to the general public, who for the space of two hours pay their respects to the Chief Magistrate of the Nation.

The Vice-President of the United States is expected to pay a formal visit to the President on the meeting of Congress, but he is entitled to the first visit from all other persons, which he may return by card or in person.

Formal Calls.

The Judges of the Supreme Court of the United States call upon the President and Vice-President on the annual meeting of the court in December, and on New Year's Day and the Fourth of July. They are entitled to the first call from all other persons.

Members of the Cabinet call upon the President on the first of January and the Fourth of July. They are required to pay the first calls, either in person or by card, to the Vice-President, the Judges of the Supreme Court, Senators and the Speaker of the House of Representatives on the meeting of Congress. They are entitled to the first call from all other persons.

Senators call in person upon the President and Vice-President on the meeting of Congress, New Year's Day and the Fourth of July, if Congress is in session at the last named time. They also call first upon the Judges of the Supreme Court, and upon the Speaker of the House of Representatives on the meeting of Congress. They are entitled to the first call from all other persons.

The Speaker of the House of Representatives calls upon the President on the meeting of Congress, on New Year's Day, and on the Fourth of July, if Congress is in session. The first call is due *from* him to the Vice-President and the Judges of the Supreme Court, but *to* him from all other persons.

Members of the House of Representatives call in person upon the President on the meeting of Congress, and on New Year's Day, and by card or in person on the Fourth of July, if Congress is in session. They call first, by card or in person, upon the Vice-President, the Judges of the Supreme Court, Speaker of the House, Senators, Cabinet Officers and Foreign Ministers, soon after the opening of the session.

Ministers from Foreign Countries.

Foreign Ministers call upon the President on the first of January and the Fourth of July. They call first, in person or by card, upon the Vice-President, Cabinet Officers, Judges of the Supreme Court and the Speaker of the House on the first opportunity after presenting their credentials to the President. They also make an annual call of ceremony, by card or in person, on the above mentioned officials soon after the meeting of Congress. They are entitled to the first calls from all other persons.

The Judges of the Court of Claims call in person upon the President on New Year's Day and the Fourth of July. They pay first calls to Cabinet Officers and Members of the Diplomatic Corps, and call annually, by card or in person, upon the Vice-President, Judges of the Supreme Court, Senators, Speaker and Members of the House soon after the meeting of Congress.

The intercourse of the other officers of the Government is regulated by superiority of rank in the public service.

The intercourse of the families of officials is regulated by the rules which govern the officials themselves.

Besides the public levees of the President, the ladies of the White House hold receptions at stated periods, to which invitations are regularly issued. The President sometimes appears upon these occasions, but is under no obligation to do so.

It has long been the custom for the President to give a series of State Dinners during the session of Congress, to which the various members of that body, the higher Government officials and the Diplomatic Corps are successively invited. In order to show attention to all, and offend none, it is necessary to give quite a number of these dinners during the session.

[The proper titles to be used in addressing the President, Members of the Cabinet, Members of Congress, Judges of the Supreme Court and other Government officials, are found in the Department on "Letter-Writing."]

DELSARTEAN DISCIPLINE

"THE end and aim of all our work should be the harmonious growth of our whole being," says Fröebel. "Know thyself," quoth Epictetus, the Stoic, and, knowing thyself, grow strong of mind, self-centered and self-possessed. "Know thyself," reiterates the modern disciple of Delsarte, since only by knowledge of self can be developed the real personality of the individual.

Grace and self-possession are the aim of Delsarte; it therefore fairly falls within the province of a work on etiquette to look somewhat into the subject. If one would control others he must first control himself, possess himself. Delsarte looked upon the nature of man as a trinity, and believed that the mental, moral and physical should be educated at the same time. Modern education tends to develop man in special directions to the neglect of others. Either the overstrained mental faculties revenge themselves by giving us the nervous, broken-down, mental type so common; or else we have the crude physical type wherein ordinary labor has exercised but a few muscles and joints.

The Three Languages.

Again, says Delsarte, "Man has for the expression of his triune nature three languages, the word, the tone, the gesture. Tones express bodily conditions, pleasure or pain. Words are symbols to interpret thought. Gestures relate to other beings and express our emotions. Of these three, the first receives undue cultivation, since we study all the words that have been said or written, while singers and actors alone cultivate tone or gesture."

Thus it comes that "the soul struggles to speak through an imperfect instrument; sometimes it ceases to struggle and finally has nothing to say."

In labor the man *moves*, special muscles do special work, but when a man is *moved*, an undulating "wave of feeling passes over him and his whole body becomes eloquent." A bow may be so careless and jerky as to be almost an insult, or it may be so gracious as to seem a caress. Again, the real self, gracious and beautiful, may strive to express itself through a set of faculties that are hardened and narrowed by decades of self-constraint on the part of himself and his ancestors.

"Physical habits have a way of making themselves felt by a reflex action on the inner nature," and with this axiom in view we feel that cultivation of the Delsartean Art of Expression becomes a vital part of our education to the end that all our emotions and all our tones may become "the outward and visible signs of an inward and spiritual nature." This principle may be called the keynote of Delsarteanism, and Edmond Russell, that modern exponent thereof, claims that as these beautiful, expressive gymnastics are for the purpose of correcting individual deviations from grace, no regular set of rules should be printed for the use of all, but that each special angularity of person or harshness of tone must be corrected by special exercises.

Harmonious Development of the Body.

Nevertheless, there are many set forms of movements by the practice of which none can fail to derive benefit both for the inner and the outer man. Other physical gymnastics seek to give strength to certain sets of muscles to the neglect of others. The rythmical movements of the Delsarte system bring into action each muscle of the body without wearying any, to the harmonious developing of all, since in all, save exceptional cases, it will be found, upon beginning this treatment, that more than half the muscles of the body are unused, while the other, and overworked half, move in stiff and angular fashion.

All students will discover it is first requisite that an "undoing process" shall precede the "upbuilding process." Stiffness of joint, or tension of muscles, whether recognized or not, must first be done away with before "the body can be molded to the expression of high thought." For this purpose the "decomposing," "relaxing" or "devitalizing" motions are given. The old gymnast doubled up the fist and, with great tension, gave a blow which jarred the whole nervous system. The "freeing" motions of Delsarte give harmonious, restful, wave movements to all portions of the anatomy.

Graceful motions are never in the nature of a blow struck straight from the shoulder, but curves and spirals constitute the lines of beauty. Nature shows us this in the free untrammelled motions of a child, or again in man, when his whole nature is so stirred to its best and sweetest depths that he is carried out of his usual tense, conscious self into unconscious rhythmic expression of his feeling. What nature does for us in times of great excitement Delsarte will do for us at all times by means of his exercises, practiced until the conscious mechanical motion becomes unconscious, automatic, and the body grows responsive to all high emotions and impulses.

Relaxing the Muscles.

In relaxing movements, the whole arm and hand, shoulder, elbow, wrist, fingers, are shaken until the joints are completely relaxed and a warm, tingling sensation passes through the entire arm. It is then dropped at the side in perfect passivity. The result is twofold—a feeling of repose and controlling power, and an absence of that nervous tendency to "fidget," or handle something, glove buttons, or watch chain, without which a morning call can scarcely be accomplished by either hostess or guest. This alone will give us a sense of perfect rest which we have never before experienced. Similar exercises are given for other portions of the body—legs and feet—a revolving of the head to limber the neck; a revolution of the shoulders and the body to gain that flexibility which is the secret of grace.

Delsartean exercises break up constrained awkward physical habits, establish in their stead restful, graceful, natural ones. Of these there are many classes.

The Delsarte relaxing exercises precede and prepare the way for all others. In their restful removal of nerve-tension they appeal especially to the overworked, nervous class.

The Delsarte sleep exercises are useful in overcoming insomnia. The Delsarte laws of expression give us a key to character, study, and the laws that underlie all art. The Delsarte work develops self-possession. The Delsarte rythmical exercises enable one not only to appear better and feel better, but, by a reflex action, to be better.

In this physical work the first object is an entire, absolute letting go of all unnecessary tension, all tension that has overstrained the muscles through an excess of effort in our daily life, though many times this effort is purely unconscious on the part of the individual. "How many a patient, trusting soul do we see with the muscles of the forehead strained and elevated until the eyebrows never fall to their normal height," or the brows are contracted until the hard lines graven between the eyes ever bespeak either pain or care.

The founders of the Benedictine nuns caught some echo of this truth when, by a rule of their order, no sister among them is permitted to wear a frown upon her brow. And the placid-faced sisterhood evidence in their sweet expressions the close relation between the exoteric and esoteric of our natures; the reflex action between the physical and the spiritual entities of our being.

Art of Breathing.

There are a few general points that may be given here to the improvement of many little habits that unconsciously enslave us and to the "letting go" of the "officious personal endeavor" that we make, as it were, to hold ourselves together—never believing that nature is more capable of the task. After the decomposing exercises comes the practice of one of the first Delsartean axioms: "Control at the center, freedom at the extremities." Without this control the newly acquired flexibility will be weak and affected.

To obtain this control the art of breathing must first be acquired. To do this properly the chest should be inflated and thrown forward by the action of the diaphragm and held as the most prominent part of the body; a position too often usurped by the inferior abdomen. The same motion which throws out the chest should draw in the lower part of the trunk, hanging it from the curve of the spine. In the proper attitude for good breathing the hips turn slightly inward and the chin goes back, but not up. There should be no effort to throw back the shoulders. Take care of the chest, and the shoulders will take care of themselves.

Position of the Shoulders.

Mrs. Edmond Russell says she would "like to make a call that would reach every man and woman in the country. 'Lift up your shoulders.' When one says this nine-tenths of them stiffen at the neck, throw themselves backward and project the body below the waist, the whole figure out of line. No, you should get the poise of a Greek goddess." Lift the chest, with the shoulders down, until it is on a line with the toes. This throws the extension on the center of the body where it should be. The heart and lungs now have full play. Close the lips; draw in the air through the nostrils, using the muscles below the diaphragm as a bellows, until the pressure against the ribs has a bursting sensation. Keep this tension firmly and steadily as long as you can; then slowly and gradually let the breath out through the lips. If you wish to sing, or recite, or even to talk, see what power is at your command.

"Try this breathing, inspiration, retention, expiration—these three movements—at night before you go to bed, when the body is free; in the morning before you dress. When you walk take in great, glorious lungsful of air until full, or deep breathing becomes a habit. Believe me, breathing properly is a certain cure for nervousness, shyness and embarrassment."

It gives command and freedom of motion, a sense of power. Keep the lips closed and breathe only through the nostrils. This is a most important fact to remember, and should always be impressed upon children. The cold air should never be taken directly into the lungs as is the case when it is inhaled through the parted lips. Children, as well as grown people, should learn to keep the mouth closed during sleep; this would prevent many lung diseases, the disagreeable habit of snoring, and the vacant, inane expression produced by an open mouth.

There is no better exercise to acquire a good habit of breathing than reading aloud. Try how much can be read easily, without strain, upon a single inflation of the lungs. Never gasp, catch up, or piece out a breath. "You may add years to your life by the simple act of breathing." Every public speaker knows, or should know, the feeling of repose and self-possession that comes over him as he calmly, silently, faces his audience long enough to draw three of these deep, full breaths. Nervousness has vanished; he and his audience have had time to become acquainted, and, having command over himself, he is able to command the minds of those before him.

Standing and Walking.

When one has learned to breathe properly, then it is that standing and walking may be practiced. Lift up the chest, inflate the lungs naturally, as in paragraph on breathing, then step up to the front of a door, letting the toes touch the woodwork. At the same time the forehead should meet the upper portion of the door, when it may be assumed that a perfect standing posture has been taken. The poise will seem at first to be a little forward of a straight line, but to disprove this it will be found that a plumb line dropped from the ear will fall through shoulder, hip and ankle. The head will be poised as if to carry a burden steadily on the crown and the weight of the body will rest on the ball of the foot, not the heel.

This position may seem insecure at first, as well as stiff and self-conscious. With some this sensation will wear off sooner than with others, according to their adaptability, and the result will be assured power for long, graceful, strengthening walks.

In walking, a common fault is to let the knees bend continuously; this gives a "flabbyness" to the whole personal expression, that always seems an outward exponent of a "weak-kneed" character. The knees, to obviate this, should be stiffened when walking. In the other extreme, most women stiffen the ankle-joint unduly, thus giving a straight up and down cramped walk, which is accompanied by coming down with all force upon the heel, thereby producing a jar throughout the entire nervous system, as well as an awkward locomotion. In this way all benefit of the strong, natural spring of the instep, which tends to lessen this jar and give grace and springiness to the step is lost, and much weariness of the flesh is the result.

Mrs. Russell says: "We have a system of levers to do our walking with, and they act precisely as do all levers. One leg is a lever to pry the body over the other leg, and the latter becomes a pendulum and swings back by force of gravity. When you walk three miles and feel as if you could walk ten, you are walking that way. When you are tired out, you are taking irregular steps and walking on your heels.

"In walking the foot should be used as an elastic arch, the ball striking the ground first, not the heel. Trying to step too far is productive of awkwardness. Hurrying is another cause. It is bad walking to lift up your foot and put it down. If the sole of the foot shows at all, it should be from the rear. What is wanting is elasticity. Swinging the arms in walking, which is universal, is absolutely unnecessary, and purely a waste of strength. Let them hang pendulum fashion."

Stair-Climbing.

"Trained stair-climbers should be the healthiest as well as the most beautiful of women, yet," says Mrs. Russell, "a town of stairs given, and I will prophesy thin, eye-circled, cross-looking women." All of this is to be laid to the fact that most women climb stairs in the hardest and most awkward manner.

"In going upstairs there should be no waddling from side to side, no trudging, no leaning forward, and no apparent weariness. The body should remain erect, the step should be taken with the ball of the foot, and the movement to the next step be made with a springing motion. This produces a graceful, poetic elevation instead of a cumbersome hauling of the body upward, and throws all of the strain upon the strong muscles of the calf of the leg. This slightly accented springing from step to step leads the true system of pacing on level ground; hence, the stairway may be made the walker's gymnasium."

Art of "Letting Go."

"Relax, relax," says Edmond Russell. "Let go the tense hold of your arms that is wearing out your vitality. You will get rest by doing this. Sleepless people will fall asleep. Stop holding yourself in a knot and relax. Hold up the chest, breathe slowly and deeply through the nose, and relax the extremities."

"Try letting go," says Mrs. Russell; "it is a great rest. You can let yourself go for a few moments in the theater, in a crowd, in church, in the street car, anywhere. It is the universal habit to hold on to one's self with a grip that would almost lift one's weight, muscles tightened, nerves strained to no purpose. The mind is too eager and fast for the body. The result is exhaustion."

"How shall it be avoided? Take the will out of the body when it is not in action. In walking, let the lower limbs do the work; the arms have nothing to do: let them be carried as attachments, pendulums if you will, but at rest." Let the hands fall easily when sitting in carriage, street car, or drawing-room.

On Corset Wearing.

The wearing of corsets meets the strong disapproval of all Delsarteans, as "control of the breath underlies gesture, walk and voice," and a tightened corset-lace necessarily cramps the breathing power. The tight, high collar is also objectionable for the same reason.

An English writer justly observes that "all the greater harmonies and higher courtesies of life must extend over the whole body." Now, in great emotions the chest expands, and especially the lower part where the ribs are freest and intended to expand most, and this part it is that tight corsets most compress to attain the artificial waist. The figure, trying to accommodate itself to the new conditions becomes deteriorated in all directions. The back grows rounded, the ribs fall in, and the stomach obtrudes itself unduly; all this to the injury of health and of harmonious beauty of form.

Mr. Russell also asserts that a forced compression of the waist damages the power of the figure as an instrument for the expression of emotions, the result of all this being an unfavorable reaction upon the mind and character of the unfortunate victims. One of his maxims is: "A beautiful woman is at her lowest plane in a tight-fitting dress; an ugly woman on her highest in drapery!"

General Remarks.

Educated men and women of to-day study social, domestic and political economy, forgetting that vital economy that Delsarte teaches is more essential to our interests and the interests of our descendants.

"Relax, relax, relax!" one is tempted to cry in unison with Edmond Russell. Give us what there is in you. Make yourself "a being whose body is the exponent of the soul responsive to every command of the spirit."

Cease limping through life on high-heeled shoes. Cease lifting the shoulders, fidgeting the hands, painfully raising the eyebrows, and contorting the face into a meaningless smile. Remember that all facial contortions leave indelible traces in their wake. The laugh, or broad smile that half closes, or squints the eyes, engraves those fine ray-like, much-dreaded lines about the eye, known as crow's feet. Remember that "laughter ages the face more than tears." Smile more often with the eyes. Let them light up and laugh for you. Trust me, in most cases a vast improvement will result, since scarcely any adult laughs well, and if there is some trait of affectation, frivolity, cruelty, or even coarseness in the character, uncontrolled laughter will be the sure exponent thereof.

Rest more. Do not try to accomplish too many things at once. Do not let your thoughts be weeks or days ahead of you and the task in hand. This would be imposing double duty upon the already strained physique. If the body is at one store, do not let the mind fly off to shop in half a dozen other stores to snatch "bargains" from the hands of other over-burdened ones.

Straighten out the frowns on your strained brows. Cease carrying numberless loose packages, and loads of heavy skirts in your hands, and struggling with the well-dressed mob to secure coveted bargains. They are dearly bought at the loss of beauty, youth and repose. One such day ages the face. If you do not believe it, ye dwellers in cities, go stand before your mirror next time you reach home, dusty, rasped, fragmentary, weary from a day of counter-shoving, neither mistress of yourself nor those about you, and the face that meets your gaze will tell its own story.

Rightly does Herbert Spencer say, "We have had something too much of the gospel of work, it is time to preach the gospel of relaxation."

And this chapter will have reached its aim if it shall be the means of inducing any to become disciples of Delsarte, restful converts of this gospel of relaxation, which is one with the Gospel of Beauty.

ART OF DRESS

"DRESS may be called the speech of the body," says Mrs. Haweis.

A woman's dress should be so much the expression of herself that, seeing it, we think not of the gown, but of the woman who is its soul. The true art of dress is reached when it serves only to heighten the charms of the wearer, not to draw attention from her to center upon her garments. One writer on beauty in dress claims that "the object is threefold: to cover, to warm, to beautify," and in dealing with this latter point farther says that, "rather than to beautify, it is to emphasize beauty." To this statement should be added that its mission is also to minimize or do away with defects.

Most dressing is done to enhance the beauty of the face, but women should remember that the tint of the complexion, the color of hair and eyes, are but a small part of the *personnel*. The physique must be taken into account. The "type" is a fact fixed and inevitable, and the woman is wise who sets herself steadfastly to "develop and emphasize its beauties and overshadow and efface its defects."

It is only by real study that a woman grows to understand and analyze her "type" and suit all accessories to her own personality; to adjust, as it were, her "relations." Art, after all, is simply, as Edmund Russell admirably defines it, "relations, the right thing in the right place."

Study your own individuality and assert it in your dress. "No woman need be ugly if she knows her own points," and some points of attractiveness every woman has. Lord Chesterfield, that cynical man of the world, assures us that "no woman is ugly when she is well dressed." That is, dressed with reference to revealing good points and concealing weak ones. Time spent in this study is gain, when one remembers in how many ways actual outward ugliness is an impediment. "The greater portion of ill-tempered, ugly women are ill-tempered simply because they believe themselves hopelessly ugly." A woman, finding her fairer friends constantly preferred despite her vain attempts to please, grows disheartened, then sarcastic, envious, ill-tempered, half unconsciously.

"Knowledge is power; beauty and knowledge combined are well-nigh all-powerful."

Stout and Thin.

Texture, color and form must all be considered in relation to the personal appearance or "type." The beautiful in itself is not always a safe guide, but its beauty in relation to the wearer must be the test. Fair, delicate, slender women make a great mistake when they overweigh themselves with rich, heavy fabrics, no matter how beautiful these may be in themselves. Instead, they should keep to clinging, draping materials, sheer lawns and shining silks.

On the contrary, the very stout woman may wear all manner of rich gownings that fall in gracious massive folds. Clad thus, her size will have about it a restful element of repose. Let her beware of closely fitted gowns. These tend to enhance the size they are supposed to conceal. Watteau or Princess robes falling from the shoulder in unbroken lines render her imposing. Little ruffles should be avoided, or frills of lace, and whatever drapery there be should fall from shoulder or hip; this gives long curving undulations that follow every movement.

The stout woman should leave black satin severely alone; reflecting the light, it reveals form and size relentlessly. "Revealed form is vulgar, suggested form poetic," says the high art of to-day, and who would not be poetic and gracious if she could? "If stout women," declares Edmund Russell, "would learn to move in grand, slow rhythm, and wear textures so heavy that the lines of their figures were concealed, they would have a grandeur and dignity that no slender woman could hope to attain."

Women must recognize their defects before they can hope to correct them. A tall, angular woman must adopt soft, fleecy materials, so made that they can float and curve about all ungraceful angles, hiding, or softening them. She of a deficient figure must never wear a plain, tightly fitting gown, unless it is relieved, and filled out with soft full vests, or veiled with falling folds of lace.

There is only an occasional perfect form that will bear the merciless revelation of the plain, tight habit, and even then the suggestion of a concealing drapery heightens the beauty of the revealed curves. "All dress should be governed by shawl instead of glove rule," assert the latest canons of costume.

Tall or Short.

There are proportionately more women that are too short, than too tall. Always a little sensitive to this defect, some try to increase their stature by high heels, which renders their gait awkward, besides being injurious to health. Others endeavor to add to their apparent height by cultivating a long waist. This they do at the expense of shortening the lower limbs, thus making themselves seem shorter than they actually are. Others strive to attain the same end by dressing the hair high, in this way too often adding to the apparent bulk of the head and giving a top-heavy appearance to the figure. It is here that a full-length glass becomes almost a necessity in the dressing-room, so that the entire effect of the figure may be observed at once, and defects of this nature detected at a glance. Sometimes a high ornament worn at the top of the head apparently increases height, but beware of any bulky style.

Long lines of drapery from shoulder to foot give the effect of height. Horizontal lines crossing the figure shorten the form.

Short, stout women, by wearing short basques that make a line about the hips, or ruffles and puffs at the shoulders, increase their bulk and shorten their stature.

Women too tall and slender use horizontal lines and puffed and ruffled effects to great advantage, thus increasing the apparent size of an arm by puffs and surrounding bands, or hips by the descriptive line of a basque.

The way of wearing the hair, also, may greatly change the whole appearance. Worn at the nape of the neck it is domestic; lower, romantic; on a level with the head, classic; on top of the head, stylish.

Decorations.

A tenet of Delsartean art asserts that, "A decoration is to make something else beautiful and must not assert, but sacrifice itself. Ornament that has no use whatever is never, in any high sense, beautiful."

A trimming with no reason for being is generally ungraceful. Buttons which fasten nothing should never be scattered over a garment. Bows, which are simply strings tied together, should only be placed where there is some possible use for strings tied together. In short, according to Mrs. Haweis, "Anything that looks useful, and is useless, is in bad taste." For instance, the dress imitating a peasant or a fishwife is never so graceful or piquant as the real costume, since the handkerchief covering the peasant's bare neck is much more picturesque than a bodice trimmed in form of a kerchief.

Slashes are at all times a most beautiful decoration. At shoulder, elbow, breast, edge of a flattened cap, the knees, cut just where a devotee of comfort might cut them to give more freedom of movement. The slash forms an unrivalled opportunity for displays of color. Deep blue, parting to display a glimpse of amber, white through black, the combinations are endless, and the whole gives the idea of a glimpse of an undergarment through an outer one. The contrast of a lining of vest, sleeve or panel is also a harmonious ornament.

Decollete Costume.

It is not the province of this work to decide the vexed question of the low-cut bodice for full dress. In this respect every woman will be a law unto herself, and every woman knows in her own mind the border line below which the corsage should not fall. All, however, do not know how greatly the hard, horizontal line of the low-cut bodice diminishes the appearance of height. Herein lies the great advantage of the heart or square-shaped opening showing the throat, since a dress high behind, or on the shoulders, gives all the height. Last, but not least, all the lovely curves of the throat are shown in this way, and any suspicion of angularity of the collar bone is hidden.

A dress should never end directly upon the skin. The line of contact should always be softened by an edge of lace, tulle, or ruching. First, for the idea of cleanliness; second, because "nature abhors sharp edges." In flowers there are contrasts of color, but they are always softened, each shade stealing a little from the other as they blend.

A regularly *decolleté* gown is properly worn only during the same hours that a gentleman's dress suit is donned, that is, "from dusk to dawn."

Sharp edges should be avoided as much as possible in the entire costume. A glove that ends exactly at the wrist bone, or a boot at the ankle joint, with a straight line, is always ugly; so are dresses when they are cut in a circle close to the juncture of the neck with the shoulder, giving the neck a decapitated appearance. The line of contrast should always be softened with an edge of lace, or a necklace, and only round, pretty throats should dare such a display.

The skirt ought to appear, even if it is not, as a portion and a continuance of the bodice. That is, "if the bodice be cut to fit the figure tightly, the skirt ought properly to be plainly gored. If the bodice be full at the waist line, the skirt also should contain fullness, for this form signifies a loose, full garment bound at the waist with a girdle."

Full waists and plain skirts, or *vice versa*, betray at once that skirt and bodice do not belong to each other. This course, however, is admissible at times, for instance, in case of the lovely, loose tea-jackets worn now, or in donning any cool lawn blouse, or dressing sacque for comfort.

The trained skirt is a most graceful garb, adding to height and diminishing stoutness, but it is never suitable for the street. For house, evening or carriage toilets it is eminently proper and pretty. All the movements of the form are softened and dignified by its sweeping undulations until one comes to feel that short skirts are really a mistake for a house gown, since so much grace and beauty of motion are sacrificed thereby.

Graceful Sleeves.

Few women have beautiful arms above the elbow. Fatness is not correctness of form, so that a short sleeve, no sleeve, or the painful strap which is all so many evening dresses can boast, is by no means always a thing of beauty.

A sleeve that falls in lace and frills just below the elbow hides many defects, besides softening, and rendering delicate, the lower arm and the hand.

A sleeve long enough to turn upward as a cuff, is much more effective than a simulated cuff, just as the thing itself is always better than an imitation. A sleeve that stops short at the wrist joint should be relieved by lace to be artistic.

Full sleeves improve every form. The very stout should never make the mistake of wearing a very tight sleeve, since to do so simply increases the apparent size of the arm. A full sleeve bound to the arm between joints gives an impression of comfort and beauty like the slashed sleeve before mentioned.

Painters have immortalized beautiful sleeves, as well as beautiful costumes. Indeed, to decide on really beautiful gowns one must study the great masters—Gainsborough, Reynolds, Watteau—until the study of costume becomes what it should be—a study of art.

Purchasing.

There should never be trying contrasts in the quality of the various articles that go to make up the sum-total of dress. To expend almost the entire allowance on a gorgeous bonnet that puts every other detail of the costume to blush, or to wear a shabby cloak with an elegant gown are examples of injudicious expenditure.

Instead, let it be remembered how many articles must be purchased and then so expend the sum to be drawn upon that it will not be exhausted on two or three expensive articles to the neglect of the necessary accessories.

An important point to be considered is the surroundings in which the garments are to be worn. Whether one is to drive over country roads or walk city streets; whether they must last one season or more. In this latter case care should be taken to choose quiet colors and inconspicuous patterns.

If the gown must serve many purposes let it be of some plain wool goods, tastefully made, hat and gloves harmonizing in tint, the whole bearing the imprint of the true lady and suitable for almost any occasion. At the same time the entire outfit will have cost no more than the dearly-purchased silk gown that left no margin for hat, gloves, or shoes, and must be worn on every occasion, suitable or unsuitable, to the discomfort of the wearer and the ruin of the gown.

If riding about in the country, choose wool fabrics that will not crease easily, or show dust, and for summer, cotton materials that will come bright and fresh from the hands of the laundress.

The Young Girl.

Sweet simplicity alone should be the guide for the young girl's costume. The dewy bloom of the cheek, the clear young eyes, the soft rosebud lips, the sweet curves of the lithe form that come but once in a lifetime, are what we want most to see.

No heavy velvets or gorgeous trimmings should be worn by any girl under twenty-one. To call attention to her ornaments is to detract from her priceless ornament of sweet and fleeting youth.

Simple muslins and wools, soft, clinging silks and gauzes should be worn. Flowers are preferable to jewels. A necklace of pearls may be worn, should the complexion warrant, but other than this is a waste of money, and a waste of beauty.

Soft colors, where the skin permits, simplicity in cut, little if any trimming, and we have the costume most fitting for a girl to wear, and when we say "fitting" we have found the key to perfect dressing.

Diamonds and Precious Stones.

Women seem to look upon diamonds as a sort of social *parole*, while, in truth, there are but few women who can wear them without detracting from their own brilliancy; without sacrificing themselves to their jewels.

Dark, brilliant eyes and dazzling teeth may wear them safely, or, very clear, cool skins with bright, blue eyes may dare them at their own risk. Yet, to "tip the ear with diamond fire" is sure to call attention from the best points of the face, and in too many cases simply effaces and outshines the face itself.

Edmond Russell severely criticises diamond solitaires for earrings and esteems the stone a difficult one to wear except when small and used in quantities as settings for other jewels.

The secret of good taste in jewels is for a woman to seek out those gems whose colors harmonize with or heighten her own tints, as she does the shades for her gown, and confine herself to them. It is quite the thing now to have a special stone, as it is to have a special perfume. For instance, the turquoise is very becoming to some (it is Mrs. Langtry's stone), garnets or rubies to others. The pearl, where it can be worn, softens the face more than any other jewel. The moonstone is very nearly as effective, as well as the beautiful opal. Rings, some authorities say, should be worn in barbaric profusion or not at all. A slender, beautifully modeled hand can afford to be guiltless of rings. One less perfect in shape, but white, can be enhanced in charm by a blaze of jewels.

Plump Women.

In the days of the painter Rubens stout women were the most fashionable creatures that walked the face of the earth. Rubens would paint none other than those of very firm build, and so artistically did he drape them, so cleverly did he pose them, and so well did he color them, that every woman aspired to sit for his pictures. To be painted by Rubens was a guarantee of beauty, grace and feminine loveliness of every description.

The Rubens woman is a stout woman of good figure. Stout women nearly always have fine forms. Their bust line is good. It is low and the neck curve full, even if not very long. The Rubens artist makes the most of these good points and conceals others.

In modern times, however, the stout woman finds that the fashions are rarely meant for her. In view of this, a number of wealthy New York women have banded themselves together in a Rubens Club, with one of its chief aims the designing of dresses for the members. For this purpose a professional designer is chosen, an artist of no mean merit.

The president of the Rubens Club, who is a woman of beauty and wealth and great loveliness of manner, had the honor of having the first gown designed for herself. This was an evening robe of great beauty, a regular Rubens gown.

The materials were dead white cashmere and dull black satin, with a very little lace and jet. The under gown, or the gown itself, more strictly speaking, fell from the shoulders in a long, loose robe. In the front there was a center trimming of black satin and lace and a heavy ruffle of lace outlined the bust and suggested the waist. A few jets were added. The back fitted closely, and around the foot extended a deep band of the black.

Over the Rubens gown fell a robe of the satin. It was caught at each shoulder and fell into a train three feet long when the wearer walked. In repose it lay around her feet, giving her height and a becoming setting.

The good points of this gown are, first, the way it showed off the very plump neck of the wearer. The fine throat line was visible, but at the shoulders, where too much massiveness takes the place of fine firm flesh, the robe was draped. The arms were likewise covered at the top, their thickest part, and, as the robe fell over them when in repose, much of their apparent size disappeared.

The robe had one very odd feature. The train was a doublet one. The back of the robe was little more than walking length, but the ends were very long indeed. This made a square court train like a monarch's robe, and could be easily brought front by the hand, for trimming or drapery when the wearer was not walking.

Black Satin and Sparkling Jets.

In choosing the color of the gown to be snow-white instead of cream color, the artist knew what he was specifying. White is a diminishing color, while cream color enlarges. The same with black satin. Satin, being full of lights and shades, is uncertain in size, and it is preferable to silk or velvet, which makes the person thicker. The jets are dressy, wicked little ornaments that wink at you unexpectedly and disappear.

Much pains are taken in choosing colors, and then comes the artist's real work. The hardest thing is to fit out his patrons with street gowns that will be conventional, and yet Rubenesque. To do this he takes advantage of the cape idea. A stout woman in a neat fitting gown, not too close under the bust, looks picturesque with a golf cape swinging from one shoulder. It gives her height. The dolmans that open in front and fall low at each side are admirable also, according to his ideas.

COLORS AND COMPLEXIONS.

"A THING should be beautiful in itself, and it should be beautiful for you." "Good dressing includes a suggestion of poetry;" but to gain this poetic grace careful study must be made of hair, eyes and skin, for a dress that is beautiful in itself, or beautiful on one wearer, may be a failure on another.

Study to "compose" your costume well; then, donning it, cease to think of it or yourself. Lead up gently to all contrasting colors that are introduced into a costume for linings of loose draperies, sleeves, or as vests. Glaring contrasts, or "spotty" effects should be guarded against. All brilliant colors in a costume should be reached gradually like a climax in music, or a highlight in a fine painting. Otherwise there is a jar, and the harmony of relation is broken.

Complexion Determines Dress Colors.

Sometimes a color used sparingly in a knot of ribbon, or glimpsed as a lining, is becoming, while the same color, used in quantity, or as a ground color of the costume, might prove inharmonious with the complexion.

It is well for every woman to choose a certain proved range of colors that she *can* bear, and to venture cautiously or seldom on new experiments. These colors will be found like a musical scale, to harmonize well in almost any combination. Thus beauty, convenience and economy are all consulted by loyalty to these proved shades.

Endless arrangements might be suggested on the economical side of the question. The light evening silk of the season before may be used for lining or form the long loose front of the tea-gown of the present. The rich draperies of last year's carriage gown may fitly furnish forth the natty velvet vest and dainty bonnet to wear with this year's street suit, and nothing be lost.

One more caution as to colors. The very delicate blonde who has reveled in palest, daintiest shades must beware of presuming too long on that evanescent bloom, lest she find herself basing the color of her dress on a flower that faded years ago. Or else, maybe, on one that has unfolded into a richer bloom, and by not adapting her color scale to the changes of time, she loses all the beauty of the present.

Another mistake women make is to forget that lovely childish curves of early youth change with the advancing years and the babyish style of dressing, so becoming then, may be worn too long. The rounded throat of the plump woman becomes muscular all too soon, and the delicate throat of the slender woman is too prone to lose its soft outlines.

The changes of color that occur almost always in cool, pale blondes are often but changes in beauty; still, these changes in complexion must be met with changes in dress.

Combinations of Color.

"A secret of artistic dressing is to match the hair as nearly as possible for day and the eyes for evening."

"The producing of an all-over effect by drapery, veiling, and headgear of the same shade is most thoroughly artistic."

These two high art axioms may be given as a safe foundation for the choice of colors, in following which no one can greatly err.

The woman of mezzo-tints, of soft half-tones of complexion, hair and eyes, loses all color and force when she clothes herself with deep, intense hues. Low, warm, unaggressive shades are needed as a background to bring out all her own best points.

"Some people," says Miss Oakey, "have many possibilities of form and color which may be brought out under special treatment, but most people have only the one possibility which can be improved upon." Certain women may be dressed in one set of colors that emphasize the whiteness of their skin; and, in still another, that bring out their own color, while others must be content with one certain range of tints.

Red Hair, with Brown Eyes.

This type of woman may wear amber, deep lined with fawn or pale yellowish pink; dark, rich red, like a red hollyhock; creamy-white (creamy-white satin with pearls and old point lace); olives and dark greens, claret, maroon, plum and gold color.

Jewels—topaz, amber, pearls and gold ornaments.

All manner of lovely combinations may be made out of these colors; especially dark amber, approaching brown, contrasted with pale fawn or gold color. Topazes for jewels. Sable furs and the deeper shade of mink are exceedingly becoming, and the same colors of the fur can be had in most dress materials. There is also a certain shade of maroon which makes red hair a positive golden, and throws into bold relief the clear white tint of the complexion even when there are freckles. These same freckles are also improved by the wearing of this maroon color.

Red Hair, with Gray or Green Eyes.

This type may wear all the above colors, adding to them all the browns and purples. Amethysts may be worn with the grays. Grays and any of the above greens contrast beautifully.

The Ineffective Type.

This style of woman has dull, light brown hair, no brilliancy of complexion, usually gray or blue eyes. The type often numbers some of our most spiritual and intellectual women, as well as, very often, our constitutionally delicate women. It is a type very difficult to dress effectively. The black of velvet may be worn, and soft wools relieved by velvet or lace; creamy white, by casting reflected lights, clears the complexion. Be careful of this however. Warm, pale pink may be worn with it. Invisible blues and greens (in other words, very dark shades). The palest possible pink may be combined with these as linings, vests or ribbons. Pale pink, lined with a pink almost white; pale, but not chalky blues. Blue should not be worn in silk, unless of a very dull or lusterless quality.

Stylish and Appropriate Jewels.

If the eyes are blue, sapphires may be permitted (a gray sapphire is best); pearls, the greenish turquoise, moonstones, intaglios, cameos, antique coins.

This ineffective type frequently, because of better health, gains a warmer glow to the skin and a richer tone to the hair. In this case there may be added to the above colors yellow-browns, fawn-browns, and a little lighter green, contrasted with the darker greens.

Brown-black hair, steel-gray eyes, fair skin with color in cheeks, may wear all greens (save the very light), cream-white, fawns, grays, browns, reds, violet, a rich pink, and all blues. If any type can wear black with impunity, this can. For jewels, any desired stone.

Black hair, very dark eyes, golden-brown skin, warm color, brilliantly white teeth, may wear rich browns, clarets, deep amber, cream-white, warm pinks and flame-color. Avoid black and very pale colors. Yellow may be worn sometimes, but with a warning here to the black-haired type in general. A writer on color wisely says that "yellow is a color that should be suspiciously approached with black hair. It is very often but a vulgar contrast." For jewels, diamonds and all rich colored precious stones.

Black Hair, Rather Sallow Skin.

This style can wear black, but it must be relieved by white laces to soften and light up the face, thus giving the "effectness of a drawing in black and white."

Dark grays, the dull reds occasionally. There is a peculiar yellow-red, dusty, unluminous, very dark, that can be profitably worn. Flame-color can be worn as linings, or trimmings, though since there is so little color in this style, no colors seem to have a true relation to it.

Dull gold is about the only ornament that can be worn, save a delicate onyx cameo. Flowers: white water-lilies, camelias, or the darkest, duskiest, damask roses, and none of these in such profusion as to appear conspicuous.

Black Hair, Clear Skin, Blue Eyes.

This beautiful combination gives a wide range of color for selection. Blues, especially sapphire shades, dark reds, pale pink, blue grays, white, both cream and blue-white, and black, solid and transparent. For jewels, pearls, sapphires, opals, turquoise, diamonds. White flowers, also violets, pansies, etc.

The woman with blue eyes should always have some blue about her. It is really extremely interesting to notice how blue brought up close to the throat and then a bow of the same in her hair intensifies the blue in the eyes, making even the pale, wishy-washy orbs a deep violet. When the blue beneath the face is too trying there must be some of the same put in the hair or hat, as the case may be. This applies to all colors.

Brown hair, warm brown skin, brown eyes, may wear browns, yellows, ambers, cream-white, rich blues, tans, fawns, all reds, olive-green and maroon; flame-color, and rose pink in small quantities. This type can wear sharp brilliant contrasts of colors if she choose, providing they keep within range. Black, blue, white and all cold, pale colors are to be avoided. The jewels may be diamonds and all rich colored stones. Brown-eyed women should wear brown for the very same reason that the blue-eyed woman should wear blue. Not necessarily entire brown costumes, but brown placed near enough the face to have the desired effect.

Dark brown hair, creamy-white skin and velvety-brown eyes, this combination is beautiful, and may wear the black of silk, or velvet with creamy lace to relieve the face. Dark reds, purples and maroons, peacock-green, olive-green, ambers, violet, rose pink, with pearls, amber, topaz, ruby, garnet, diamonds.

Chestnut Hair, Fair Skin, Blue Eyes.

This type can wear almost any color, except mauve and mysterious, pale colors. To wear yellow, she must contrast it with brown or subdued green.

Chestnut hair, gray or green eyes: this type must be more cautious, especially if the complexion be pale or sallow. Olive-green (not too brown), relieved with palest pink. White contrasted with old gold. Dark and light blues; purple with white; lilac and burnt cream mingled (pongee is burnt cream shade). Black with yellow greens. Red in small quantities. In almost every eye there is a touch of green. In some cases it is the predominant color, and when that is the case green should be worn.

Blonde, fair hair (pale gold or flaxen), blue eyes, with or without a rose flush: this is one of the few types that can wear blue-white. All cool, refreshing colors; cold silvery blues, pale greens, pale grays, black, even the shiny black of satin, are all becoming. Heliotrope, purple, cool violet, pink and lavender may be worn. It may be mentioned here that, while there are many other colors she *can* wear, the cool blonde will never be better dressed than when adhering to the colors that rightfully belong to her, and to her alone. Her style is never more charming than when arrayed in sheer, floating, gauzy materials. But since winter must come, silks, velvets and all wools are at her disposal in the desired shades. Amethysts, emeralds, sapphires and opals should be her jewels.

Almost Any Color.

The golden blonde gradually deepens in color as time passes on; she has usually gray-green or hazel eyes, and a warm, rosy skin. It is a type that has a wide range of color from which to choose.

Warm reds and even flame-color can be worn, but ambers, yellows and fawns will be the more harmonious. Warm pink, too, black, brown, warm greens, cream-white, turquoise-blue, violet, purple and warm gray.

This same type with pale, clear skin, instead of the roseate blue, must choose very different shades. Olive-greens, all soft yellow-greens, cream and transparent white, pale peacock and turquoise-blues, pale amber, mauve pinks, shades of amethyst and heliotrope are all suited to this type.

Pearls, opals, moonstones, turquoise and topaz, all flowers may be worn, also pansies, sweet peas, and pale tinted roses.

All blondes, save the cool blonde, deepen in color as time goes on. Let them watch for this, drop their palest tints, and adopt a few warmer hues.

Occasionally, we see a blonde in whom this deepening process has turned the hair to a golden brown, brought out the warm golden tints of the skin, and with it the blue eyes. Here the mistake is often made of ignoring the blue eyes. This should never be done. Fawns and old golds are good for this type.

Browns, deep, rich pinks, blues, all greens but the palest, bluish grays, cream-white and pansy-purple.

Gray Hair.

Premature gray hair has a picturesque and charming effect, often giving beauty to what might otherwise prove a commonplace countenance. There are several types to be considered. Greenish gray hair, premature or natural, accompanied with brown, or dark gray eyes, and a skin in which the brownish tints prevail, can wear all dark greens and olives, blue, browns, and dark amber, warm yellows and dark, dusky reds, yellowish-pinks, dark blues and purple, especially the brownish-purples, also cream-white. Gray or black is to be avoided. This range of color will, of course, be chosen from, in accordance with the age of the wearer. For jewels, reddish topaz, and amethyst are beautiful for this type, and tea-roses a most effective flower.

Gray hair with a lighter, clear complexion and, perhaps, some color in the cheeks, can wear the loveliest harmonies in grays. Black can also be adopted and any of the first mentioned colors except brown.

A pale complexion with gray or blue and snowy hair, will be elegant in the black of lace or velvet.

Prematurely gray with fine clear complexion, either pale or roseate, together with blue eyes, is a magnificent type. The gray hair gives the brilliancy of powder, and diamonds combined with turquoise can be worn with fine effect; pearls also.

The Black Gown.

Women, as a rule, consider their wardrobe incomplete unless it embraces at least one good black gown. "So very convenient, you know, and suitable for so many occasions." In many respects this is very true. But there are several points to be considered. First, there are some types that should never wear black. Again, there are others that must carefully discriminate between the black of velvet, wool, satin, or lace, and the transparent black of grenadine and gauze. While to all comes the caution that, after thirty years of age, no woman can safely wear all black without thereby ageing her face.

Black certainly whitens the skin by contrast, but it brings out and deepens every line. Only plump, fair, unlined faces can safely bear the contrast.

In wearing black, the material whose tone is most becoming to the skin, must be chosen. For instance, very few skins can bear the glossy black of satin with its reflected lights. Black, however, may be softened by a profusion of cream laces or jetted until it scintillates with every motion, and for evening wear the bodice may be cut low, thus removing it from direct contrast with the face.

Various Hints.

Blondes may, if they choose, wear yellows in harmony with their hair. This possibility was first daringly acted upon by Worth with most charming results.

Blue eyes can always be deepened by wearing the appropriate shade of blue. White can be worn by women of all ages, and in almost all materials is it becoming. For evening wear and for day wear it is most satisfactory. Southern women make a point of dressing in it altogether.

For evening wear, where the complexion renders it possible, a very pretty effect is produced by wearing colors that relate or melt into the skin tints, such as pinky browns, soft drabs, ashes of roses or warm, creamy tints, like the heart of a tea-rose.

The Choice of Colors.

Much more lies in choosing a becoming color than people generally imagine. There is an old story told about some celebrated man, whose lifelong devotion to his wife was considered somewhat remarkable, as she was a very plain woman. One of his friends asked him what had been the first thing about her that had attracted him. He said: "A pink shawl that was lying on the back of the chair in which she was sitting made so pleasing a contrast to the white frock she wore that I thought only of that, and upon asking for an introduction to her solely on account of the pink shawl, I was then introduced to a wonderful fascination of manner and grace of mind which have enthralled me ever since."

A woman's surroundings of necessity play a great part in her appearance, but it does not by any means follow that luxurious furnishings have any more effect than the very simplest and plainest, particularly if they do not throw out well the beauty of the coloring. What shades of ribbon to choose, what colors to wear are far more serious matters than the majority of people realize.

The most stunning gown in the world, if it be unbecoming, will not be half so efficacious as the simplest and plainest of gowns of a becoming color and cut. This is emphatically a picturesque era, and wide latitude is allowed in the choice of what is becoming. But big hats, big sleeves, very stand-out skirts and a general fashion-plate air do not do for every woman, and she who has her gown made on the simplest possible lines will create more sensation in a roomful of very much gotten-up women than if she attempted to vie with them.

Harmony and Contrast of Colors.

- The following is a list of colors which contrast and harmonize:
- White contrasts with black and harmonizes with gray.
- White contrasts with brown and harmonizes with buff.
- White contrasts with blue and harmonizes with sky-blue.
- White contrasts with purple and harmonizes with rose.
- White contrasts with green and harmonizes with pea-green.
- Cold greens contrast with crimson and harmonize with olive.
- Cold greens contrast with purple and harmonize with citrine.
- Cold greens contrast with white and harmonize with blues.
- Warm greens contrast with crimson and harmonize with yellows.
- Warm greens contrast with maroon and harmonize with orange.
- Warm greens contrast with purple and harmonize with citrine.
- Warm greens contrast with red and harmonize with sky-blue.
- Warm greens contrast with pink and harmonize with gray.
- Orange contrasts with purple and harmonizes with yellow.
- Orange contrasts with blues and harmonizes with red.
- Orange contrasts with black and harmonizes with warm green.
- Orange contrasts with olive and harmonizes with warm brown.
- Citrine contrasts with brown and harmonizes with green.
- Citrine contrasts with crimson and harmonizes with buff.
- Russet contrasts with green and harmonizes with red.
- Olive contrasts with white and harmonizes with black.
- Olive contrasts with maroon and harmonizes with brown.
- Gold contrasts with any dark color, but looks richer with purple, green, blue, black and brown than with the other colors. It harmonizes with all light color, but least with yellow. The best harmony is with white.

DRESS FOR SPECIAL OCCASIONS

"THE beautiful is the suitable." "A woman careless of her dress is either unloved, or unhappy." "Dress is to the body what good sense is to the mind." "Dress is really a department of manners," and appeals to the eye with the same force that gracious words and softly keyed voices appeal to the ear. Costliness is not the measure of the beauty of dress. Nay, rather suitability, harmony, becomingness, unobtrusiveness, fitness for the place and person are the qualities that make it perfect.

And because these canons of good taste are so frequently sinned against it has seemed best to give the proper dress and appointments for the proper times. Not as to particular styles for they are fleeting as the breath of fashion, but as to general principles which are well nigh changeless. Once certain of these fundamental principles, embarrassment and self-consciousness are banished.

Dress at Home.

It is, perhaps, the dress at home that tells most of the care and character of the wearer. Much regard is given to the dress for other occasions, but here comes the test of delicacy and refinement, the criterion of the individual.

Neatness is the first requisite, suitability the second. There is nothing more of an offense to good taste than seeing the delicate fabric, the ribbons, the laces of a once elegant toilet, degraded to the uses of the kitchen, spotted and soiled almost beyond recognition.

Have gowns adapted to the tasks for which they are intended. The neat gingham, the plain wool gown, are pretty and appropriate for the morning wear of any lady who must superintend the workings of her own household. Aprons, gloves, dust caps, which can be quickly doffed and will leave her neat and presentable for the stray morning caller without the necessity, on her part, of a change of costume, and on his, of a tedious waiting.

For afternoon the prettiest of toilets may be worn in the shape of house-dresses, or tea-jackets made of otherwise useless remnants of bright silks, and ribbons may be used to wear with otherwise presentable skirts whose original bodices have been long outworn. Trains, medium, are always pretty in the house, hence tea-gowns, from the richest to the most modest in cost, are always in favor. Avoid very short skirts for the house; they are awkward, and belittle you from a mental as well as a physical standpoint.

Observe the utmost neatness in every detail of the toilet for home or street. It is an old rule, but a very good one, that a woman may be judged "by her boots, gloves and pocket-handkerchiefs." To this may be added "finger nails," and last but not least, skirt edges. "No matter how elegant the general get-up may be," asserts one fastidious critic, "if a woman's skirt binding is muddy, frayed, or pendant, she is, to my mind, not a gentlewoman."

The General Fitness.

The style of the person should have much to do with choosing the style of dress for any occasion. Only people lacking the slightest originality of mind would think of blindly following the dictates of fashion without any reference to their own physical style.

Very short women should not wear very large hats. Women with very thin faces should avoid wide hat brims and many plumes. Women with large, full faces should not go to the extreme in wearing small bonnets. To do so is but to exaggerate the defect in each case. No matter what the extremity of style may be, there is always a happy medium from which to choose.

Flying curls and a great superabundance of ribbons and fluttering ends belong only to a young girl. To persist in an extremely youthful style of dress long after the passing of youth, instead of adding to the apparent youth of the wearer, simply defeats its own end by exaggerating the defects it was meant to conceal.

Small, thin women should not wear too much black. Let them wear a profusion of fluffy laces about the throat; soft, puffy vests, or, as one writer observes, "learn something from Sara Bernhardt and her consummate skill in concealing bones."

Short, stout women should see that all adornments, such as folds, plaits, etc., keep as much as possible in perpendicular lines. It is a mistake to think that perfect plainness will disguise the breadth, it rather emphasizes it. On this style of woman a loosely-fitted wrap has a better effect for the street than a tight, plain garment.

Common-Sense Sleeves.

A very stout or a very thin woman should never wear extremely light sleeves, no matter what the style may be. The stout woman should also avoid an elbow sleeve with loosely falling ruffles, and the trimming, if possible, should run in lengthwise folds or bands. This precaution tends to decrease the apparent size of the arm. The slender woman, on the contrary, is much improved by the puffed elbow sleeve ending with a fall of lace.

Let women learn to put on belts so that they will slip downward in front and up in the back. This does everything for the waist in making it look slender and graceful. If yokes are worn, it is well to remember that a deep yoke is more becoming than a narrow one. If it is short in front, it looks awkward, and if it is short behind, it gives a round shouldered effect.

Where a rich toilet is worn for any occasion, be sure that everything is in keeping. If the gown be of velvet do not wear with it a linen collar or cheap lace. If real lace is beyond the means there are always the filmy tulles and *crepe lisse*. If jewelry is worn, it should be of the best, be it much or little. The fan, also, for such a costume should carry out the idea of luxury.

Cheap, fanciful, pretty things have their place in connection with soft wool, or pretty cotton costumes, but "lightness or grace is one thing; magnificence or luxury, another."

A very young girl should never wear rich, heavy fabrics; they are unsuited to her youthful face and ways.

The evils of tight lacing are so pronounced that it would seem almost unnecessary to remonstrate against them in this age of enlightenment, were they not so continually forced upon our view. Nothing could be more unbecoming to the women fair, fat and forty, who are usually the ones to adopt this custom; an inch less in waist is hardly gained at the price of an unbecoming flush, a labored breathing, and a serious injury to the health, besides the lack of grace that comes from binding and constricting any portion of the human form divine.

Gloves and Shoes.

To have many dresses is always a mistake even among the very wealthy. They are constantly going out of fashion and unless the owner is continually seen at balls, receptions and other gatherings, they are entirely unnecessary.

The glove of to-day is fitted comfortably. Nothing is more indicative of a lack of taste than to crowd the hand into a glove that is several sizes too small for it. The same might be said of the foot, and with more reason, since a painfully tight shoe not only injures the health, comfort and complexion of the wearer, but is ruinous to all grace of carriage.

There is nothing marks the true lady as much as the perfection of neatness and style in gloves and shoes. To be well gloved and to have one's feet neatly clad, no matter how plain the attire, is to be well dressed.

(Other hints on this subject will be found in the departments of "Art in Dress" and "Colors and Complexions.")

The umbrella, too, must be carefully chosen. If it is possible to have parasols and umbrellas for different occasions, then there is no difficulty of choice, but where one must answer for all occasions of the season, let it be a plain, dark or black silk. This will be suitable at all times, but if the fancy of the moment, as to pale and delicate colorings be consulted, the result is too often painfully incongruous. In buying gloves, shoes or umbrellas, it is worth while to invest in a good article. There is no economy in the poorer grades.

Artifices of the Toilet.

All artificial aids to beauty should be sparingly used, and have no place whatever upon the toilet table of the young girl. Powder and paint are so obvious to the eye, that their use, or rather abuse, by some otherwise sensible women, is a continual wonder. A dust of rice powder is sometimes excusable, but there can be no possible apology for the "made-up" faces one sees upon our streets. They deceive no one and have no excuse for being. The woman who stands in the pitiless glare of the footlights must needs add color to replace that stolen from her face by the strong white light of day, but others have no such excuse for "frescoing" the face. It is a sin alike against good taste and good breeding.

There are various simple preparations that can be used to clear the skin, and various massage treatments to smooth out the cruel little lines that time writes on all faces, and kindly unguents to fill out the hollow cheeks and temples, and thus keep the outlines of youth a little longer. And there is wholesome living and vigorous exercise, and daily and revivifying baths to call the flush of health to the cheek; and loving thoughts and kindly deeds to keep the eyes soft and bright, and thus to set the inroads of time at defiance for many years. And since a woman is no older than she looks, and since the prerogatives of youth are dear to the heart, it is her bounden duty to keep herself sweet and young.

There is one excusable addition to the personal charms and that is where nature has denied the grace of luxuriant locks. This lack can be so cunningly supplied by the hairdresser's art that detection is impossible, and as it ever has been, and ever will be, that a woman's hair is a glory unto her, there can be no reason against her hiding from view any lack of it when it is done in an artistic fashion.

When to Wear Jewels.

Mme. de Maintenon declared that good taste simply indicates good sense, but many women who boast of good sense seem not to have the slightest idea of the times and places for wearing precious stones.

It is conceded by all authorities that articles of adornment consisting of or containing jewels or precious stones should never be worn in the street. Exception is made in favor of rings and watches. The woman who wishes to adopt correct form in dress will never wear any but the simplest little pin to fasten her gown at the throat during the morning hours and on the street.

For ceremonious visits, a pretty and ornamental pin of gold is proper, or of gold and enamel, but even then it should have a useful purpose; it should fasten some part of the toilet. The enameled and gold wreaths of myrtle or of forget-me-nots are extremely pretty for these simple pins. So are the true love-nots or a flower of enamel upon gold, but without the all-prevailing diamond dewdrop or center.

For dinner, a woman may wear the richest gems, it being understood that the function is a ceremonious one, and that she shall wear a low gown. Should she dine in a more democratic way and the men of the family do not wear evening dress, she naturally will wear a high gown or one possibly open a little at the throat. She may wear a pin with a single gem under these circumstances.

For balls, operas or entertainments of corresponding splendor, a woman, when she is not herself the hostess, may wear any number of well-chosen jewels. It is quite correct to be sumptuous in this particular, but well to remember that jewels, like flowers, harmonize or do not harmonize, and that emeralds and turquoises, for example, may not be worn in conjunction, because, as the French say, "they swear at each other."

It is not good form to wear ornaments made in the form of beasts or reptiles. The sacred emblem of the cross set in shining jewels and worn at ball or rout, shows a most pitiable ignorance of the eternal fitness of things.

Well bred young girls are limited as to jewels—a string of pearls for the slender neck, a ring with the natal stone or an armament of turquoises and pearls, a little gold love manacle about the wrist, that is all, and quite enough until after marriage. A bride may wear for the marriage ceremony either diamonds or pearls—not in profusion—but never gold ornaments.

Use of Scents and Flowers.

The use of various scents is more sinned against than any other toilet accessory. Only the faintest suggestion of perfume should be allowed to hang about the garments of a well-bred woman or girl. To wear any redolence on the person in the shape of sachet bags is unpardonable. To many people strong perfumes are extremely unpleasant, and those who have regard for the feelings of others would forbear their use for this reason alone, even were it not a sin against the canons of good breeding as well.

When perfumes are used, it is a dainty custom to choose one favorite scent and to use that, and that only, so that in time the sweet, illusive odor becomes almost a part of the personality.

Flowers, fresh, dewy flowers seem the natural adornment of youth especially, and to forswear the pretty custom would appear an uncalled-for giving up of the sweet thought which dedicates the flowers of the field to their human prototypes. Yet there is reason in the custom that has, in great measure, withdrawn them from the heated ball-room and the artificially illuminated dinner table.

Corsage bouquets, in dancing, become an early ruin. Carried in the hand at a ball, they are speedily tossed aside on the nearest point of refuge and left there to ignominiously fade. When flowers are worn at an evening entertainment, choose those that will best stand the light and heat.

The Face Veil.

In spite of the protestations of oculists, women continue to regard veils as an essential part of their toilets; first, because they are becoming; and, second, because they keep their hair in order. The plain tulles and nets, which come in all colors, single and double widths, are always pleasant to wear and less trying to the eyes than the coarser meshes. The veil of Brussels net wrought in sprigged designs is a failure. It is becoming to nobody, and is essentially inartistic.

Women with dark hair and eyes and a brilliant color look well in veils with the dots larger and nearer together. If the skin is clear, white veils are very becoming, though apt to give an impression of a made-up complexion. The woman with fair hair and blue eyes, and without color, generally looks best in a large meshed black veil, with the dots—if dots are worn—far apart. A navy blue veil makes the skin look clear and fair, and a gray veil should never be worn by the pale or sallow woman.

When to Wear Gloves.

The question of when to wear gloves is a much disputed point in the etiquette of dress. They are worn to dinner parties, but custom prescribes that they shall be removed in sitting down at the table. After using the finger-bowl, the gloves should be resumed before leaving the table, or else immediately after returning to the drawing-room. To wear gloves while assisting to pour tea for an "at home," is out of place, but it is very usual to wear them while receiving in the afternoon, though their omission at such a time is pardonable. The visitors, of course, wear both gloves and bonnets.

At a "stand-up" evening supper it is not usual to remove the gloves since there is really no time or place to do it, where each one is expected to leave as soon as possible to make room for the next. Remove the hand only of the right glove and tuck it back under the wrist.

Dancing parties always call for gloves, preferably light in tint. To wear gloves while playing cards is also an unnecessary affectation of elegance. Walking, driving, shopping and all outdoor events, such as lawn parties, etc., call for gloves. Tint and quality of these are to be regulated by the occasion or the costume.

When to Wear Low-cut Gowns.

This question has but one answer, "Never by daylight." In this respect the rule that governs the wearing of a man's dress suit—"from dusk to dawn," is applicable. Even on those occasions when the jealous daylight is shut out and candlelight reigns, dress suits and full *décolleté* gowns are not permissible. A concession can be made by cutting the corsage a little low in the throat, and by elbow sleeves or almost no sleeves.

For every social function held from midday to a late dinner hour, young girls, especially, should wear their gowns cut high with long sleeves, except on some gala occasion, when the rule may be somewhat relaxed as above.

Even at balls, evening parties, late dinners, the young girl's evening dress, if *décolleté*, should be very modest in cut. Where a dinner and dance follow a large afternoon reception and the men who are invited are apt to arrive at dinner in full evening dress, a girl's dress may be somewhat elaborated, but not to the extreme of ball costume.

Ball Dress.

For the ball-room the most elaborate dress is to be worn; *décolleté* corsage, flowers and jewels are all appropriate. Those who dance should wear pale colors and light, floating fabrics, leaving the heavy silks and velvets for those who do not indulge in this amusement.

A low-cut corsage is not expected of elderly women unless they wish it. Chaperons can wear an elegant dinner dress if they desire; velvets or brocades, cut square in the neck, with a profusion of fine lace and rich ornaments. In short, she should be as different as possible from her charge.

If an elderly woman of full figure wears a low-necked dress, a lace scarf or something of that sort should be thrown over her shoulders.

Gowns cut dancing length or with train, are appropriate for the ball-room, but where much dancing is to be indulged in, trains are very much in the way.

Opera Dress.

For the opera the most elegant dressing is desirable. Ladies may wear evening gowns, and men dress suits. If they occupy boxes this is almost an obligation. Light colors render the house more attractive—are, in fact, a part of the whole spectacle. Jewels and flowers are there, and those who wear visiting or street costume are in the minority.

If a man wear a dress suit it is expected that the woman will show him sufficient respect to wear an evening gown. The man's costume is donned out of respect for the occasion and the woman, and she betrays utter ignorance or remissness of duty when she does not return the compliment in kind.

High hats are an abomination at opera or theater. Where anything is worn upon the head it should be in the shape of a tiny bonnet, a dainty confection of tulle, flowers and ribbon.

This is especially necessary where a public conveyance must be made use of to reach the place. At an opera matinée the bonnet must be worn in connection with an elegant visiting or reception costume.

Middle-aged women wear the same costume at the opera that they would at a dinner party.

Theater Costume.

To dress for the theater is a much simpler matter than for the opera. Display is not required here. Elegant visiting or promenade costume is appropriate. Dressy little bonnets or small hats, gloves, either matching the gown or light in tint, complete the theater toilet. If a large hat is worn to the theater, common courtesy demands its removal that those in the rear may see the stage.

Dress for concerts admits of a little more display than for the theater. A silk gown with a little lace and jewelry, and white or light kid gloves.

Dinner Dress.

A lady's dinner dress may be elegant as her fancy dictates. But if she is hostess she should never try to eclipse her guests. Trained gowns are eminently suitable, and may be worn by maids or matrons alike. Full length trains are not necessary, and even demi-trains need not be worn by very young women. But the soft sweep of a train lends an added grace to a woman's gown, and this is one of the few places where it can be appropriately worn. The corsage may be cut square, or heart-shaped, or opened at the throat in any pretty way, but never so low as for a ball dress. Sleeves are usually half length, and bracelets are given an opportunity for display. Long gloves must be worn. As to color, all shades, from the safe selection of a black silk or velvet, down to the palest tints, are in order, the only proviso being that color and material suit the style of the wearer. An elderly lady inclined to stoutness, and with a florid cast of countenance, is at her worst in light silks or satin. They heighten her defects, while darker shades subdue her coloring and serve to decrease her apparent size and superfluous breadth.

For a young girl, a simple dress of wool goods in white, or pale becoming tints, is all that is necessary. Open it slightly at the throat, soften it with a little lace, show the pretty arms in a demi-sleeve, and it is far more suited to her youth than an over-elaborate gown.

If the dinner is held by daylight and the men wear morning dress the ladies must confine themselves to high-cut gowns turned in slightly at the front and fastened with a simple pin of gold enamel, with, perhaps, a single gem at its heart.

Traveling Notes.

A dress for traveling should be plain and serviceable; a tint should be chosen that does not show soil or dust. A duster, an ulster or over-garment of some kind made of pongee silk, linen or whatever material is in vogue, should be worn to protect the costume from smoke and dust.

TRAVELING COSTUME.

The hat should be plain and a veil worn to shield the eyes from cinders when traveling by railway. A pair of slightly smoked spectacles are very good for this purpose. Carry an extra wrap and a hand-satchel to hold the needed toilet articles. Let everything else go in the trunk. A woman burdened with "big bundle, little bundle, bandbox and umbrella," is a burden to herself and a terror to others. Let the satchel contain a flask of some invigorating toilet water—Florida, lavender or whatever is most refreshing, with a soft sponge to bathe the face, hands and wrists, and thereby many a headache can be warded off. If traveling in a sleeping coach, a larger valise should be carried and ought to contain a pretty loose gown of dark silk or wool to serve as a slumber robe, since clad in this one may safely venture from berth to dressing-room without exciting observation.

The rule for traveling dress is that there should be nothing about a lady to attract attention, but this is relaxed in case of ladies traveling a short distance for a brief visit, who are privileged to wear the dress that suits their purpose.

Bridal Dress.

The conventional bridal dress is pure white, whether the material be satin, silk or muslin. It may be made trained or walking length. If a veil is worn the gown is cut *en train*. White satin slippers must be worn and white gloves. Rip the fourth finger of the left-hand glove ready for the ring; the maid of honor will turn this back at the proper moment. Natural flowers are carried and a wreath is worn with a veil. The veil should sweep to the edge of the train and may be simply a cloud of sheerest tulle or filmy lace worth a king's ransom. It may be worn over the face or not, as fancy dictates. Sometimes a white leather or pearl bound prayer-book is carried instead of the bouquet. This custom has the advantage of having the prayer-book as a memento of the occasion, while the flowers wither. A young girl, known to the writer, carried with her to the altar the same prayer-book that her mother before her had carried on her wedding day.

The wedding dress, no matter what its material, must be cut high in the neck and with long sleeves. This in deference to the fact that a marriage is not simply a gala occasion, but the turning point for weal or woe in the bride's life, and a solemn sacrament of the church, and not to be celebrated in the garb of frivolity.

Where flowers are worn, orange blossoms are particularly appropriate, though no German maiden would think of donning the bridal veil without its attendant myrtle wreath. Any white flowers, however, are appropriate.

Where jewels are worn the choice is absolutely confined to pearls and diamonds (not in too great profusion). Instead of flowers, the veil is sometimes fastened with a star or sunburst of diamonds.

Widows, no matter how youthful, are not privileged to wear the white bridal robe, the veil, nor the orange blossoms. However, the most exquisitely delicate tints may be chosen for their adornment.

If the marriage is private and the bride leaves immediately on her wedding trip she can be married in her traveling suit. At other private weddings, where no trip is taken, the bride usually wears a pretty reception or visiting costume of silk or wool, choosing some color that will be appropriate for after-wear.

The bride's mother, whether the wedding be at home or in church, wears an elegant reception gown. Even if she be in deep mourning she lays aside its sombre shades for this one hour. Invited guests should also avoid mourning garb.

Bridemaid's Dress.

The bridemaids' dresses are often all of white, but frequently color are chosen, sometimes all alike; again, two by two of different hues. The material of these gowns must be much less expensive than that of the bride's. Their bouquets or baskets of flowers may be either white or colored. They sometimes wear lovely picture hats with broad brims and drooping plumes.

What Wedding Guests Wear.

If the wedding reception is held in the evening, full evening dress is worn; reception gowns being suitable for the elder ladies. (See "Ball Dress.") Where children are present, the girls are dressed in sheer muslin or lace over silk slips, and adorned with fluttering ribbons. The boys in fanciful costumes, such as pages' suits, etc. If it is a morning reception, rich visiting or promenade costumes should be worn, small dress bonnets and white gloves.

Ordinary Evening Dress.

This applies to small parties at home or with friends, to receiving calls at home or in making an evening call. It should be appropriate to the season. Pretty wool goods, exquisitely made, in winter; organdies, grenadines and mulls for summer; laces, a modest bit of jewelry or a simple flower, and one is sufficiently well-gowned.

If the gathering is a little more formal, reception dresses may be worn by the matrons, while the young ladies garb themselves as for receiving at an afternoon tea.

If gloves are worn at all on such an occasion they must be light colored. They are really unnecessary, unless the taste of that especial "set" is very strongly in their favor. If in doubt, it is well to go furnished with a pair for use in case one finds all the guests gloved, and has not the moral courage to remain the exception.

Dress for Church.

Well-bred people attend church in simple costumes, free from display. These may be of rich materials, but they are quiet in color and make. Jewelry, other than a simple pin, should not be used; earrings, of course, if one is in the habit of wearing them, but not diamonds. The church is not the place to flaunt elegant attire in the face of less fortunate worshipers in the "I-am-richer-than-thou" style that marks the *parvenu*.

Receiving Calls.

A lady with regular days for receiving calls wears a reception dress as before described. Casual callers she receives in her morning or afternoon house dress. Her morning dress, if she superintends her household affairs, should be plain and neat, and be so protected by cap and apron that by doffing these, she will be presentable in a moment.

Where there are no household cares, a daintier morning dress may be adopted, but let it be suitable to the occasion, not some old, half worn finery revamped for the occasion. If visiting, a still richer gown may be worn, and for a late breakfast at a watering place one may be quite luxurious.

Calling or Visiting Costume.

For morning calls dress quietly in promenade costume. Wear light-colored gloves unless in deep mourning. If driving, carriage dress may be worn. For day receptions the dress may be more elaborate and the bonnet more "dressy."

By not carefully distinguishing between the gowns for different occasions and over-dressing at all times, women lose all the advantages of contrast in style. If lace and silk are worn indiscriminately, what is there left for the full dress function?

Walking Dress.

This should be plain—tailor-made is the best—walking length, and of good material. "Fussy" styles should not be chosen for street wear, and the hat or bonnet should be rather plain and harmonize with the gown.

Carriage Dress.

There is much more latitude for display permitted by the carriage dress. Rich materials, elegant wraps, costly furs, are all allowable here.

Coaching parties, too, have grown to be occasions for most gorgeous costuming. Every hue of the rainbow is to be seen as the lofty tally-ho rolls past, until, so great has become the license of color and richness of material, that the "four hundred" are calling a halt, and soberer tints are beginning to mark this amusement.

Do not wear too many fluttering ribbons, especially if occupying that coveted position—the box seat. It does not add to the skill and accuracy of the driver at a critical moment to have a fluttering ribbon cut like a whip-lash across his eyes.

Dress for Lent.

This should be the sort of gown most appropriate and becoming to the attitude of repentance. The gowns, of course, are simple, quiet affairs. Symphonies in gray, poems in black and white, must, says one writer, "reflect in their construction as well as color the soberness of the event which they will grace. A train is always admissible for the Lenten robe—that is, if it is for house wear. Otherwise the skirt must be short—quite short enough, indeed, to give one's churchwomen a glimpse of a dainty gray or black walking boot."

Any of the heliotrope, mauve or pansy shades, also, are appropriate expressions of the sorrow of the fashionable woman, thus giving a color scheme capable of the most exquisite effects. White cashmere is well suited for the house; and very little draperies, but long, straight lines, give the sought-after effect, and thus the dainty chrysalis rests during the forty days that precede the unfolding of the gorgeous wings of the Easter butterfly.

Dress for Riding.

The riding-habit should be made of broadcloth or some other suitable cloth. The skirt should be weighted by sewing shot in the lower edge of the left-hand breadths. Equestrian tights should be worn. The habit is sometimes worn over another dress-skirt, when, in case of dismounting or accident, the habit-skirt can be slipped off and the rider still left properly attired.

Very long skirts are not worn. The habit should fit perfectly and button to the throat. Linen collar, a pretty tie and linen cuffs are worn, and a leather glove with gauntlet. The hat should be plain, and of the prevailing fashion.

Lawn Parties.

The dress for these occasions has been already described; sufficient here to say it should be light and graceful, and the bonnet or hat ornamental and effective.

Picnics and Excursions.

Light-weight wool goods, or heavy cotton or linen material that will wash and not tear easily, is most suitable for these occasions. Linen or cotton duck is very serviceable.

Croquet, Archery, Skating, Etc.

All of these semi-athletic games call for bright, pretty costumes, short enough to give the freedom of movement necessary to excel in the game. For summer out-of-door games, pliable gloves should be worn, and a hat to protect the eyes from the sun. For skating, rich, warm materials, fur trimmings, fur caps, and warm, furred gauntlets should be worn.

Bathing Dress.

Bathing calls for a costume of some material that will not cling to the form when wet. Flannel is appropriate, and a heavy quantity of mohair also makes a successful dress, as it resists water and has no clinging qualities. An oil-silk cap should be worn over the hair. The cut of the dress should be modest; the costume loose and full, and it should be made with a skirt. The neck should be cut quite high.

Yachting Dress.

This is a pretty, nautically devised and ornamented suit, made of warm materials and those that will stand sea water.

Dress for Gentlemen.

The subject of dress, while not so complex for a man as for a woman, must still receive a certain amount of care at his hands, for no gentleman can possess complete disregard of reigning styles without thereby sacrificing a certain amount of dignity in the estimation of his associates.

As far as the cardinal points of the toilet extend, a man is bound by the same laws of exquisite neatness that are incumbent upon a woman. The same care of teeth, finger-nails, hands and hair is necessary. Don't neglect the small hairs that sometimes project from the nostrils and the apertures of the ears. Use a small pair of scissors.

A gentleman will have spotless collars, cuffs and handkerchiefs, irreproachable gloves, nicely blackened shoes and thoroughly brushed clothes. Hair oil must never be used; it is ill-bred.

Clothes of plain colors are always in good taste, and so is pure white linen. The fancy dotted and striped collars, cuffs and bosoms, so often worn, are not as good taste.

Jewelry should be used very sparingly. Utility should be apparent in the articles worn. Watch chain, sleeve buttons and studs (one or three, as liked) are necessary. Where one stud is used, the stone, though not conspicuous for size, should be a very fine one. A scarf pin is sometimes worn, and one ring is allowable, but not too large or showy. Don't use quantities of perfumery, it is very bad taste.

Keep a dressing-gown for use in the dressing-room or the sickroom. It is not a proper garment for the table or the sitting-room.

Wear the hat properly and squarely upon the head, Wear a coat at all proper times—in the sitting-room, drawing-room, and at table.

Lastly, a gentleman avoids all conspicuous styles of dress, and confines himself to quiet colors and well-fitting, well-cared-for garments.

Evening Dress for Gentlemen.

The evening dress for gentlemen varies very little from year to year, and the time of wearing it varies not at all. From "dusk to dawn," in other words, a gentleman wears a dress suit during the same hours that a lady wears an evening dress.

Gentlemen's evening dress consists of black trousers, a low-cut black or white vest, dress or "swallow-tail" coat, and white necktie. The linen must be immaculate. A young man wears a standing collar; an elderly man, if he choose, may wear his favorite style, with due deference to the reigning style. One or three studs adorn the bosom.

Properly speaking, white or very light kid gloves are a part of evening dress, but to say whether or not they shall be worn always at a formal dinner is hardly safe. If worn, remove them at the table; but at a ball they are indispensable. On all doubtful occasions it is well to be provided with a pair, to use if wished.

Evening dress is to be worn at balls, large dinners, parties and the opera. It is never worn at church, save in case of an evening wedding. It is never worn anywhere on Sunday. In a small town a dress suit on any occasion is apt to seem an affectation. Never wear a dress suit anywhere before six o'clock in the evening.

"A gentleman never looks more thoroughly a gentleman than in an evening dress," says one writer on etiquette, and it is well for those to whom the occasion is liable to come to learn to wear one gracefully and easily.

In France a dress suit is worn upon nearly all festive occasions. In England the same customs prevail for its use as in our own country.

Morning Dress for Gentlemen.

Black cutaway, or Prince Albert coat (frock coat), black vest, white in summer, light-colored trousers, silk or some other style of stiff hat, and a black necktie. A light coat is never worn with black trousers. This morning dress is worn at church, morning receptions, informal parties, garden parties, when making calls, and at places of amusement.

Wedding Dress for Gentlemen.

At morning weddings, that is, all weddings before six o'clock, the gentlemen, bridegroom, best man, and all, wear morning dress with light-colored ties. If gloves are worn, light-colored ones must be selected. If there is a formal reception held in the evening, evening dress and white or very pale gloves may then be worn. At an evening wedding, evening dress is expected.

Gloves for Gentlemen.

Gentlemen wear gloves when walking, riding, or driving, at church and all places of amusement, when making calls, and at receptions, balls and evening parties. White or very pale tints for balls and weddings; delicate tints for evening parties; any shade preferred for the other occasions.

General Hints.

A silk hat should only be worn on appropriate occasions. Worn with a rough business suit, or on a picnic or mountain ramble, it is in the worst possible taste. It should appear only with frock coats, dress coats and a fine quality of cloth.

Felt or straw hats should be worn with short coats or business suits.

The mourning weed, conventionally speaking, is worn only on a silk hat; but there is no good reason why those who wish to wear mourning for lost friends should always be in dress of ceremony so to do.

Diamonds should not be worn during business hours by men who are obliged to stand behind counters or engage in any toil.

Business suits should never be worn to an evening party in the city, though in small country gatherings they might be permissible.

Even various styles of outing suits are allowable in some of the informal gatherings at summer resorts.

"Nice customs courtesy to great kings," or to occasions.

Evening Suit for Boys.

This is black cloth with the rough surface that is seen in the material used for grown-up, evening clothes. His trousers are the proper width and show a slight but not too pronounced crease. His waistcoat is cut low, and over it he wears an Eton jacket of black cloth that is accentuated by the deep white linen collar which turns over it, and which is attached, like his cuffs, to his immaculate white shirt.

He scorns all jewelry but a little watch and the white enamel buttons that are in his shirt. His silk hat has a lower and a somewhat broader crown than that made for an older gentleman.

A suit like this is worn by a boy from the time he is twelve until he is eighteen, and then he is supposed to assume the regulation evening dress worn by men.

LETTER WRITING

"LETTERS are the memory of friendship, and are to be reckoned among the chief links in the social chain that binds parent and child, lover and sweetheart, friend and friend, in harmonious accord."

A letter may, from a business point of view, make or mar the fortunes of its sender, while none the less surely, from a social standard, will our epistles approve or condemn our claim for consideration. Every position in life, and every occasion which may arise therein, demand more or less exercise of our epistolary powers, and while but few can hope for the grace, the wit, the repartee that sparkle in the missives of a de Staël, a Récamier, a Walpole, a Macaulay, every one can and should learn to write a clear, concise, intelligent, appropriate letter.

A Rare Accomplishment.

To do this properly is a social accomplishment, and one of the greatest boons that education confers. A graceful note, a kindly, sparkling letter, are each the exponent of a true lady or gentleman, though it must be confessed, since our country furnishes no so-called "leisure class," the art of letter-writing has, in great measure, fallen into feminine hands, the cares of business and professional life ofttimes preventing the sterner half of creation from mere friendly exercise of the pen. It is among women, therefore, that we will find in the present, as we have found in the past, the best and most fluent of correspondents.

A certain dread of letter-writing, however, seems to haunt a large class of people. This dread, arising either from imperfect education, a lack of practice or a fear of "nothing to say," can be overcome in great measure by careful study of the few main requisites of the art, as embraced in style, orthography, forms to be adopted and stationery to be used for certain occasions.

The Style

Of course, is a subtle something inherent in each individual, not to be entirely done away with in any case, but to be improved by a careful study of good models, such, for example, as the letters of the above mentioned authors. To read the best prose writers also cannot fail to work an improvement. For instance, the writer once, after an enthusiastic study of Taine, was rewarded by the assurance from a literary correspondent that her letters were thoroughly "Tainesque" in style.

By judicious reading and carefully taking thought, an abrupt style may be softened and more graceful, flowing sentences substituted for its short, sharp phrases; while a redundant style, by the same care, may be pruned of its exuberance.

The chief charm of a letter consists in it being written naturally and as one would talk. "We should write as we speak, and that's a true familiar letter which expresseth a man's mind as if he were discoursing with the party to whom he writes," says Howell, and, ancient as the words are, no better advice can be given to-day.

Write easily, and never simply for effect; this gives a constrained, stilted style that will soon cool the correspondence. Let your thoughts flow as they would were you conversing with your friend, but do not gossip; give friendly intelligence only when certain of its truth. This will not seem too much when it is remembered how written words sometimes rise up in judgment against their authors when the spoken words would long since have been forgotten. A lapse of time will brush the bloom from our sentences and nothing can bring back again the tender grace that transfigured the over-sweetness of some little written sentiment, or redeem it from the realm of the bombastic in our eyes to-day. Then "let your communications be, not exactly 'yea and nay,' but do let them be such that you would not fear to hear them read aloud before you, for more than this 'cometh of evil.'"

A PLEASANT SURPRISE.

Grammar and Orthography.

These should receive most careful attention. "A great author is one," according to Taine, "who, having passions, knows also his dictionary and grammar." And a good letter-writer, as well, must "know his dictionary and grammar" to render his missives presentable.

Grammatical errors are almost unpardonable, and a misspelled word is an actual crime in these days of dictionaries. Punctuation and capitalization, too, must be looked after, and the whole letter give evidence of thought and care on the writer's part.

Handwriting, Paper and Ink

Are all of importance, and etiquette has prescribed certain formulas for these adjuncts of a good letter, that, however the vagaries of fashion may invade the outer borders of the realm epistolary, are always correct and in good style.

The paper in best taste is thick, white or creamy-tinted, unruled and of such a size as to fold once for fitting square-shaped envelopes, creamy-white like the paper. Never use envelopes so thin in quality as to permit the writing to be seen through from the outside. The square envelope is not a necessity; the slightly oblong is also used, the paper being folded twice to fit this size.

This paper would be suitable and in perfect style in any portion of the civilized world, and on any occasion, and no one with any pretensions to good breeding should be found unsupplied. This is an item in which we cannot afford to economize, for one judges a lady or gentleman, unconsciously, by the contents of his or her writing desk, as exemplified by the letters sent from their hands.

Monograms are not entirely "out," but they are only used by those to whom their own especial design, through long use, has come to seem almost a part of themselves. All fleeting fancies in stationery should be passed by on the other side, or, at most, left to the wayward tastes of "sweet sixteen," or to some few whose very eccentricities are part of their fame. Sarah Bernhardt, for instance, uses blue paper framed in a pale gray line on the top of the page, and the flap of the envelope is a tragic mark, above which her initials are traversed by a scroll bearing her motto, "*Quand méme.*" She is as exact, however, in the formulas of her letters as any dowager of the old school. The Royal Highnesses of England use the paper and square envelopes before described; initials, monograms and crests are left to foreigners and outsiders, and the Orleans family, of France, are severely plain in their choice of stationery.

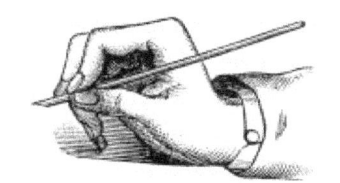

INCORRECT MODE OF HOLDING
THE PEN.

PROPER MODE OF HOLDING THE
PEN.

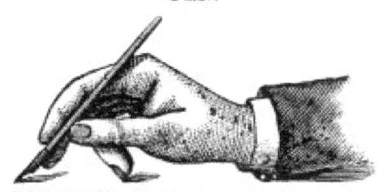

CORRECT POSITION OF THE HAND.

Given the correct paper and envelopes and plain, jet-black ink (no other tint should ever be used), the penmanship must next be considered. It is very well for Madame Bernhardt to write an elegant, graceful hand that is absolutely impossible to decipher, and for General Bourbaki to indite his epistles in a microscopically minute script, but less important people will do well to render their chirography as perfect and legible as possible, and not to flourish.

Avoid always too near an approach to the clerkly, commercial hand. A talented foreigner once remarked to the writer upon his astonishment at the predominance of this hand in America. "I do not like it," he said; "the clerk sends me in my rates, the landlord my bill, and the young lady her reply to my invitation, all in that same commercial hand. There is no individuality, no character, in such writing." And there was too much reason in his remonstrance. We are not quite "a nation of shopkeepers," and there is no reason why this business handwriting should so permeate all classes of society.

The lines should be straight, and as ruled paper is not permissible in formal notes, invitations or punctilious correspondence, savoring too nearly of the schoolroom and the counting-house, some little practice may be necessary to keep the lines even. Should this prove impossible, let a sheet of paper with heavily ruled black lines that will show through the writing paper, be kept in the desk and slipped beneath the page as a guide. It may also be inserted in the envelope to keep the superscription or address perfectly straight.

PROPER POSITION OF A LADY IN WRITING.

The lines should be rather far apart, and the fashionable hand just now is not the pointed English style, but somewhat verging on the large, round hand of the last century; the ladies, as a rule, indulging in a rather masculine style.

Thin foreign note paper may be used for letters abroad, unless the most formal. This is usually ruled. So is the commercial note used for business letters.

These forms answer for ladies and gentlemen alike. There is no particular objection to gentlemen using in their informal friendly letters, business note with printed letter head, but for ceremonious occasions they must be bound by the foregoing forms.

Very faintly perfumed paper is the prerogative of the ladies. Gentlemen are denied this privilege and a lady avails herself of it with discretion, selecting a favorite odor and adhering closely to it, so that correspondents could tell her missives with closed eyes, by their very fragrance.

Where black-edged paper and envelopes are used by persons in mourning, the width of the black border varies according to the nearness of the deceased relative or the length of time since the loss, though some never use more than the narrowest line of black, while others still, with the most perfect propriety, discard it altogether. Its use is a matter of taste simply, and must cease so soon as the mourning garb is dropped. Never be guilty, however, of writing a letter of congratulation on black-edged paper, even if in mourning; use plain white for this purpose. At the same time, it is never necessary to write a letter of condolence on black-bordered paper, unless the writer himself is in mourning.

IMPROPER POSITION. PROPER POSITION.

The careful writing of a note or letter is a mark of respect to the recipient, and blots, erasures and mended words should never be permitted to disfigure it. Erasing cannot be done without marring the entire page and a mended or rewritten word is an offense to the eye. To copy the letter afresh is the only real remedy, and those who value their own standing will not grudge the pains spent in the composition of a letter that shall be a credit to the writer and a pleasure to the receiver.

This comes under the general recommendation of doing everything you do as it ought to be done. There should be no slipshod way of writing a letter by which you are to be judged.

Figures and abbreviations are often used. Few numerals are allowable, except the dates, the street number and the hour of the day. Very large sums of money are also stated in figures unless they begin a sentence, when all numbers must be written out fully. Figures are also preferable in uneven sums of money too long to be written with one, or at most two words; per cent., as well, is rulable in figures. Degrees should be either written "75°", or "seventy-five degrees." Fractions, given alone, should be in words, and all other numerals occurring in a letter must follow the same rule, except quotations from stock and market reports. For extra precaution, sometimes sums of money are written, followed by figures representing the same, in parenthesis.

Common Abbreviations.

Abbreviations proper to social and formal letter-writing are few in number. Honorary titles, such as Dr., Prof., Hon., Rev., Messrs., Esq., Capt., etc., are usually abbreviated as above, though very good authorities advocate, and with much reason, the use of the full word "Reverend," as also the titles "Honorable" and "Professor." The scholastic titles are also abbreviated by the proper initials, as A. M., M. D., LL.D., following the name. The names of months, of states, the words "County" and "Post Office," when used on the superscription are also abbreviated.

The use of A. M., M., P. M., to mark the divisions of the day, technical abbreviations, and the usual e. g., i. e., viz., etc., are too familiar to the users to need mention. Further than the above, brevity is *not* always the soul of wit.

The letter itself, as a whole, is now to be considered, and to facilitate its writing there should be some one corner in every home devoted to this purpose. The incentive to letter-writing is always damped, the happy thought we would send our friend takes flight, if we must find the pens upstairs, the paper down, the ink bottle in the pantry, empty or not, as the case may be, and our patience wherever it may be after the search is ended.

A SCRAP OF A LETTER.

Letters would be more frequently written, more punctually answered, and half the unreasonable dread of writing done away with, were this matter attended to properly. Let the writing desk stand in some well-lighted corner of sitting, dining, or "mother's" room, and let it be stored with all articles necessary to the exigencies of correspondence. Should the desk prove beyond the depth of the family purse, then, let its substitute be found in a firm, good-sized table or stand, with a drawer where necessary supplies may be kept. Two or more sizes of note paper, unruled, with envelopes to match, for the elders of the household; writing tablets and commercial note, together with plain envelopes, for the school-children and everyday uses; a good dictionary, a tray with pen rack and inkstand thereon, and a goodly supply of pens, will complete a corner that will do more toward the family education in good breeding and culture than any other expenditure that can be made, and will render letter-writing the pleasure it should be, instead of the dread it too often is.

If one possesses a permanent address, street, number and city may, with great propriety, be engraved on the paper at the top of the sheet. If this is not done the address should always be written clearly on all letters. It is too much to expect one's friends to remember the private addresses of all their correspondents, and time is too precious to be spent searching out some missing letter in quest of street or number, in default of which more than one letter has gone unanswered.

The date of a letter, month, day, year and city is first in place. This should be written on one line, beginning, according to length, more or less near the center of the sheet and ending at the right-hand margin. In business letters, unless the printed letter head fixes the place, this line should not be more than one-quarter down the page; while in social or formal letters it should be one-third the distance down. If it should be desirable to give the county also, the date may be allowed to occupy two or more lines, as follows:

MENDOTA, LA SALLE CO., ILL., May 29, 189—.

In the same manner a city number and address may be given:

309 POST STREET, OTTAWA, ILL., January 30, 189—.

In writing from hotels, the following form should be adopted:

THE ARLINGTON, BINGHAMTON, N. Y., October 3, 189—.

Some, in polite letter-writing, prefer to give the address at the conclusion rather than the beginning of the letter. Under these circumstances the prescribed form would be:

Truly your friend, MARY N. PRESCOTT.

FRANKLIN GROVE, Lee Co., Ill., January 14, 189—.

There are several ways of writing the figures that compose the date of a letter. Many business men and others use this form, 1—2—189—. or, 1/2/9—, for January 2, 189—. Others still would write as follows: Jan. 2nd, 1896. Taste and habit will decide the matter for each. To give the name instead of the number of the month is, perhaps, more elegant.

The address, supposing it to be a business letter would come next in order, beginning at the left-hand margin, and our letter would stand thus:

TIPTON, IOWA, April 1, 189—.

MR. WILLIAM H. HILL,
307 Wall Street, New York.

The salutation is a matter wherein there is great latitude of usage. In conformity with custom, some title is to be used in addressing correspondents, and this title differs greatly in accordance with the degree of acquaintance, or friendship, with the party addressed. It should always begin at the left of the page. In the business letter just above, the form might be as follows:

TIPTON, IOWA, April 1, 189-.

> MR. WILLIAM H. HILL,
> 307 Wall Street, New York'
>
> DEAR SIR: (or, SIR:)

Or, if there should be a firm name, the address would be as follows:

> Messrs. WILLIAMS & HILL, 307 Wall Street, New York.
>
> DEAR SIRS: (or, SIRS:) (or, GENTLEMEN:)

Again, if wished, the salutation might be omitted and the address made to serve as title. Another form is this:

> MR. WILLIAM H. HILL, 307 Wall Street, New York. MR. HILL:

The following form, though causing an unpleasant repetition of the name, is often adopted in business letters to unmarried ladies, probably to escape the problem that the choice of Miss or Madam offers to so many:

305 BEACON STREET, BOSTON, MASS., February 10, 189—.

> MISS MARY WRIGHT, Cherry Valley, Ill. MISS WRIGHT:

Or, omitting the name, the simple address may be used. However, there need not be the slightest difficulty in addressing an unmarried lady, even should she be in her teens, as "Madam," or "Dear Madam," it being a general term as applicable to women without regard to age or condition, as "Sir" is to their brethren. This will be easily seen when it is recollected that it is a derivation from *ma dame*, my lady, and since our language is deficient in any equivalent term to the pretty French *Mademoiselle*, or the German, *Fraülein*, and, as "Dear Miss" is obsolete, we must be content to utilize "Madam" on all necessary occasions. There is another form much used where the address is omitted:

> 305 MICHIGAN AVENUE, CHICAGO, July 10, 189—.
>
> MISS HALSTED. DEAR MADAM:

Or, if on friendly footing, simply: DEAR MISS HALSTEAD:

If two young ladies are to be addressed, the term "Misses" should be used, as:

> HAVANA, ILL., February 20, 189—.
>
> MISSES TAYLOR & WATSON, Stenographers,
>   159 Church Street, Rockford, Ill. MESDAMES:

The "Mesdames" may be omitted and the address used alone, but its addition indicates more polish. The translation is "My Ladies." Some substitute for it, simply "Ladies," which is quite proper.

The prefix "Dear" may be omitted wherever desirable, but never write "*My* dear Miss Halstead," "*My* dear Madam," or "*My* dear Sir," unless intimately acquainted.

In writing a social letter the address is omitted or added at close of the letter. A gentleman in private or professional life would be addressed as:

> FREDERIC GUY, Esq. DEAR SIR: (or, SIR:)

Or,

> HON. FREDERIC GUY. DEAR SIR: (or, SIR:)
>
>   Respectfully yours, JOHN GRACELAND.

The use of titles will be explained farther on, but here it may be said that two titles are very seldom given to the same individual at once. For instance, never write Mr. Fred. Guy, Esq., nor Hon. Mr. Fred. Guy. There are some exceptions to this rule, as where the Rev. Mr. Churchill and the Hon. Mr. Brice are addressed under circumstances where their Christian name is unknown, and where a married lady makes use of her husband's title, as: Mrs.

Capt. Jones; Mrs. Judge Snyder, and where the Rev. Prof. Dr. Kemp shows by his titles the weight of his learning. Never deny an individual the titles that are rightfully his. They show that he has fought and conquered men, or books, to win them, and they are the well-earned meed of his endeavor. But never, if you have titles, be guilty of bestowing them on yourself; leave that for others.

A gentleman writing to a married lady would address her in friendly correspondence as, "Dear Mrs. French," or, "My dear Mrs. French." To an unmarried lady, "Dear Miss French," or "My dear Miss French." A lady addresses a gentleman in the same fashion, as "Dear Mr. Courtney," or "My dear Mr. Courtney," or "Dear Dr. Courtney."

The Proper Salutation.

Nearer degrees of intimacy, of course, formulate their own laws in this regard, but even here, be it said, that discretion may be exercised to advantage. It will also be observed that if the word "dear," or any like term, begins the salutation it is capitalized; otherwise, not. Thus: "My dear Friend;" not "My Dear Friend." Authorities on etiquette differ somewhat on this score, different works in the author's possession taking exactly opposite sides, the weight of evidence, however, falling on the form given here.

The complimentary conclusion, "Yours truly," "Very truly yours," "Very respectfully," etc., should begin about the middle of the page on the next line below the body of the letter. The first word only should be capitalized, and the expression followed by a comma. The signature should come on the line below and end at the right-hand margin of the page. The address also is sometimes, especially in social notes given at the conclusion, where it should begin, one or two lines below the signature, at the left-hand margin of the page, occupying two or more lines, according to its length, as:

DEAR MISS LOTHROP:

In reply to your kind note, I would say, etc.

Cordially yours,
MARION KENT.

2 Arcade Court, Chicago, Ill., October 5, 189—.

Another very formal style would be:

21 DELAWARE PLACE, BUFFALO, N. Y., June 1, 189—.

DEAR MISS LOTHROP: In reply to your kind note, etc.

Truly yours,
GEORGE HARLAND.

>To Miss Julia Lothrop,
>
>>110 Beacon Street, Boston, Mass.

The conclusion of a letter gives the writer fully as much latitude of style as the salutation. Some graceful little phrase should follow the subject-matter of the letter and lead up to the conclusion, thus:

>I am, with love to the family, and remembrances to all my friends, Yours cordially,
>
>>Mary Roe.

Salutation and conclusion should always correspond in formality or friendliness with one another, thus: Mr. John Bright. Sir: would appropriately conclude with: I am, sir, Respectfully yours, Frank B. Folsom.

A friendly letter beginning: Dear Bright: or, My dear Bright: would terminate thus: Cordially yours, Frank B. Folsom.

Other forms for closing business letters are: I am, respectfully, James Ross. Or, Respectfully, James Ross.

These forms do away with the personal pronoun "Yours," which, although custom has in reality rendered it a pure formality, still retains a certain meaning in the minds of some, as the man, who, in a long correspondence, with his wife-that-was-to-be, never signed a letter otherwise than "Truly yours." "What more could I be," he queried, "than hers truly, body and soul?" and with this feeling could their married life have been other than it was, beautiful to look upon?

Never abbreviate the conclusion to "Yours, etc.;" it has too much the careless, thankless sound of "Thanks," and neither can be sufficiently condemned.

Letters beginning, My dear Margaret: or, My dear Daughter: might end, respectively: Ever yours, or, Your friend, Jane Brown. And, Your affectionate mother, Gertrude Mason.

A gentleman, writing to a lady, could say: Very sincerely (or respectfully) yours, P. H. Gould. Or, Yours, with sincere regard, Henry Grayson.

The address need not be added unless the acquaintance is very slight. At times a more elaborate closing is desirable and graceful, as when the correspondent is very much higher in station, or older in years, or you have been the recipient of some great favor at his or her hands:

>I am, dear madam, with the most profound esteem,

> Yours sincerely, JAMES TALBOT.

Or, to a gentleman, under like circumstances:

> I have the honor to be, sir, Yours most respectfully, JAMES TALBOT.

Such closings as "Obedient, humble servant," are quite too much for Republican simplicity, and even in writing to no less a dignitary than the President:

> TO THE PRESIDENT,
> SIR:
>
> Very respectfully,
> JAMES TALBOT,

really fulfills all requirements, though one may consult his own taste in making use of the two complimentary conclusions given above.

A lady in writing to a stranger should always suggest whether she is married or single. This will prevent mistakes and annoyance, and can be done in two ways. Respectfully, (MISS) FRANCES CLAYTON, Or, more elaborately: Respectfully, FRANCES CLAYTON. Address, MISS FRANCES CLAYTON, 21 St. Caroline's Court, Chicago.

A lady never signs herself as Mrs. Helen B. Hayes, or Miss Gertrude Vance, without, at least, putting the titles in a parenthesis. Primarily, a woman is Helen Hayes or Gertrude Vance, and should sign herself as such. The "Miss" or "Mrs." signifies simply an incident in her existence, and is added, as it were, in a note, to prevent mistake on the part of others. A failure to observe this rule indicates a lack of culture. Neither does a gentleman ever sign himself Mr. Brown, but George G. Brown, or G. G. Brown.

Use of the Husband's Name.

A married lady should always be addressed by her husband's name preceded by "Mrs.," except in case of well-known names, such as Mrs. Potter Palmer, or Mrs. Isabella B. Hooker. A widow is no longer called by her husband's given name, but reverts to her own christened cognomen, preceded by "Mrs." Thus, Mrs. James H. Hayes in her widowhood is, to every one, Mrs. Helen B. Hayes. An exception to this would be in the case of such well-known names as Abraham Lincoln, or James G. Blaine, where custom grants the widow the right to bear the beloved title.

The superscription or address should be written plainly (if speedy delivery is expected) upon the lower half of the envelope, the flap being at the top. The title and name form one line with about an equal space at each end. The writing should be just below the middle of the envelope. The street number, the name of the city and the state each form a separate line, one below the other, and each should begin a little to the right of the one above, so that the last line will approach nearly to the lower right-hand corner of the envelope. The county or number of post office box may be given in the lower left-hand corner. Where there is no street number the county, or even the box number, may be written directly beneath the name of the town.

The stamp should be invariably placed squarely and right-side up in the upper right-hand corner. A request for return in a given time may be written, if necessary, in the upper left-hand corner.

A physician is addressed thus: DR. ALBERT YOUNG, Watseka, Iowa. Or, ALBERT YOUNG, M. D., Watseka, Iowa.

In addressing the wife of a doctor the following formula may be used: MRS. DR. ALBERT YOUNG, Watseka, Iowa.

The strictest etiquette, however, would involve writing: MRS. ALBERT YOUNG, care of Dr. Albert Young, Watseka, Iowa.

THE PLACE FOR STAMP AND SUPERSCRIPTION.

Either of the above forms may be taken for addressing the wife of a professor, an army or United States official, a minister or a legal dignitary, always remembering that the longer is more elegant, as: MRS. MELVILLE B. FULLER, care of the Hon. Melville B. Fuller, Chief Justice of the United States, Washington, D. C.

The President, however, would be addressed: To the President, Executive Mansion, Washington, D. C.

This is the simplest form, and as such, in the best taste, but it is sometimes written: To the President of the United States, HONORABLE GROVER CLEVELAND.

"His Excellency" was formerly used in addressing the President and the Governors of States, but it is largely abandoned as inconsistent with the lack of titles in our country. The same rule is observed in writing to the Governor of a State: To the Governor, Gubernatorial Mansion, Springfield, Ill. Or, To the Governor, ROBERT P. MORTON, Albany, N. Y.

A member of the Cabinet: To the Honorable, the Secretary of the Interior, Washington, D. C. A State official has the following address: DR. JOHN C. WYATT, Secretary of the State Board of Charity, Springfield, Ill. In addressing one person in care of another the form would be: MRS. JOHN DRAPER, Grand de Tour, Ill. Care Dr. I. S. Prime.

A note to be delivered by a friend is always unsealed and usually addressed: MISS FLORENCE WARDEN, Vassar College, Poughkeepsie, N. Y. Kindness of MR. G. A. RHODES. A still better form is to simply use the address of the person without farther preamble.

Always fold a letter sheet so that the opening lines face the reader on unfolding.

Punctuation Marks.

Punctuation and capitalization are very necessary matters in the art of letter-writing, but in these days of common schools, and all but compulsory education, it is to be supposed that some knowledge of these important facts will have been gained. It will not be amiss, however, to mention a few of the most necessary rules.

The four chief punctuation points are the comma, semicolon, colon, period. In the days of our grandmothers children were taught to "mind their stops," with this rule for a guide: "Count one at a comma, two at a semicolon, three at a colon, and four at a period, or 'full stop.'"

In punctuating the date, address, closing and superscription of a letter, certain rules are necessary. One of these is that a period follows all abbreviations, such as those of title, state and county, and separates and follows all initials, whether abbreviations of names or titles; while the slight pause occurring between such abbreviations is marked by a comma, and the end of the date, like the end of a sentence, is closed by a period; for example: 540 West Main St., Galesburgh, Ill. Or, Poughkeepsie, N. Y., Jan. 10, 189—.

A colon suggests something more to follow, hence in the salutation of a letter we find a colon at the end, signifying that the body of the letter is yet to come, as: "Dear Sir:" or, where the communication begins on same line of salutation, we find both colon and dash, as: "Dear Madame:—Yours of," etc.

Commas are used frequently to divide long complex sentences, and the sentence is somewhat further broken by the use of the semicolon between its more decided sections. Abraham Lincoln once said: "I throw in a semicolon whenever I am at a loss what pause to use; it always fits."

The complimentary close of the letter is followed by a comma and the signature by a period. A period also separates and follows two or more initials, as: Yours truly, (Mrs.) ADELINE D. T. WHITNEY.

Writing the Superscription.

A very long complimentary conclusion should be punctuated like a sentence, as: I am, dear madam, with the most profound esteem, Yours truly, JAMES TALBOT.

The superscription on the envelope is to be punctuated according to the above given rules. An interrogation point (?) should be used at the end of all questions. It is in truth, as the small boy said, "A little crooked thing that asks questions." The exclamation point (!) expressing astonishment, the dash and parenthesis, need only be employed by those thoroughly understanding their use. Quotation marks (" ") should always be placed at the beginning and end of words quoted from another; slang, or any fashionable "fad" if written, should be quoted.

As for capitals, one should begin every sentence, all names of persons and places, all appellations of the Deity, the first word of every line of poetry, and show themselves in the pronoun "I," and the exclamation "O."

Sealing wax is to be used, or not, as inclination directs, but neatness and skill are necessary in its use, or an unsightly blotch will result, than which the self-sealing envelope is far preferable. A heavy cream-white envelope sealed with a large, perfect seal of rich red, or bronze-brown wax with a clear monogram or initial stamped thereon, is always pleasing to the eye. To very slightly oil the seal will prevent it adhering to the wax and thereby spoiling the impression. In a foreign correspondence, the self-sealing envelopes are better since in tropical countries the great heat often melts the wax, and it is always liable, during transportation in the holds of vessels, to become cracked and loosened from the paper by the weight of other goods, and close packing in the hold.

Final remarks are scarcely necessary, but it might be suggested that it is rather fashionable to write one's full name, as more elegant than initials. A lady never signs herself simply by initials. Mary Creighton Cutter should so write her name, or, at least, Mary C. Cutter. Never M. C. Cutter. A gentleman is privileged to do this in business or formal letters, but in any others, instead of L. B. Bancroft he is Lucius Bright Bancroft or Lucius B. Bancroft.

Points to be Remembered.

Margins are no longer a necessity even in the most formal letters. Sometimes in writing a long, friendly, not formal, letter, instead of utilizing one side only of the paper, it is written across the sheet upon the first and fourth pages, and then lengthwise upon the second and third, though of course it is perfectly correct to write upon the pages consecutively.

Tautology, or a continued repetition of the same word, is a disagreeable and inelegant fault in writing, as: "If John will *come* home, we will all *come*, but if he fails to *come*, we will not *come* until he can *come* also."

One other point remains to touch upon. Any one that has ever glanced at the "Correspondence Column" of any paper will see how often young women ask if it is proper to write to gentlemen who have requested the favor of corresponding with them, and which should write first. This point is rightfully one that should be settled by the mother or other guardian of the girl; but let it be said here that while this is the only country in the world where a so-called "friendly correspondence" is or can be carried on between young men and young women with, or without, any particular object in view, even here it is well to be careful. Girls are sometimes a little too confidential, and all men are not gentlemen, outward polish notwithstanding. A friendship too easily won or too fully expressed is not always prized, and while manly men are supposed never to boast of the number of their correspondents, yet club-room walls, could they speak, would stamp many a man as less than a gentleman.

Titles.

The proper use of titles forms an important item in letter-writing. The slightest hesitancy on this point shows a lack of culture on the part of the writer that lowers him at once in the eyes of the recipient.

The ordinary social titles used are simple and familiar. These are: Mrs., Madam, Miss, for women; Mr., Esq., Messrs., Sir, for men, and Master for boys.

Of course, in writing to an acquaintance, while the outer address retains all its formality, the commencement will be whatever is warranted by the degree of friendship between the parties.

Domestic Titles.

By the constitution of the United States it is provided that no titles of nobility shall be granted by the government. Neither shall a person holding a governmental office accept any title from any king, prince or foreign state, except express permission be given by Congress. The President of the United States and the Governor of Massachusetts are the only citizens possessing as officials a title by legislative act. This title is the same: "Excellency." Governors of other states are given this title by courtesy only. However, this title may be omitted at discretion, and indeed the simpler form given is far more suited to our Republican simplicity of manners.

The following list will be found a complete guide in the use of all honorary titles sanctioned by custom in the United States:

Ambassadors, Foreign, to the United States, are addressed officially by the titles recognized in their own countries, and if they have no title, as "Mr.—— ——," followed by title of office. United States ambassadors to foreign countries, officially as "Mr.——" or "Hon.——," followed by title of office. There are but four ambassadors sent out by the United States, the ministers to Russia and England having been but lately invested with that title.

The Hon. John Jones, United States Ambassador to the United Kingdom of Great Britain and Ireland, or to the Court of St. James.

Archbishop (Roman Catholic)—Letters addressed: "The Most Reverend —— —— D.D., Archbishop of ——."

Associate Justices—Addressed with: "Hon., name and name of office", but spoken of as "Mr. Justice ——."

Bishop—Addressed: "The Right Reverend —— D.D., Bishop of ——." The address of Protestant Episcopal and Roman Catholic Bishops is precisely the same. Bishops of the Methodist Episcopal Church are addressed as the "Reverend Bishop ——, D.D."

Cabinet Members—Addressed as: "Honorable," usually contracted to "Hon.," as: Hon. James Johnson, Secretary of State, Washington, D. C.

Cardinal (Roman Catholic) is addressed in writing, and spoken of as: "His Eminence——, Cardinal (Bishop, Priest, or Deacon, according to rank) of the Holy Roman Church," spoken to as, "Your Grace."

Chief Justice—Addressed as: "Hon. Chief Justice of the Supreme Court of the United States."

Chief Justice's Wife—Addressed as: "Mrs. Chief Justice——," by virtue of a social custom that is largely observed. This custom does not extend to daughters.

Clergymen—Addressed as: "The Rev.——," spoken to as, "Mr. ——." If a doctor of divinity, addressed as, "——, D.D.," or "The Reverend—— , D.D.," and spoken to or of as, "Dr.——."

College Degrees.—All recipients of regular or honorary degrees should be addressed by name followed by abbreviation of degree: A.B., A.M., Ph.D., M.D., D.D., as, "——, A.B."

Congress, members of—Addressed: "Hon.——, M.C."

Esquire.—Justice of the peace, as well as some grades of lawyers are addressed in writing and spoken of as "——, Esq." Any gentleman may be so addressed, but "Mr." is preferable.

Government—Official communications from—Always begin "Sir."

Governor.—May be addressed as "His Excellency the Governor of ——." Spoken to, "Your Excellency." See, also, other forms given before.

Governor's wife is by courtesy addressed, "Mrs. Governor——." This usage does not apply to daughters.

Judges—Addressed by courtesy with the title, "Honorable," contracted to "Hon.," and the name of the office usually follows, as: "Hon.——, U. S. Senate."

Legislature, members of.—Address as, "Hon.——," followed by name of office.

Mayor.—"The Hon. Mr.——, Mayor of——."

Minister, American—Addressed as: "Hon.——, American (or U. S.) Minister to France."

Municipal Councils, members of.—Courtesy grants the title "Honorable."

Officers of Army and Navy.—Addressed by name, followed by title of highest rank attained, and, if in command of a military division, naval squadron or station, or on retired list, by a signification of the fact, as: "————, Major General U. S. A., Commanding Military Division of the Atlantic;" "————, Rear Admiral U. S. N., Commanding European Squadron;" "————, General U. S. A., Retired."

President.—Addressed as "His Excellency the President of the United States." Spoken to as, "Your Excellency."

President's Wife.—Addressed by courtesy, "Mrs. President——." Usage does not apply to daughters.

FORMS FOR LETTERS

Lord Chesterfield says in those inimitable letters to his son, that "style is the dress of thoughts, and let them be ever so just, if your style is homely, coarse and vulgar, they will appear to as much disadvantage as your person, though ever so well proportioned, would if dressed in rags, dirt and tatters."

So true is this that graceful commonplaces, either spoken or written, are far more apt to produce a pleasing impression than weightier matter awkwardly uttered, or uncouthly expressed. Hence, the length and familiarity of the friendly epistle should never be carried into the short, concisely worded business letter, while the social note, though brief, should differ greatly in its gracefully turned phrases from the formal note of acceptance, regret, application, or introduction.

The following forms are to be looked upon, not as copies, but chiefly as suggestions that may be used to solve some doubtful point.

Social and Friendly Letters.

These are less subject to rule than any other class, and the models here given are simply to show how flowing and easy the style may be between friend and friend, or how gracious and instructive from parent to child. In the friendly letter great freedom of detail is allowable, especially among near relatives. "You do not tell me half enough," writes H. H. from Europe. "I even want to know if the front gate is off its hinges." But do not render a friendly letter so long as to tax the patience of the reader. "Samivel Veller" discovered one of the secrets of letter-writing when he made that famous love letter of his short, "so she vill vish there vos more of it." Neither railing, nor fretfulness, nor too great egotism, is wise in letter-writing, for written words have a sad fashion of outlasting the mood in which they were penned, nay, even the hand that penned them.

Letters of Introduction.

These are left unsealed, that the bearer may be permitted to read the contents. They are brief, so that if read in the presence of the person introduced, the slight embarrassment may be shortened as much as possible. They usually contain a reference to the occupation or character of the individual in order that some slight clue may be given to the recipient in beginning a conversation, and usually conclude with some pleasant, complimentary phrase.

One simple form would be:

> EVANSTON, January 1, 189—.

My dear Miss Kimberlin:

This letter will introduce to you my friend, Mr. Otis Van Orin, a member of the Corps of Civil Engineers, to be located near your home for several months during a partial survey of the new railroad. May I not be assured that you will extend to him some of the hospitalities of your delightful home, thus being to him that "friend at court" so desirable to the stranger in a strange land? Trusting that this will be the case, I am,

Very sincerely yours,
Charles H. Calcraft.

Another, from a mother introducing her daughter to an old friend, would read:

Waterbury, Conn., March 10, 189—.

Dear Frances:

My daughter Madge will present this letter in person, as she is about to enter school in your town for a several years' course of study. Under these circumstances, and in memory of our own lifelong friendship, may I not ask that you will help her to forget some of the sorrow of this, the first parting her happy, young life has known? Trusting that you will do this for the sake of auld lang syne,

I am, as ever, your friend,
Margaret M. Blatchford.

Mrs. Frances H. Page,
Portland, Me.

A still briefer form would be:

Baltimore, Md., November 20, 189—.

Dear Denton:

My friend, Louis Ross, will present this note. Any kindness you may show him will confer a favor upon

Yours truly,
Frank P. Breckenridge.

To Mr. James Denton,
Ottumwa, Ill.

The envelope to a letter of introduction should be addressed as follows:

   Mr. James Denton, Ottumwa, Ill.

Introducing Mr. Louis Ross.

Letters of introduction should not be sent indiscriminately, as no one has a right to force a possibly undesirable acquaintance upon a friend, while, at the same time, the individual asking such a favor should be thoroughly convinced that he is entitled to the privilege. Letters of introduction, where they are between ladies, may be left by the caller, together with her card. She must not, however, ask to see the lady of the house, who is expected, shortly after the receipt of such a missive, to call in person, and should endeavor, during her stay, to include her in a portion of her social plans for the season; circumstances, of course, governing the extent to which these attentions should be carried.

A gentleman, in presenting a letter of introduction to a lady, may, if she should be at home, make his first call when sending in his letter and card, whereon should be designated his hotel or place of residence. If this should not be the case, she will answer by sending her card with her reception day engraved upon it, or, if that be too far distant, a note, stating when he may call, should be sent; it may also be expected that her husband, son or brother will call upon him and offer what civilities are at command. Even should neither card nor note be sent, it is still permitted him to call once more. His responsibility ceases here, and if no attention follows he may conclude his friend has overstepped the limits of a slight acquaintance in giving him the letter of introduction.

A Letter of Recommendation

to some position or appointment is very much the same as one of introduction. Its reception, however, does not necessitate social attentions. The form is very simple:

   644 Broadway, New York, November 22, 189—.

Dear Mr. Hill:

> Recognizing, as I do, that your position in commercial circles will give your influence great weight, I take it upon myself to introduce to you Mr. Philip Palmer, a graduate of one of the best business colleges in New York City, and a young man of integrity and capacity. Any recommendations which you can grant him will be looked upon as a favor by

Your friend,
MILTON JONES.

To WILLIAM HILL,
Elmira, N. Y.

A general letter of introduction, intended for the perusal of strangers, would read somewhat as follows:

> *To whom it may concern:*
>
> This is to certify that the bearer of this letter, Miss Marietta Hope, was graduated with high honors from Vassar College, and has since taught in the schools of this city. As her principal for a number of months, I can truthfully recommend her as capable of filling any position for which she may apply.
>
> JAMES H. BLANCHARD,
> Principal of Livingston School,
> New York City.

Letters of Condolence

should be written very soon after the occurrence of the sorrowful event, and, while brief, should not be cold and formal; neither should they touch the opposite extreme, and, by dwelling with maddening iteration upon the fresh sorrow, harrow anew the stricken soul of the mourner. The occasion should never be seized upon as a text for a sermon on resignation, nor should frequent reference be made to various like bereavements suffered by the writer. These comparisons only wound, for "there is no sorrow like unto my sorrow," has ever been the cry of the stricken soul. And when friends have done their little all, each mourner still feels the truth of Lowell's lines:

"Condole if you will, I can bear it,

'Tis the well-meant alms of breath,

Yet all of the preachings since Adam

Cannot make Death other than Death."

Yet friends cannot deny themselves the privilege of a few loving words, and a letter on the loss of a beloved daughter might be as follows:

CAPE MAY, June 1, 189—.

MY DEAR MRS. SUTHERLAND:

I cannot resist my desire to write you a few words of love and sorrow; only a few, for my heart is full and words seem very weak. Thank God, my friend, for the nineteen beautiful years that ended that morning in May.

If you could but know how sweet and tender a recollection she has left enshrined in the hearts of her friends, and all the loving, gracious utterances that are offered to her memory! It is well with Alice in heaven; that it may be well with you on earth, in the days that are to come, is the prayer of

Your loving friend,
MARIE.

To a friend who has sustained a financial loss might be written:

TONAWANDA, N. Y., November 12, 189—.

MY DEAR BLAKE:

The first announcement that I had of your severe financial loss was through the morning paper. I can only express my sorrow at the event and my indignation over the falsity of the cashier in whom you placed so much confidence.

Hoping that you have employed the best of detective skill, and that you will succeed in recovering a portion, at least, of the sequestrated funds, I am,

Yours sincerely,
GEORGE G. PARSONS.

MR. FLETCHER BLAKE,
President of the First National Bank, Aurora, Minn.

It must be remembered that letters of condolence, unlike those of congratulation, are not expected to receive an early answer, and, in case of very deep affliction, may remain seemingly unnoticed, save perhaps, after a time, by cards of thanks.

Letters of Congratulation

should be sent immediately upon the occurrence of the fortunate event that calls forth congratulatory wishes; they should be brief, gracefully worded and contain no mention of other matter. The occasions in life that call forth such missives are numerous: birthdays, engagements, marriages, anniversaries, business successes, etc., each, or all, should win some congratulatory notice. The formal congratulation is in set terms, usually written in the third person, and may be used between individuals but slightly acquainted; for example:

> Mr. and Mrs. Stuart congratulate Mr. and Mrs. Fielding upon the successful conclusion of Mr. Harold Fielding's college course and express the pleasure with which they listened to the delivery of his eloquent oration on Commencement Day.
>
> 81 St. Caroline's Court, July 1, 189—.

This, in common with all congratulatory letters, should be replied to at once, and, wherever any missive is written in the third person, the reply must follow the same fashion. An appropriate answer for the above form would be:

> Mr. and Mrs. Fielding unite in sending thanks to Mr. and Mrs. Stuart for kindly praise awarded their son Harold on the late important event in his life, and also for the exquisite flowers they sent to grace the occasion.
>
> 891 Michigan Avenue, July 2, 189—.

A friendly congratulation in the first person is less stately, as, for instance, one friend might congratulate another upon his marriage:

> GEORGETOWN, D. C., January 10, 189—.
>
> DEAR JACK:
>
> "And so they were married and lived happy ever after," of course. At least, that is what you and Mrs. Julia anticipate at this present time, and is what I, knowing you both, do confidently predict. Accept my heartfelt congratulations, and believe me
>
> Your true friend,
> RICHARD DOE.
>
> To JOHN MYERS, Esq.,
> Yankton, Da.

Answer to the foregoing might be:

> YANKTON, Da., January 20, 189—.
>
> DEAR DICK:
>
> Julia and I received your congratulations with pleasure, my only regret being that I cannot return them in kind.
>
> "Gather roses while ye may,

Old Time's a-flying."

A word to the wise, etc., and let me speedily have occasion to felicitate you in like manner.

Your friend and well-wisher,
JOHN MYERS.

MR. RICHARD DOE,
Georgetown, D. C.

It should be mentioned here that while one congratulates a gentleman upon his engagement, or marriage, and may congratulate his parents upon the same occasion, it is inadmissible to congratulate a lady on a similar event, or to extend the congratulations to her parents. Well-bred mothers have been known to resent this solecism keenly. You may, and indeed are expected to, offer to her, and her parents, all manner of good wishes for future happiness, but be sure not to congratulate.

Almost any success, or pleasant happiness in life, may be made the subject of a congratulatory letter, but a multiplicity of forms is unnecessary here.

Proposals, Engagements, "Naming the Day,"

And other letters of this description are important affairs that may all be transacted through the medium of correspondence, but it is to be hoped that a matter so closely personal will quicken the imagination and inspire the pen of the dullest swain.

Let him woo his Dulcinea swiftly and tempestuously, as King Hal wooed Kate, or let him serve twice seven years as Jacob served for Rachel, but let him never search out printed forms whereby to declare his passion: nor fit the measure of his love to the lines of the "Model Letter-Writer." As to "naming the day," 'twere a wordless lover indeed who could not say, as the poet says:

"Sun comes, moon comes,

Time slips away.

Sun sets, moon sets,

Love, fix a day."

The note has become a factor in modern social life. We send a note when we send a gift, when we ask a favor, when we acknowledge a favor, when we offer an apology, when we postpone an engagement, and when we give, accept, or refuse an informal invitation. These forms will be given here for reference, excepting those pertaining to invitations, which are discussed in their place.

Notes Accompanying a Gift

should be brief, prettily worded, and strictly confined to the subject in hand; for instance, a gentleman sending flowers to a lady might say:

> Mr. Irwin, hearing Miss St. John express a preference for roses, hopes that he may have the pleasure of seeing her wearing the accompanying cluster this evening at the Opera.
>
> 91 Ashland Boulevard, October 2d.

The wearing of the flowers would be all the answer required by this note.

With a birthday gift an appropriately worded note would be as follows:

> AT HOME, August 1st.
>
> DEAR NETTIE:
>
> Remembering that your birthday is at hand, I send you this little painting as a token of my love, together with wishes for many happy returns of this day.
>
> Your friend,
> MARIE ST. JOHN.

These little notes should always receive an answer, as, for instance, this last might be appropriately replied to thus:

> 632 CORSON STREET, August 2, 189—.
>
> MY DEAR MARIE:
>
> You cannot think with what delight I received your beautiful birthday gift, rendered tenfold dearer by the knowledge that it is the handiwork of my friend. With many thanks,
>
> I am, as ever, yours,
> NETTIE D. CATON.

Notes of Apology

are a frequent necessity. They should be written with promptness, evince a repentant spirit, and should be acknowledged pleasantly and forgivingly. Always remember in such a note to explain the cause rendering the apology necessary. For instance, an unfulfilled engagement might be apologized for thus:

DEAR MISS MASON:

I cannot sufficiently regret that I was unfortunately prevented from keeping my engagement to drive with you on Wednesday. An important telegram, received but a moment before the time set for our "outing," left me but a brief five minutes to catch the first train for R——, where affairs, permitting no delay, awaited my attention.

Dare I hope that I have your pardon for so great a seeming negligence?

Very respectfully yours,
JOHN H. CURRAN.

This note being written in the first person will be replied to in the same manner by the recipient:

MR. CURRAN (or, DEAR MR. CURRAN, according to the degree of familiarity):

I accept your apology as quite sufficient, and beg that you will give yourself no further uneasiness over so unavoidable an occurrence.

I am, sincerely,
GERTRUDE MASON.

Notes of Postponement

are always to be sent when the necessity arises for deferring any social gathering. Write them promptly, and explain the unavoidable reasons for the postponement; for example:

DEAR MRS. BRIGGS:

It is with great regret that I inform you that our exhibition of private theatricals is indefinitely postponed on account of the sudden and serious illness of Miss Hope Ledyard, who was the chief star of our little company.

The "Lady of Lyons," with the "Lady" left out, would be like "Hamlet," with the noble Dane missing, an impossible performance; and, as there was no one else so capable of filling the part as Miss Ledyard, we are resolved to await her recovery.

Your friend,
ELIZABETH STUART.

Notes of Request or Refusal

are frequently necessary, but care should be taken neither to make an unreasonable request, nor to return an unjustifiable refusal. Should denial seem imperative, strive to imitate that English statesman who could refuse more gracefully than others could grant. The following examples will suffice:

> DEAR MRS. WINTERBLOSSOM:
>
> You remember the little picture, a Sunset View, that I admired so much the other evening at your home? Would you have any objection to lending it to me for a copy?
>
> Should you have even a shadow of dislike toward my proposition, do not hesitate to refuse at once. So many people are averse, and justly so, to having their paintings duplicated that I feel my request almost an impertinence.
>
> Believe me, truly yours,
EDITH GRANGER.

Refusal to the same:

> MY DEAR MISS GRANGER:
>
> I dread to answer your note, since it must be a refusal of your request, for the little painting is the property of a friend of mine, who has left it, together with a few others, in my care during her tour in Europe. The fact that she has a morbid dislike to having duplicate copies made of her pictures, forces me to deny a request that, were the painting in question mine, I would gladly grant.
>
> Sincerely your friend,
HELEN WINTERBLOSSOM.

Business Letters

need especial care in writing. They are to be read by men with whom time is precious and the demands upon it numerous. Hence they should be brief, clearly worded and straight to the point. Such a letter is much more certain of speedy attention and prompt returns than the rambling, incoherent missive of the unaccustomed writer. If you want ten yards of ribbon of a certain color and quality, say so, but do not lose the order in a maze of irrelevant matter; for instance:

MENDOTA, Ill., April 4, 189—.

MESSRS. BLANK & CO.

Please send me:

10	yards of black silk, at $1 per yard	$10 00
14	yards of green cashmere, at 75c. per yard	10 50
1	pair black kid gloves	1 50
1	pair tan kid gloves, undressed	2 00
	Total	$23 00

Enclosed find money order for the above amount. Goods to be sent by American Express. By filling the above order quickly as possible, you will greatly oblige,

MARY MCNETT.

Address: MRS. W. D. MCNETT, Mendota, Ill.

If there is any special reason for filling an order hastily, such as a birthday gift or wedding present, mention the fact briefly, and care will be taken that it is sent in time. Always make use of money order, draft or registered letter, when sending other than very small amounts of money by mail. Should you have anything to say in such a letter aside from the affair in hand, attend first and briefly to the matter of business, and then add whatever remarks may seem necessary.

Answers to Advertisements

should also be concisely worded, as for example:

61 DELAWARE PLACE, February 19, 189—.

MRS. GENERAL CHANNING:

Seeing your advertisement for a governess in to-day's "Herald," I wish to inform you that I am a graduate of Wellesley, and have, for the two years since being graduated, taught French and German in the college.

Any references which you may desire as to my efficiency for completing the education of your daughter will be furnished you by the College Faculty.

Hoping to hear favorably from you,

I am, respectfully,
(MISS) ELIZABETH STUART.

A letter of inquiry might be something as follows:

DR. J. H. GRATIOT:

In making some inquiries relative to the present residence of a friend of mine, Miss Grace Gage, a mutual acquaintance of ours, Mrs. Emmons B. Corthell, of this place, gave me your address, suggesting that you could afford me the desired information.

This being the case, would you be so kind as to send the lady's present address, or, by handing her this note, permit her personally to furnish the desired information. Any communication addressed, from now on, to 1267 Madison Avenue, will find and greatly oblige,

(MISS) KATE G. COX.

A letter of resignation, being a rather formal document, should be worded very much as follows:

To the Directors of the Owatonna Public Library.

GENTLEMEN: I hereby tender my resignation of the Librarianship of the Owatonna Public Library, said resignation to take effect on the —— day of —— 189—.

Thanking you for the kindness and thoughtfulness with which you have acceded to my wishes and requests during my late term of office,

I am, respectfully,
GEORGE H. GRAHAM.

OWATONNA, Minn., August 1, 189—.

Some Don'ts and Do's for Letter-Writers.

Don't write an anonymous letter; it is a cowardly stab in the dark.

Don't pay any attention to an anonymous letter; it is not worth your regard.

Don't conduct private correspondence on a postal card. Many persons consider this an insult. A purely business message may be thus sent, but even then the slight saving in postage is small recompense for the delay so often attending the delivery of postal cards.

Don't use a postscript; it is unnecessary, old-fashioned, schoolgirlish, and in a particular, punctilious letter the omission of any important matter necessitates the rewriting of the entire letter rather than the use of a postscript. In very friendly letters one may be permitted to add the forgotten paragraph in the form of a postscript, omitting, however, the obsolete abbreviation, "P. S."

Don't write on a half-sheet of paper unless the nature of the correspondence permits the use of the ordinary business letter-head. If the note is short, write only on one side of the paper, but don't tear a sheet in half for economy's sake. The rough, torn edges, denote haste, ill-breeding, or carelessness on the part of the writer.

Don't use tablet paper for ceremonious letters.

Don't write on both sides of the paper to any but very intimate friends or relatives, they being disposed to tolerate slight departures from formality on our part.

Don't meddle with foreign nouns or verbs unless conversant with the language itself; incorrect and ungrammatical usage is too apt to be the unhappy result. Even foreign names and titles should not be used without the exactest care as to their orthography and application.

This rule should be especially remembered with reference to all matters destined to pass through hands editorial.

Don't erase misspelled words in letters of any moment. Recopy the entire missive.

Don't quote too constantly.

Don't underscore your words, unless they express something very important.

Don't send enclosures in a letter written by some one else; only the greatest intimacy can excuse this practice. Write your own letters and send in a separate envelope.

Don't write a letter in a towering passion; you would not care to have it confront you in some cooler moment.

Don't cross the writing in your letters. Life is too short and the time and eyesight of your correspondent too precious for this.

Don't fill up every available blank space and margin of your letter with forgotten messages. If these are very valuable, add an extra sheet to your letter, thus saving its appearance and the patience of its recipient.

Don't divide a syllable at the end of a line. The printer may do this, not the letter-writer.

Don't fall into the habit of using long words in a letter, they show a straining after effect. One should "say," rather than "observe," "talk," rather than "converse," if one's missives are to be easy, well-bred and readable.

Don't refold a letter, the marks always remain to show your carelessness. Fold it correctly the first time.

Do remember to answer all important questions in a letter clearly and decisively.

Do burn the great majority of your letters after answering. Those that are to be kept should be filed away in packages adding date and writer's name on corner of envelope and by a word or two suggesting the topics with which they deal. This will save time in referring to them.

Do answer your friendly letters with reasonable promptness. To do otherwise is a breach of etiquette. An unanswered letter is an insult, a cut direct. Business letters, of course, must be replied to at once.

Do send a postage stamp when you write a letter of inquiry, the answer to which is of interest only to yourself. A stamped and addressed envelope would be a still better enclosure.

Do, if you are an absent son or daughter, write home promptly and regularly; the comfort this will be to the parents at home, and the pain they suffer at any negligence on your part, cannot be overestimated. Husbands and wives, when separated for a time, would do well to follow this same advice.

Do date your letters carefully. Events and proofs of the greatest importance have hung upon the date of a single letter.

Do put sufficient stamps upon a letter to make sure of no extra postage falling to the lot of your correspondent.

Do put your address plainly in all letters. This ensures a prompt answer and, in case of miscarriage, a speedy return from the Dead-Letter Office.

Do, if a business man or woman, have your address on the outside of your envelope. This will make sure of your uncalled-for letters returning to you immediately. It is well to do this in any case where a little uncertain as to the exact address of your correspondent.

Do read your letters over carefully before sending, that no errors may be overlooked.

Do give every subject a separate paragraph instead of running the whole letter, social items and sentiment, all into one indistinguishable whole.

Do begin the first line of each paragraph, at least one inch from the margin of the page.

ARTISTIC HOME DECORATIONS.

THE greatest art work the individual has to do is the building of a home. "A small and inexpensive house may be the House Beautiful," says Edmund Russell.

A famous architect once wrote that he could furnish a plan for a house of a given size and cost without knowing whether the owner was a millionaire or a day laborer. But if he wanted a *home* the case was different. "I desire then to know his antecedents, how he made his money, the size of his family, the number of his servants, and how his daughters spend their time: whether they are domestic, musical, literary or stylish. I want to know the number and quality of his guests, whether he drinks wine with his dinner, and his views on sanitary questions; for this home-building is not mere spending, it is the shaping of human destiny."

In a home things must be beautiful and true and good, and as a celebrated art critic says, "related to us, belonging to us, expressing us at our best; our taste and culture, our personal likings, our comforts and needs, and not merely the high-tide mark of our purses."

Fireplaces and Windows.

We are all of us by nature fire worshipers and the altar of every home is, or should be, the glowing, open fire. Next to this are the great, clear windows meant to admit the glorious glances of the fire worshiper's sun.

As to the first, "if you can have but one, the house or the fireplace, give up the house and keep the fire. If you wish to test the soundness of this advice, build a house, furnish it extravagantly and supply furnace heat to all but one room, and in that room build upon an ample hearth a glowing fire of hickory logs, and in the presence of that genial blaze, upon the bare floor of that unfurnished room, will gather the united household." The broader this family hearth the better. The old English baronial halls with their mighty fireplaces and their great stone hearths had more of light and beauty than all our modern improvements.

ARTISTIC FIREPLACE.

Next come the broad, open windows. Better one window five feet wide than two of two and a half feet. Better for light, warmth or interior furnishing, and better for the illuminating effect upon the whole apartment.

Stairways.

Stairs are a necessity, and their comfort and sightliness depend on several features. Steps must be broad and deep, landings wide and windowed, if may be. If they must be crowded into a narrow hallway it is better that they be made deep and sloping as space permits, and then inclosed with an archway and curtain at foot instead of a door. This also saves heat. But where the great square reception hall can be devoted to them they may be made a thing of beauty.

Woodwork.

Says one writer, "There is a widespread illusion gone out through the world that to have everything in a dwelling 'finished in hard wood throughout,' as the advertisements say, is the only orthodox thing. Paint smells of turpentine and heresy." In this respect it is useless to deny that there is solid comfort in the permanency and genuineness of oak, walnut, or ash, that paint is powerless to give.

But the natural color of woods in many cases may fail to harmonize with the scheme of color to be carried out in the furnishings of the apartment.

WINDOW DECORATION.

In such case, the woodwork should be subjected to delicate, harmonious, painted tints, or polish or gilding, as the case may be.

There is a great variety of woods from which we may choose, but to obtain from them the finer shadings and combinations of color is difficult, not to say impossible.

There is no necessity for making the woodwork that is to be painted unnecessarily substantial or elaborate. Woods such as white maple, holly, poplar, for the light effects; black birch, cherry, mahogany, for darker.

"One fallacy among people," says an architect, "is an immovable faith that the first duty of a human apartment is to look as high as possible. A cathedral, or the rotunda of the Capitol, must have height to produce an overpowering effect. But in an ordinary room of ordinary size, comfort, convenience and prettiness are more to be sought after than height."

Ordinary woodwork must be painted in such shades as will debar it from occupying the prominent position to which positive beauty is alone entitled. Give it a similarity to the ground of the paper, but a little darker, and the rounded surface of any fancy moldings, a shade or two darker. Paint the doors the same, except the panels, which may be decorated, in which case they must be painted the tint of the furniture as a background for the design. This may be very simple, a band of color, a vine in outline or flat color. Trace the outline of wild vines, or ferns, anything graceful. Originality is not demanded. There are good reasons why window casings should start from floor or base, since in this way a visible means of support is given to the entire window, which otherwise has a suspended, insecure look. The panel underneath may be of wood or plaster.

Doors.

Doors are the greatest problem in a room. They monopolize the space on the floor and wall that should be free for pictures and large articles of furniture, and otherwise completely demoralize the apartment. To do away with this inconvenience substitute heavy curtains whenever an impassable barrier is unnecessary; closet doors, for instance, and those between parlors. Again, doors that are much open may be made to slide into the walls. Then, for ornament and as a screen, the doorway may be furnished with hangings, costly or not, as the purse may dictate.

The outer doors are intended as a defense from intrusion from without. It is not really good taste to have these doors of plate glass as that militates against the primal idea of strength and protection.

A Door Divan.

Chairs and sofas we have without end in variety and beauty. Every alcove and nook in every possible sort of room has been thought of and provided for except the one place that exists in almost every house and is the one place where people are always wanting to sit—that is the doorway itself. Folding doors between communicating rooms are seldom closed. An ordinary chair within a few feet of the space never looks well. It shows its back to one room or the other and is in the way.

A divan is an addition to any decorative arrangement of either room. It does not interfere with any graceful drapery that may be arranged at the door. It is decidedly useful, convenient and gives a certain touch of the unusual to the room.

An Improvised Bookcase.

A superfluous doorway or window too often mars the effect of a room, and the present day architecture, as found in cheap apartments and houses, frequently abounds in this sort of generosity.

To surmount the difficulty a very useful inclosure can be constructed by placing two uprights and a few shelves within the door jamb, or against it, as the case may be. Staining or painting them to match the rest of the woodwork is a small matter, while arranging brass rods and pretty curtains is not much more.

Screens.

Screens are a necessary object of household adornment. It is not requisite that they should be expensive, but the uses to which they can be put are legion. A plain frame of hard wood, or pine stained, rectangular, three or four inches wide and one inch thick, furnished with feet, and with or without castors, is all that is necessary. Covering may be done with a great variety of materials, cheap or dear. Ornamentation may be applied, embroidered, sketched, outlined, or painted. If the screen is made in two or three parts to fold like clothes bars, feet will not be necessary.

A rustic fire-screen is a unique affair, handsome and useful where there are open fires, as a shield from heat in cold weather, and as a screen for the emptiness of grate or fireplace during the summer. It is formed from natural branches, two straight and two crotched ones, from which all the smaller branches and twigs have been cut away so as to have but little more than protruding knots. When these are well seasoned, rub, brush and rebrush, both with a soft brush and a stiff one, to remove from every crevice in the bark every loose particle of moss and dust. Then, with liquid gold, gild the bark all over, or, if preferred, gild only the bare wood where it is exposed at the ends and where the limbs are cut off, and give a touch of gold to every crack or protuberance, or, if a smoother finish is desired, remove all of the bark and smoothly gild or enamel the whole surface.

The screen, suspended from the upper crosspiece, is a fringed silk rug woven on a hand loom, as old-fashioned carpets were woven. It falls freely from the top, its own weight keeping it in place, but it might be tied to the standards—half way down and at the upper corners—with bows of braid, soft ribbon or with heavy tassel-tipped cords, or a smaller rug without fringe might be suspended by gilt rings and finished at the bottom with a row of tassels in mingled shades.

In a small apartment, where the radiator is an objection, hang on the wall over it a large picture, placing before the unsightly heater a screen of not too high dimensions. If a space is too large for your picture, hang on either side a bracket, on which place a quaint jug or jar.

For a sewing-room, or, in fact, any apartment where the weekly mending is done, a darning screen is wonderfully commodious. Its conveniences consist of two capacious pockets, to hold stockings or any garment fresh from the laundry and needing attention; a handy shelf whereon to place one's sewing, a tidy little cushion with scissors and loosely swung by ribbons to one side.

ORNAMENTAL SCREEN.

It is a delightful bit of property to serve one, while seated at an open window in summer time or upon an upper veranda with one's work, looking out over the sea with the perfume of flowers in the air.

Trim the skeleton screen to harmonize with the fittings of the room.

A carpenter constructed the framework for the two panels, with the bar across the top, and the little shelf for twenty-five cents. The pine used was an old packing box. The panels must be three and one-half feet high and eighteen inches wide, made of strips three inches broad. The shelf should be eight inches wide and twelve inches long.

Four yards and one-half of chintz in cream-tinted ground, sprinkled with Dresden nosegays gaily dashed with pink and delicate green color, eight cents a yard. Four grades of delicate pink silesia and two and one-half yards of unbleached muslin for interlining, made an item of fifty cents. Hinges and corners and nail-heads of brass, satin ribbon and tacks, by considerable calculation, can be pressed into the amount of seventy-five cents.

A Saturday morning industriously spent in the upholstery of the little screen presented it in completeness.

Screens can be used to protect from drafts of air, by day or night, to keep the sun from an exposed spot on the carpet, to shade the light from weary eyes, to temporarily close archways that have no doors, and to conceal a door that is not often used. They will divide a large room into two small ones when a sudden influx of company arrives, or even close in a corner for the same hospitable emergency. They make delightful nooks in sitting-rooms for the little folks' playhouse, or they may screen off, from the morning caller, a temporary sewing-room in the back parlor, and in sleeping-rooms, occupied by more than one person, a cosy dressing-room may be made by their use.

Draperies.

The new swinging portieres that have appeared have a handsome swinging crane fastened to the wall near the ceiling, upon which a portiere or curtain is suspended. This can then be swung back against the wall or swung out to make a cozy corner or to shut off one portion of a room from another. These swinging portieres can in many cases be made to take the place of screens and often fit with great advantage where a fixed portiere of the old sort could not be used.

The handsome cranes are of course more or less expensive, but a home-made substitute will answer the purpose very well. It is not exactly home-made, however, for the services of a blacksmith may have to be called in to bend the three-eighths inch iron rod into shape for use. The ends are bent to fit into screw eyes or other sockets fastened to the wall, upon which this improvised crane can be swung. The portiere is suspended from the iron rod by rings.

Denim is one of the best of all fabrics for a portiere in rooms constantly used. It may be washed out and will look quite as well as new. If you want a variety put one entire width in right side out, and split another and join to the first section, putting the side pieces wrong side out. Sew the seams, then fell them and featherstitch the outside of the seams in colored linen. Then with a teacup or saucer draw some circles, intersecting or lapping at one edge. Work these with linen in short stitches and make eccentric lines or spider-web lines from the central design. The edges may be hemmed or featherstitched or done in button-hole and cut out in scallops. It is better to have the edge of the facing instead of making a turned-in hem.

Then denim, as a floor covering, wears far better than low-cost matting and never becomes disagreeably faded; for, being made for hard usage, it but takes a quieter tone when other blues would surely fade into unpleasant, soiled-looking hues.

Some Useful Bits of Furniture.

A settee table of oak has an adjustable top, which can be turned over by the removal of two pegs, making a high back to the bench, whose deep seat is utilized as a household linen closet. These tables are in great demand where the saving of space is an object and come in various sizes. They can be purchased without the top and used as a window seat. One in a pretty studio of a woman artist in New York was most artistically treated. It was painted a dull green. The back and the lid of the seat were upholstered in an effective gold colored tapestry drawn over a padding of hair and held down by gimp and gilt nails, making a most artistic seat or table, as its use for either was required. Another one was stained green, and on the back and lid of the seat was used natural toned burlap, with stenciled griffins in dark brown as a decoration.

These tables may be treated in various ways to suit their surroundings. It is suggested in *The Decorator and Furnisher* that one stained the natural oak and upholstered in green rep, turcoman, corduroy, burlap or denim would be most attractive, or for green, substitute brown in the same materials and put on with dull brass nails, making an effective seat for a hall.

Another, painted white and enameled, would be charming in a blue and white dining-room. Upholster in dark blue denim with white nails, and fill with a number of pretty pillows in various designs of blue and white, and one of vivid scarlet to give a warm touch, which is needed in these coldly decorated rooms.

The lovely liberty chintzes in dark blue and white, and sometimes yellow, red and white on blue, are good to use on these settees, which are first painted black.

A Hanging Desk.

The economy of space necessary in apartment living has brought about the evolution of some remarkable pieces of furniture that may be useful in small houses anywhere.

The writing desk may be included in the list of household wonders directly attributable to the necessity of fitting that most useful household article in a six by ten apartment. When closed, it really occupies the very smallest amount of room imaginable, and for the young students' use, or in flat bedrooms, where space is at a premium, it is unique and valuable.

The material may be oak or such wood as one fancies. Pine enameled in white or black is as good, so long as it matches the woodwork or furniture of the room. Two strips of the wood, each two inches by three feet, are attached to the wall by long screws. Across the top of these are placed three shelves about five inches wide, supported by brackets of brass. Between the two upper ones partitions are glued in to form pigeonholes.

From four to six inches from the lower end of each of the strips of wood is firmly placed a strip about two inches wide, to which is hinged the shelf that forms the desk. This is upheld when open by brass chains, and is thus made firm. When it is desired to close it, it is merely shut to the wall, the chains falling into place. The ledge upon which the lid is hinged forms a firm place for the inkstand and other necessary fitments of a desk.

Against the wall, between the supporting strips, may be fixed a Japanese panel or some tapestry or silk, as taste may dictate. A picture can be so fastened to the panel as to form a good letter or cardholder.

The whole affair is simple and easily managed. Any good carpenter will make the necessary woodwork for a very small sum.

A Window Desk.

One of the most convenient and altogether satisfactory contrivances quite in the power of a woman to manipulate is a window desk.

Take a board about fifteen inches wide and saw it the length of the window sill. Put small iron hinges on it and screw it to the sill, so that it can hang down against the under wall when desirable.

Tack a narrow strip of wood under the board, near the front edge. Resting on the floor and wedged under this cleat there is a prop of planed wood, slender and neat looking. You can put a beading around the board, with small brads and stain it cherry or some other color.

The sill holds pens, pencils and inkstands, and a large blotter laid on the board, is a most desirable writing pad. This idea comes from an art student in Paris, who dotes on her window desk.

It will be found useful in the nursery as a place for pasting pictures, drawings, etc., and when done can be swung down and out of the way.

A Hall Chest.

A pretty hall chest is one of the things that may be successfully produced at home. In a seaport town, the chest of some ancient mariner is easily procured; otherwise, one of similar style and make must be fashioned for you by a carpenter. As it need only be made of soft wood the cost is not great. After it has left the carpenter's hands it may be decorated with the applied ornamentation in scroll design, which is now obtainable ready to put on, and afterward treated to a coat of stain.

Old oak is the most satisfactory, or it may be ebonized, if preferred. Polished brass corners and hinges may be added, and a row of brass nails set around the edge with good effect. The convenience of these chests for hall use has been accepted. They beautifully conceal rubbers, mackintoshes, a storm shawl and various unsightly but useful impedimenta of the hall rack, and if, in addition, a seat is desired, a strip of dark leather with a light pad beneath it may be set on with brass nails across the middle of the lid.

Cozy Corners.

They are so easy to arrange. Have your carpenter make a double right-angle bench, with a high, straight back. The seat must be two and a half feet wide, and the top of the back five feet from the floor. This now looks like an ungainly three-sided square, or rather oblong, for it is better to have one side somewhat longer than the others. The wood should be stained cherry or oak, to match the other furniture in the room, and oiled and polished so as to be smooth and of rich appearance; or, use hard wood, black walnut, ebony, mahogany.

The seat and inside back may be thickly and prettily upholstered, and then piled high with pillows, or, the wood having been nicely finished, the upholstery may cover the seat only. Be sure and have the seat made low, otherwise the Cozy Corner will be uncomfortable, its name will be belied, and no one will hie to what might have been the favorite seat in the room.

Now, where shall we place the corner? Put it in the space next to the grate fire, and since you have had this place in view, the side to fit in there should be made the requisite number of feet and inches so as to actually fit.

Placed in this part of the room, two sides of the corner are against the wall, but the third side presents a bare and uninviting appearance. This may be avoided by suspending a silk or gauze hanging close to its side, in the same way that the back of an upright piano is often screened. The seats should be piled with sofa pillows, and in the inclosure a few hassocks would not be found amiss.

The word cozy suggests warmth and pleasantry, as well as comfort. Therefore, this corner is always by the fire, and those occupying it are presumably cheery and happy.

It is just the place to rest in, just the place to read in, just the place for you and your dearest friend to chat in, just the place to play a game in, as bags, balls, etc., could easily be tossed from one seat to the other; just the place to lay plans in, for you are in no hurry to move, and so your plans, not being hurriedly completed, would be more apt to prove satisfactory; just the place to nap in, just the place to frolic in. Indeed, just the place to add to our already comfortable homes if we would have them one remove nearer the ideal home than they now are.

Plenty of Pillows.

All cosy corners and all couches are incomplete without numberless pillows of all sorts, shapes and sizes.

A serviceable pillow, and one that can be laundered, is of blue denim, with a band of Irish point embroidery running around the four sides of the square with the edge toward the center. A ruffle of denim with a narrow embroidered insertion to match the edge, completes this sensible head-rest.

An Indian silk pillow is always pretty, and is pleasant next to the face when one is lying down.

An open-work scrim with rows of ribbon placed upon the plain stripes, made over a contrasting color of silk, with ruffle of sheer lace over the color of the pillow, is effective and bright looking.

Any one who is fond of an Oriental effect can have it in the pillow by sewing silks and satins hit and miss, as in making an old-time rag carpet, then having it woven with black linen chain.

One who is expert with crochet needle can have a creation worthy of handing down for ages to come. Crochet a number of artistic wheels or medallions of knitting silk in a golden yellow shade; join together, making a square the size of the pillow desired. Place this lace cover over a contrasting shade of yellow, finishing the edges with yellow silk pompoms placed close together.

Yellow cheese cloth perfectly plain on both sides, with two ruffles of the same and a fullness of lace between, makes a dainty and inexpensive pillow; the under ruffle being six inches, lace ruffle five inches, and the top ruffle of cheese cloth three inches in width.

For the woman whose tastes run to the elegant, a pillow of silk-faced velvet and satin ribbon is grateful. A novel pillow is the clover pillow, but to carry out the idea as originally designed one must await the coming of the season when clover is at its fullest and sweetest blossom. Then gather the large red clover heads. Take as many as would fill a large washtub, sprinkle a pound of fine salt over them, and stir them well, about once a day, until they are thoroughly dried, without falling to pieces. This is the filling for a pillow made of white linen duck, embroidered with a straggling design of clover.

The convenient and ornamental floor pillow is especially adapted for the summer home, the piazza, the lawn or the lounging-room. The frame, which is made of good springs enclosed in a strong linen covering, is on casters, and can be readily moved from place to place. Covered with Baghdad stripes, tapestry, or any artistic material, it makes a Christmas present that would please the most fastidious taste.

A Corner Closet.

Lack of closet room in a house is a fruitful theme for complaint in these days of contracted space. Architects there are who are willing to sacrifice every consideration, not excepting internal utility, for picturesque outside effects.

In such cases recourse must be had to wardrobes, but as these are expensive, the busy fingers of the housewife must be depended upon to improvise substitutes. If there is a corner in the room with sufficient space (sometimes the architect denies us this small boon) it may be utilized in the manner herewith described.

REPLICA OF A GRECIAN VASE.

Two strips of wood as long as you desire and four inches wide by one inch thick are screwed in the angle of the wall about six feet from the floor; boards are cut off to fit in the corner and resting on these strips; this will form the roof. A brass or wooden rod is then run across the front of this board from wall to wall and from which the curtain is suspended by rings. Cretonne, chintz or printed cotton, will make a good list to choose from, and are inexpensive. One may screw upon the underside of the roof and on the cleats as many hooks as are required, and, if desired, a shelf may be introduced about fifteen inches below the roof, and on that attach the hooks. Such an emergency closet will often be found a great convenience, and the cost will be trifling. It will be well to stretch a piece of muslin or paper across the upper side of the roof to keep out the dust.

A home-made Japanese cabinet may be readily made of the common materials found about the house, such as boxes of hard or soft wood. The smoother the boxes, the better; but they can be planed, if they are not.

The shelves are so arranged as to accommodate the different sizes of Japanese bric-a-brac. The small cabinet in the upper left-hand corner is simply a smooth bit of the board, finished with two ornamental hinges, either brass or bronze. The escutcheon is of the same. The circular panel can be either of Lincrusta, bronzed, or to make it a little more unique, a circular hole can be cut in the door, and a pretty blue Japanese plate inserted, held in place at the back, and the door lined. The supports are easily obtained by a visit to a factory where they have a turning lathe. The ornamental finish at the bottom is of lightly carved wood, if one can do these things, or a strip can be purchased at a carpenter shop or wall paper store. Still another way out of the difficulty is to get just the length of Lincrusta and tack it on neatly.

Before the hinges and escutcheon are put on, the staining should be done, and the simplest way out of the difficulty is to purchase Pik-Ron, stain whatever color or wood you require, then afterward give it a coat of varnish, coach varnish giving a durable finish that is heavy and beautiful, or the whole cabinet may be covered with the stamped Japanese cotton goods in gilt and colors, each shelf being covered before being put in place, and the uprights gilded or stained. Still again, if the work is of pine, it may be stained a rich bronze, and left with dead finish, which is a very fair imitation of Japanese woodwork.

Piano Decoration.

An upright piano should be placed with its back to the room. This position is not only good from a decorative standpoint, but a performer likes to be shielded by the instrument. Here are enumerated various graceful ways to cover the polished bareness of this musical instrument.

To hang a square of tapestry over the back from a brass rod is exceedingly striking. If possible, let the painted subject relate to music or sentiment, and have it sufficiently large to cover the surface of the piano.

If the tapestry is very fine work its surface should be unspoiled by additions. Across the top of the piano lay a scarf of Liberty silk, or another painted panel. The only bric-a-brac that combines with this drapery is a pair of candelabra, the quainter in style the better.

Algerian stripes, Baghdad tapestry or Persian prints make good backgrounds. Their cost is $1.25 a yard, and width fifty inches. With this as a foundation many schemes may be carried out. Bas-relief heads in plaster can be swung on it without injuring the wood of the piano. Medallions of Beethoven, Mozart or Wagner can be purchased for $1 each. A long panel of cherubs goes well, or a line of Delft or Japanese plates.

A low settle has a comfortable resting place underneath this. Either a box seat upholstered in dark, contrasting stuff, or one of the $4.50 green wooden settles, sold to artists, would serve. A number of cushions placed on the seat against the piano add to the coziness and grace of the decoration.

Lighting.

Rooms should be lighted from the sides, if possible. The great central chandeliers, casting their downward shadows, age every face in the room by emphasizing every line, and bringing out every defect sharply.

Decorating.

In decorating a room a harmony of the shades of one color should be used. Beware of spotty effects. It should really, according to Edmond Russell, "be conceived, as a piece of music is, in a certain key. There should be sympathy and harmony. Even the pictures should be chosen with as much regard to their surroundings as to their individual merits."

Another important item in the decoration of the home is considering the choice of ground tones with reference to the complexion of its hostess. Guests appear there but casually. She is always there, and no one should elect to occupy a room, whose color tones either totally efface what little color one may possess, or else, by an exaggeration of natural ruddiness, be made a rival of the setting sun.

The effect of color upon the appearance is so important that every change of color, changes not only the color of the skin, but that of the hair and eyes as well.

Edmond Russell once studied a room with reference to complexions, mixing his paints to a relative hue with the general tone of complexions, making it duller and grayer, so that standing near it the skin looked clear and fresh beside it.

"I made the tone," he said, "a little greener and colder than flesh, so that one looked lighter and warmer and was enriched by the contrast. Any who stood in front of that wall looked five or ten years younger than they were."

In using a flower, or other design, for a frieze or dado, they should be conventionalized. This term is used to signify the modification of a real object with its surroundings. The more formal they are the better; no attempt at shading or perspective is necessary, and the square and compass should be used as much as possible in their designing.

In decorating a room, a dark floor is the beginning, and the walls grow lighter as the ceiling is approached. The richest effects should be congregated at the mantel, with the fire as its central object.

"The ability to combine is a rare one." Ruskin writes truly that, "one rarely meets even an educated person who can select a good carpet, a wall paper, and a ceiling, and have them in harmony." There is too much of a temptation to adopt beautiful things simply because they are beautiful, without pausing to consider the weightier matter of their eternal fitness, or remembering that a thing intrinsically beautiful in itself may become hideous by inharmonious proximity or combination with another beautiful object.

Home of the Soul.

A mystic German writer calls a house, properly ordered, the "home of the soul," carrying out the idea that the house in which an orderly soul lives, is only an expansion of the body built and adorned out of her passing experiences. "All sorts of delicate affinities establish themselves between her and the lights and shadows of her abode; the particular picture on the wall; the scent of flowers at a particular window until she seems incorporated into it."

In other words, one's environments, as one's dress, must be in harmony with their individual type, or a permanent discord will result; for instance, Emma Moffett Tyng speaks of a "pond-lily type of woman, soft color, gray blue eyes, pale brown eyes," appealing to her as to the "effect" of the gorgeous, redecorated interior of her home, with flames of color in hangings and rugs, and "her Egyptian gown with its glow and glint of purple and gold. All these things were artistic and beautiful, and perfect in their relations to each other," but in their relation to her nothing could have been worse. The woman, herself, was eclipsed, obliterated. "A Cleopatra, dark and flashing, would make the picture complete. But such a colorless woman needs repose in her surroundings; the low tones of blue and gray, the palest flush of the sunset heavens."

Some Lovely Rooms.

Edmond Russell has treated two rooms exquisitely. A gold and ivory parlor, tinted, walls and ceiling in a grayish white with a greenish tinge, and this is mottled with gold flecked lightly over the surface. The broad frieze is adorned in free, simple style with leaves and blossoms of magnolia. Everything in this room should be light and delicate in color. The soft gold and ivory would be nullified by heavy walnut window casings; red and green carpet, red or blue plush furnishings, or vivid hangings would ruin the effect. Pictures in such a room should be preferably water-colors with pale gray mats, and gold or white frames. Oil paintings are only permissible when dreamy and vaporous in tint. Light, delicate colors in upholstery, creamy madras for curtains. The carpet may be a little darker, verging on some of the delicate, woody browns. Any bric-a-brac should be in pale shades of yellow or rose.

The tender lights of this room seem to clear and soften the complexion of the occupants.

Another is a dining-room of copper, bronze and terra cotta shades. A pale tint of copper to the background overlaid with dashes of bronze and strong copper color. The frieze is a succession of pine boughs, lightly fringed with their needles. Above the sideboard is a panel representing magnolia blossoms, and their heavy polished leaves, with brown in stem and shadows. The effect of this color scheme is to give a suggestion of warmth and cheer. The gold and copper used in flecking the wall are merely the two shades of the common bronze powder.

RICH PIECES OF FURNITURE.

Still another nest of a sleeping-room comes to mind, a creation of Moscheles. Floor covered with white bearskin rugs, furnished with a delicate tint of robin's-egg blue. Toilet table strewn with every imaginable luxury in old ivory and silver. Panels in the wardrobe and doors filled with paintings by Burne-Jones, classic figures given the preference.

These rooms are given as examples of harmony of coloring. Great expense is not always necessary to secure this artistic harmony. Money goes a long way, but good taste and ingenuity will go just as far, with a minimum of expenditure.

There is a little room, a symphony in green and gold, created by one girl's taste, a pale seafoam green that is delightful to the eye. The woodwork, banded with a narrow strip of gilt, is of this color, and the enterprising young woman painted it all with her own hands. The curtains at the three windows are of the freshest and purest white muslin, prettily ruffled. They are the kind that always look as if they had just been laundered and they are tied back with pale green ribbons that make them look the more exquisitely neat. The floor is covered with plain matting, which particularly recommended itself, by the way, because it was inexpensive.

As to Furniture.

Every article of furniture in the room is of the prevailing green and there are no off shades, for they were all painted from the same can of paint. The bedstead was nothing but common pine, made to order at the factory, and it is of a quaint design that originated in the same fertile brain that is responsible for all the rest of the perfect appointments. The headboard is in the shape of a shield and there is painted thereon a spray of wild roses to bring to the sleeper over whom they bend sweet dreams of perpetual summer time. And the white counterpane and snowy pillows in the setting of green and gold make it a most inviting place of repose.

The chairs were resurrected from the débris in the family attic. There are two heavy old-fashioned ones of curly maple, and they are cushioned with a brocaded green and gold material that exactly match the green of the furniture. Then there is a comfortable little rocking chair cushioned with the same material and painted in green with many stripes of gold.

But it is the dressing table that is the most charming of all the unique devices that make the room attractive. It was a battered old washstand at first, but now it is a work of art. It is painted, of course, in green and gilt, and there is a spray of wild roses on the front. Above it is a green and gilt framed mirror with a spray of the favorite wild roses again overhanging the top part. Over mirror and washstand and all is draped a canopy of white muslin. Among the other articles that find place on the table is a little fairy lamp with a shade of green tissue paper that gives the softest light imaginable.

A comfortable green window seat in the corner is well supplied with pillows covered in green and gold brocade, and up and around the window there clambers an old English ivy.

There is an oddly fashioned bookcase in another corner. You would never guess it, of course, but it was constructed out of two dry goods boxes. It is painted green inside and out and fitted up with four shelves. A green silk curtain hangs from a brass rod, and about the edge of the bookcase is a gilt cornice. The top is covered with bric-a-brac.

For pictures there is an etching or two on the wall in green and gold frames, and you have a room the very sight of which is cool and refreshing, and which cost its owner some time and some planning, but very little money.

Pictures.

Be careful of the pictures and their relations to the walls. Rooms should rather be a setting for a beautiful moving picture of the shifting groups of people in it.

Too much gilding, too many gaudy oil paintings attract the eye and distract the mind.

There is a simple picture in my room, red curtains, a white-robed child kneeling, that is all, but everything in it harmonizes, and it harmonizes with the furnishings of the room, and my eye is often drawn toward it.

One authority objects to portraits as a decoration. "Their presence, if at all impressive, is too stimulating."

Picture frames should never be so gorgeous as to distract the mind from the picture. "Frames are to protect the picture and relate it to the walls."

Group etchings together and put engravings in the portfolio. Over low bookcases pictures should be large, and in this form they give a style to the room. Water colors look admirable if treated in this manner, and if two bookcases are put together so as to form one, divide the pictures by a bracket, on which place a jar of some unique pattern.

SELECTING PAINTINGS FOR HOME DECORATION.

Small rooms require medium-size pictures, which can be hung one above the other, and three may even be placed on line with good effect. For an ideal head in oil the frame should be of broad gilt. Hang it in a good light, and on one side group two small water-color pieces in the fashionable white band frame. For an oblong picture a small sketch under it looks well equipped.

A very large and beautiful picture sometimes sets the keynote of color for the apartment. Otherwise, subordinate them as decorations to the colorings of the room, as in the ivory and gold room.

In a room where there are to be many pictures, give rather a neutral color to the walls, merely as a picture background. Where there are finely decorated walls pictures are rather out of place, since one decoration spoils the effect of the other.

Mottoes.

The motto, whose revival is noted in the above title, is the expression in architecture of some sentiment suitable to the place to which it is applied. It is more frequently and more noticeably in domestic architecture than elsewhere that the motto is found. Scarcely a country house of sufficient size to boast a hall and fireplace but announces in script or text a welcome to all guests or some appreciation of the comforts of its four walls. The favorite place for this motto is over the fireplace, either above or below the mantel shelf, and of all the old ones, "East or west, home is best," with its variety of expressions, is the favorite. "A man's house is his castle."

"Home is the resort

Of love, of joy, of peace."

"A man's best things are nearest him;" "Our house is ever at your service;" "You are very welcome;" "Take the goods the gods provide thee"—any one of these will as appropriately welcome the stranger as the friend.

Over the mantel of one's private room the restful motto, "Duty done is the soul's fireside," may find appropriate place.

HOW TO BE BEAUTIFUL.

TO begin at the beginning: to insure a good complexion strict attention must be paid to the diet. Wholesome, well-cooked food must be eaten; regular exercise in the open air is another point, and the body must be bathed three hundred and sixty-five times a year. It may be considered almost supererogatory to remark that not any amount of cerates, washes or powders will cover or obliterate blotches, pimples and blackheads caused by unwholesome food or uncleanly habits. We may not be able to afford elegantly-appointed bath-rooms, but we all can indulge in a daily bath.

A quick and simple method for the busy housekeeper, which need only occupy a few moments, is as follows: buy a yard of coarse Turkish toweling, and make of it two mittens. Have a bowl of warm water, in which dissolve some borax. This is soothing to tired nerves, besides rendering the skin soft and white. When ready, slip on one of the mittens, wet it thoroughly, rub well with soap, and quickly wash the body all over. All the impurities of the body are now on this mitten. Lay it to one side. Put on the other mitten, and wash the body again. The mittens may be washed and hung to dry, ready for the next bath. Rub the skin briskly with a rough towel until it glows.

If this treatment is followed daily, with a tub-bath weekly, you will not complain of those tired, nervous headaches, your face will lose its sallowness, and your walk will gain in sprightliness. Here let us say, for the benefit of those who are obliged to live in rented houses, or who have no facilities for a bath-room, that a folding bathtub is now offered. It folds up somewhat after the manner of a folding bed. When closed it looks like a cabinet, and is nicely finished in oak. In connection with it is a tank and heating apparatus. The water may be heated with gas, kerosene or gasoline.

Lemon juice, diluted, is a famous whitener for the skin, as are all vegetable acids, such as tomato, cucumber and watermelon. Oftentimes something is needed to heal as well as whiten. For this, take two tablespoonfuls of oatmeal and cook it with enough water to form a thin gruel, strain, and when cool add to two tablespoonfuls of the gruel one tablespoonful of lemon juice. Wash the face with this at night, allowing it to dry on the skin. This is excellent for a shiny face.

Another very soothing preparation to use at night is made of one ounce of glycerine, half an ounce of rosemary (fluid), and twenty drops of carbolic acid. This is excellent for any irritation of the skin, and also for prickly heat. The face must always be well washed with water and pure soap before applying any of these preparations. If the skin is oily, bathe with diluted camphor (a teaspoonful to a pint of water), but it is injurious to a naturally dry skin.

Treatment for a Rough Skin.

A wash for a rough face is two ounces of water, one ounce of glycerine, one ounce of alcohol, and half an ounce of gum of benzoin, to be dissolved in the alcohol first. Apply at night. For wrinkles—do we see some of you looking interested?—take some clippings of sheep's wool and steep in hot alcohol. It is said that the grease thus obtained is identical with an element found in the human bile. I know that if rubbed on the skin it not only removes but prevents wrinkles, making the skin soft and pliable. These remedies all have the merit of being harmless, which cannot be said of all cosmetics.

Let us give one more recipe, and that is for brightening the eyes. When you are tired and warm, and your eyes are dull, take a cloth and wring it out of very hot water, as hot as you can bear it. Lie down for ten minutes with this cloth spread over your burning face and tired eyes. You will be surprised to see how the tired lines will fade out and how the eyes will shine, and when your "dearest" comes home he will pay you a compliment which will more than reward you.

Reducing Flesh.

The real mode of life and diet should be changed if the fat would be reduced. If necessary, procure a pair of scales and weigh the different foods that are taken into the system. Reduce the diet then to about four ounces of starch or sugar material per day, one and a half ounces of fat, taken chiefly in the form of butter, and about six or seven ounces of albuminous food, such as lean meat or fish. This is the minimum that should be resorted to, and the patient can take more of each at first and reduce the diet gradually to this point. The proportion of the different food compounds, however, with the exception of figs, dates, grapes and nuts, should also be eaten daily, and one-third of a pound of some of the following vegetables: asparagus, turnips, cucumbers, parsley, watercress, celery, kale or cabbage. Fluids have a fattening tendency, and they must be taken in small quantities.

The drinking should be confined to tea, coffee or water, and never should be taken at mealtime, nor within one hour of a meal. This is peremptory, for food will produce fat much quicker and surer when watered by some good beverage.

Refreshing Sleep.

What is the correct method to pursue in preparing for a trip into dreamland, for there is a right as well as a wrong way? The business of disrobing should be so systematized that attending to all the little niceties included in the process will become, after a while, second nature. There is something more to be done, let us assure you, in addition to putting your hair up in curl-papers and dabbing a bit of cold cream on your face, if you would wake up in the morning looking as fresh as a rose. In the first place, do not put off these important preparations until you are so heavy-lidded that you are ready to give everything belonging to the toilet the go by. And now for the first step. Early in the evening your sleeping apartments should be thoroughly aired by dropping the window from the top and raising it at the bottom.

The current of fresh air is especially important when the room has been, as so many sleeping apartments are, in constant use all day. Ten minutes will be quite sufficient for toning up the atmosphere. Now close the window and allow the room to become thoroughly warmed, that you may not experience a chill while taking a rub down. Prepare a big bowl of tepid water, into which you sprinkle a small quantity of ammonia or borax. Take a Turkish towel, which is much better than a sponge, wring it out as dry as possible, and, grasping a corner in each hand, give the spine a vigorous rubbing. Have at hand another Turkish towel, and as you bathe the body in sections, dry as quickly as possible.

From the points of your rosy toes to the curve of your soft throat you are a blushing model of the charming effects of the bath. When finished, slip over your head a soft little shirt, high neck and short sleeves (a white silk or lisle thread is the best), the rosy skin beneath giving it the appearance of being lined with pink silk. Then comes the nightrobe, and next the pajama or lounging robe, which may be of anything, from flannel to eider down.

Tuck your feet into a pair of bedroom slippers, and your are ready to attend to minor details. Never think of retiring in any article of clothing which you have worn during the day. Such a barbarous custom has nothing whatever in common with health and refinement. Neither is it well to discard everything but your nightgown, for it is exceedingly dangerous to chill the system by night draughts.

How to Take Care of the Eyes.

Avoid sudden changes from darkness to brilliant light.

Avoid the use of stimulants and drugs which affect the nervous system.

Avoid reading when lying down or when mentally and physically exhausted.

When the eyes feel tired rest them by looking at objects at a long distance.

Pay special attention to the hygiene of the body, for that which tends to promote the general health acts beneficially upon the eye.

Do not depend on your own judgment in selecting spectacles.

Old persons should avoid reading much by artificial light, be guarded as to diet and avoid sitting up late at night.

After fifty, bathe the eyes morning and evening with water so hot that you wonder how you stand it; follow this with cold water that will make them glow with warmth.

Do not give up in despair when you are informed that a cataract is developing; remember that in these days of advanced surgery it can be removed with little or no danger to vision.

Never read in bed or when lying upon the sofa. Sit with your back to the light as much as possible. Attend to your digestion. Do not work longer than two hours without closing your eyes and resting them for five minutes. If your eyes are weak, bathe them in water to which a little salt and a little brandy have been added.

The Hair and How to Take Care of It.

If the hair has that soft, glossy look that tells of regular care, and if it is well kept, with every pin in its place, you may rely upon it that its owner possesses the instinct of ladyhood.

Each hair has tiny prongs or tentacles, something like those on the cockle bur, which catch the dust; hence the especial need of brushing. At a lady's school in England, some twenty years ago, the girls were required to brush their hair for fifteen minutes daily in the long dressing-room, and they were timed at this exactly as if it were any other exercise.

Occasionally the hair and the scalp need washing, as the face, though less often if the brushing be carefully attended to. When, however, it begins to seem dirty, give it a good shampooing. Wash both hair and scalp thoroughly in a washbowl of warm water in which has been dissolved a tablespoonful of powdered borax; then rinse it well in clear warm water; you will be surprised sometimes at the complexion of the water.

Many women dread the shampooing because of their liability to take cold in the process. Let such a person choose a room where the air is warm and dry. After wiping the hair thoroughly dry with towels, and pinning a fresh one around the neck and shoulders, let her get some one to come and make a breeze with a large palm-leaf fan upon her hair while she is engaged in carefully disentangling it with a brush and comb, occasionally giving the scalp a little vigorous rubbing if it begins to feel chilly. The fanning greatly hastens the drying process. Another plan is to lie down with the hair spread out on cushions in the sunshine. Be sure to get it thoroughly dry before putting it up.

An Excellent Head Covering.

A very pleasant step, though not a necessary one, next to take is to have a little thin silk mob-cap (of some pretty shade of silk, so that it is becoming rather than disfiguring, if needful, to wear about the home), lined, and thickly wadded with cotton-batting, well powdered with heliotrope or some other delicate sachet powder (these come in ten or fifteen-cent packages), and wear this from one to three hours. Here, again, those thousands of minute tentacles come into play; they catch and retain (one would almost think they close over them) the atoms of the perfume when they are thus freed from dust, and when the hair is soft and light in its new cleanness—and it is astonishing for how long a time the hair will retain that faint, delicate aroma which is so truly lovely in a woman's hair; and all to be obtained in so simple and innocent a way as with this little mob-cap, put on at the right time.

A good rule for ensuring the regular brushing of the hair which may be taught to children (and perhaps good for busy women also), is to brush the hair with fifty long strokes both at morning and at night.

Much also depends upon the brush. Let it not be stiff enough to hurt the scalp. Choose a brush of medium stiffness, with bristles long and close together, and nowhere will it pay better, "in the long run," to give a good price for a good article than in a woman's hairbrush which she proposes to use as described above.

Do not use a fine-tooth comb. Frequent washing will remove the dandruff in all cases, and without the injury caused to the scalp by the fine comb.

It is also well to clip the ends of the hair regularly once a month, keeping it smooth and even, besides, as is thought by some stimulating the growth and keeping it in a more healthy condition.

Perseverance in this treatment will give the hair a fine natural gloss, and a healthy tone. It will tend to prevent its falling out, and will also help to preserve its natural color much longer than if it were neglected.

"Show me a woman," said a wise matron the other day, "though she be in the busiest farmer's kitchen in America, who may always be found with her hair neatly and carefully arranged and with a fresh linen collar, and I will show you a lady in mind and manners. Those two points always settle the rest in my opinion!"

Recipe for the Complexion.

A mixture for preserving the complexion, easily made at home, is as follows: take a wineglassful of the best French orange flower water. Add a tiny pinch of carbonate of soda and two teaspoonfuls of glycerine. Melt a piece of camphor the size of a pea and three teaspoonfuls of cologne water and add to the orange flower water. Shake the whole for five minutes. Apply to the face every night.

Care of the Lips.

The Cupid's bow in dainty curves has always been symbolical of a perfect mouth, and lips most kissable have never been represented as other than pink and perfect.

No other portion of the face, however, so quickly responds to symptoms of ill-health in the body as do the lips. Fever blisters are the disfiguring reminders of a cold; dry, broken or bloodless lips show that one is out of sorts, even more certainly than heavy eye or dejected mien, and it is a woman's duty to endeavor to restore them to their soft, rich redness, which is the outward and visible sign of good health.

To do this the general system must be toned up, diet regulated, and a regular house-cleaning gone into; but there are certain defects of the lips that can be overcome without all this trouble, because they arise from a woman's own fault. Many of us, from nervousness or habit, have a way of biting our lips which will surely result in swelling, bruise or dryness that is both uncomfortable and unpleasant to look at.

Therefore, the first step is to break off so pernicious a practice by watching one's self very carefully. Next, anoint the poor, bruised members with some healing salve of a pure make.

Do not, however, think to cure chapped lips by anointing them after being out in the air. The time for treatment is before the mischief is done, putting on a little cold cream every time you start out for a walk, which you will find highly beneficial and will keep your lips in winter just as sweet and rosy as when the milder zephyrs of summer rule the air.

Remedies for the Lips.

A writer whose knowledge of such subjects is beyond question says that glycerine and rose water should never be used to soften the lips, as this remedy has one great drawback, namely, that it induces the growth of superfluous hair, a warning which all women will gladly heed, for no one desires to pose as a bearded lady. When cold sores appear rub them with cold cream, being careful not to break them, and they will soon disappear.

The reason that they usually cling so long is, that they are tampered with by rubbing or biting, and therefore cannot have a chance to heal properly, as they would if left alone. The same writer who warns us against glycerine and rose water is a strong advocate of hot water, and affirms that there is scarcely any ailment that will not succumb to its healing virtues. Therefore, with cold cream and hot water one should be able to present to the world a pair of rosy lips free from any unsightly blemishes.

Smoothing Out the Wrinkles.

Wrinkles are, of course, the special detestation of every woman, and when they begin to make their appearance, one of the most perplexing questions is as to how they can be removed, or at least the evil hour of their coming be put off for a time. There has recently been a good deal of nonsense printed in various channels as to this subject, and one of the most cherished fads is that the steaming of the face will remove them. This is one of those half-truths which are simply deceit and disappointment.

Wrinkles appear because the fine muscles of the face lose their tone, the tissue shrinks, and the skin fits itself to the depressions which are thus left. It is a mistake to suppose that wrinkles can be wholly eradicated, especially those which are due to advancing years. Let us "grow old gracefully" and accept the inevitable with the best grace possible. A cheerful disposition will do wonders toward lighting up the face and making one's friends forget or overlook entirely the signs of advancing years. But wrinkles frequently come on prematurely, and prove extremely vexations. It is unquestionably true that a proper, thorough and careful course of face massage will do a good deal to help things, where the skin has become dull and lifeless, as will especially happen in cases of general decline or ill health.

From two to four times during each twenty-four hours the face should be gently but systematically rubbed, the best method being to employ a fine towel or a bit of red flannel. The finger ends answer very well, but it is quite difficult to use them without weariness. It will be noticed after a few days that the skin is gaining in tone and rigor, when the degree of vigor employed may properly be increased.

Bad air is one of the most potent causes of wrinkles and the remedy, of course, as the getting of good air. Excellence of the highest degree may not be attainable; if not, let us get the best we can. With good air should come good living and plenty of nutritious food, especially that which has fat-producing qualities.

Massage of the face is well recommended, using a light, gentle, circular motion of the fingers, while much may be done by cultivating flexibility and voluntary motions of the muscles of the face, especially those affecting the wrinkled portions. And it may not be amiss, though it be a delicate matter, to suggest that an overworked, thankless, hopeless life will inevitably wrinkle the fairest face with furrows that no agency this side of the grave can remove, till the cause shall have been lifted.

The Feminine Waist.

We have already had occasion to discuss the question of small waists and the abuse of proportions that tight-lacing frequently entails. We have only to consider now the caprices of fashion with regard to length. Sometimes this fickle goddess sends our waists up under our arms, and then a reaction sets in, and they lengthen gradually till the points and basques of our bodices reach very nearly to our knees. Of the two extremes, the more sanitary, as well as the more artistic, is the former, but these considerations have little effect on the arrangements of fashion.

The weight of clothing should hang as little as possible from the waist. Many women believe that it is better that it should come from the hips than from the shoulders, but the testimony of all medical men is clear and indisputable on this subject. Nor is it upon hygienic grounds alone that this is objectionable. This weight from the hips destroys all freedom of movement, just as the tight corset deprives the body of all the suppleness and flexibility given it by nature.

The belt is, on a perfect figure, an interruption to harmonious lines that could well be dispensed with. On an imperfect figure it is excusable, when associated with a form of bodice that seems to require to be confined, such as the loosely plaited or gathered bodice sometimes worn. Over a tight bodice the belt has no reason for being, and is absurdly out of place. For this and also sanitary reasons we feel inclined to condemn it.

Beautiful Arms.

Beautiful arms are a powerful weapon in the armory of beauty; but though most women appreciate to the full the charm of this possession, the fact remains that in America undeveloped arms are the rule, and rounded, dimpled symmetry the exception. Lately, however, the gymnasium is producing charming arms.

Exercise is essential to the development of the arms: exercise, that is, of the arms themselves. Gymnastic exercises that bring the muscles of these into play should be, as far as possible, encouraged in girls, as tending not only to their improvement in this particular, but as being beneficial to the general health.

Arms disproportionately large as compared to the rest of the frame are, on the other hand, at least equally disagreeable with those we have been discussing. Very large arms carry with them a suggestion of coarseness that is unpleasant as associated with a woman. It is, as we have said before, impossible to give the exact proportions which one portion of the human frame should bear to the rest. The ideal arm, however, should gradually decrease in size from the shoulder to the wrist, the outlines being marked by those inward curves which are also noticeable in well-formed shoulders. The wrist should be slender without being thin, the bone at the outer side being well covered and indicated rather by dimples than otherwise.

There is an old rule for measurement that approaches accuracy in some degree. We give it for what it may be worth, advising our readers not to pin their faith to it too implicitly. Twice round the thumb, once round the wrist; twice round the wrist, once round the neck; twice round the neck, once round the waist.

The roundest arms in the world fail to be beautiful if they are red. There are beautiful white arms, brown arms, copper-colored arms, and even black arms, but beautiful red arms are not. This fault is seldom to be found with the arms of ladies, which are so constantly kept covered as to be protected from the influences of weather. It is characteristic of a cook, a dairymaid, a housemaid, a field-hand, to have red arms, and it is probably from this association that they have fallen into such extreme disrepute.

The use of violet-powder may be condoned when it modifies the contrast between red arms and white evening dresses. The application being only temporary, it can only very slightly affect the well-being of the pores, but it should be very carefully used, or it will come off on the coat sleeves of the partners of the red-armed one.

When the arms are very thin the sleeves should not be too tight, though, as a rule, thin arms do not look at all badly in tight sleeves. When the arms are too long, their apparent length may be diminished by crossway trimmings on the sleeve. When, on the contrary, the arms are disproportionately short, a lengthwise trimming will remedy the defect. The sleeve of to-day is a blessing in disguise for ladies with thin arms.

The leg-of-mutton (*gigot*) sleeve was invented to conceal defects in the arm, and to make the waist appear small by contrast with the size of the sleeves. Puffs at the shoulder give grace and delicacy to the neck and head. The pagoda sleeves, copied from the Chinese, being wide and open, cause the hands to appear smaller by contrast with the aperture from which they emerge; but when the sleeve is exaggeratedly large and wide, the effect of the contrast is lost, the sleeve losing itself in, and mingling with, the rest of the draperies. The epaulette worn some years ago is useful as giving width to narrow shoulders. The Louis XV., or *sabot* sleeve, tight to the elbow, and ending in a frill of lace, is perhaps the most becoming of all sleeves to a really pretty arm, while the sleeve open to the shoulder is the most trying to a defective outline.

Treatment for the Hands.

The hands of growing girls are often red and clumsy, and girls who are beginning to take thought of their appearance are sometimes in despair about them, not being aware that they will grow whiter and whiter with every year. The ideal hand is white, certainly, but not dead white. It should have a dash of healthy flesh-tints. The tips of the fingers and the portions that surround the palm should be tinged with pink. The fingers should taper towards the nails, the most approved shape for which is the "filbert," so called from its resemblance to the oval form of the nut of that name, and the similarity of the direction of the lines of the nail to those on the wood of the nut.

Scissors and Nail-brush.

The appearance of white spots on the nails is caused by knocks or blows. To obviate the appearance of such spots the hands must be taken care of and the nails disturbed as little as possible. When the nails become stained or discolored, a little lemon juice is the best agent to employ as a corrective. It is equally valuable in discoloration of the skin.

The care of the nails, should be strictly limited to the use of the knife or scissors to their free border, and of the ivory presser to their base, to prevent the adhesion of the free margin of the scarf-skin to the surface of the nail and its forward growth upon it, The edge of scarf-skin should never be pared, nor surface of the nail ever scraped, nor should the nails be cleaned with any instrument whatever except the nail-brush.

There is no rule for the management of the nail of greater importance than that which prescribes the pressing back of the edge of the scarf-skin which forms the boundary of the base of the nail. This margin is naturally adherent to the surface of the nail, and has a tendency to grow forward with it and become ragged and attenuated. When allowed to do so, the ragged edge is apt to split up into shreds, and these projecting from the surface, are pulled and torn, and often occasion a laceration of the skin and a painful wound. The occurrence of these little shreds, denominated *agnails*, may be effectually prevented by the regular use of the presser once or twice a week. It must be used with gentleness.

The following is said to be an excellent preparation for making the hands white; and as it cannot possibly injure them, we give it a place here. Take as much scraped horseradish as will fill a tablespoon; pour on it half-a-pint of hot milk. Use it before washing, allowing it to dry on the hands before applying the water. Redness and chapping are sometimes caused by the hands being imperfectly dried. The greatest care should be taken in drying them, more especially in cold weather, and when the hands are exposed to cold winds.

If the hands become rough from any cause, the following may be applied with good effect: Half fill a basin with fine sand and soapsuds, as hot as can be borne. Brush and rub the hands thoroughly with hot sand. The best is flint sand, or the powered quartz sold for filters. It may be used repeatedly by pouring the water away and adding fresh. Rinse the hands in a warm lather of fine soap, then clean cold water. While they are still wet, put into the palm of each hand a very small piece of almond cream and rub it all over them. This, again, forms a strong lather. After drying the hands, rub them in dry bran or powdered starch till every atom of moisture is absorbed, and finish by dusting off the bran or starch. This will make the hands very soft and smooth.

To Cure Burning of the Skin.

Occasionally the hands and face become red and flushed while the feet are cold. This very uncomfortable state of things may be effectually remedied by bathing the feet in hot water with a tablespoonful of Kretol in it. This will frequently be found an immediate cure for headache, but must not be attempted just before going out in cold or damp weather. A simple remedy is to wash the face and hands in very warm water, as hot as can be borne. This will frequently dispel the burning sensation and induce a cooler condition of the skin.

A slice of raw potato rubbed well into them will remove stains from the fingers and hands. Lemon juice is also effective in this way, and, if not used immoderately, may be applied without fear of evil consequences. For chapped hands and lips the following will be found efficacious: Equal quantities of white wax (wax candle) and sweet oil; dissolve in these a small piece of camphor; put it in a jam crock, and place it upon the hob till melted. It must be kept closely covered. It should be applied to the hands after washing, and previous to drying them.

A few drops of glycerine poured into the palms of the hands after washing, and rubbed all over them before drying with a towel, is perhaps the best and simplest remedy for chapping; but if good soap is always used, and the hands well dried and protected by warm gloves against the cold, the chapping will be prevented, which is preferable to the very best cures.

Remedy for Chilblains.

Chilblains may be cured very speedily by rubbing into them morning and evening as much spirits of turpentine as they will absorb. This must not be applied to broken chilblains, but if taken in time it will prevent their breaking. The water in which potatoes have been boiled is an excellent remedy for chilblains on feet or hands. These members should be put into the water while it is as hot as can be borne. The same specific applies equally to what are called "whitlows," or "felons" a gathering in the region of the fingernail that is extremely painful, and to which some are constitutionally liable.

When the feet are large, the owners should never be tempted into wearing any but the very plainest boots and shoes. Ornamentation of any kind makes the foot look larger. Even a pretty foot looks its best in a perfectly plain satin slipper, with only a small rosette with buckle on the toe. This rosette must not, however, be permitted to the large foot. It may, certainly, be worn on the place intended for the instep, when that ornamental rise in the outline of the foot is totally absent. Lines of white stitching on the boot make it look larger than it really is. The best boot for a large foot is one in which the toe-cap comes well up on the foot. Its lines are thus broken up, and the apparent length diminished. A pretty foot, on the contrary, looks better in a boot that has no toe-cap, the "upper" of which is made all in one. This displays to advantage the beautiful outline of the foot, and the gentle but decided curve of the instep.

The possessors of large feet should be particularly careful to have their boots perfectly cleaned and very glossy. The feet look much smaller when this is the case than when the boot has a rim of mud around the sole and a shadow of dust upon the uppers. Where the instep is defective or totally absent, a pretence at one may be made by blacking that portion of the sole of the foot that is immediately adjacent to the heel. This causes a kind of optical illusion which is favorable to the flat-footed.

Patent leather is a most objectionable material for wearing upon the feet. Through it ventilation is absolutely impossible. So much for the sanitary part of the subject; and as to convenience, this is as much in the shade as sanitation, for patent leather "draws" the feet much more than any other kind. Of late, ladies and children have begun to borrow this material from gentlemen, but as much smaller shoes can be worn with comfort in any other kind of leather, it is not likely to become universally popular. Large feet should never be clad in satin.

Foot-Wear.

The fit of the stocking is almost as essential to the perfection of the foot as that of the boot or the shoe itself. It should be large enough to allow freedom to the toes, and not so large as to wrinkle on the foot. In a well-fitting stocking the foot can be more accurately measured than otherwise, and the comfort of the foot is sadly impeded by an ill-fitting one.

The feet should be bathed every morning, and for those who walk much, a daily change of stockings is advisable. This daily change is more than advisable, it is necessary, for persons who suffer from perspiring feet. Regular washing of the feet preserves their strength and elasticity, and helps to keep them in shape. At least once a week they should be washed in hot water, with plenty of soap, rubbing them with a ball of sandstone, which will be found a very useful article for toilet purposes, also a tablespoonful of Kretol in the water. The nails should then be carefully pared, and, in drying the feet, much friction should be used in order to stimulate the skin to healthy action.

When corns appear, they may be accepted with resignation as lifelong acquaintances. Seldom, indeed, do they quit the victim, who has invited them by ill-advised pinchings and squeezings. All that one can do is to keep them under control by constant care. The treatment recommended is the same as that used for warts—viz., to pare the hard and dry skin from the tops, and then touch them with the smallest drop of acetic acid, taking care that the acid does not run off the wart upon the neighboring skin, which would occasion inflammation and much pain. This should be done once or twice a day with regularity.

We should, no doubt, easily get rid of all our corns if we could make up our minds to do without shoes, or even to wear them of such a large size as would prevent all pressure upon the corn. This disagreeable effect results quite as often from badly made boots as from injudiciously tight ones. There is a particular knack to be observed in paring a corn. It should be cut in such a manner as to excavate the center, while the hardened sides are left to protect the more sensitive portion against the pressure of the boot. When the corn is small and yet young, the best application is a piece of soft buff-leather spread with adhesive plaster and pierced in the center with a hole of exactly the size of the summit of the corn. There are two varieties of corn, the hard and the soft. The latter occurs between the toes, and is quite as painful as, and less easily guarded against, than the hard variety.